2015
CyberArts

ARS ELECTRONICA

HATJE
CANTZ

Hannes Leopoldseder · Christine Schöpf · Gerfried Stocker

Prix Ars Electronica
CyberArts 2015

International Compendium Prix Ars Electronica

Computer Animation / Film / VFX – Hybrid Art – Digital Musics & Sound Art
Visionary Pioneers of Media Art – u19–CREATE YOUR WORLD
[the next idea] voestalpine Art and Technology Grant

Contents

VISIONARY PIONEERS OF MEDIA ART

u19–CREATE YOUR WORLD

[the next idea] VOESTLPINE ART AND TECHNOLOGY GRANT

Prix Ars

Electronica 2015

The Creative Outbreak

Everything changes, nothing remains as it is

Hannes Leopoldseder

Cities have always been the driving forces behind the economic and cultural development of a region, of a country, of a continent. That's how it's been since time immemorial and this has not changed in the 20th and 21st centuries. But one thing does distinguish this day and age: the speed of that development. One of the most radical upheavals in human history is the upshot of the internet, an innovation that is only 40 years old.

According to a McKinsey study entitled *Urban World,* big cities worldwide will be developing into megacities, and today's megacities, in turn, into super-megacities. In ten years—that is, by 2025—the world's 600 largest cities will be where 65 percent of the world's GDP is produced. Over the last century, the economic heavyweights have undergone a decisive change. On this subject, the McKinsey study states: "But since the mid-1980s, the pace of that shift—from the United States and Europe toward Asia—has been increasing dramatically. We expect this trend to continue, so executives and policy makers must be prepared to respond."[1]

Especially in cities, we are seeing the interplay of three major trends that reciprocally impact each other: mobility, speed and innovation.

All major automakers are striving at supercharged speed to bring out the car of the future. The triumvirate of mobility, speed and innovation is particularly relevant to the auto industry. Europe, and Germany in particular, is still the foremost producer of high-quality vehicles, whereas Asia leads the pack when it comes to automotive affordability. Of course, the luxury market segment in Asia plays an increasingly important role. All major automakers have one immediate objective: the self-driving car with an invisible robot on board. The latest study by the Boston Consulting Group predicts that, beginning in 2017, there will be more and more self-driving cars on the road, and autonomous motoring will create a $42 billion market by 2025.[2]

Mercedes-Benz's biggest innovation is dubbed the F015 Luxury in Motion, a model that has been shrouded in mystery for years now. In this car, four passengers can relax in what amounts to a cozy salon and chat while the vehicle morphs into a self-driving robot and thus dispenses with a driver. The Mercedes' interior got rave reviews in *Autorevue,* which called it a "setting for digital experiences." The driving is left up to an extended-sense sensor linkup featuring eye-tracking and gesture steering, radar and ultrasound sensors and stereo cameras.

Mercedes-Benz CEO Dieter Zetsche said: "Critics claim that the car's best days are behind it. My opinion is the exact opposite. The technology of self-driving cars is progressing rapidly."[3]

What comes after the automobile? Is the self-driving car the *non plus ultra* of future mobility? Many ideas and projects are pointing out directions of potential development. Here are a few examples:

- Japan's zero-emission Aero-Train: a metropolitan tramway hovering ten centimeters above the ground that can carry 335 passengers at a speed of 500 kilometers/hour will go into operation in 2020.
- Downtown cable cars and aerial tramways are already in operation in numerous cities, including Caracas, Venezuela, La Paz, Bolivia, New York and Portland, USA, Algiers, Algeria, Chongqing, China (population: approximately 30 million) and Nizhny Novgorod, Russia. In fact, an outstanding Austrian company is the international leader in this market. Doppelmayr Garaventa installs aerial tramways, gondola lifts and other mass transit systems in urban settings and all types of rural and mountainous landscapes in 89 countries worldwide.
- "Are Flying Cars the Future of Transportation?" is how the US-based *Forbes* magazine headlined an article datelined Vienna about the AeroMobil,

a spectacular flying car developed in Slovakia by Juraj Vaculik and Stefan Klein. On May 8, 2015, an AeroMobil crashed in the Slovakian city of Nitra; the pilot/driver was able to parachute to safety and sustained only minor injuries.[4]

- Elon Musk, co-founder of PayPal and CEO of the California-based Tesla Motors, has conceived a futuristic, revolutionary high-speed transportation system. The Hyperloop incorporates reduced-pressure tubes in which pressurized capsules ride on an air cushion driven by linear induction motors and air compressors powered by solar cells. The capsules containing the passengers move at 1,300 kilometers/hour: Vienna-Salzburg in fifteen minutes; Vienna-Linz in eight. Dirk Ahlborn, CEO of Hyperloop Transport Technologies, presented the Hyperloop project in May 2015 at the Pioneers Festival in Vienna. The mass media is already calling Elon Musk the new Steve Jobs, the Da Vinci of the 21st century, a visionary in mass transit, space travel and the energy sector. His dream: private space travel and affordable flights to Mars. He aims to use his lithium-ion batteries as the basis of reasonably priced cars with a range of 800 kilometers. But Musk's mission in life is Space X, an effort to assure humankind's survival in colonies on other planets. Wherever he looks, Elon Musk peers far into the future.[5]

Christoph Keese, a German journalist, economist and vice-president of Springer SE, spent several months together with a group of Springer staffers in California's Silicon Valley plumbing the mysteries of the digital world. In the book that was the outcome of this research, Keese describes in dramatic terms how Europe is falling behind in digitization. "This culture is developing at tremendous speed into the lead culture of the Digital Age. Living in Germany during the Internet Revolution is a little like having spent the 19th century in Lisbon: pleasant living conditions but far away from where the action is and detached from the Industrial Revolution."[6]

And even if this comparison does smack of journalistic oversimplification, it nevertheless contains a kernel of truth about the current technological and social situation. We Europeans scrutinize every development and every innovation from a critical distance at first. And often, following protracted debates on the pros and cons, the opportunity is no longer there—others have swiftly opted in and taken action. The best example of this is one of history's most significant innovations, the World Wide Web. Twenty-five years ago, on December 25, 1990, Tim Berners-Lee presented the World Wide Web. Whereas its decisive development by Tim Berners-Lee and Robert Cailliau was done at CERN in Switzerland, Europe failed to recognize its significance. In America, the WWW was professionalized at lightning speed and proliferated worldwide. A similar process took place in mobile telecommunications, though not American but rather Asian enterprises have emerged as the big players in this field.

A look at the market value of the world's largest internet companies in 2014 (calculated in May 2015) reveals a gloomy picture for Europe: Apple $529bn, Google $377bn, Facebook $157bn, Amazon $144bn, Tencent $132bn, eBay $66bn, Priceline $63bn, Baidu $59, Yahoo $35bn, Salesforce.com $30bn.[7] These ten high-tech companies offer a broad spectrum of products and services oriented on the future and customers worldwide. Ninety percent of these companies are based in the USA; ten percent , Baidu and Tencent, are in China. None of these top enterprises is European.

Business consultant Roland Berger took a close-up look at the world's twenty leading internet companies, thirteen based in the USA, seven in Asia. In response, he launched Terra Numerata, a digital entrepreneurship platform to give Europe a fresh start in innovation, creativity and networking.[8]

All over Europe—Austria included—everyone is talking about the digital revolution. But parallel to this are feelings of uncertainty. In the USA, innovation evokes curiosity, but in Central Europe it's a cause for anxiety. Austrian delegations consisting of political leaders, executives of start-ups and government agency experts visited Silicon Valley high-tech companies in 2015. They were surprised by the digital world and talked about a necessary cultural shift, but these words have to be followed by deeds. Austrian State Secretary Harald Mahrer at least enunciated the goal: "It would be possible to make Austria Europe's start-up country number one by 2020."[9]

For more than 35 years now, the Ars Electronica Festival has been dedicated to elaborating on the technologies of the future and their impact on our lives. This year's festival theme—POST CITY—Habitats for the 21st Century—will focus attention on metropolitan life in transition: mobility, the city as transportation hub; work, the city as workplace; citizens, the city as community; resilience, the city as stronghold. These considerations touch upon everyone's life. In each of them, the accent is on innovation, creativity and speed. POST CITY will, no doubt, also take up the current discussion of so-called post-media.

The University of Applied Arts Vienna recently set up a master's program that emphasizes the cityscape: Social Design—Arts as Urban Innovation. This course underscores the necessity of urban innovation in the transition process: "Especially universities are predestined to formulate these new, distinct perspectives on the inherent logic of cities and the corresponding dynamics of their processes."[10]

One indication of the extent to which digital competence has become de rigueur in the workplace is the fact that a quantitative measurement of it has been developed in the USA and is increasingly taken into account by human-resource managers: the Klout score. An algorithm computes this rating on a scale of 0 to 100, whereby prospective employees with a score under 40 can pretty much forget about their chances of getting hired. The score measures a person's online identity.

This tool was launched in 2007 by Joe Fernandez and has gradually established itself in the USA. Klout's slogan is "The Standard for Influence," which is to say it is an actual measurement of the clout a person wields in social media, a factor of growing importance in hiring new staff members.[11]

The more digital competence is called for, the more a person has to develop the personal touch—human qualities, a people-oriented attitude, consideration of others, and thus characteristics that differentiate a human being from a machine. At the same time, humans are being equipped with ever-more-powerful technology—to upgrade our hearing and seeing, the way we move, in our hearts and, above all, in our brains.

Nick Bostrom, a Swedish neuroscientist and philosopher at St. Cross College Oxford as well as director of the university's Future of Humanity Institute, has created impressive scenarios of a coming revolution that he sees emerging as the result of so-called superintelligence.[12]

On this subject, he poses two questions situated at the nexus of science fiction and reality:

1. Will a machine ever have the same intelligence as a human?

   Nick Bostrom first defines human-level machine intelligence (HLMI) as a form of artificial intelligence "that can carry out most human professions at least as well as a typical human." According to Bostrom, there is a 50 percent probability of achieving HLMI by 2040, and a 90% probability by 2075.

2. Will a machine's cognitive performance ever be greater than that of a human being?
   Nick Bostrom defines superintelligence, the term he uses to refer to this level of development, as "an intellect that is much smarter than the best human brains in practically every field." In addition to the predictions cited above, Bostrom makes another one for 2105. According to this scenario, there is a 75 percent probability that superintelligence will have been achieved and, thus, the intelligence of robots will then exceed that of humans.[13]

This means that children born in 2015 might well experience the emergence of superintelligence and especially humankind's protracted confrontations with intelligent machines' penetration of all spheres of life as well as all the upshots of this. These include radical changes in the world of work and thus the consequences attendant on the transformation of jobs. The machine is leaving humans behind. Or will we succeed in upgrading and enhancing our own intelligence too?

Nick Bostrom also goes into this question at length, in the process elaborating on several variants. One approach is whole-brain emulation (WBE), which will supposedly be able to engender "intelligent software by means of scanning and modeling the computational structure of an actual brain." Another possibility of stepping up the human brain's performance is via nutrition, training and genetic manipulation.[14] The conclusion: many questions remain unanswered.

It is nevertheless proper to start posing these questions now, as Bostrom is doing. What will happen when digital superintelligence emerges and asserts its dominion over the Earth? Would a superintelligent machine be capable of this? Is this actually conceivable or purely science fiction?

Yes, there is plenty to discuss. What are the prospects for human life, our everyday life? What will the world of work be like? Robots and robotic systems are almost totally pervasive today, though Nick Bostrom's futuristic scenario is not yet in sight. But it is looming on the horizon.

Nevertheless, what is no longer just a future prospect but already in our midst is this inviolable postulate of modern life: the creative outbreak. Everything changes, nothing remains as it is.

1 Urban World: Cities and the Rise of the Consuming Class http://www.mckinsey.com/insights/urbanization/urban_world_cities_and_the_rise_of_the_consuming_class
2 BCG Study: https://www.bcgperspectives.com/content/articles/telecommunications_technology_business_transformation_mobile_revolution/
3 Joachim Becker: *Die Neuvermessung der Welt: So fahren wir in die Zukunft* [Remapping the world: the route we're taking into the future], in: *Süddeutsche Zeitung*, No. 7, 10, January 11, 2015, p. 72
4 http://www.faz.net/futuristischeesflugautostürzteab
5 Ashlee Vance / Elon Musk: *Wie Elon Musk die Welt verändert [How Elon Musk is changing the world]. Tesla, PayPal, Space X*, Munich 2015, pp. 293, 297ff. Uwe Jean Heuser: *Der Raketen-Mann* [The rocket man]. http://www.zeit.de/2013/26/unternehmer-elon-musk
6 Christoph Keese: *Silicon Valley: Was aus dem mächtigsten Tal der Welt auf uns zukommt* [What's coming our way from the world's most powerful valley], Munich 2014, p. 11
7 http://de.statistica.com/statistik/daten/studie/umfrage/marktwert
8 http://www.rolandberger.at/press/releases/Terra_Numerata_en.html
9 Gerald Reischl: *Die Welt ist unser Markt* [The world is our market], interview with Harald Mahrer in *KURIER. Futurezone*, No. 146, May 28, 2015, p. 22
10 http://www.dieangewandte.at/jart/prj3/angewandte/main.jart?=en.
11 http://www.lithium.com/company/; http://klout.com
12 Nick Bostrom: *Superintelligenz: Szenarien einer kommenden Revolution* [Superintelligence: Paths, Dangers, Strategies] Berlin 2014
13 Ibid., p. 37 ff
14 Ibid., p. 131

Prix Ars Electronica 2015

Christine Schöpf, Gerfried Stocker

Nearly 3,000 artistic and scientific projects from 75 countries were submitted for prize consideration to the 2015 Prix Ars Electronica. These impressive figures once again underscore the significance of the world's most time-honored competition in the digital media arts, and also reflect the diversity of the concepts and forms of artistic expression in these genres.

Following the reconfiguration last year of the Prix Ars Electronica and the decision to stage four of the seven categories on a biennial basis, we are honoring excellence in the following fields in 2015: Computer Animation / Film / VFX, Digital Musics & Sound Art, Hybrid Art, [the next Idea] voestalpine Art and Technology Grant, u19 – CREATE YOUR WORLD and Visionary Pioneers of Media Art. A grand prize (including a Golden Nica statuette and €10,000), two Awards of Distinction and 12 Honorary Mentions were awarded in each category. The Golden Nica in u19–CREATE YOUR WORLD comes with a €5,000 first prize. [the next idea] voestalpine Art and Technology Grant is € 7,500 and support from the Ars Electronica Futurelab to help the winner further develop his/her idea.

Several factors have gone into the unique status that the Prix Ars Electronica has enjoyed since its inception 29 years ago:

Firstly, the interdisciplinarity of digital media art that's reflected in the respective categories which bring them together in a simultaneously staged competition. Thus the Prix Ars Electronica's results each year provide a broad overview of the complexities of what's happening in media art right now.

Secondly, the way the Prix Ars Electronica has responded to the rapid development of digital media over the course of almost three decades by introducing new categories, jettisoning old ones and repositioning others. It began in 1987 with computer music, computer graphics and computer animation. Now the Prix Ars Electronica honors outstanding work in seven categories, four of which are staged biennially. They not only cover all the essential genres of media art today; we also go beyond this spectrum to scout the latest experimental fields of creativity such as Hybrid Art at the nexus of art and science.

Thirdly, the internationality of the Prix Ars Electronica: here, every year, a wide array of global cultural approaches and points of view coalesce into multifarious political, artistic, sociological, ecological, economic and participative takes on what is transpiring in our world.

Fourthly, there is the most recent addition to the Prix Ars Electronica—the Golden Nica awarded annually to one of the Visionary Pioneers of Media Art, outstanding men and women whose artistic creativity and bold experimentation have not only laid the foundation for media art as we know it today, but also made a major impact on our current social reality with all its forms of communication and cultural techniques. The aim of this prize is to increase awareness of the recent history of media art and to give recognition and respect to those who have made their mark on it.

Fifthly, the selection of the prize-winners in each competitive category every year is done by a jury made up of five prominent experts in that particular field, with each juror being entitled to nominate five works. The choice of the recipient of the Visionary Pioneers Golden Nica is the result of online balloting by all artists who have themselves been Golden Nica prize-winners since 1987.

One final quality that has defined the Prix Ars Electronica right from the start is the openness it has displayed towards projects from the worlds of art, science and R&D, as well as towards works submitted from professional studios of the entertainment industry or university labs. Moreover, the u19–CREATE YOUR WORLD category welcomes student productions and ideas by young people. This makes for a confluence of highly diverse positions, perspectives and forms of expression, and assures the Prix Ars Electronica a broad spectrum of participation in the decades to come.

The Prix Ars Electronica has been sustained over the years by public subsidies and private sponsors. First and foremost is the City of Linz, which has provided financing to the Ars Electronica Festival, the Prix Ars Electronica and the Ars Electronica Center since 1979. We also gratefully acknowledge the ongoing support from the Province of Upper Austria. A sponsor since the inception of this endeavor is voestalpine, the source of funding for [the next idea] – voestalpine Art and Technology Grant. We also wish to express our appreciation to the OK Center for Contemporary Art, Casinos Austria, Cubus, KulturKontakt Austria, Rotary Club Linz-Altstadt and Linz AG for their support and cooperation over the years.

The prize-winning projects will be presented to international audiences in exhibitions, concerts, performances, speeches and workshops staged in conjunction with the Ars Electronica Festival, and documented in this book as well as online in the Ars Electronica Archive.

Computer Animation

/ Film / VFX

The Ironic Mirror

Gaëlle Denis, Joe Gerhardt, Sabine Hirtes, Erick Oh, Rob O'Neill

This year 722 entries were submitted to the Computer Animation / Film / VFX competition. The total projects were divided randomly into seven groups of roughly 90 entries and each juror (Gaëlle Denis, Joe Gerhardt, Sabine Hirtes, Erick Oh, and Rob O'Neill) in addition to the curators of the Ars Electronica Animation Festival Christine Schöpf and Jürgen Hagler, pre-selected 15 projects to be viewed by all jury members. Jury members were also invited to nominate five pieces that Ars Electronica would pick to submit their films to the competition. The jury members met in Linz, Austria, at the Ars Electronica Center and spent three days watching, discussing and selecting from the pool of 126 pre-selected and nominated entries. The first step was to address any technical issues with the pre-selection process and to watch projects that could not be viewed at home.

Next, in the first round, the jurors reviewed the projects to select those they felt should go on to the second round. Projects were selected based on aesthetic, narrative and technical criteria in addition to notions of originality, innovation and depth of concept. We were specifically looking for pieces that were innovative and could only be seen at Ars Electronica, that bring the audience something new and innovative, were technologically surprising and that bring a personal artistic vision of the world. Regardless of whether it was a narrative or abstract piece, we were looking for work that communicated a very unique and specific outlook. When traditional techniques such as stop-motion or traditional hand-drawn animation were employed, we searched for work that was forward-looking in its representation of the richness of those techniques and that pushed them in novel and unique directions. The jury also strove to represent diversity amongst the artists, making sure to acknowledge work from female artists, artists from under-represented regions of the world, and student work. In each successive review round, the jurors dug deeper into the submissions and narrowed the field down to around the 25 projects for the final round.

The jury noticed a number of trends in the work submitted. One trend included the use of animals as metaphors for human issues. While this is certainly not a new trend in animation it was often paired with narratives about alienation in a post-human world. Humans were often removed from the works altogether, with many pieces illustrating the natural world reclaiming or haunting what humans have left behind. Isolation and alienation were themes we found in many of the works. This isolation, whether created by time, war, emotions or an unknowable divide, is something that many of the artists seem to be grappling with and digging into for narrative works. The process of "making art" in and of itself was another narrative trend we noticed. Certainly, in a world where arts funding is shrinking, the act of creation itself is a challenge on the minds of artists.

In computer animation, it was clear that deep, complex and subversive narratives outweighed pure demonstrations of technical prowess that might have been successful in the past. In a field where anything visual is possible, the question now is what can be said with this powerful medium? In that respect, we saw many projects that used advanced visual effects to tell very intimate and personal stories. We sincerely hope that this trend continues. As narrative devices, sarcasm and irony were well used tools for telling stories about complex political, historical and social challenges. Irony, in particular, was often used to soften the emotional impact or to throw light on complex situations. Coupled with a dark sense of humor, irony brought an introspective levity to many of the works. The works acknowledged were all very contemporary and many were reflections on and critical examinations of the crises and subjects of today. Works confronting subjects related to war, oppression, media manipulation and the insecurities of the modern world very much resonated with the jury. Another trend we noticed was the movement of deconstructed methodologies. In many cases, traditional techniques were subverted

through lo-fi approximations or subversive deconstructions of established and well-worn methodologies. These works illuminate and comment on the process making way for a post-technical form of animation production that favors narrative over technique.
In the end, and after some long and vibrant discussions in the final round about the remaining 25 works, it was time to pick the top fifteen. Personal favorites slipped away as consensus was built and, in the end, the jury reached a selection that was unanimous and satisfying. The twelve Honorary Mentions, two Awards of Distinction and the Golden Nica were awarded after a long deliberation weighing this collection of strong and inspiring work.
Of particular note this year is that the Golden Nica for Computer Animation / Film / VFX goes, for the first time, to a non-linear piece. In a way, many of the trends we saw culminated in the selection of *Temp Mort / Idle Times* in that it was a complex yet deconstructed narrative that wove together many overlapping emotional stories into a truly compelling work.

Golden Nica

Temps Mort / Idle Times · Alex Verhaest

Temps Mort / Idle Times by Brussels-based artist Alex Verhaest is awarded the Golden Nica for its complete achievement in visual, interactive and innovative qualities. Verhaest uses animation to bring to life a reinterpretation of a classical 15th century master painting exhibition in the form of a series of interactive movies. This visual experience offers enormous potential to elucidate the internal turmoil of the family of characters. The details of the setting add a haunting and mysterious backstory that intrigues us and prompts us to ask more questions. Like a projection of our own world, the work is an invitation into a place of illusion, a study of complex, alienated characters through intriguing dialogues, neurotic monologues and subtle animated elements.

Awards of Distinction

Bär · Pascal Floerks

Pascal Floerks' Diploma film *Bär* [Bear] from Filmakademie Baden-Württemberg is a very personal story about the artist's relationship with his grandfather, who he visualizes as a powerful bear. But the bear can also be seen as a strong metaphor for a whole generation and reveals its deep and tormented past. By integrating the true-to-life CG bear into original photographs of the time, a touching and complex story about World War Two, loss, disappointment and the small things that make up the sum of a lifetime is told.

The Reflection of Power · Mihai Grecu

The Reflection of Power by Mihai Grecu begins with the now familiar North Korean tourist trail, with its sanitized public monuments and epic staged performances. But something stirs beneath the surface, which turns our voyeuristic impressions of the city into a physical manifestation within the movie. Islands of totalitarian architecture and social housing become symbols of the politically remote state within a drowning isolated world. This work has been awarded an Award of Distinction for its subtle yet powerful intervention of visual effects within a hauntingly real world documentary.

Honorary Mentions

Omote / Real-Time Face Tracking & Projection Mapping · Nobumichi Asai

Nobumichi Asai has been exploring projection mapping for many years through various projects taking place on the stage or in architectural spaces. This time Asai goes further with his experiments by delving into an exploration of the human face. Heavily inspired by Japanese traditional Omote masks, Asai invites us all to experience the beautiful yet impressive live performance of real time facial mapping. In Japan's classical musical plays, performers use Omote masks to express a multitude of dramatic expressions, opening onto inner emotions and revealing something more than just the graphic image. Asai's work is intriguing, powerfully presented and fascinating, as if the soul were suddenly revealed on the surface. The face becomes a canvas for a work of digital art.

10964579043769284765O · David OReilly
Another brilliant cutting-edge piece of art from the visionary artist David O Reilly. *10964579043-7692847650* is a collection of six different short films featuring David's own iconic aesthetic and classic black humor, placed in an URL space as a main platform to interact with the viewers. From the horse that couldn't fit into society trying to find a way to communicate with his friends, to a couple arguing by repeating each other's sentences, each piece brings the viewer to a new level of anxiety. Even if they all appear random and disconnected, they are executed in such a unique and emotional manner that, at the end of the day, they all portray a certain part of our lives that we can deeply relate to even if we don't admit it. This is definitely David's signature approach to filmmaking. He has done it again in a smart and innovative way.

Symphony no. 42 · Réka Bucsi
With its unique style and sarcastic vision of the world, this surreal dark comedy observes irrational connections between humans and nature. Made in 2D animation, this non-narrative Hungarian graduation short film weaves small events and intervening free mental and visual associations with an efficient sound design to create a captivating piece. Réka Bucsi reinvents an intuitive way of editing non-related scenes together, illustrating a way to express absurdity about life and, with great sensitivity, about our own society.

World of Tomorrow · Don Hertzfeldt
For his new work, Don Hertzfeldt has produced his first all digital animation, yet hasn't lost any of his signature "no-fi" graphic cartoon style. With Hertzfeldt's familiar existential probing, this hilariously funny sci-fi film explores many far future themes such as human cloning and the transferring of our memories when we die. The jury was impressed by the imaginative depth of the storytelling coupled with the well-performed voice acting that produced a truly compelling work. The writing combined with the aggressively imaginative concepts and stark visual style have earned *World of Tomorrow* an Honorary Mention.

Marilyn Myller · Mikey Please
After the multi-awarded *The Eagleman Stag*, the great storyteller Mikey Please comes back with another creative piece in his unique black and white animation style, showing a playful, well-crafted piece of dark humor. Marilyn, the hero of the film struggles with her creative process, becoming a sort of Fellinian character in *8½*, enabling her to tackle the pressure of her own creative spirit. The dream is the nightmare, the reality becomes surreal. The spectacular rhythm and detailed animation takes us into her frantic and poetic mind. The ending is left open about the achievement of Marilyn Myller as an artist. Was it all a dream? Or did Marilyn (and Mikey Please) intend to create a biting critique of an often pretentious art world.

In The Distance · Florian Grolig
While living a peaceful life with his chicken in the penthouse of an island-like building, danger and combatants of an unseen war are looming in the distance for the protagonist of this sensibly designed and beautifully animated short film. Though the protagonist can keep the immediate danger to his life at bay and is not involved in the approaching war, he is finally forced to leave his home. Only via the sound and the effect on his environment, the slow destruction of his home, and finally the killing of his chicken by stray bullets, is the fate of millions of people displaced from their homes shown, leaving the audience deeply moved. Florian Grolig, an already acclaimed German animator, succeeds in telling a highly complex and moving story about the aftermath of war in a very unpretentious and unadorned way.

Reid Willis – Placed (official video)
Fernando Lazzari, Popscience
The music video for Reid Willis's track *Placed* by Fernando Lazzari, a London-based designer and filmmaker, is a surreal and poetic animated painting. Like a visualization of the Romantic poems of Lord Byron and his contemporaries the piece explores and celebrates the closeness of life and death. In

a way the visual mood also reflects Romanticism: skull adorned sperm-like flying creatures explore the world of untouched serene landscapes and indulge themselves in life by dancing and playing. Highly aesthetic, beautifully lit, and with perfectly integrated CG creatures, this film is a feast for the eyes and lets you linger on contemplating transience and the endless circle of life and death.

Descent · Johan Rijpma

Johan Rijpma's work explores the ephemeral forms emerging from simple gestures, such as the spilling of water or dropping of objects, with stop-motion animation. Fragments of collapsed space and time are deconstructed and reconstructed from various points of view with great simplicity and beauty. In *Descent* a broken clay pot becomes the source for a most unexpected claymation regeneration. The work is deceptively complex, with elegant camera moves and playful timing. Reminiscent of contemporary 3D printing yet using traditional animation techniques in a most unusual way has gained this work an Honorary Mention.

Do Not Touch · Moniker

Obedience and willingness to give our data away is the subject of this exceptional interactive music video. Set up as a game, the participants joyfully reveal themselves without ever noticing. An ironic and significant statement in these times of endless data mining, the work also reveals our internal struggle between our innermost needs and our adherence to social standards—even when nobody is looking. By starting with simple orders to move to certain areas of the screen, the participants are slowly and harmlessly guided to give away more and more information about themselves. A very telling metaphor for our careless handling of crucial and personal information contained even in the simple gestures of our hands on the computer mouse.

Deichkind "Denken Sie Groß" · Till Nowak, Timo Schierhorn, Christian Hartmann (UWE)

Think Big is a music video for Deichkind, a well-known German electro-punk hip-hop band. This is a hilarious and ironic statement about the megalomaniac approach that modern societies, politics and individuals sometimes suffer from. The young kid in the video is creating an abundantly illustrated and imaginatively constructed, absurd world of bigger, better, faster. Not only is it a twist on the idea of the adolescent YouTube tutorial but it also pokes fun at the assumed ease of commercial animation. Christian Hartmann (UWE), Till Nowak and Timo Schierhorn have transformed the lyrics, obviously with relish, into a visual firework of an imaginative and colorful conglomeration of at first sight abstruse but in the end meaningful ideas.

Augmented Hand Series
Golan Levin, Kyle McDonald, Chris Sugrue

The whimsical *Augmented Hand Series* utilizes innovative computer vision, and custom software to subvert our familiarity with our own bodies by altering our hands in a real-time and utterly convincing manner. The jury was impressed by the results of the work but also by the captivating documentation of this remarkable installation. The video of the work not only gave us a sense of the wonder felt by participants but made us long for a chance to feel the sensations that the work attempts to produce. By playfully challenging our perception of our own image, the work taps into notions of phantom limbs and our proprioceptive sense of where our appendages are in space in a seemingly magical way.

YouTube Smash Up · Parag K. Mital

YouTube Smash Up is mash-up collage in motion and an endlessly generative snapshot of pop music. The work resembles the style and content of Robert Rauschenberg's artwork when he played with the iconography of American pop culture. Only this collage is not composed by an artist but by a cleverly and artistically programmed algorithm, written and explored by Parag K. Mital. This work brings into focus how copyright law will automatically treat works of art in the future when our computational tools for remixing media are able to understand so much more about the content rather than simply by reading the textual headers. The work explores how the simple manipulation, alteration and replacement of digital artworks can also explore and challenge our audiovisual perception of them.

Temps Mort / Idle Times

Alex Verhaest

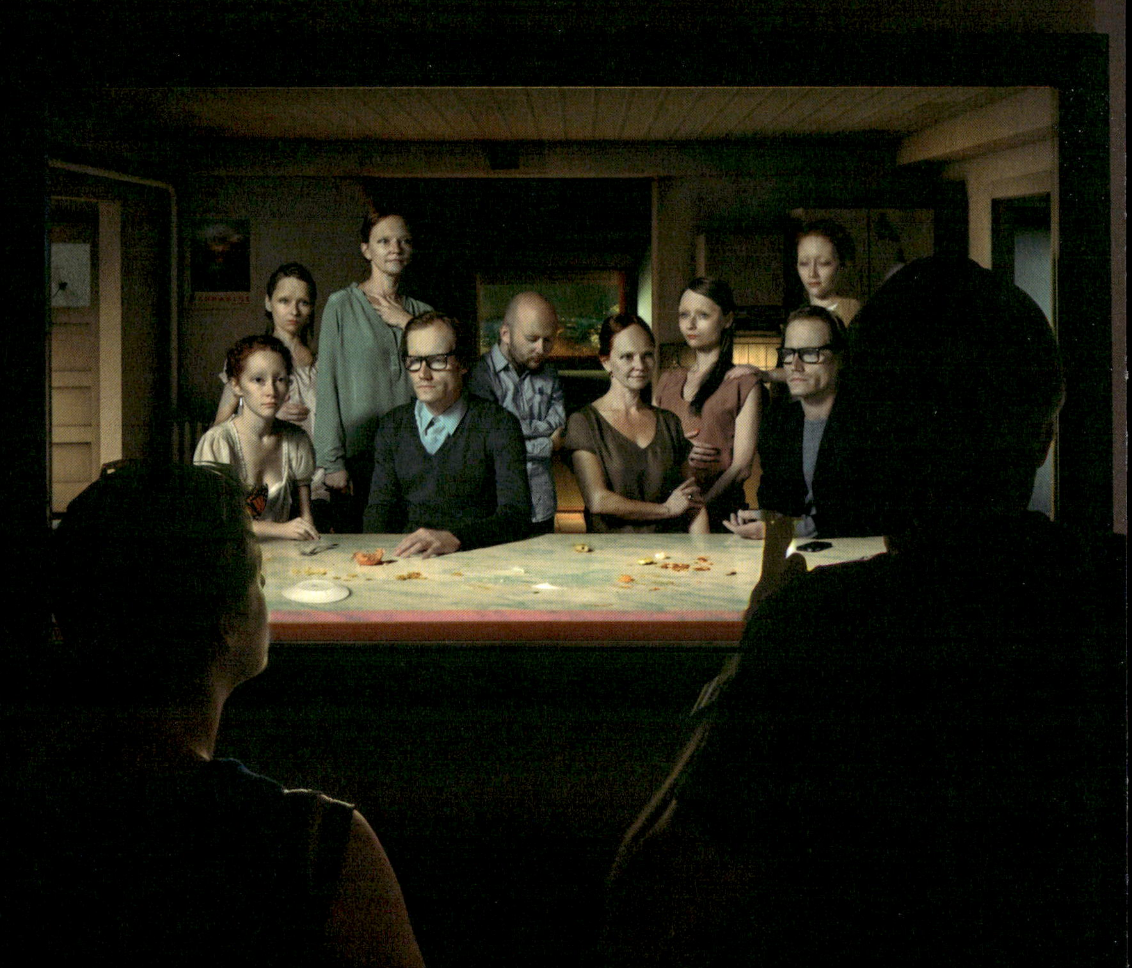

Alex Verhaest's works are visual explorations and investigations of the nature and boundaries of language, communication and social conventions and the potential of contemporary storytelling. The basis of each project is a narrative script, existing or newly written, around which she creates a body of standalone works by analyzing its storyline and exploring the limits of what constitutes communicable language. Her highly pictorial work operates by the juxtaposition of painting, video and contemporary technology.

The script of *Idle Times / Temps Mort* operates as the narrative backbone for a series of works on the suicide and character assassination of an absent *pater familias*, and the incapacity of the family members to communicate on, and to deal with this tragic event. The protagonists of *Idle Times / Temps Mort*, the 'mourning' relatives (Hélène, Dolores, Peter and Madeleine) and the storyteller (Angelo) are introduced via a series of five Character Studies: a series of portraits that visualize the internal emotional struggle and inability of the surviving relatives to adopt an adequate attitude. Hélène is about to cry but she doesn't. Is she trying to cry because she needs to, or because society expects her to do so? Dolores is pregnant and about to give birth to the first grandchild of the deceased father. Her portrait suggests a mental state which balances between salvation, expectation and disappointment and fear.

https://vimeo.com/alexverhaest/tempsmorttrailer
http://www.dauwensbeernaert.com/artists/alex-verhaest/

The character studies also operate as standalone works that investigate the pictorial, historical and psychological potential of portraiture. On the one hand the protagonists seem to operate in a timeless or even futuristic and parallel universe, on the other hand the aesthetics of the works refer to old master paintings (e.g. Cranach the Elder) and contrast with the technology and data carriers (Ipads) used for these works. The combination of these temporal aspects gives the works a universal and timeless yet very contemporary dimension.
This art historical dimension of the character studies is also present in another series of five works: the Table Props. Each character study corresponds with a so-called Table Prop. At first sight, these works remind us of classic still lives of Pieter Claesz and Willem Claesz Heda. A broken plate, a fallen glass, bread crumbs and leftovers suggest a hasty departure, or memento mori. Upon closer inspection, each Table Prop is literally a *tableau vivant*, a very subtle video loop without beginning or end. Table Props operate as allegoric representations of the protagonists of *Idle Times* and their mental states. Again, the combination of contemporary technology and classic themes results in an alienating visual anachronism.
Idle Times / Temps Mort also includes two interactive works, which engage the direct participation of the viewer and explore another aspect of Alex Verhaest's work. Indeed, the title *Temps Mort / Idle Times* is derived from the feeling of missing out when using (or not using) a networked device, such as a smartphone or laptop. Verhaest feels that using a networked appliance generates a sort of buffered time zone, where her sense of time is suspended between physical presence in her environment at a particular moment and the time in which others send an e-mail or update their Facebook status. This caused her to reflect about layers in time, about our ever-failing relationship with it and the depth perception of memory as a container of the past and present.

The View is a life-size interactive animation loop. As the title of the work suggests, visitors are welcomed by a view: the view from an apartment located in an unknown city. Upon closer inspection the viewer is however confronted with (the reflection of) another person: Hélène, one of the protagonists of *Idle Times / Temps Mort*. Even though *The View* is not intended to deliver a specific ethical or philosophical message, it irrevocably questions the duality and relation between the Other and the Self and the concept of intersubjectivity.
The Dinner scene brings together all protagonists of *Idle Times*. The composition and setting of the work refer to a *Last Supper* scene. The relatives are represented twice, on the left and right of Angelo, the storyteller. The relatives are depicted before and after the suicide of the absent father. When the visitors call Peter (via a phone number given on a business card handed out during exhibitions), they activate a conversation, or at least a series of monologues between / of the family members. The relatives do not communicate or interact, they are making small talk to break the awkward silence. Even though Alex Verhaest takes a neutral stance on the usage of social media or networked devices, *Dinner Scene* does illustrate the discrepancy between the multitude of means to communicate and social platforms (which only allow for a binary state of mind: like/dislike) on the one hand and our inability to communicate and interact on complex state of minds and tragic events on the other.

Direction, writing, CGI and post-production: Alex Verhaest
Senior post-production assistance and compositing: Dustin Kershaw
Overall assistance: Sam Monballiu
Interaction design advisor: Bas Withagen
Recoding to html: Jean Joskin & Present Plus
Sound: Sonogents & Wouter Verhulst

Actors:
Hélène Devos
Mieke Versyp
Dolores Bouckaert
Angelo Tijssens
Pieter Genard

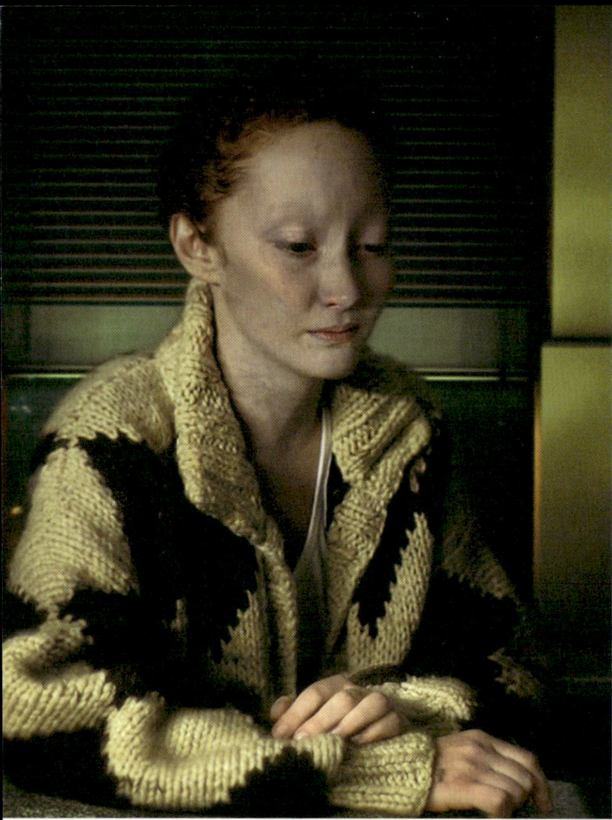
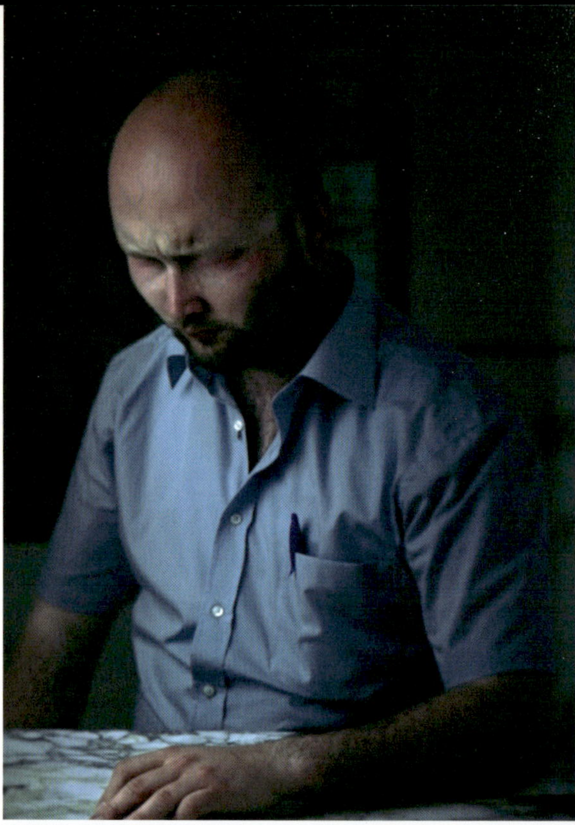
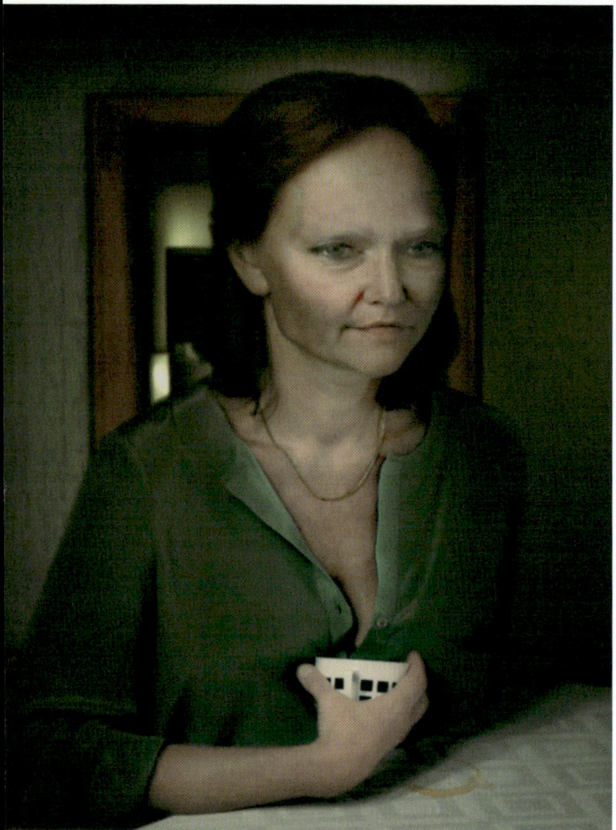
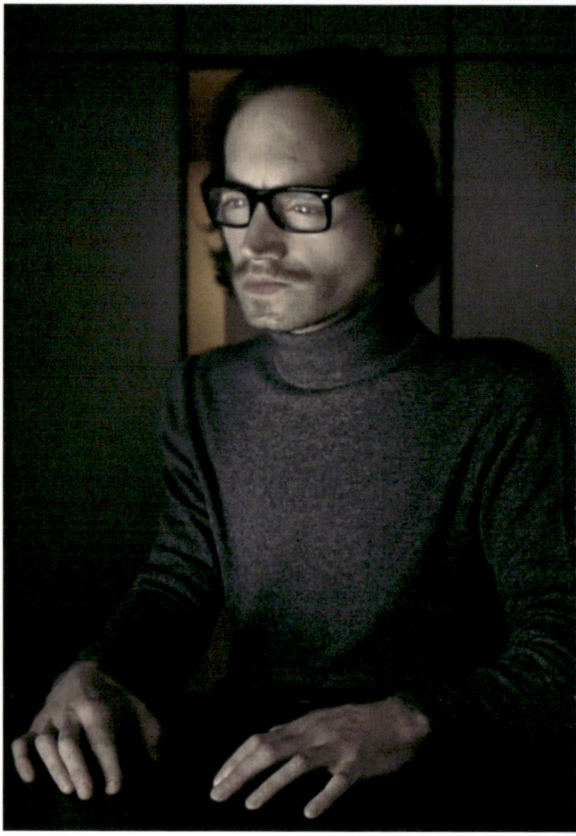

https://vimeo.com/alexverhaest/tempsmorttrailer
http://www.dauwensbeernaert.com/artists/alex-verhaest/

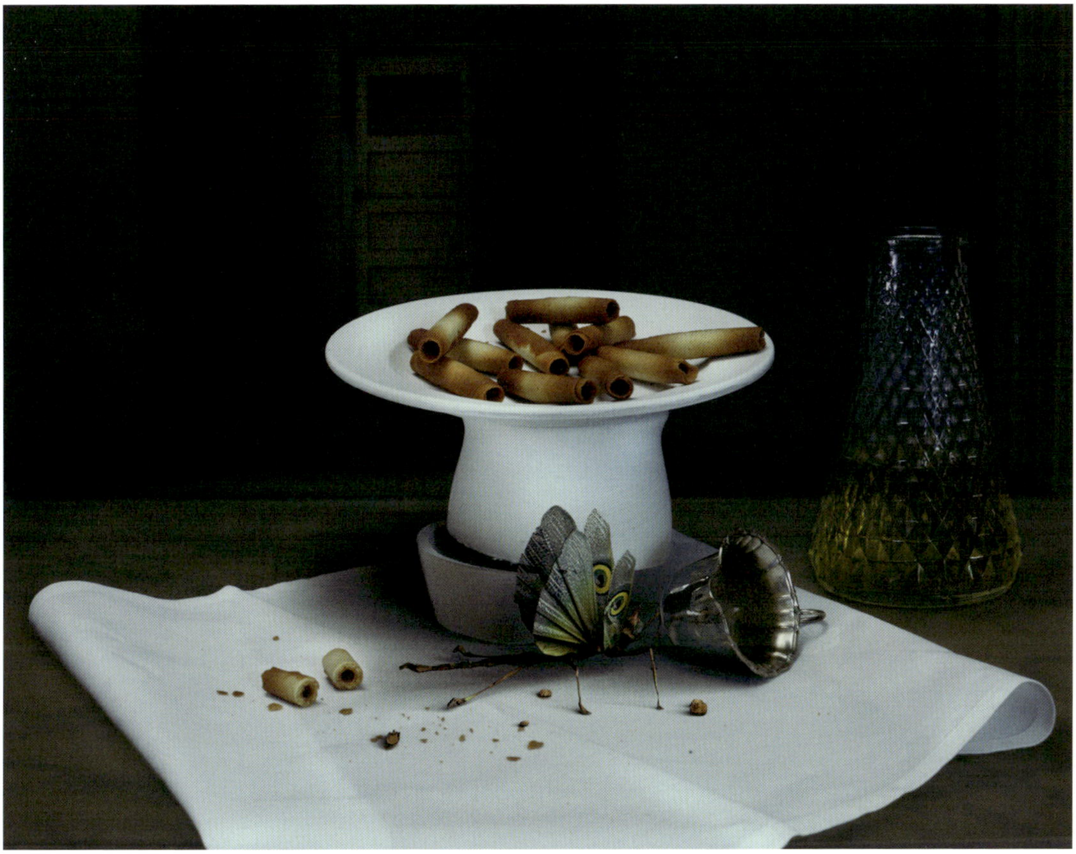

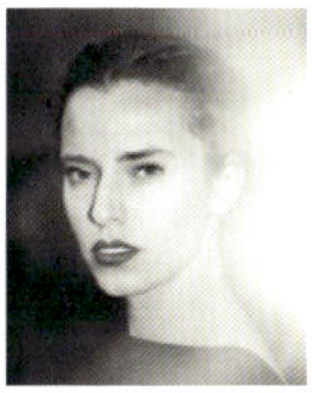

Alex Verhaest (BE). During her MFA year, Verhaest traveled to China where she discovered the Asian hacker subculture. She was invited to participate in a six-month residency at the island6 Arts Center in Shanghai where she joined the former artist collective Platform for Urban Investigations. She then traveled to Mexico DF, Eindhoven and Salvador da Bahia where she participated in group shows by the collective at the Museo de la Ciudad de Mexico, the Van Abbe Museum and the Museo de Arte Moderna. In 2009 she decided to focus more on her own practice and to leave the collective, which resulted in participation in several group exhibitions around Belgium and the Netherlands. In September of 2013, her debut solo *Temps Mort / Idle Times* opened at Grimm Gallery, Amsterdam. She is currently represented by Dauwens & Beernaert, Brussels, and Envoy Enterprises, New York. Her work has been selected by several arts and new-media festivals and competitions; i.e. the FILE electronic language festival in Sao Paolo, the New Technology Art Award in Gent, TAZ Oostende and Arts Festival Watou, and her work is featured in the Akzo Nobel Collection. Alex Verhaest recently won the prestigious Japanese Media Arts New Face Award.

Bär

Pascal Floerks

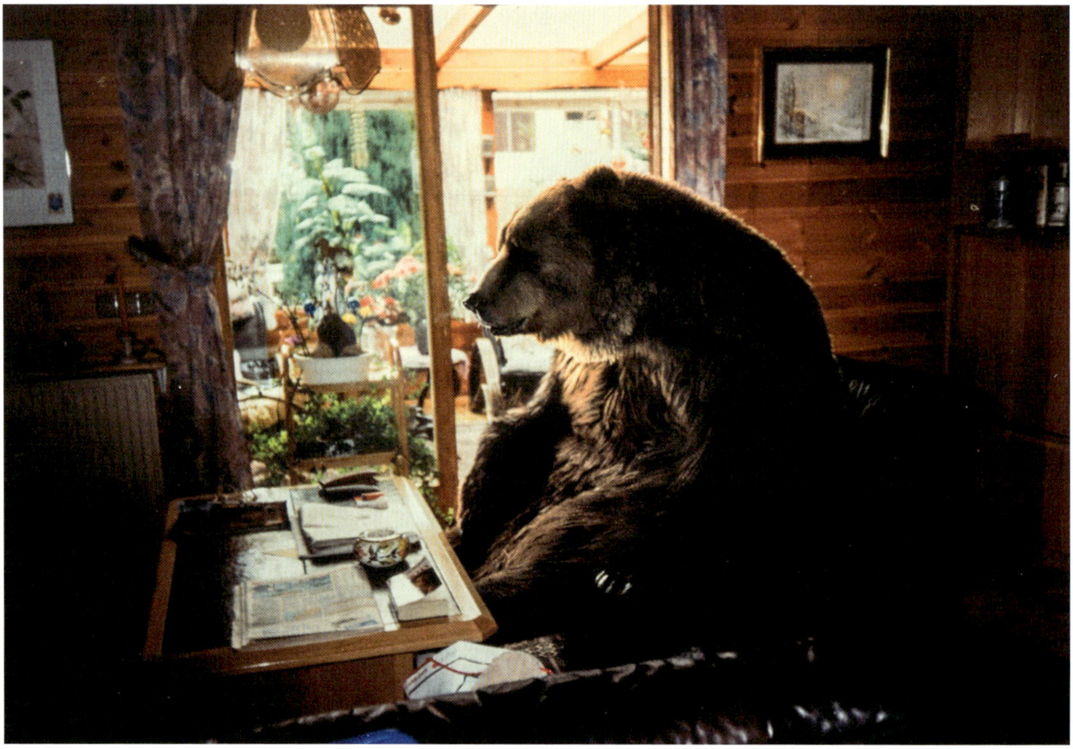

Bär [Bear] is a film about my grandfather. It's a film about his personality, about his past as a WW2 soldier and it's about me, his grandchild, and the way I saw him. I always found it fascinating that he would never talk about the war. Though everyone in the family knew about his past, no one knew any details. But it was always with him. Most that I know is part of the story of *Bär*.

My motivation to make this film was that I felt very sad about the fact that I would never be able to ask him those questions, to never solve the mysteries around him and not just around him, but all the witnesses of the war area that we keep losing until there's no one left to ask. Therefore I wanted to make a film about all the grandfathers and their mysteries of the past.

So to tell the story about my grandfather but leave it open for own personal projections I chose to picture him as a bear. I chose to not make a full animation film about it, first because of time restrictions, but later I realized that those photos would be all I needed to tell the story, and also picture the fact that everything is in the past. So the minimalistic approach also helped me to sell the story, which was really good as I was also involved in other projects at that time, being more in a technical role. I was helping myself with family photos at hand, going through the big library with the help of my grandmother. All color photos (except a few at the end of the film) are actual family photos. I had to go and shoot some of the photos for the last part of the story myself. The war photos were gathered from a

http://www.floerks.de
http://www.floerks.de/portfolio/bar/
https://vimeo.com/118812044

German photo library. Luckily that library was available online, so I could find the photos I needed quite fast. Then I replaced my grandfather or a soldier on the photo with a CG bear. One of the most common questions is: Why a bear? For me that was very clear from the beginning. I found bears to be very pretty animals, cute, huggable, very well established in our society thinking of Teddy Bears. At the same time a bear is a very dangerous predator. So the bear was perfect for what I wanted to tell.
From the technical side, I started creating a ZBrush model of a bear, made a riggable, retopologized version of it, created a basic rig in Maya so I could pose him for the different photos. Fur was a good adventure as I had never done a fur project before. I tried different solutions but ended up using yeti fur for Maya, which was a great choice. After lots of grooming and combing and texturing and shading, matching the lights of the photos, I rendered the bear in Arnold for Maya. This gave great quality in a short amount of rendering time. Final compositing was done in Nuke and sometimes Photoshop.
The final step was to put all the photos on film slides, project it onto a nice canvas and film the slide show. Though I tried going all digital for this, I found that going the analog way gave a much more satisfying result. All filming had to go through one last step of editing. Combined with the sounds and music of Christian Heck, the film finally came together.

Director: Pascal Floerks
Producer: Julia Smola
Music/sound: Christian Heck
Script translation: David Mass

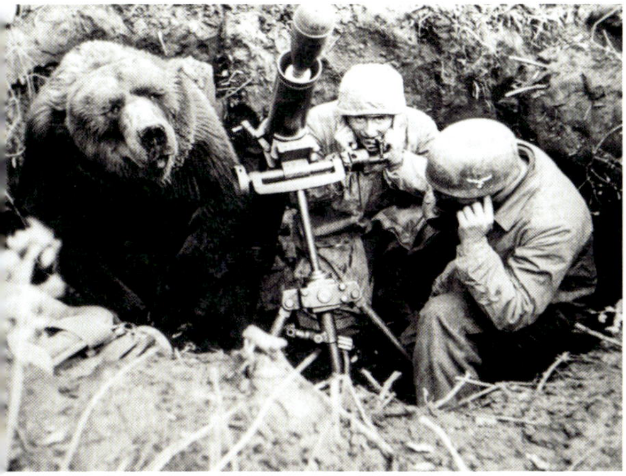

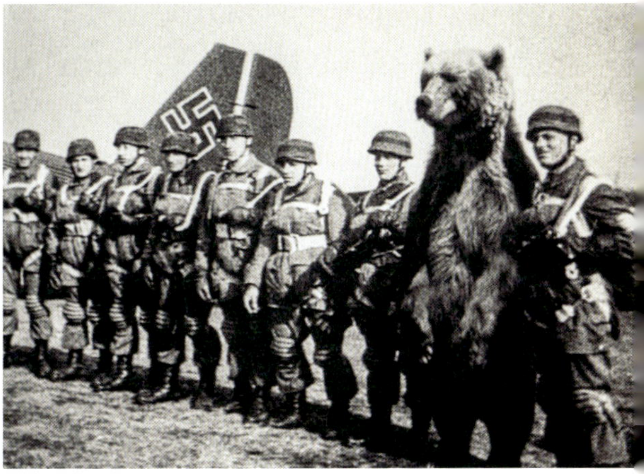

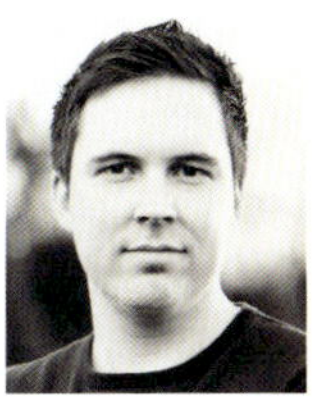

Pascal Floerks (DE), born 1982 in Worms, discovered his passion for animation early on, making his first films as a child. After successful completion of a media management degree at the Business and Information Technology School Iserlohn, he wanted to explore the creative side of media production and so decided to continue his education at the Filmakademie Baden-Württemberg. He gained plentiful experience as a character TD on numerous student projects and also professionally at Blue Sky Studios in the US. Back home in Germany, he has contributed to a multitude of projects for studios such as Polynoid, Woodblock and Studio Soi, most recently as lead character TD on the Oscar-nominated film *Room on the Broom.* In March 2014, Pascal concluded his studies at the Filmakademie with the completion of his film *Bär.*

The Reflection of Power

Mihai Grecu

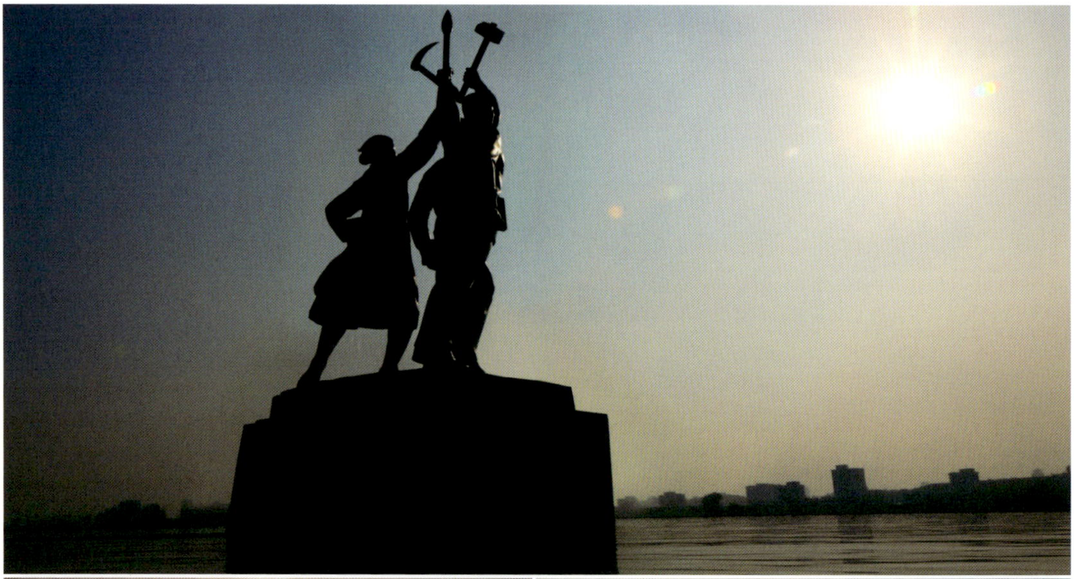

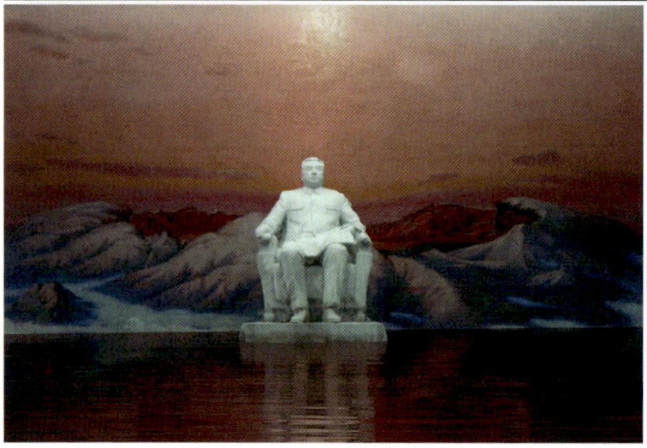

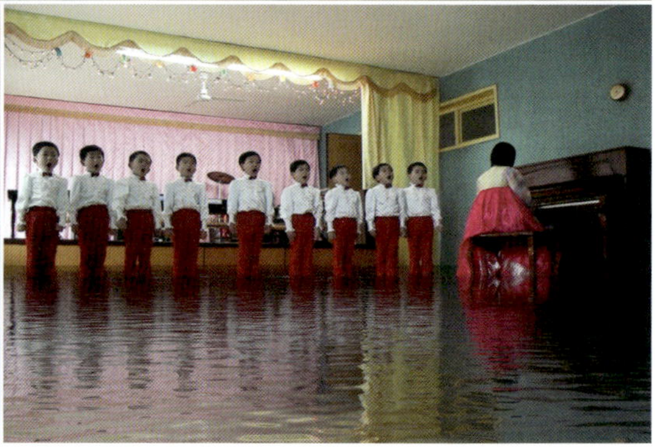

This film is a rare glimpse into one of the most reclusive places of the world, Pyongyang, the capital of North Korea. Slowly, an unknown anomaly devours this strange city. But the city's atmosphere of eternal celebration never changes no matter how obvious the approaching end. The people keep absurdly demonstrating the same preset patriotic behavior. The visual poetry of the film rests upon metaphoric relations being created between architectural objects, including symbols of the North-Korean regime, and the natural phenomena sent to dissolve them. The film supposes history to be a chain of situations that seem to be unshakable until they are gone forever.

Director: Mihai Grecu
Production: Bathysphère Productions
Producer: Nicolas Anthomé
Script: Mihai Grecu
Camera: Mu-jin
Editing: Mihai Grecu, Seto Momoko, Clémence Diard
Sound editing: Mihai Grecu, Guiz Maubert
Sound design: Mihai Grecu, François Martig, Yann Leguay
Mixing: Simon Apostolou
Animation and special effects: Mihai Grecu, Manea "Dexter" Alexandru

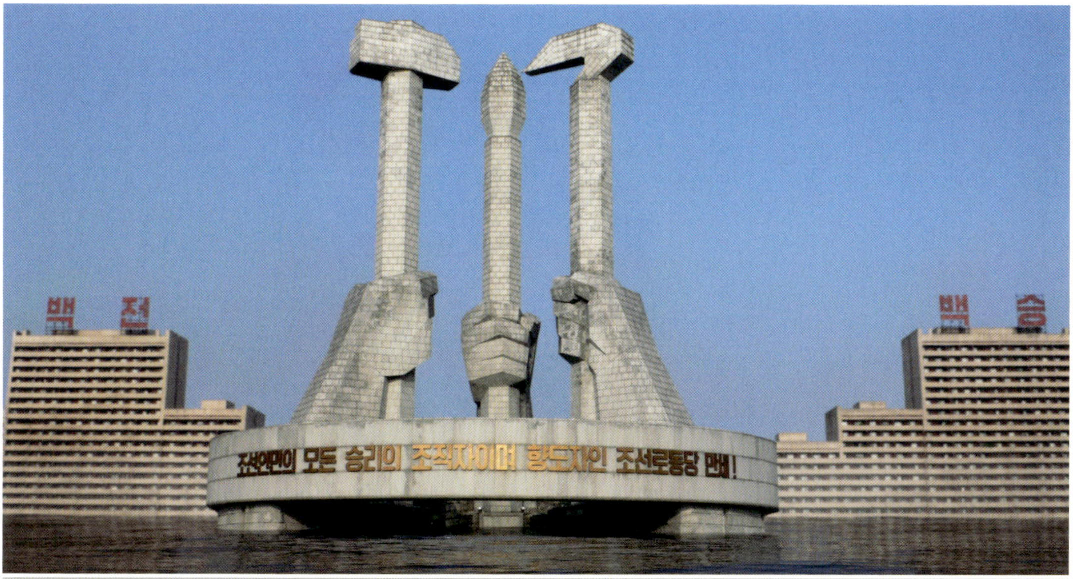

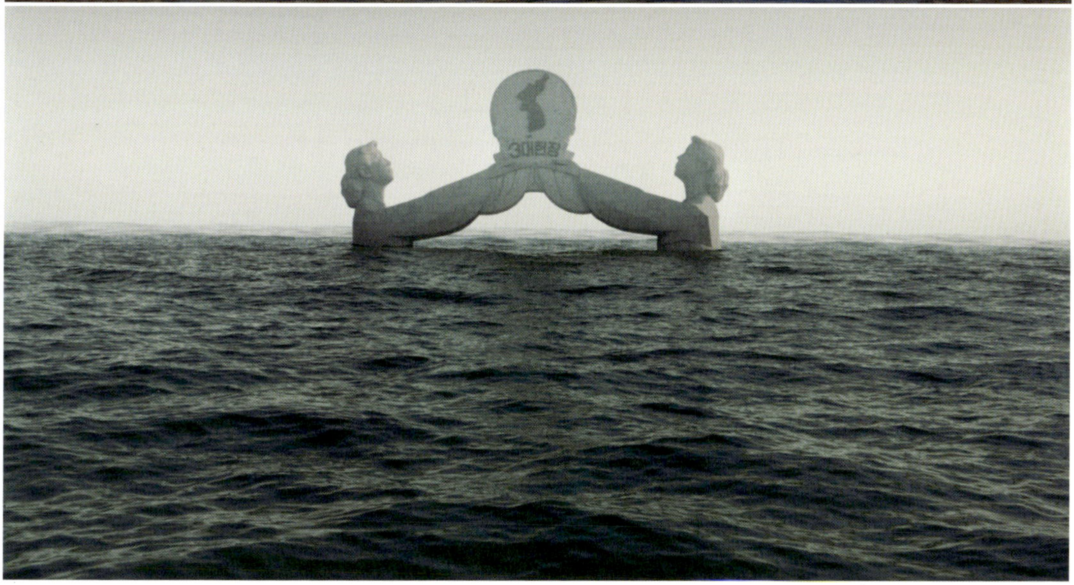

Mihai Grecu (RO/HU) was born in 1981. After studying art and cinema in Romania and France, at the Fresnoy Studio of Contemporary Arts, he has been developing a complex personal visual language. By mixing symbolic images with highly metaphorical situations and surreal atmospheres, his works challenge the viewer's perception as well as contemporary imagery, with recurring themes such as environment, war, water and metamorphosis. His film-poems have been shown in numerous film and new media festivals worldwide (Rotterdam, Festival of New Cinema in Montreal, Clermont Ferrand, Videobrasil) and exhibitions *(Dans la nuit, des images* at the Grand Palais in Paris, Mois de la Photographie in Paris, Hengesbach Gallery in Berlin etc.).

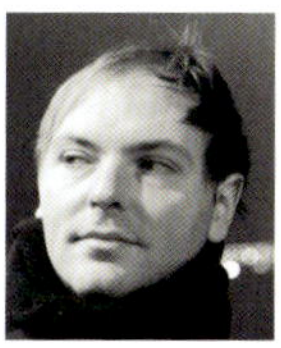

Augmented Hand Series

Golan Levin, Kyle McDonald, Chris Sugrue

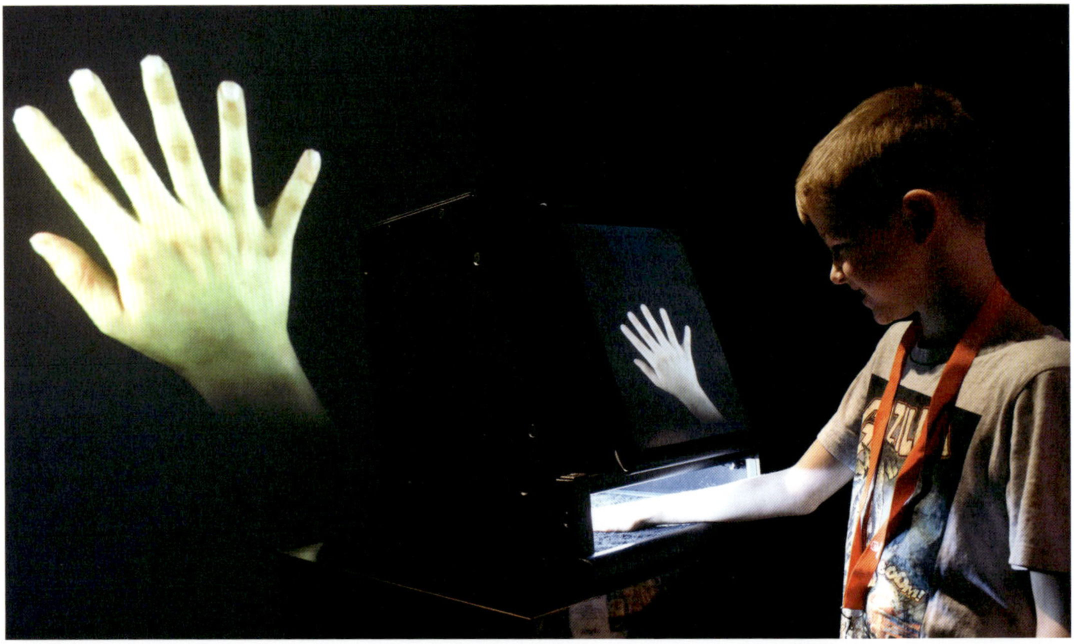

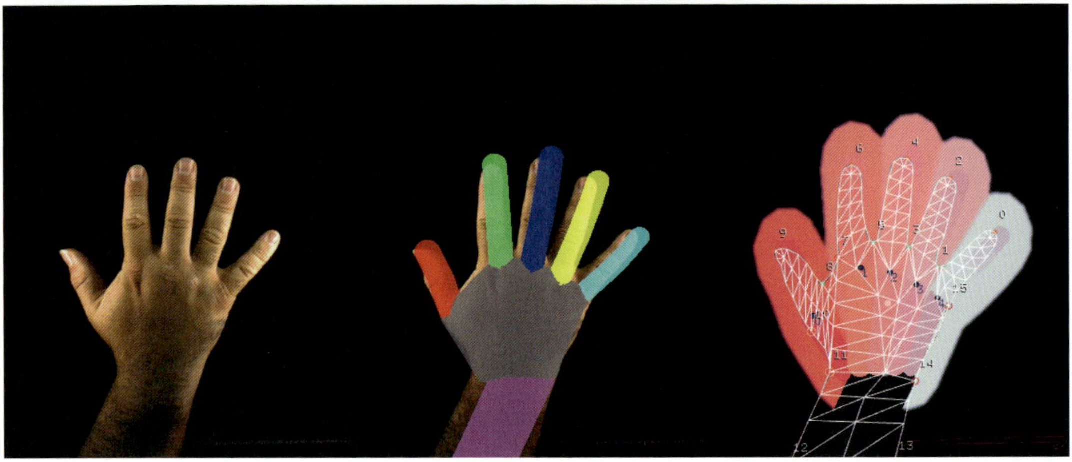

The *Augmented Hand Series* is a real-time interactive software system that presents playful, dreamlike, and uncanny transformations of its visitors' hands. Conceived as a tool for muddling embodied cognition, the installation consists of a box into which a visitor inserts their hand, and a display that shows their "reimagined" hand, altered by various dynamic and structural transformations.

The system uses the real-time posture of the participant's real hand as the moment-to-moment baseline for its transformations. Participants are free to use either of their hands and, within certain limits, the system works properly even with visitors who wiggle their fingers, or who move and turn their hand.

Critically, the project's transformations operate within the logical space of the hand itself. That is to say: the artwork performs "hand-aware" visualizations that alter the deep structure of how the hand appears—unlike, say, a funhouse mirror, which simply distorts the entire field of view.

The hand is a critical interface to the world, allowing the use of tools, the intimate sense of touch, and a vast range of communicative gestures. Yet we frequently take our hands for granted, thinking with them, or through them, but hardly ever about them. Our investigation takes a position of exploration and wonder. Can real-time alterations of the hand's appearance bring about a new perception of the body as a plastic, variable, unstable medium? Can such an interaction instill feelings of defamiliarization, prompt a heightened awareness of our own bodies, or incite a reexamination of our physical identities? Can we provoke simple wonder about the fact that we have any control at all over such a complex structure as the hand?

About twenty different transformations have been developed. Some of these perform structural edits to the hand's archetypal form, cutting-and-pasting the visitor's digital body; others endow the hand with new dimensions of plasticity; and others imbue the hand with a kind of autonomy, whose resulting behavior is a dynamic negotiation between visitor and algorithm. These scenes include:

Plus One: The hand obtains an additional finger.
Minus One: The hand has one finger omitted.
Extra Knuckle: Each finger has an extra phalange.
One Knuckle Fewer: Each finger has a phalange omitted.
Two Thumbs: The thumb is copy-pasted to the other side of the hand.
Transposed Thumb: The thumb is relocated to the other side of the hand.
Fractal Hand: Each finger terminates in a small hand.
Throbbing Fingers: The fingers appear to throb, as with a heartbeat.
Variable Finger Length: The fingers' length changes over time.
Meandering Fingers: The fingers take on a life of their own.
Procrustes: All fingers are made the same length.
Lissajous: The palm is warped in a periodic way.
Breathing Palm: The palm inflates and deflates.
Vulcan Salute: The third and fourth fingers are cleaved.
Angular Exaggeration: Finger adduction and abduction angles are amplified.
Springers: Finger movements are exaggerated by bouncy simulated physics.

The *Augmented Hand Series* was conceived and developed by Golan Levin, Chris Sugrue, and Kyle McDonald, with additional software assistance from Dan Wilcox, Bryce Summers, Erica Lazrus, and Zachary Rispoli. The project was commissioned by the Cinekid Festival, with support from the Mondriaan Fund, and developed at the Frank-Ratchye Studio for Creative Inquiry at Carnegie Mellon University.

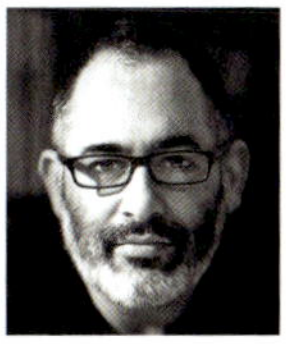
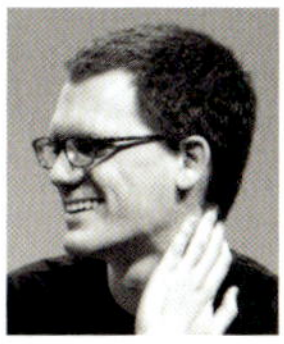
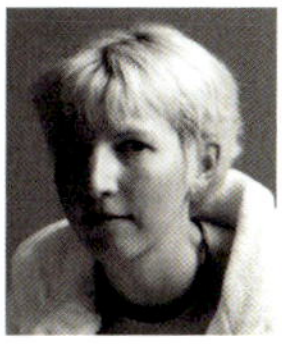

Golan Levin (US) explores the intersection of abstract communication and interactivity. Blending equal measures of the whimsical, the provocative, and the sublime in a wide variety of media, Levin applies creative twists to digital technologies that highlight our relationship with machines, expand the vocabulary of human action and awaken participants to their own potential as creative actors. Golan is Associate Professor of Electronic Art at Carnegie Mellon University. **Kyle McDonald** (US) works with sounds and codes, exploring translation, contextualization, and similarity. With a background in philosophy and computer science, he strives to integrate intricate processes and structures with accessible, playful realizations that often have a do-it-yourself, open-source aesthetic. Kyle is a member of FAT Lab, community manager for openFrameworks and an adjunct professor at the NYU ITP. **Chris Sugrue** (US) is an artist and engineer who develops interactive installations, audio-visual performances and experimental interfaces. Her works experiment with technology in playful and curious ways and investigate topics such as artificial life, gestural performance and optical illusions. Chris teaches new media arts at The Parsons School of Design in Paris.

Deichkind "Denken Sie Groß"

Till Nowak, Timo Schierhorn, Christian Hartmann (UWE)

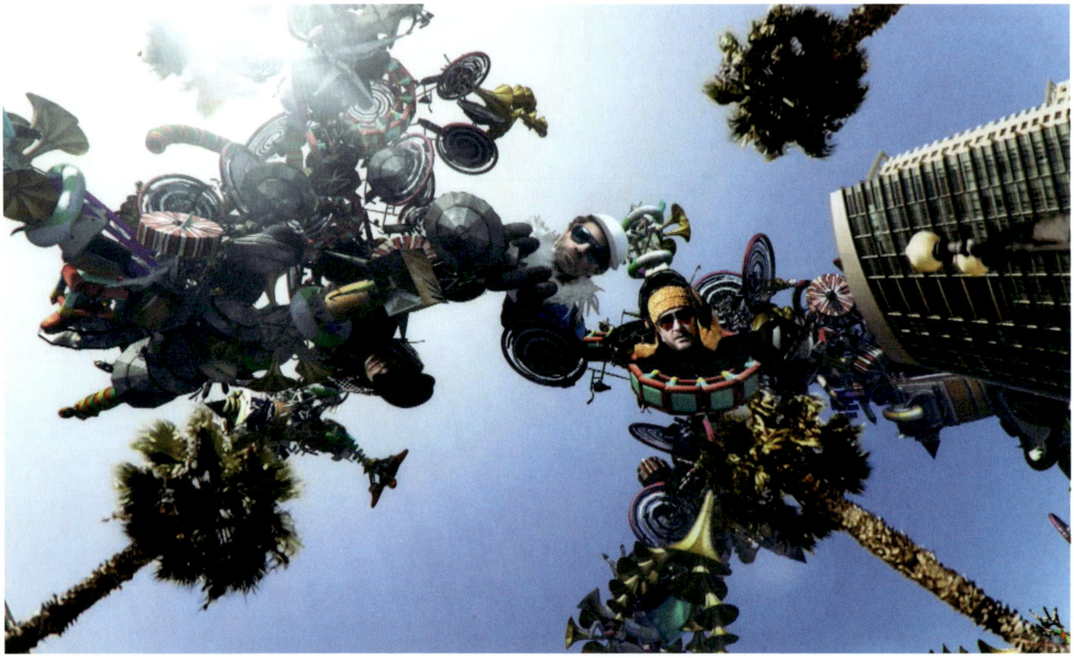

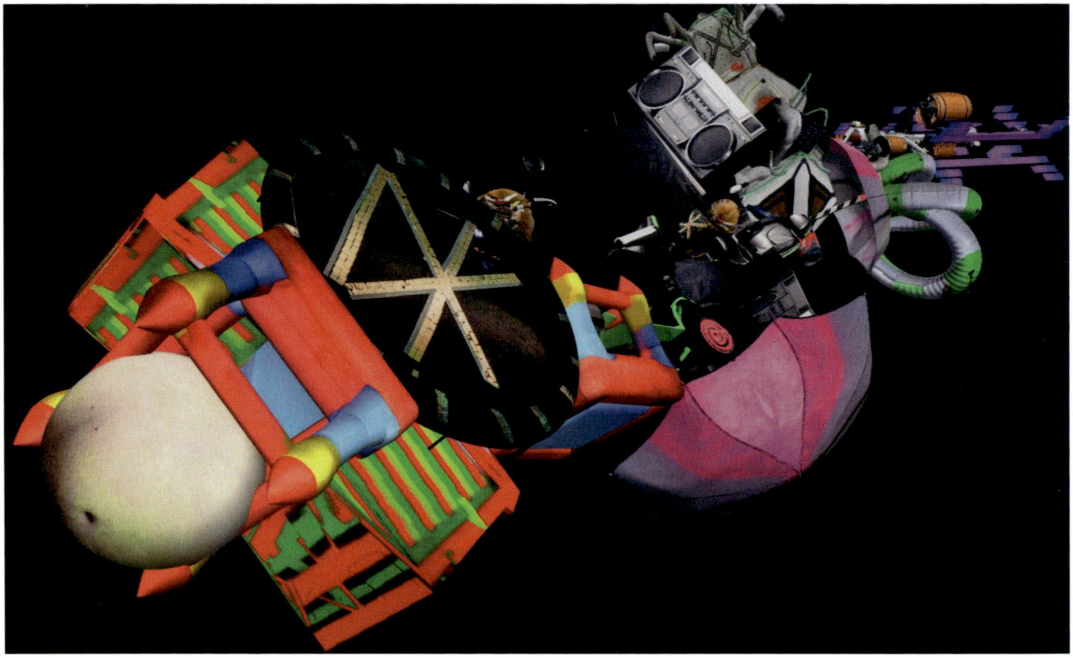

https://www.youtube.com/watch?v=cnEQjaOjBXs

The song *Denken Sie Groß* ("Think Big") by the German band Deichkind is a motivational guide to megalomania. In the video a ten-year-old boy gives an internet tutorial on how to make an award-winning music video. Using 3D animation software, he builds a digital sculpture from archive photos of the band. He reassembles the band's biography and sends the continuously growing entity on a world tour. World domination instead of homework.

Famous for their DIY approach, Deichkind started in small clubs using garbage bags, duct tape and everything they could find backstage to add excitement to their shows. Following that concept for nearly fifteen years, they have grown into one of Germany's biggest live acts, with truckloads of high-tech equipment, all of which they invented themselves. The photographs used in the video show various of these gadgets, props and costumes, spanning their entire career. The items have been digitalized, morphed and reconstructed by a little kid, to form some sort of entertainment Godzilla that grows ad infinitum. The digital world is increasingly being conquered by teenagers and kids. In countless online tutorials they teach adults and professionals the proper use of modern technology. The world is in their hands and their imagination knows no bounds.

Timo Schierhorn and UWE, who have been collaborating with Deichkind since 2012, became interested in working with Till Nowak after seeing his short film *The Centrifuge Brain Project*. Nowak's absurd extensions of found footage realism especially attracted their attention. When they met Nowak and caught a glimpse of his unique 3D modeling workflow, the idea was conceived of recording his working process and making the video a tutorial. The production was realized over a period of six weeks. For the first three weeks Nowak used an HD recorder to capture his daily modeling routine. The footage was passed to Schierhorn and UWE every two to three days for editing. For the remaining weeks Nowak worked on the more elaborate compositing scenes that would conclude the video, while continuously exchanging files and ideas with his workmates, who would finish the edit and the sound design. The concept of using sound effects emerged during the editing process. Incorporating industrial sounds, from knitting machines to large hydraulic systems, helped make the fast-paced modeling sequences more accessible and also added a subtle touch of overstatement to the story.

The intro and interlude scenes were shot on location by Schierhorn and UWE in week five. Elliot D., the boy in the video, had no acting experience. To keep the performance as real as possible, the lines and dialog were mostly improvised. The video was color-graded and finished two days prior to its release, with Nowak still handing in reworks of the final compositing shots. The programs used in the production are Autodesk 3Ds Max, SynthEyes, Adobe After Effects, Crazy Talk Pro and Final Cut Pro.

Directors: Till Nowak, Timo Schierhorn & UWE
3D artist: Till Nowak
Cast (boy): Elliot D.
Grading and finishing: Sebastian Nevermann , Oliver Krupp
Editing and sound effects: Timo Schierhorn, UWE
Production: Auge Altona
Post-producer: Oliver Krupp
Post-production and finishing: mookwe GmbH

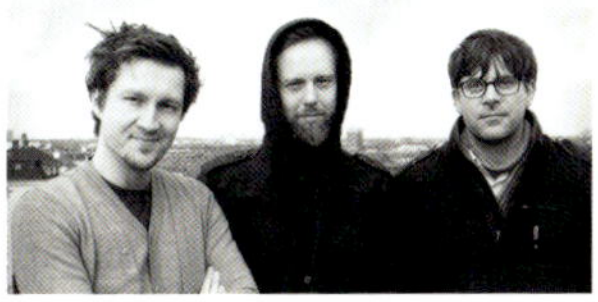

Christian Hartmann (UWE) (DE) born 1980, is a musician and director from Hamburg. He works as a songwriter, producer and touring musician for several bands, such as 2raumwohnung, Nobelpenner and Deichkind. From 2012 he became increasingly involved with directing, especially in the field of music videos. **Till Nowak** (DE), born 1980, is a digital artist, designer and filmmaker based in Hamburg. Since 1999 Till has worked as a professional computer graphics artist on his own independent projects and as an efficient one-man production company for high-profile clients. Till graduated in media design at the University of Applied Sciences in Mainz in 2005. His work has been exhibited in hundreds of international film festivals, featured in books and at SIGGRAPH 2006, 2007, 2009 and 2011 and has received more than 60 awards. **Timo Schierhorn** (DE) born 1979, is a video artist and filmmaker from Hamburg. His film *Night in Olympia* was awarded the 2010 German Film Critics' Prize for Best Experimental Film. In 2013 he made a documentary about the reunion tour of the band Slime, and has made music videos for Deichkind, Die Goldenen Zitronen, Die Vögel and other bands.

Descent

Johan Rijpma

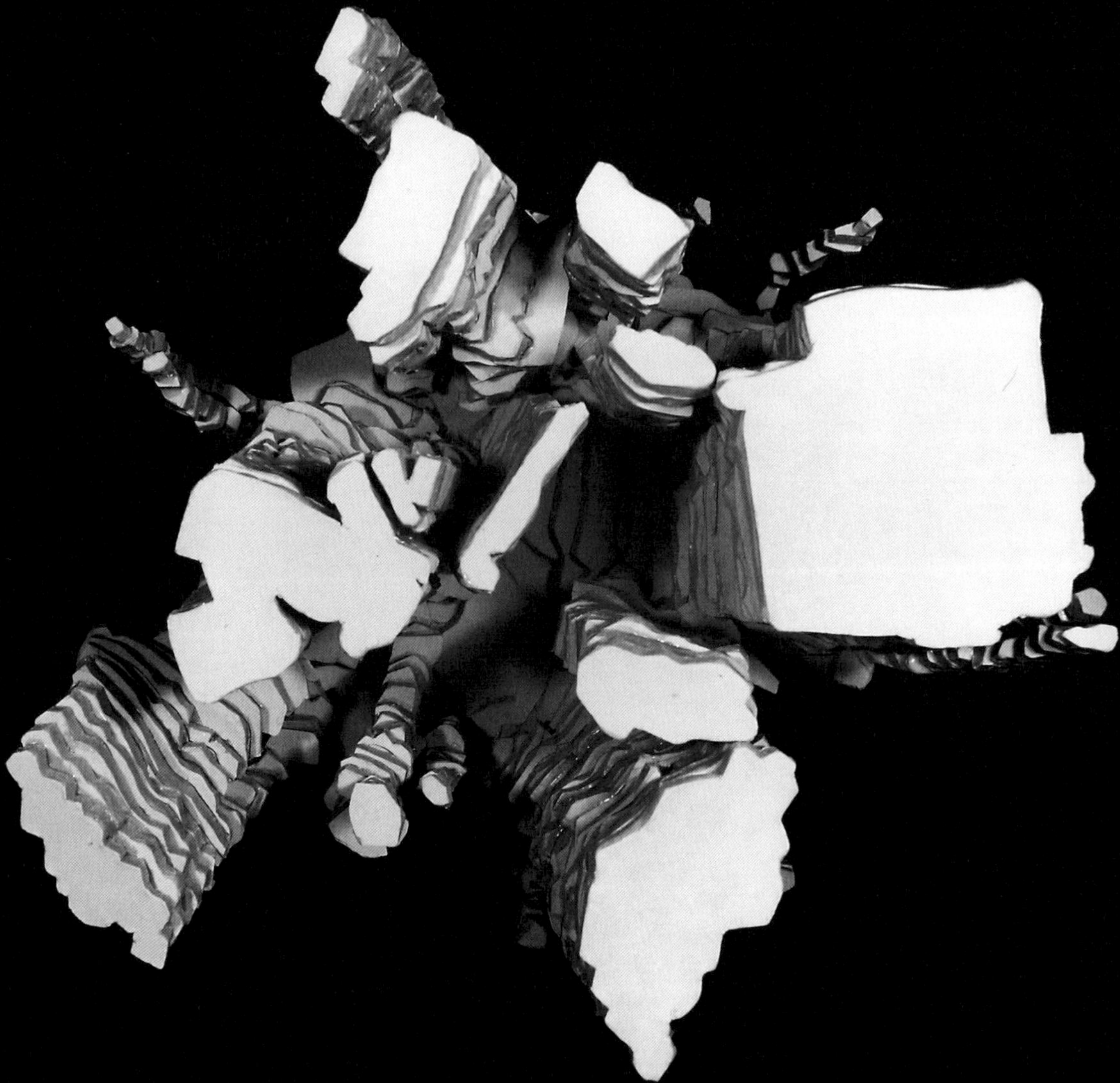

Descent is an experimental film that focuses on the moment when a cup falls and breaks into pieces. By capturing this moment and by making new connections between reality and representation, destruction can simultaneously be the creation of something new. Something that through the force of gravity and the act of observing seems to shift into higher dimensions.

The film is structured in different steps. The first is simply the cup falling to the floor and breaking. Then all of the frames of the clip (of the cup breaking) are stacked onto each other. This happens in real life, all the pieces of the cup are traced frame by frame and are turned back into clay to make a sculpture of all the stacked frames. As this new form emerges, gravity starts to shift and the new sculpture (all of the frames of the clip of the cup falling and breaking) also breaks, and its pieces are re-used to build another sculpture in the same way as the previous one. And so the cycle of creation and destruction continues. In each cycle of the process the camera translates the destruction of the sculpture into a series of two-dimensional pictures representing the destructive moment. This representation is then turned back into a real-life and into a higher-dimensional form, turning from a two-dimensional representation into a three-dimensional object. From this perspective it is possible to consider each cycle in the process to be a step to a higher dimension. Starting with a three-dimensional cup and after nine cycles arriving at a twelve-dimensional sculpture that visualizes, and reflects on its own creative/destructive history. According to M-theory (the current theory in physics that attempts to explain all of the particles and fundamental forces of nature in one theory) the universe has eleven dimensions, which proves that the sculpture is theoretically impossible. All the nine sculptures in the film were made from the remains of their predecessors, and because each sculpture had to be destroyed in order to create the next one only the last sculpture still physically exists. Not only the film but also the last sculpture could therefore be considered to be the final work descending from its ancestors in other dimensions and containing all matter.

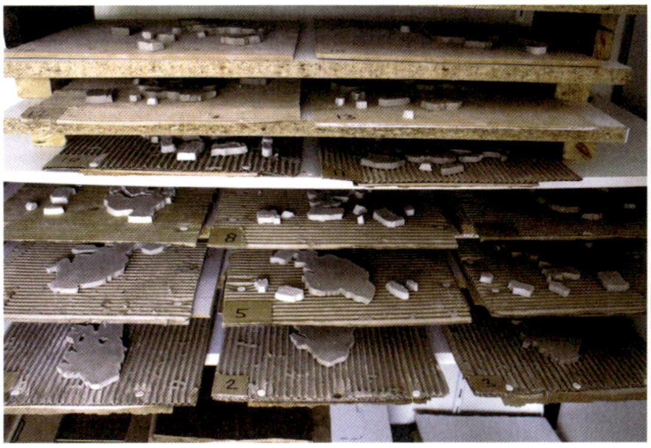

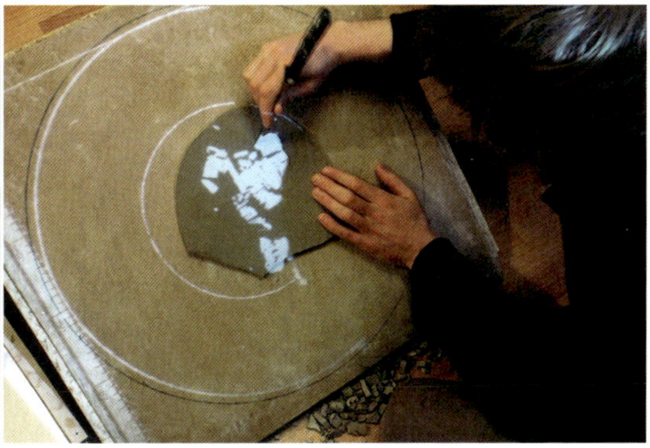

Johan Rijpma (NL), born in 1984, obtained his MA at the Utrecht School of the Arts (Faculty of Art, Media & Technology). In his work he forms creative collaborations with often simple subjects from his daily surroundings in an experimental and playful way. Within his systematic and analytical procedures he reflects on the relationship between his own presumed control and the unpredictability of everyday life. Video, animation and photography are primarily the means by which he creates and captures unusual, seemingly simple but often meticulous processes.

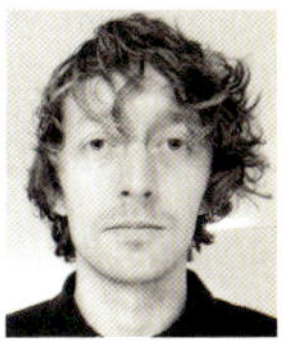

Do Not Touch

Moniker

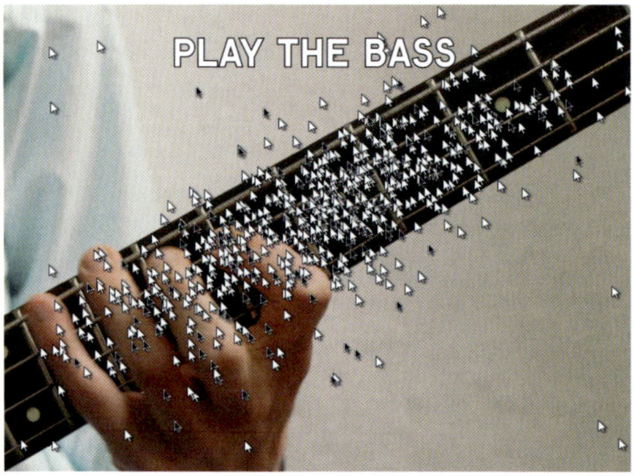

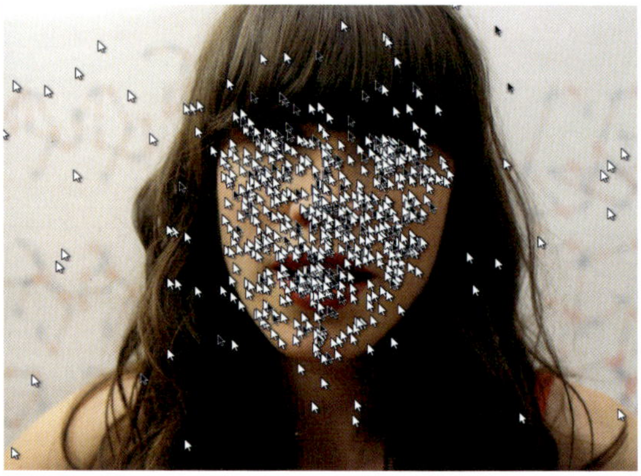

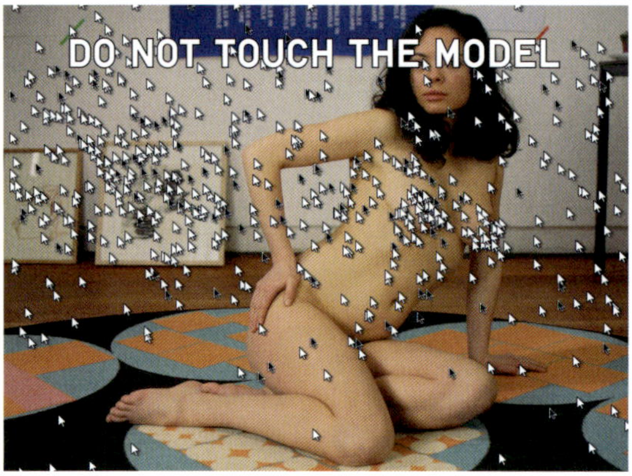

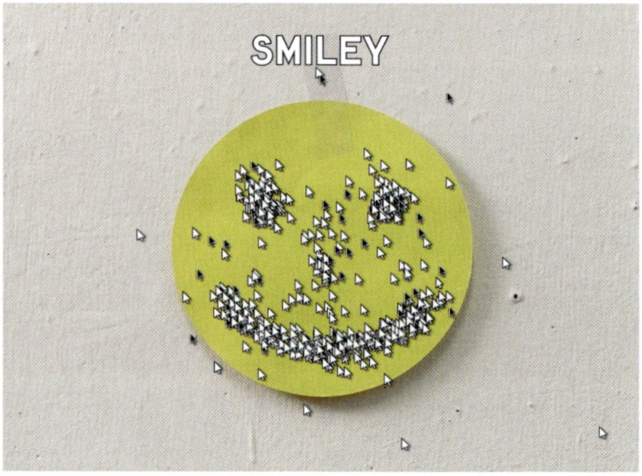

Do Not Touch is an ever-changing interactive music video for the track *Kilo* by the Dutch band Light Light. After the earlier projects *One Frame of Fame* and *Now Take A Bow,* which invite online audiences to participate using their webcams, *Do Not Touch* celebrates and laments the end of the cursor. For decades this inconspicuous arrow has been the essential interface allowing people to communicate with their computers. In recent years the cursor, along with the clicking and dragging necessary to operate the mouse, is being replaced by a finger swiping across a touchscreen.

The *Do Not Touch* video starts with the message "Your cursor will be recorded" and invites users to participate by moving their cursor. They are asked to answer questions like "Where are you from?" and "Where would you like to go?" by pointing at maps shown in the video. Further, users are asked to perform small tasks like "Catch the green dot" while a green blob moves around the screen, "Form a mask," which should be formed on top of the face of one of the singers and "Do not touch the model." While taking part, users see hundreds of cursors moving about in the background. These belong to others who have participated in the past. Together all the cursors form a swarm, displaying distinct behavioral patterns. It becomes apparent that many users do their best to complete the tasks, moving in line with the others and following instructions. Some, however, do not. They don't take part at all or move about at random. Others explicitly do not follow the instructions, doing the exact opposite instead. Cursor movements are recorded and automatically uploaded to the video. A new video is rendered every hour displaying the cursors of the last 1,000 participants.

http://donottouch.org
http://studiomoniker.com/

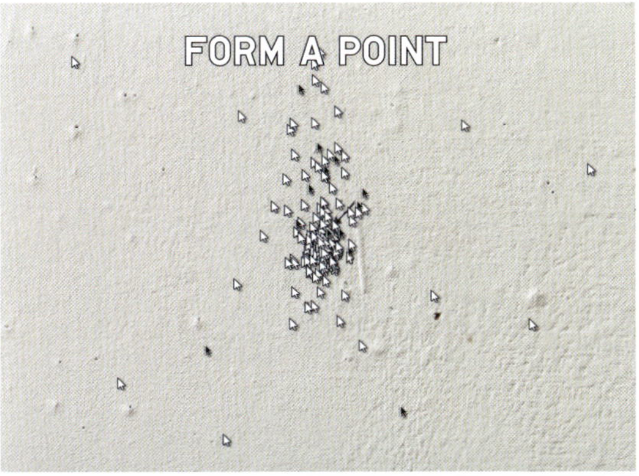

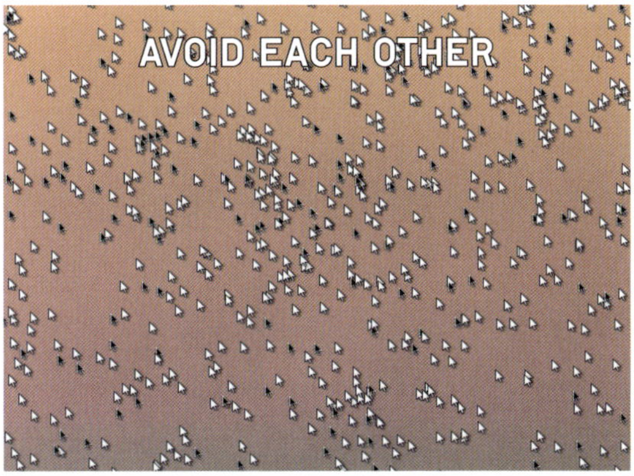

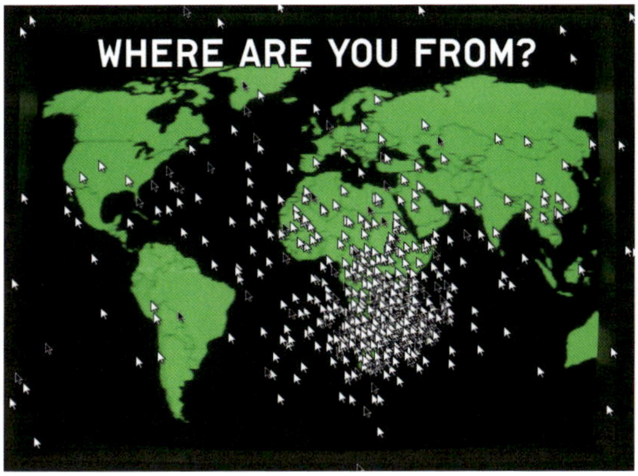

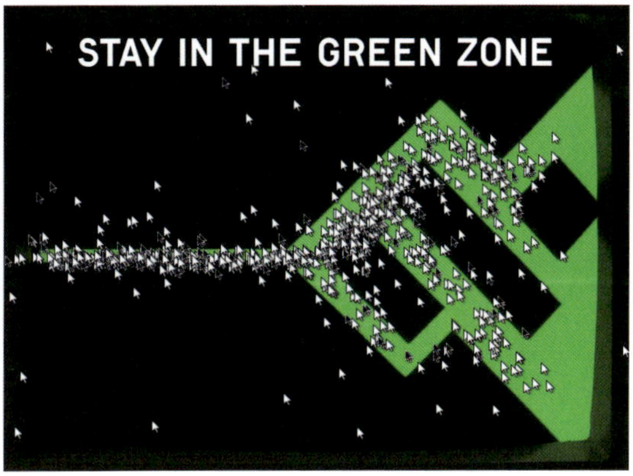

Cast: Björn Ottenheim, Daan Schinkel, Alexandra Duvekot, Thijs Havens, Roberta Petzoldt
Director: Moniker
Line producer: Vargo Bawits, Flickering Wall
DOP: Sal Kronenberg
Focus-puller: Marinka Schippers
Styling: Ogenda ter Haar
Make-up: Paulien Hartman
Still photography: Adina Renner
Editing: Moniker
Grading: Sal Kroonenberg and Moniker
Do Not Touch was generously supported by TAX-videoclipfonds

The Amsterdam-based interaction and media design studio Moniker was founded in 2012 by **Luna Maurer** (DE), **Jonathan Puckey** (UK) and **Roel Wouters** (NL). With Moniker, they explore characteristics of technology, how people use it and how it influences people's daily lives. Often the audience is asked to take part in the development of their (on- as well as offline) projects which are set in motion through the actions of others and trigger a sense of play. Together with Edo Paulus, they authored Conditional Design *http://conditionaldesign.org/*. From 2013 Moniker continued the workshop tradition with their Thursday Afternoon sessions. *http://thursdays.studiomoniker.com/*

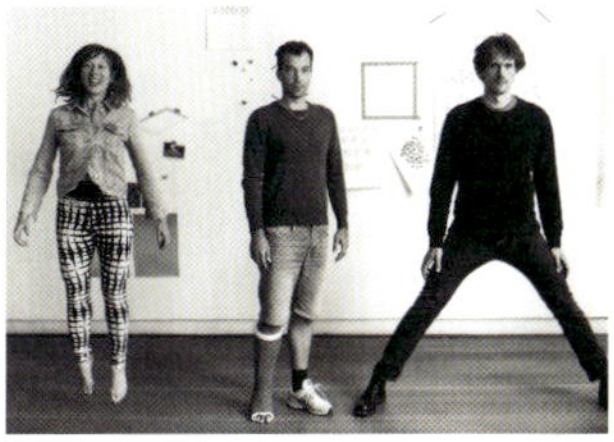

In the Distance

Florian Grolig

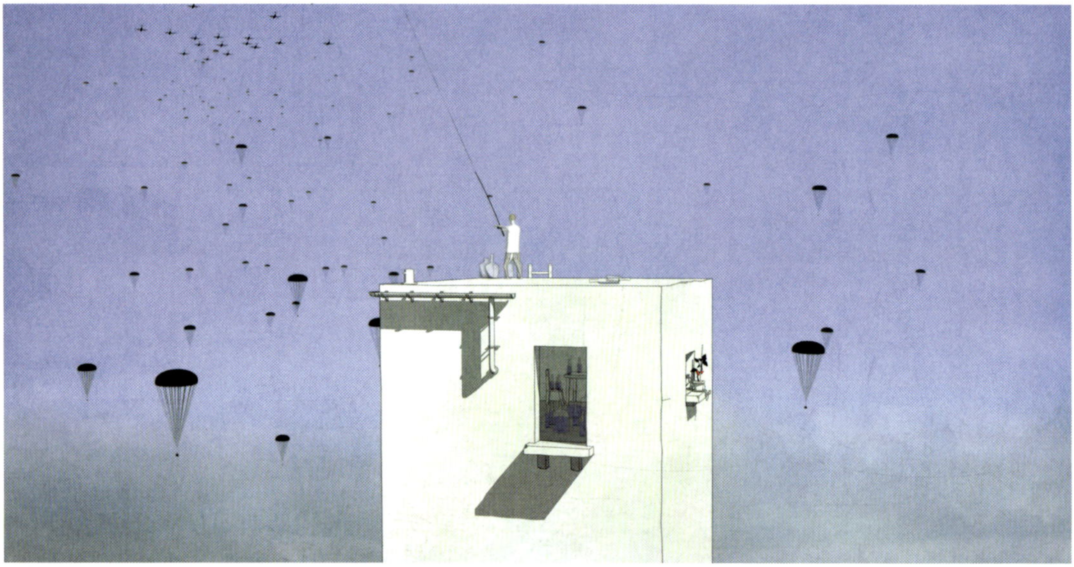

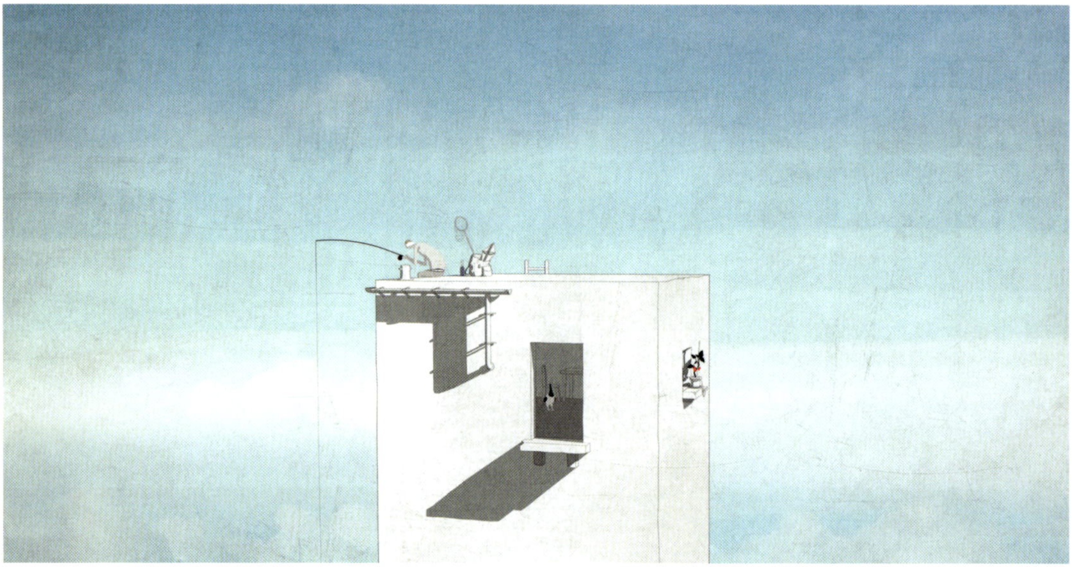

Actually, he has everything he needs—a window to peer out of, a plant growing and flourishing in the sun, a chicken to keep him company. But all around him the noise keeps getting louder, the planes are flying lower, the bombs striking closer to his home. And the people too, they're becoming more intrusive, want to come up to where he is. But he'll have none of that. After all, it's not his war. All he wants is to be left alone. What emerges here, in only a single shot, is a scenario that, though full of individual elements, impressions and events, nevertheless leaves it up to each viewer to put these components together into a complete story. Where exactly is this lonely man's house located? Which country is the plot set in? What war is this an account of? These questions dominate the film all the way to its open ending.

Text: Filmbewertungsstelle (FBW)

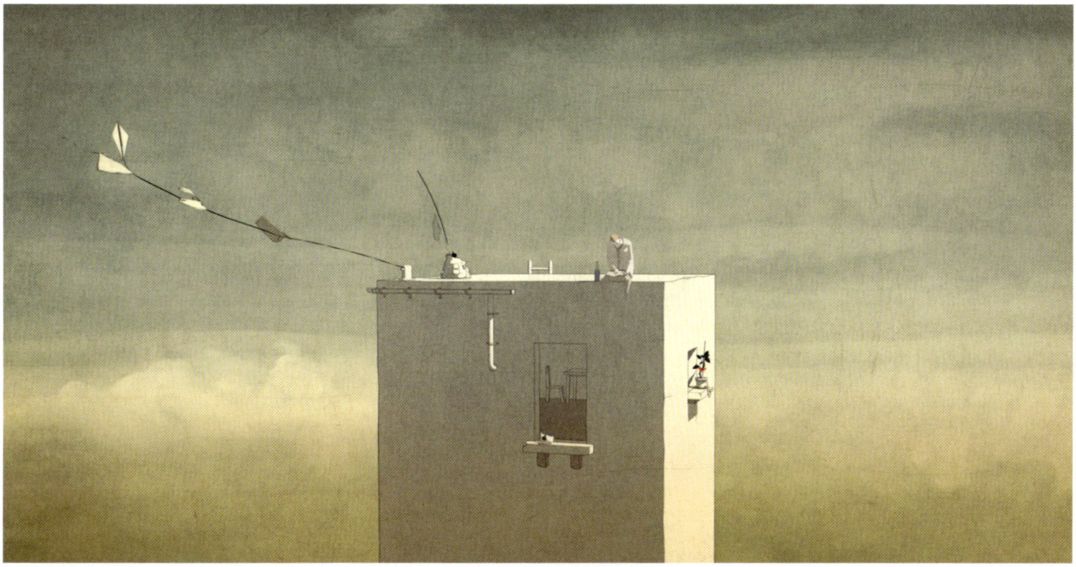

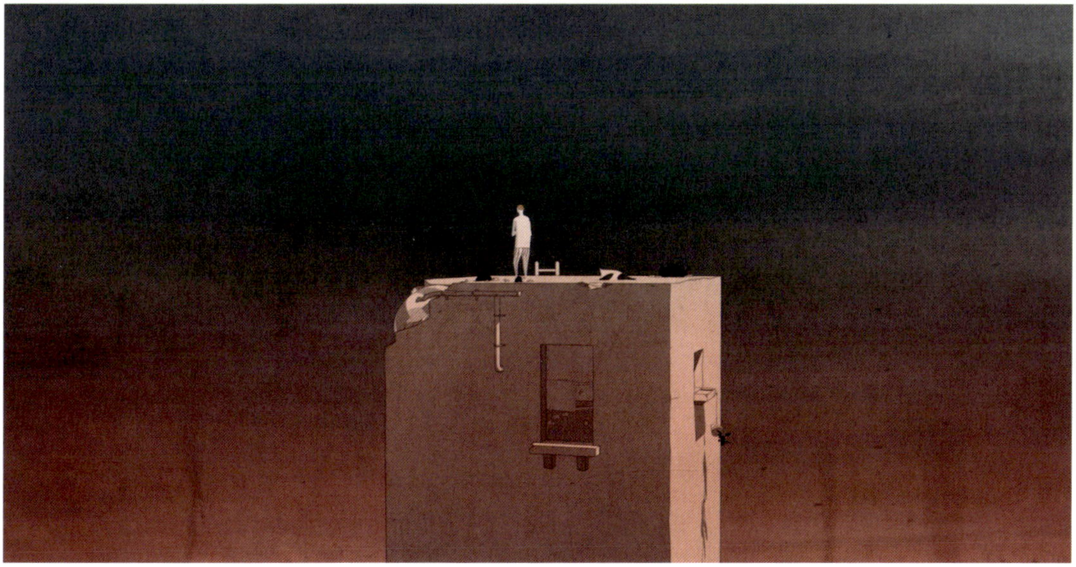

Director: Florian Grolig
Animation: Julian Vavrovsky
Sound design: Tobias Boehm, Christian Wittmoser
Funded by FFA and KjdF

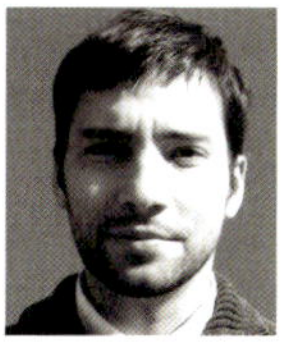

Florian Grolig (DE) is an animation filmmaker and game designer. He graduated from the School of Arts and Design in Kassel and made several award-winning short films as well as commissioned animation. In 2012 he co-founded the Black Pants Game Studio where he was responsible for concept and game design of their first game, *Tiny & Big in Grandpa's Leftovers*. Currently he is living and working in Berlin, making new animation shorts and developing games with "metameta".

Marilyn Myller

Mikey Please

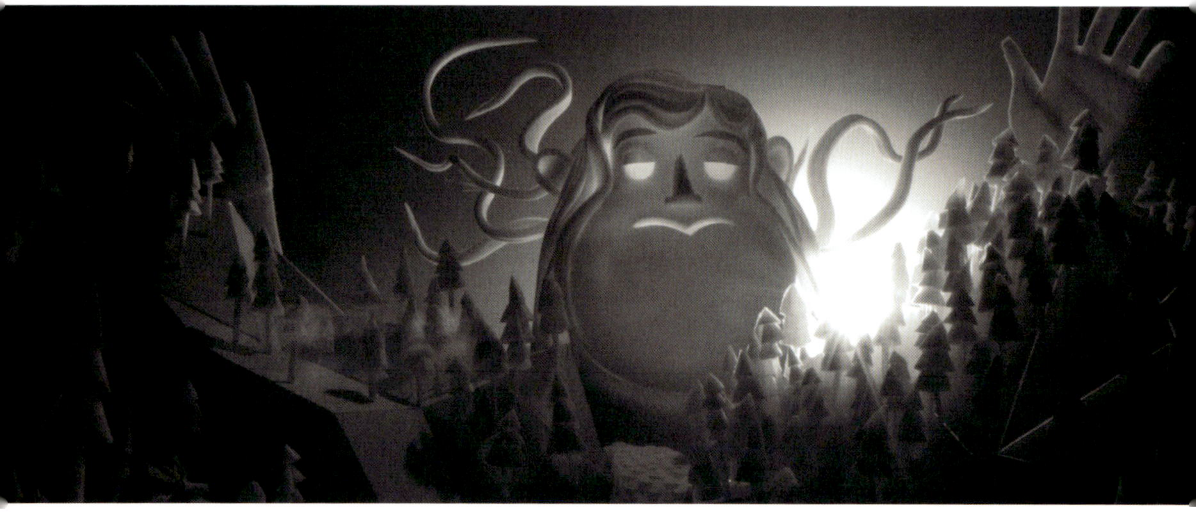

Marilyn is trying really hard to make something that is good. For once her expectations and reality are going to align, perfectly. No, it will be even better than she imagined. It will be epic. It will be tear-jerkingly profound. It will be perfecter than perfect. Nothing can go wrong. From the BAFTA-award-winning director of *The Eagleman Stag* comes the follow-up film: *Marilyn Myller.* One year in the making, the six-minute stop-motion short features the voice of comedy wiz Josie Long, one zillion hand-carved tiny things, literally tens of carved foam puppets, two eyefuls of in-camera, long-exposure light trickery and a pair of tiny dolphins, smooching.

Mikey Please describes the production process: "The film was developed during a three-month residency in Japan in 2012. I started by working with some pre-existing scripts, trying to wrestle them into something that I felt confident enough to dedicate a year of my life to. But, over that time, the process of being locked in this tiny room on the 34th floor of a Tokyo skyscraper, trying to devise something earth-shattering and profoundly beautiful, became more interesting than the scripts themselves. It's such a weird process. I think anyone who's ever made anything—from baking a cake to flying to the moon—can relate to that feeling of expectation and the difference, good or bad, between aspirations and what we actually end up with. So the film slowly morphed into a meditation on what it means to make something. It's a pretty personal piece of work, it feels odd to talk about it, but I guess that's the point and hopefully what makes it interesting. It's a pretty rigorously planned out affair. A lot of wonderful animation is made just by feeling your way through it in the moment, like an improvised performance. It's called "straight ahead" animation. But in my work, which is usually more heavy on narrative, I start with a piece of prose writing. Then it needs to be put into script format, boarded, animaticed (a moving storyboard) then sometimes we'll even roughly animate the shot first before attempting the real thing. Stop-motion is pretty time consuming and there's no apple-z, so yeah, if you want a specific outcome, you need to plan the heck out of it before leaping in. Everything in the film was built from naturally white materials: polystyrene,

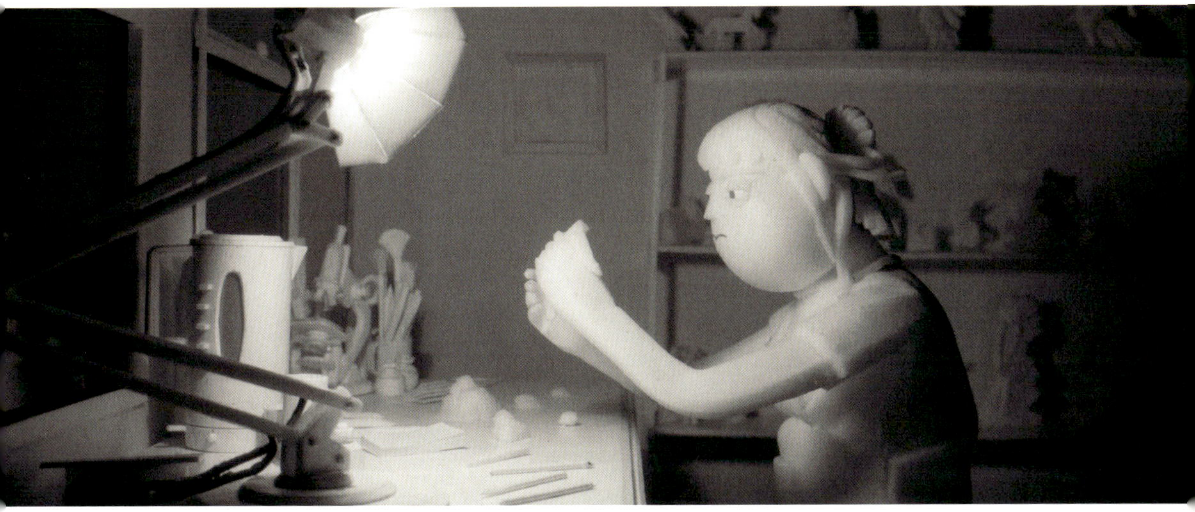

paper, plastazote, plaster, ping-pong balls, styrene and styrofoam. The most difficult aspects to model are the soft-edged, smooth rounded surfaces like the characters' faces—it's not what the material naturally wants to do. The largest technical challenge was the lighting effects—trying to strike the balance between organic and animate-able. We used lots of long exposures while moving the light source, but the results tended to be very loose, and when you're doing that frame-by-frame, it quickly becomes complete chaos. So we developed a process of using stencils and running the light sources behind them, controlling the line edge, and found it struck just the right balance of chaos and control."

Director: Mikey Please
Produced by: Blink Industries, Hornet Films
Executive producers: Peter Medlock, Michael Feder, Bart Yates, Mikey Please
Supervising DOP: Matthew Day
Produced by: Jan Stebbins, James Stevenson Bretton, Mikey Please
Animated and DOP'd by: Mikey Please, Dan Ojari
With animation from: Tim Allen, Steve Warne
Model-makers: Jen Newman, Nadia Oh, Katy Beverage, Dan Ojari, Mikey Please, Carmen Mason, Anna Ginsberg, Laura Bateman
Set design: Nadia Oh, Mikey Please, Jen Newman, Dan Ojari
Mixed by: Simon Harris @ Offset Audio

Mikey Please (UK) is a London-based animation writer and director. With two phenominally successful shorts under his belt, racking up a BAFTA, BAA, numerous other accolades and screenings at over 400 festivals worldwide, Mikey is now developing his first feature film, *Zero Greg,* with Film Four and Warp Films. Alongside fellow RCA graduate Dan Ojari, Mikey has recently opened up Parabella studios to continue his commercial work starting with a beautifully crafted campaign for Twinings. He is represented commercially by Hornet Inc. in New York and Blink Ink in London.

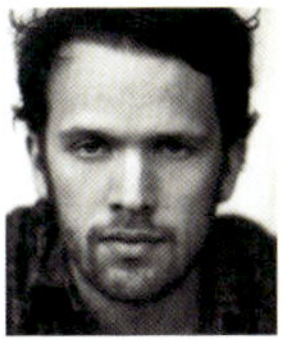

Boo George

Omote Real-Time Face Tracking & Projection Mapping

Nobumichi Asai

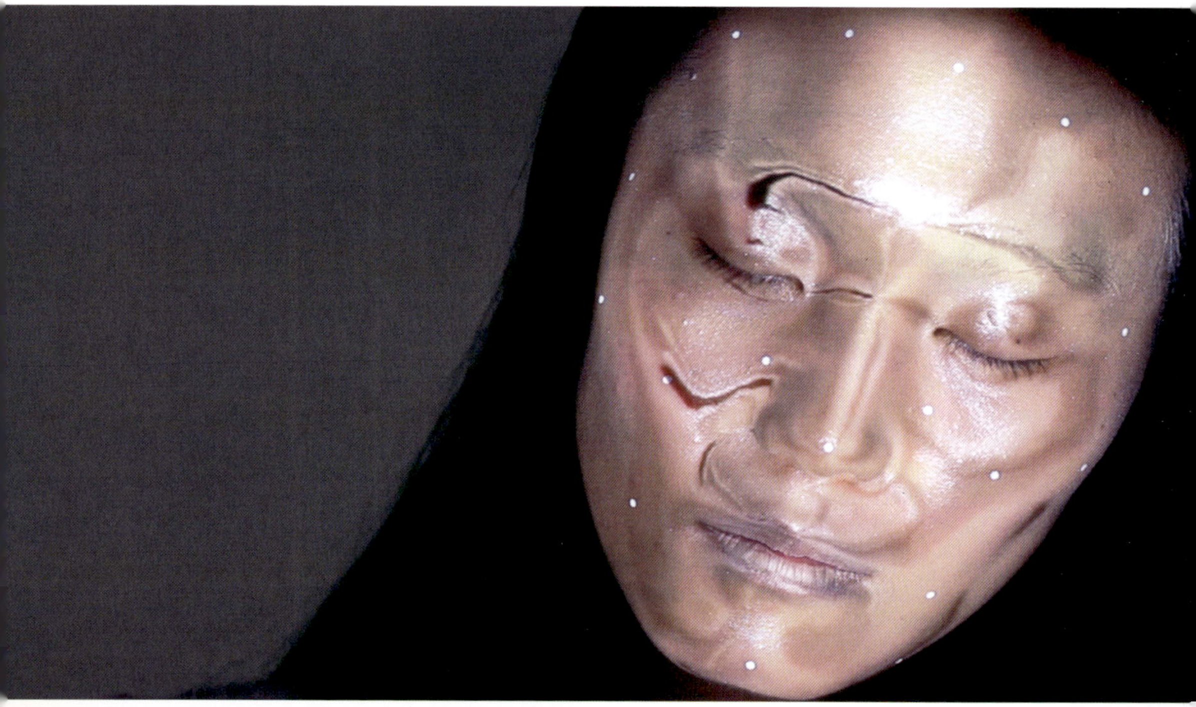

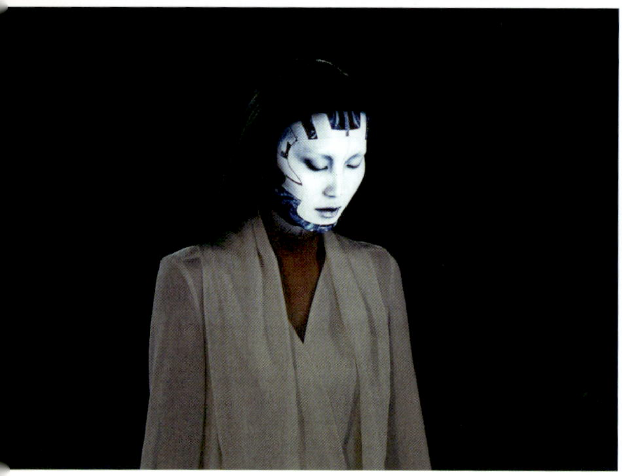

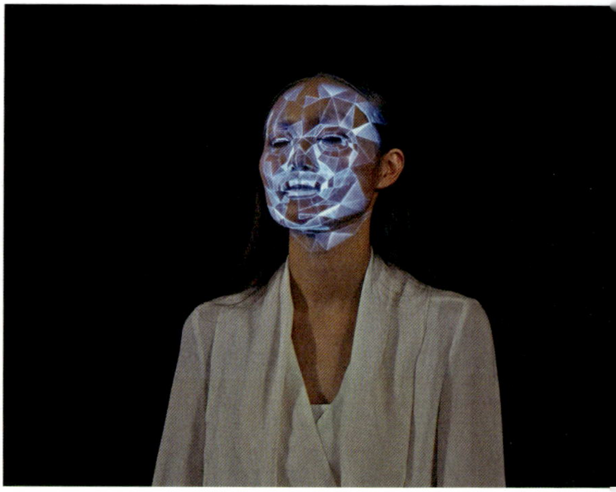

Omote is a collaboration between the Japanese media artist Nobumichi Asai, make-up artist Hiroto Kuwahara and the French digital image engineer Paul Lacroix.
Producer, director, technical producer: Nobumichi Asai (WOW)
Art director and make-up artist: Hiroto Kuwahara
Technical director, programmer: Paul Lacroix (Transit Digital Works)
CG designer: Jin Hasegawa (Spade)
CG designer: Takashi Ishibashi (Spade)

http://www.nobumichiasai.com
https://vimeo.com/103425574

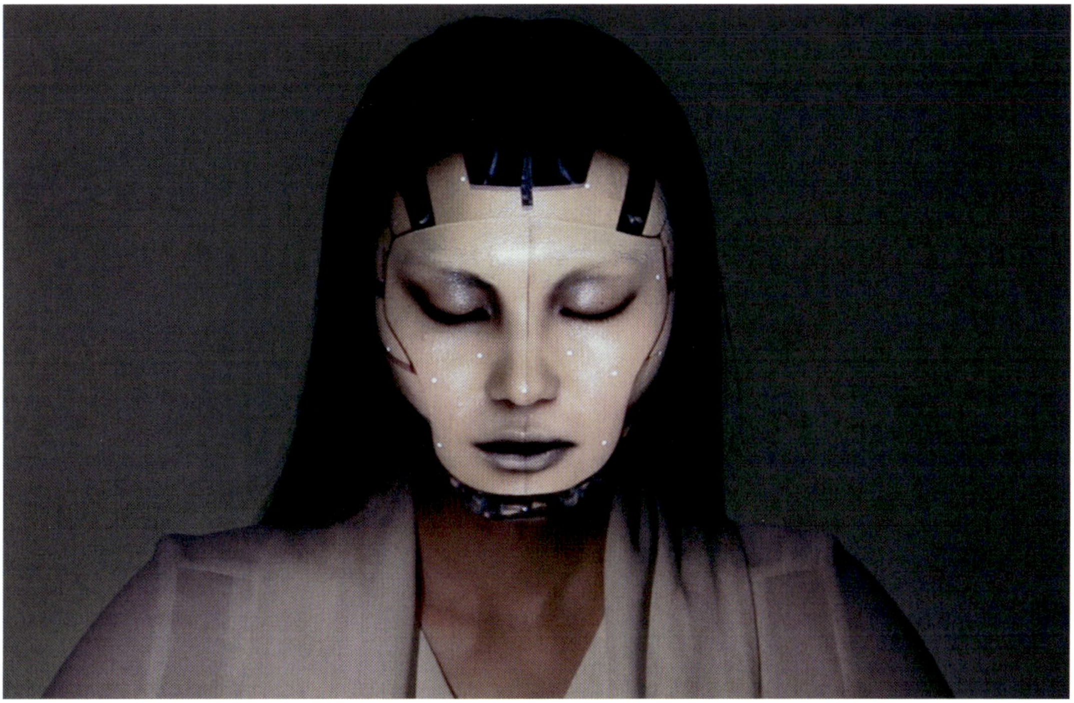

Omote is a Japanese word for the face or a mask. The face is considered to be a mirror that reflects the human soul, a separation between *omote* (exterior) and *ura* (interior), and in *Nogaku*, Japan's classical musical plays, performers use masks *(omote)* to express a multitude of dramatic emotions. As we spent more time on the project, we became more aware of its similarities with *Nogaku* masks *(omote)*, and explored further possibilities by integrating the latest technology and classical Japanese art. I have always considered the face to be the most delicate yet powerful medium for art. The face has evolved in order to convey emotions, and it is the only body part that effectively communicates and reacts to the most subtle changes and conditions. I became interested in the possibility of face mapping and its potential in expressing something extraordinary. The team also wanted to express Japanese beauty to the world. Japanese women have bewitching, ethereal and sophisticated qualities that are unique. Additionally, Japanimation is also an art form, a subculture that is unique to Japan. I personally like manga and animation and looked for particular motifs from it. For this project, we used OptiTrack sensors for a swift response, and developed an original C++ program. To reduce minimal latency (delay), we devised ways of integrating the whole process into one program. This created amazing effects.

Nobumichi Asai (JP), graduated from Tohoku University, Department of Science. He belongs to WOW (www.w0w.co.jp) and works on music videos, CM, and projection mapping as a planner and producer and technical director. He is noted for combining his science background and artistic skills to create original and innovative works. He has also been active in mapping projects since creating Seikei 3D Projection Mapping, the first large-scale projection-mapping project in Japan. His work has been awarded many prizes and has been shown worldwide.

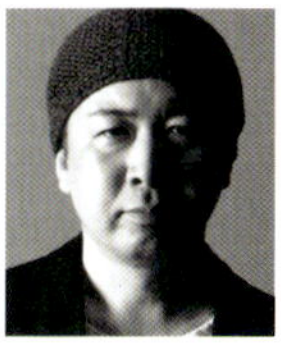

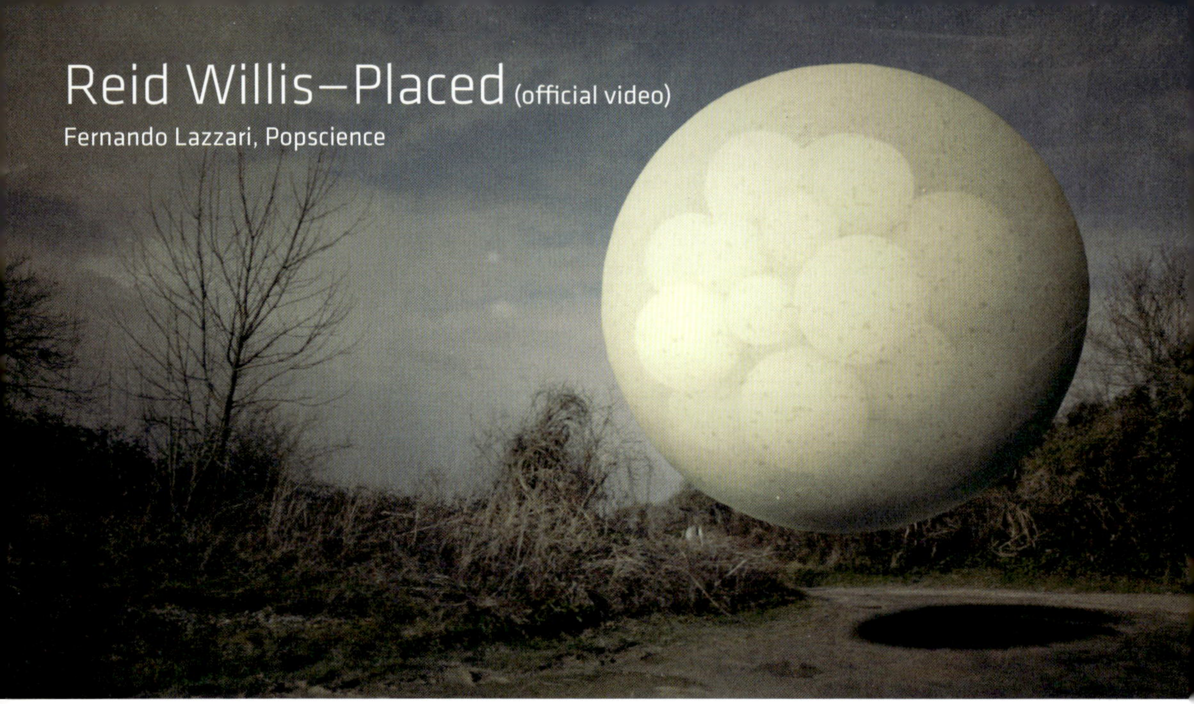

Reid Willis–Placed (official video)

Fernando Lazzari, Popscience

Official music video for the first track of Reid Willis' album *The Sunken Half.* The video was originally inspired by the work of American photographer Robert Adams, in particular his pictures of vast empty landscapes. Later in the process, inspiration came also from the surrealistic work of English graphic designer Storm Thorgerson and Japanese artist Koji Shiraya's *After The Dream* series. The very ambiguous quality of the music track–oscillating between the happy and the sad, the bright and the spooky, inspired the creation of objects that make reference both to birth and death at the same time. The big sphere that floats above the land works as a "presence" (Led Zeppelin's *Presence* album cover by Thorgerson is a reference) that momentarily affects everything happening on the planet. The actions are deliberately ambiguous and do not really have a clear consequence, but rather suggest ideas that lend themselves to different kinds of interpretations. Eggs, sperm, skulls, stones and fabric all act together in the context of nature to create a mood that some find unsettling, some beautiful. There is no linear narrative, but a shot by shot, line by line, poetic approach. The backgrounds were shot on the Isle of Wight, UK, a place of natural allure and a very special light in the month of February. The west side of the island features some corners of desolate, timeless beauty that were perfect for the track. The backgrounds were shot on a Canon 5D II on a tripod, with a variety of lenses and using the Cinestyle color preset that provided a slight HDR look, which resembles an illustration rather than a photograph. This look proved very appropriate for the project and made it to the final version with little color correction. All 3D objects were created and animated in Cinema 4D using a combination of dynamics, mograph, deformers and displacements. They were lit, textured and rendered using V-Ray, and later composited in After Effects, where some color correction and texturing was added.

Design, direction, animation: Fernando Lazzari
Music: Reid Willis

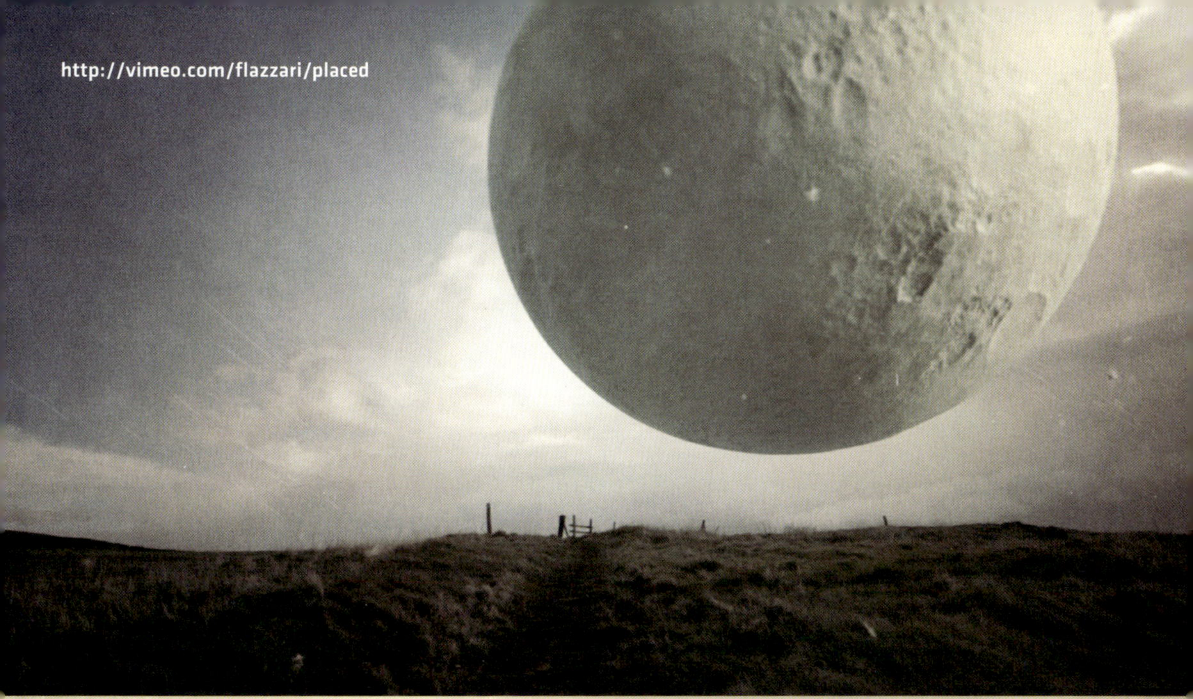

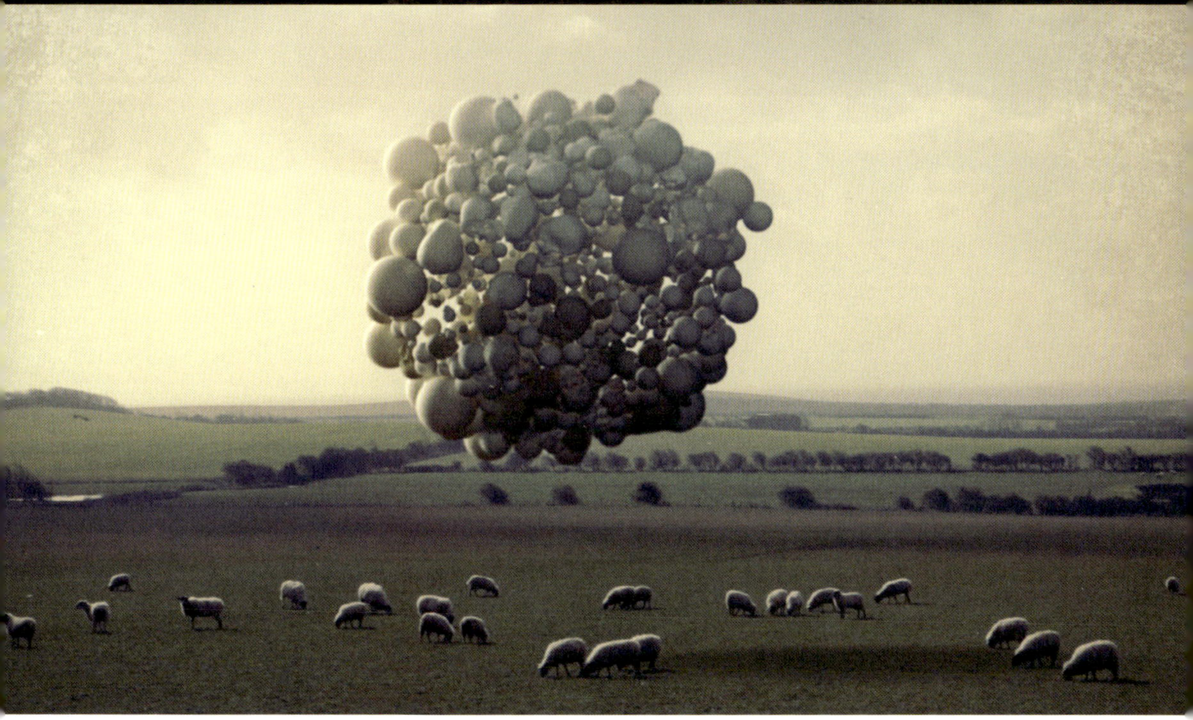

Fernando Lazzari (UK),is a London-based designer and director with a strong, refined visual style and a unique combination of creative and technical skills. With a solid background in design, film, typography, photography and animation, his work has been recognized with multiple industry awards. His work ranges from short-format logo animations and idents to longer experimental videos where image and sound converge to create strong, poetic audiovisual experiences. Key to his style is the juxtaposition of live-action landscapes, both man-made and natural, with 3D graphics and typography.

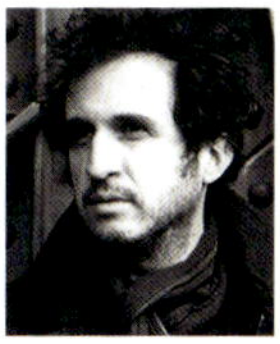

Reid Willis—Placed (official video)

Symphony no. 42

Réka Bucsi

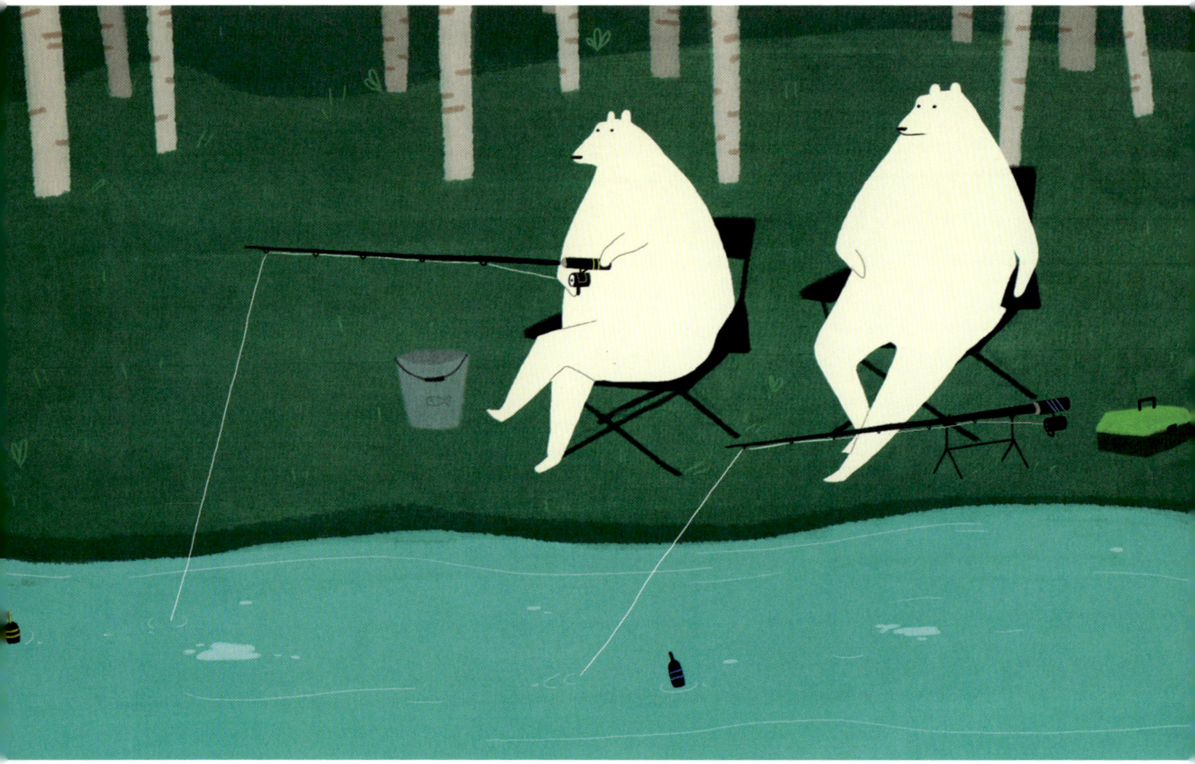

The film applies an unconventional narrative. It presents a subjective world through 47 scenes. Small events, interlaced by associations, express the irrational coherence of our surroundings. The surreal situations are based on the interactions between humans and nature. Differences between human and animal diminish, everyone is doing their job and leaving traces. Every small movement affects another, building an unpredictable, irrational system. I found it important not to interpret or highlight particular things, so the characters and situations of the film can exist independently. I tried to stay neutral, to reveal, to present rather than form an opinion. I do not wish to offer a solution or a moral. The basic idea of the film lies in an interesting human habit: when witnessing an unknown situation, we unconsciously put it in context according to our own ideas. I wanted to utilize this and have the viewers automatically find their solutions for the given situations. The scenes are interlaced by diverse visual, auditory, sensory or other impressionistic associations. It was important to create a temporal and spatial structure that can tie together all the different locations and characters, so that the viewer can travel seamlessly. Although the first phase of the making of *Symphony no. 42* was completely intuitive, in the course of the development a more concrete theme developed and the scenes started to arrange themselves around it. These 47 observations focus on the interactions between humans and nature. Differences between human and animal diminish, everyone is doing their job and leaving traces. Every small movement affects another, building an unpredictable, irrational system. I find it soothing that the world around us is often irrational, and I also find it very funny to observe how we live alongside all these creatures. It is interesting for me how much we compare completely different life forms' behavior to our own. This arrogance is very inspiring for me, as I find

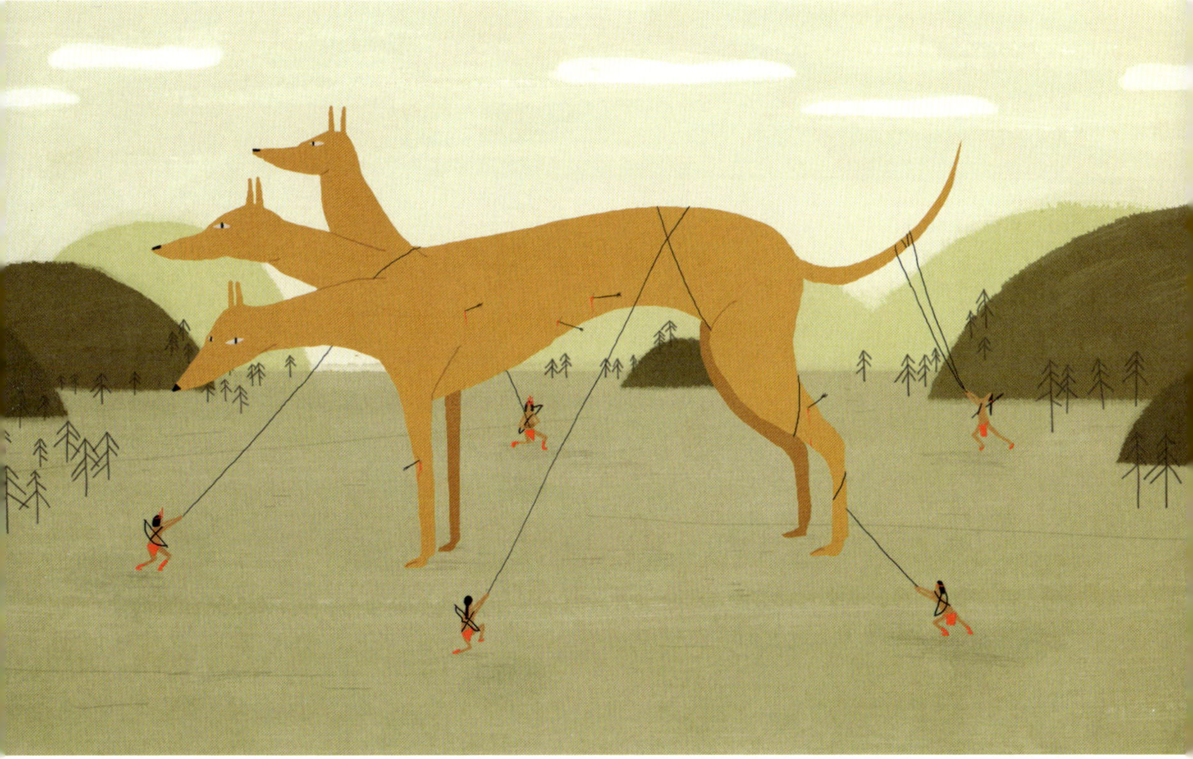

it cute, funny and sad in the same time. The fox, with its attempt to describe the material world, the rules of tiny particles that secretly determine our everyday life, sets another world in motion. We wander further and further, to the Milky Way in the fortune-teller's crystal and its cosmic scale. After peeking into 47 scenes, we fall back to the forest, from which we saw the same universe in the form of a star-studded sky. *Symphony no. 42* was animated frame by frame, backgrounds were painted using a digital tablet. From the very beginning of the process there was a big focus on sound. I started working with Péter early on, asking for his ideas concerning sound. I wanted to have as much recorded sound as possible, to make this flat, minimal, 2D world more relatable, more 3D. We traveled around Sri Lanka for two weeks recording most of the sounds for the forests in the film. The whole production from writing until end of post-production took around a year.

Animation: Nándor Bera, Réka Bucsi, Krisztián Király, László Tóth, Sándor Vágó; Producer: József Fülöp; Director, design, writing: Réka Bucsi; Sound design: Péter Benjámin Lukács

Réka Bucsi (HU), born in 1988, is an independent animation filmmaker and illustrator. From 2008-2013 she attended MOME (Moholy-Nagy University of Art and Design Budapest), animation department. Her graduation film *Symphony no. 42* was selected for the Official Shorts Competition at the Berlinale, Sundance Film Festival and was shortlisted for the 87th Academy Awards. From 2011-2012 she attended Essemble, a digital filmmaking training program. 2013/2014 she attended Animation Sans Frontiéres (ASF), the European animation production workshop. Réka is represented as a director by Passion Pictures, Paris.

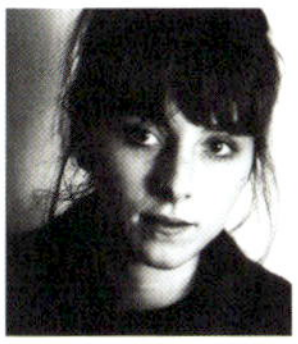

Sándor Fegyverneky

World of Tomorrow

Don Hertzfeldt

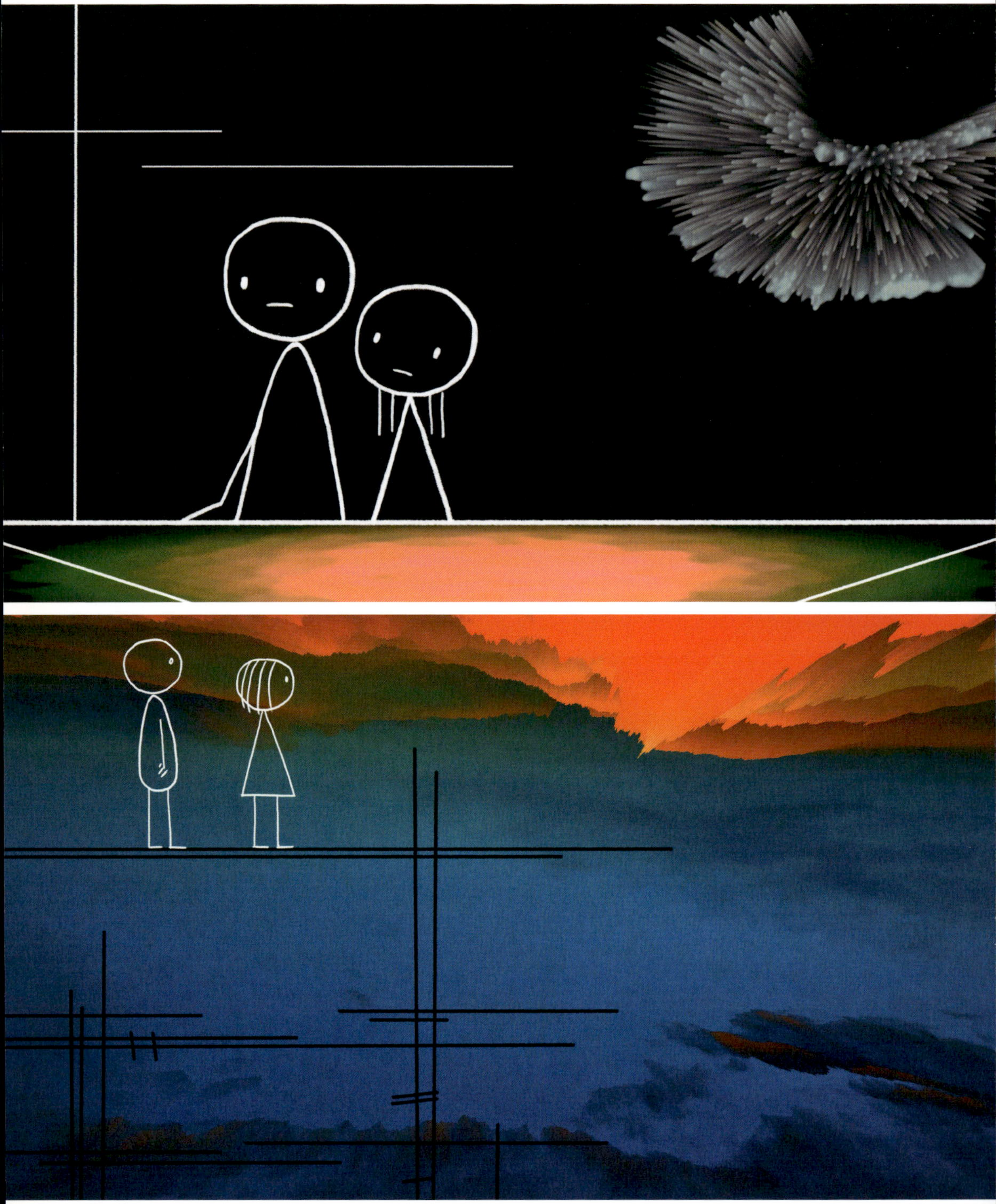

http://www.bitterfilms.com
https://vimeo.com/ondemand/worldoftomorrow

A little girl is taken on a mind-bending tour of her distant future. *World of Tomorrow* is Don Hertzfeldt's first digitally animated film, after twenty years of animating with paper, pencil, and 35mm.

An introduction from director Don Hertzfeld:

Hi everyone! In early 2014 I began work on a secret project called *World of Tomorrow.* It was originally just an exercise to teach myself the basics of digital animation: after nearly 20 years of working with paper, pencils, 35mm film, rocks, and fire, I'd never actually drawn anything on a tablet before. Animating this way at first seemed a bit like trying to read a children's book in a foreign language ... it all seemed vaguely familiar somehow, but was sort of weirdly scrambled. I'm also pretty sure I bent the software to do things it was in no way designed for. But the writing and the visuals soon began to grow, as they always do, and I made two new rules for myself: get through shots as fast as you possibly can, and do everything differently.

Carrying on with this spirit, for the first time I'm releasing a new movie online: *World of Tomorrow* will continue to play theaters all over the world like the 35mm stuff did, but going digital now means we can bring it to everyone else as soon as possible. As an independent, those theatrical tours and DVD sales directly funded the next films. and the prevailing gloomy attitude towards selling shorts online seems to be 1) huh? but there's no market for shorts online you fool, and 2) people will steal it anyway. But if we continue to believe there's no market for shorts without ever trying to do anything to challenge it, nothing will change. And I still believe people simply want to support the things they'd like to see more of ... because hey, without all of you over the years, I surely would've had to give up and gotten a real job back in the 90s.

Finally, I'd like to introduce my amazing two leading ladies. The wonderful Julia Pott (animator & illustrator herself), appears in her first acting role, and proves that there is a viable side career for her should she ever tire of endlessly drawing little animals wearing scarves. Julia performs opposite my niece, Winona, who was four years old when I recorded her. I learned very quickly that you cannot direct a four-year-old. You cannot even expect a four-year-old to recite lines back at you. You just sort of have to let the four-year-old happen. So I recorded her as we drew pictures together and talked about the world. We live very far apart, I only see her about once a year, so we only had the time for a couple of sessions. And with these recordings—her candid thoughts, reactions, and questions—plus a bit of rewriting, I was then able to create the character you are about to meet ...

The text was originally written for the Vimeo online release of *The World of Tomorrow*

Cast:
Emily: Julia Pott
Emily Prime: Winona Mae

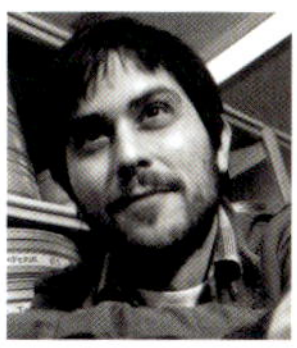

Don Hertzfeldt (US) is an Oscar nominee whose animated films include *It's Such a Beautiful Day, Billy's Balloon, The Meaning of Life,* and *Rejected*. His work has played around the world and most recently appeared on *The Simpsons.* Seven of his films have screened in competition at the Sundance Film Festival, where he is the only filmmaker to have won the Grand Jury Prize for Short Film twice. After creating animated films for nearly twenty years using traditional tools (pencil, paper, and 35mm cameras), *World of Tomorrow* is his first 100% digital production.

YouTube Smash Up

Parag K. Mital

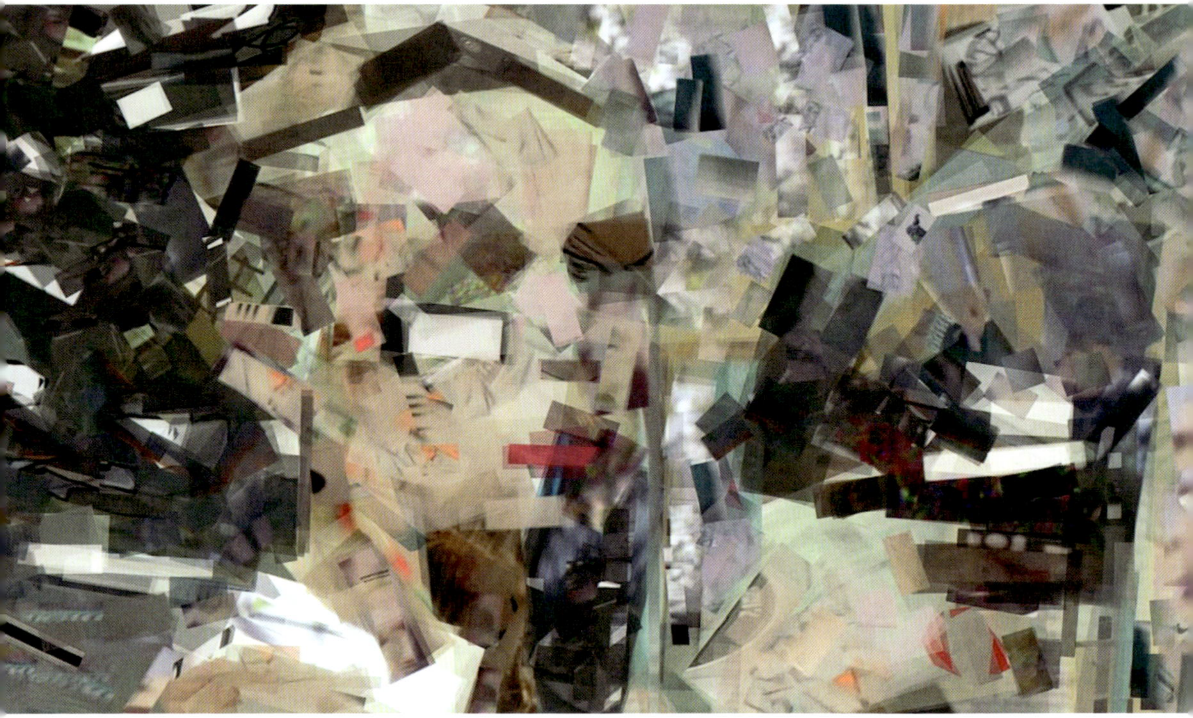

YouTube Smash Up attempts to generatively produce viral content using video material from the Top Ten most viewed videos on YouTube. Each week, the Number One video of the week is resynthesized using a computational algorithm matching its sonic and visual content to material only from the remaining Top Ten videos. This other material is then re-assembled to look and sound like the Number One video. The process does not copy the file, but synthesizes it as a collage of fragments segmented from entirely different material.

Using YouTube's interface, the videos are also textually tagged with popular culture's "most viewed" artifacts, i.e. the database containing the Top Ten YouTube videos. This process attempts to inject the video into the community, masquerading as an innocent tribute video. The video's audience, often viewers hoping to find the original Number One video, are almost certainly disturbed by the videos, as illustrated by the video's overwhelmingly negative "like" ratio, and by comments such as, "now im [sic] blind", "Will someone kill me in my sleep because I watched this video?" and another commenter's reply to the previous comment, "me 2 [sic]".

Despite their poor reception, likely due to their cut-up and abstract nature, most smashups have been the subject of copyright violations from YouTube's automated copyright infringement detection system, Content ID. In each case, Content ID flags the videos as duplicates of the Number One video, rather than flagging any of the content actually used from the Number Two to Ten videos. This automated system attempts to automatically discover copyrighted content in newly uploaded videos, informing the original content holders if it finds anything. Most likely the content-rights holders never watch the supposedly infringing videos, and instead forward a cease-and-desist notice threatening a lawsuit. Despite the powerful language used by the content-rights holders, the videos were all put back online after multiple rounds of fair-use arguments and even more cease-and-desist notices.

The videos manipulate a level of representation indistinguishable by a robot perception, a space be-

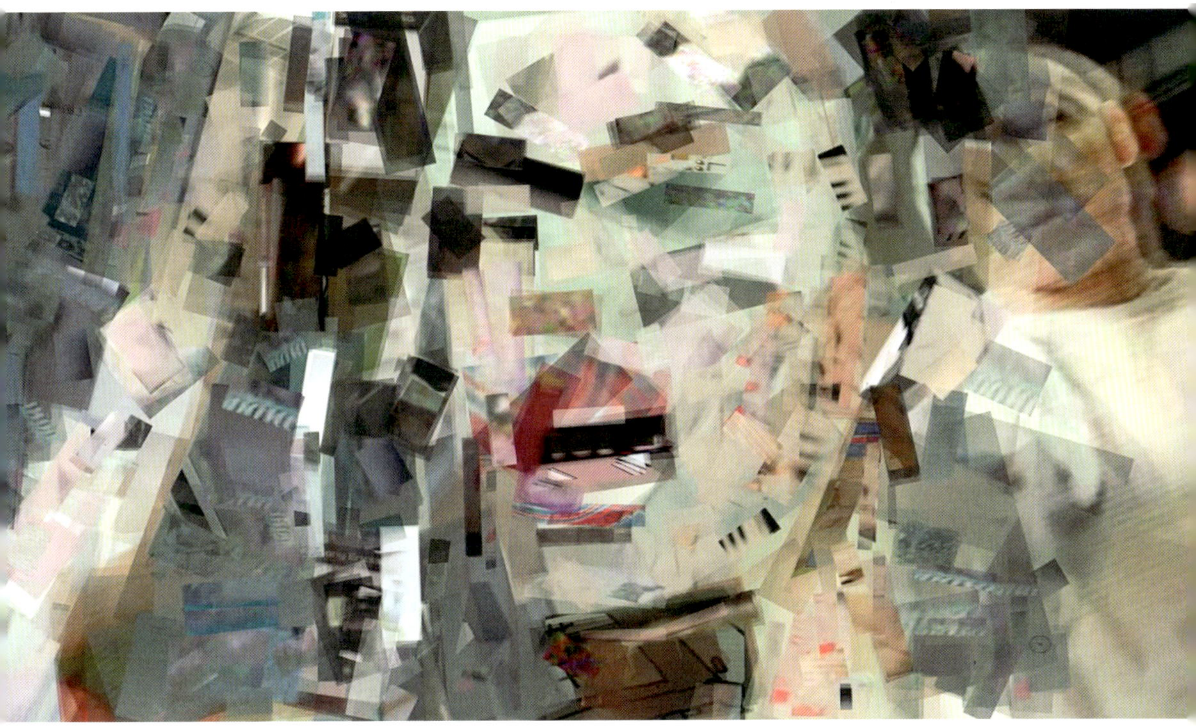

tween pixels and perception, juxtaposing cultural fragments at a proto-object layer in an entirely automated process: Miley Cyrus's lips collaged against the background of a troupe of dancing animals or Psy's forehead dancing without the remaining pieces of Psy. Within this space, a disjunct between a state-of-the-art robot perception and those of unsuspecting YouTubers is revealed, asking what constitutes a copyrightable cultural artifact, as algorithms become increasingly more intelligent and as data continues to be manipulated by even more complex pattern-recognition and information-retrieval algorithms. Finally, the videos attempt to probe a dystopian future of automated content generation, when computer algorithms are not only capable of modeling cultural artifacts but also producing them, further embracing their present role as mere content curators.

Programming, concept, execution: Parag K. Mital
Carried out during a PhD on "Audiovisual Scene Synthesis", funded by the Department of Computing, Goldsmiths, University of London, under the supervision of Mick Grierson and Tim Smith.

Parag K. Mital (US) is an artist and interdisciplinary researcher obsessed with the nature of information, representation and attention. Using film, eye-tracking, EEG, and fMRI recordings, he has worked on computational models of audiovisual perception from the perspective of both robots and humans, often revealing the disjunct between the two, through generative film experiences, augmented reality hallucinations and expressive control of large audiovisual corpora. Through this process, he balances his scientific and arts practice, with both reflecting on each other: the science driving the theories, and the artwork re-defining the questions asked within the research.

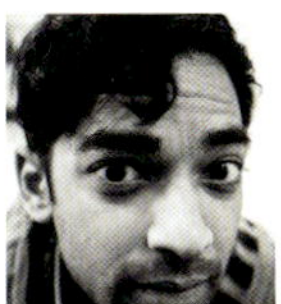

109645790437692847650

David OReilly

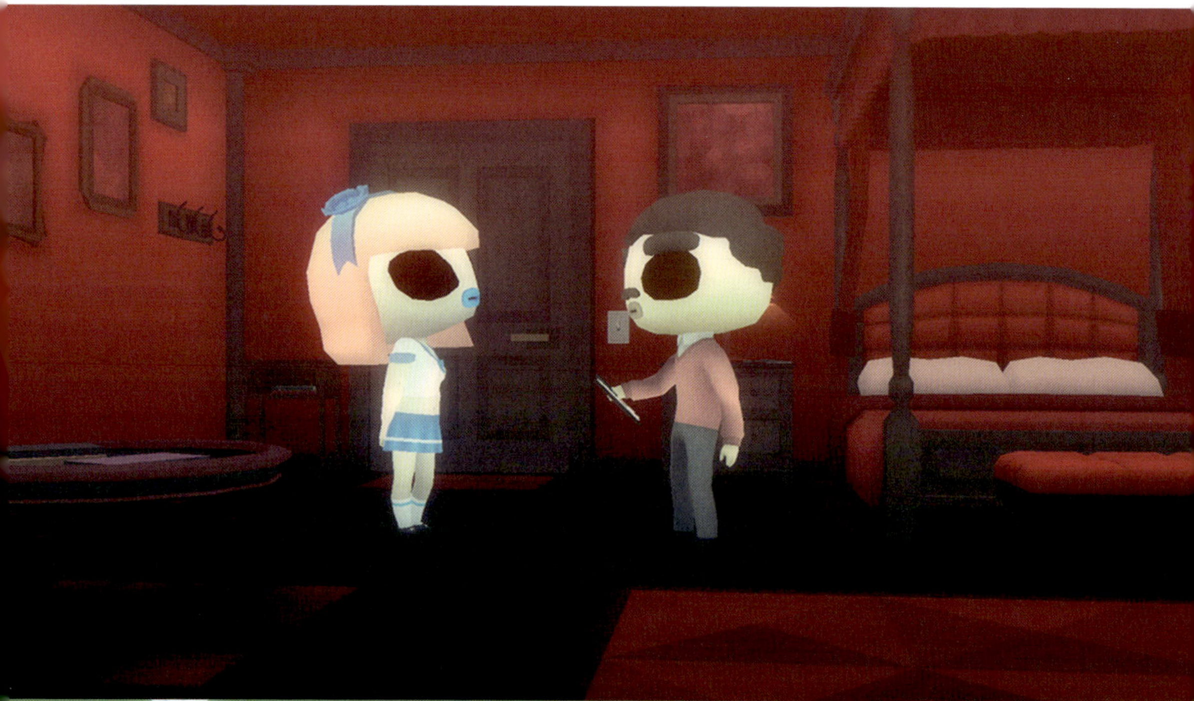

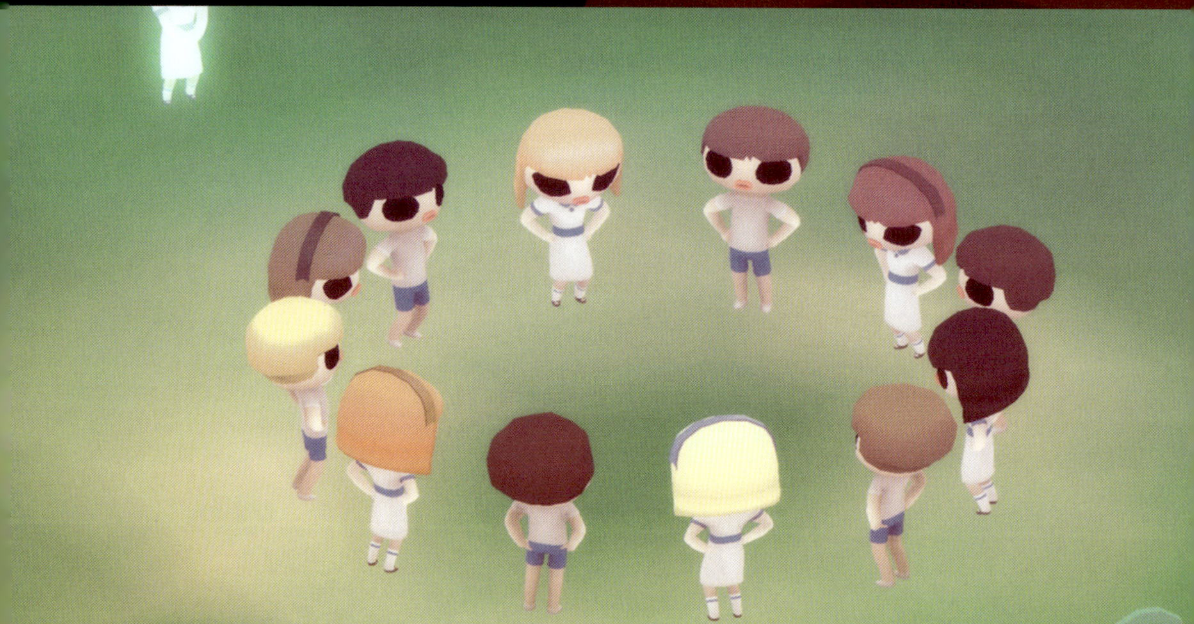

http://109645790437692847650.com
http://www.davidoreilly.com/

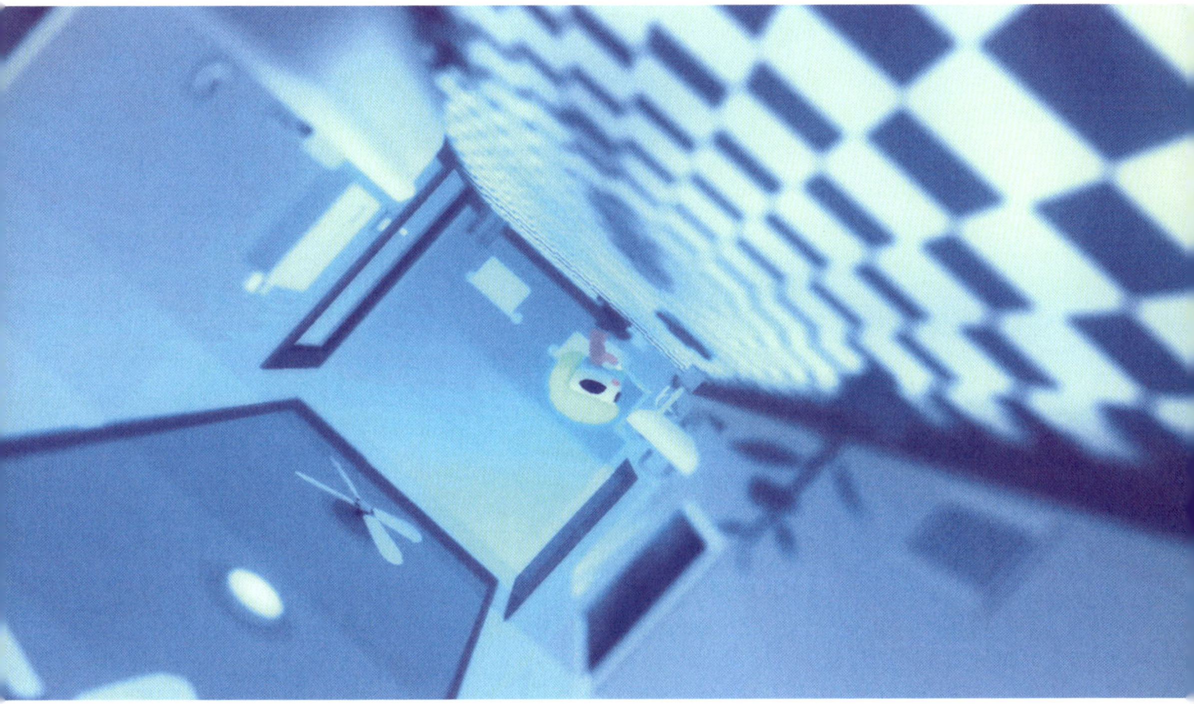

109645790437692847650 is a collection of absurdist short films, strewn across the internet as the meandering dreams of a dying AI.

David OReilly (IE) is an Irish-born filmmaker and artist based in Los Angeles. Creator of the influential short films *Please Say Something* and *The External World*, his animation work has garnered over 80 awards including Berlin's Golden Bear, the Cartoon D'Or and awards at Sundance and the Venice Film Festival. David's short films have been the subject of several retrospectives internationally. He has lectured at Pixar, Harvard, Yale, USC, CalArts and at many other conferences, institutions and film festivals around the world. In 2012 he wrote, directed and produced a special episode of the Emmy-Award-winning show *Adventure Time*. He also created fictional video games in Spike Jonze's Academy-Award-winning film *Her*. In 2014 he released his first video game *Mountain* and wrote for the acclaimed animated sitcom *South Park*.

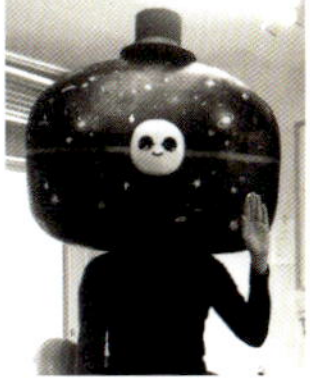

Hybrid Art

Towards A Collective Hybrid Vigor

Jens Hauser, Susanne Jaschko, Jurij V. Krpan, Victoria Vesna, Filip Visnjic

"The first hybrid is the human. And living in paradox. A mix of mind and matter, a translating device, a handshake from mind to matter and vice-versa, humankind is in a permanent state of hybridization, consciously and unconsciously."

Derrick de Kerckhove, in G. Stocker/C. Schöpf (eds.), *HYBRID—Living in Paradox,* Ars Electronica 2005, Hatje Cantz, Ostfildern-Ruit, 2005

It is a decade since *HYBRID—Living in Paradox* was presented as the Ars Electronica festival theme. For anyone using this word "hybrid" loosely, and in relation to culture in particular, it would be a good idea to access and review the catalog archived online, as there is not much that can be added other than to point to the foundation that has been already laid down by the festival organizers. To briefly summarize, the overarching premise is that hybridity is an evolutionary principle that has consistently driven natural as well as technical developments—all "new" things are hybrids rather than innovations and most of all expressions of our times. The show was curated by Derrick de Kerckhove, head of the Marshall McLuhan program at the University of Toronto, and dealt with such topics as Al-Jazeera, Islam, multiple identities, robotics, ecology and genetic engineering. Jens Hauser wrote a seminal essay on *Bio Art—Taxonomy of an Etymological Monster* (p. 182/188) and the foundation for this new category was in place.

This theme anticipated the creative soup that we are now fully living in, where machine and flesh have already merged, cultures and ideologies are clashing face to face as well as online, autonomous warfare is waged, top-down technologies have reached their limit and science is learning to return to bottom up systems that nature has been employing all along. We have by now acquired full global awareness of the implications of interconnectivity and emergent self-organized systems and have to confront our learned anthropocentric arrogance for the survival our species. Ten years later we see that the works submitted this year have emerged as more advanced and complex in form, with a surprising level of modesty or even humility, giving us a sense that perhaps there is some hope to be held on to and that hybrid art can indeed play an important role in this transitory age.

Jury Process

The jury group that was called to task represented multiple points of view and our first challenge was to agree to how we would conduct the review of so many submissions coming from multiple approaches. Jens Hauser was helpful, as he was involved from the inception of this category and his close knowledge of the history, previous applicants and tendencies made it easier to lay down the working principles for the selection process. Having a brief at the beginning from someone with a solid memory of the past process and awarded artworks, the group quickly agreed that this category is a fluid, moving target that will continue shape shifting and should not be pre-determined. Instead of deciding what we are looking for in advance, we first considered a large number of projects, taking a bird's eye view and seeking out the currently emerging trend, the connecting invisible thread and bringing to light what is taking shape at this present moment in time.

All three award-winning projects have a great degree of humility, with an awareness of the larger incommensurable constraints confronting humanity. In order to address these complex issues that transcend disciplinary boundaries, all involve multiple collaborators and renounce the central artist genius as creator in favor of the larger goal. These works are produced with large teams from various disciplines and the artists involved and taking the conceptual lead all demonstrate long-term commitment to the process. Thus the artworks we were particularly impressed with go beyond the spectacular—from launching satellites to learning from other species and co-creating a new reality that will help us move ahead as a collective in a more conscious manner. Finally, these works also span three continents, pointing to the cultural diversity or hybridity of our times—necessary to confront the global environmental issues not limited to our planet but looking to cosmos as a part of the holistic system.

Golden Nica

Plantas Autofotosintéticas · Gilberto Esparza

This year's winning art project *Plantas Autofotosintécas* by Mexican artist Gilberto Esparza condenses all the above-mentioned criteria: the artist has mobilized a large network of trans-disciplinary competences, carried out both technological and sociological research over a long period of time, shares the knowledge gained in workshops with a large community and concerned populations, and presents us with a complex hybrid ecosystem in which, despite the technological skill, the human species is not at the center. The jury acknowledges Esparza's *Plantas Autofotosintécas* as an outstanding example of an artistic embodiment of the progressive convergence of hardware, software and wetware, while addressing issues of wastewater management and the need for symbiotic ecological solutions both materially and philosophically. Conceived as an ecosystem ironically relying on human pollution, the artist uses sewage as a source of energy, thanks to autochthonous bacteria in microbial fuel cells, which not only purify the water but in turn also produce the energy necessary to power light sources for aquatic plants to photosynthesize. The plants become entirely independent of natural light and habitat companions for other species such as protozoa, crustaceans and micro algae. Against the grain of ever more sophisticated and accelerated engineering, Gilberto Esparza's artistic practice avoids the use of engineered organisms, drawing instead on their "natural technical" capacities. The artist consciously stages the inherent paradox in new technologies' greenwashing discourses that always comprise an instrumental common feature in human wishful thinking: they harbor the promise that new technologies might undo damage to the environment caused by past ones. The *Plantas Autofotosintécas* are themselves human constructs and, as such, point to the destructive, polluting character of these, while at the same time they interlace with natural processes, evolving through technology into symbiotic ecosystems to become independent of their creator. Aesthetically, this trans-species network enables its participants to compensate and overcome their innate biological limitations, and to become increasingly self-sufficient in the process. While the somehow literally living-nature cultures continue the ever-recurring historical fascination with staging aliveness in cultural history, here, unlike many artificial-life art and robotic projects in recent decades, Esparza breaks with the posture in order to conceive his wetware robots to carry out useful tasks mainly for our own species. If they are said to express autonomous and intelligent behavior, the latter might not mean the mimicking of human cognition, but rather the system's decentralized intelligence to clean up humankind's mess in times of major atmospheric crises.

Awards of Distinction

The two projects that the jury selected for Awards of Distinction are *ARTSAT1: Invader* by ARTSAT: Art and Satellite Project and *Teacup Tools* by Agnes Meyer-Brandis and are complementary to the Golden Nica artwork and in very different ways address similar issues. Both works are collaborative across the arts and sciences, involve long-term commitment and ultimately transcend the disciplinary boundaries with shared visions.

ARTSAT1: Invader

ARTSAT: Art and Satellite Project

The jury was particularly impressed by the specific open and collaborative approach of the art project *ARTSAT: Invader.* The interdisciplinary group ARTSAT managed to design, build, program and launch the first nano art satellite into space, thus turning an exclusive expert technology into a personal and artistic medium. The jury acknowledges the group's efforts to create an "open" satellite whose data is not only accessible to the builders, but also to other stakeholders and collaborators such as the international amateur radio community. In the same spirit, the ARTSAT API software package was not only developed for the *Invader* art satellite, but has been designed to be adaptable to other nano satellites with the aim of promoting and expanding the use of satellite data by artists and designers as well as the general public. Invader is an extraordinary example in the legacy of hybrid projects located between art, technology and science. It suggests and fosters a new kind of "satellite culture" that explores the highly poetic and creative power of cosmic space for the public. During its flight it performed and produced a number of individual art pieces ranging from generative poems to images. The exhibition of art pieces produced on the basis of the data collected on the satellite's journey can be seen as one of many possible manifestations of the *Invader* project. The artwork's minimal and clear aesthetics speak once again of both the sophistication and modesty of the artists involved and their particular ability to condense the vast amount of data into distinct individual experiences.

Teacup Tools · Agnes Meyer-Brandis

The decision to honor this work was related to the jury considering previous, related works by Agnes Meyer-Brandis that address issues of climate-related sciences. Coming from a sculptural background, she successfully bridges the factual evidence derived from scientific research environments with fictional, almost surrealistic responses. The *Teacup Tools* installation was inspired by her interaction with a cloud scientist Dr. Ulrike Lohrmann, who told her about her research in Antarctica and mentioned how surprising it was that when she drank the tea outside it did not give off any steam at all—the Antarctic air was so clean that there were not enough aerosols to create a visible cloud above her cup. The *Teacup Tools* installation represents an in-between presence in public space that can be funny and serious—at once commenting on the estranged objects of scientific measuring devices in natural environments and the alarming measurement data that we are presented with. One imagines being caught off guard seeing these teacups in unexpected environments and by extension learns more about the climate of the moment. This strategy is a difficult balance to achieve and the jury felt that it was successful in its odd way—to drink tea and see clouds made of anything falling from the sky—aerosols, residues, rain and data computation—is to ingest the environment and the message all at the same time.

Honorary Mentions

Drosophila *titanus* · Andy Gracie

Drosophila titanus is an ongoing project that, through a process of experimentation and artificial selection, aims to breed a species of fruit fly that would be theoretically capable of living on Saturn's largest moon, Titan. While being a virtually impossible project to complete "successfully", *Drosophila titanus* sites itself as a process within the ongoing discourse surrounding the complex relationships between art and science. By necessity the project has to adhere to a rigorous scientific methodology. However, it endeavors to extract artistic metaphor, poetry and ambiguity from these apparent creative restrictions. The author is upgrading the transdisciplinarity of astrobiology as such, with incredibly subtle artistic strategies that can enable the viewer to catalyze the ontology of life in space on a tiny artistic setup. The jury recognized the poetics of the project investigation stems from the miniature model of possible beyond planet Earth.

Hare's Blood +
A transgenetic performance project
Klaus Spiess, Lucie Strecker

Stage director Lucie Strecker and medical researcher and anthropologist Klaus Spiess combine the bodily presence of actors, dancers, audience members, manipulated yeast cells and genetic sequences obtained from "artistically philosophical animals" in novel ways. In *Hare's Blood +*, announced as a "transgenic performance", the duo proposes a convincing way to combine micro bio-politics with hybrid diegetic theater/performance time, and to dramatize economic value fluctuations in stock market and art market logics, as well as in livestock of transgenic cell cultures which can be speculated on as part of the performance: having extracted DNA from hare's blood from one of Joseph Beuys' multiples, and activating its genes in living cells, Strecker and Spiess stage the conflict between bio-banked commodities in their actual biotechnological presence. Both materially and spiritually referencing the figure of the hare—to which Joseph Beuys once explained pictures in the 1960s—they confront Beuys' desire for a counter-economy with the omnipresent human drive to create monetary value.

Light Barrier
Kimchi and Chips—Elliot Woods, Mimi Son
Kimchi and Chips' *Light Barrier* installation creates phantoms of light in the air by crossing millions of calibrated beams; creating floating graphic objects which are animated in space. Their study of digital light is concerned with a visual mechanism, and as artists they have developed a unique visual language of light and space. The "phantoms of light" in *Light Barrier* are shaped into mesmerizing volumetric projections as beams of light pass through haze. The artists draw ephemeral three-dimensional forms in space in conversation with a carefully crafted and synchronized musical score. Extensive computation and mathematical models, hacked projectors and calibration routines enable Kimchi and Chips to eloquently layer physical space with brush strokes of projected light.

Mirage · Ralf Baecker
Mirage by Ralf Baecker is a projection apparatus that combines optics and artificial neural network research to create a synthesized landscape that registers the magnetic field. At the same time, the machine uses a wake-sleep algorithm to consolidate its neural network, as an analogy for dreaming—suggesting a form of life in the machine. The project presents itself as an anamorphosis, a physical lens to observe and enter a different realm, both physical and digital, that we as humans cannot sense. The jury enjoyed the artwork's capacity to access viewer intelligence by removing the perceptual elements of the piece and focusing on the light as manifestation of the "in-between" scenario that glues together sun, earth and us using the invisible forces of magnetic fields. *Mirage* is a beautifully crafted machine and a hermetic system that intelligently brings together complex algorithmic behaviors with machine poetics.

Myconnect
Saša Spačal, Mirjan Švagelj, Anil Podgornik
Myconnect is an interspecies connector that emerged as an aspiration to enable human beings to transgress their own species and connect with them on perceptive and physiological levels. On entering the installation one joins with the otherness, another multiplicity i.e. the fungal mycelium. In the *Myconnect* capsule, a person's nervous system is integrated into a human-mycelium interface feedback loop via their heartbeat signal. Mycelium's oscillations are produced by electrical resistance and correspond to the incoming, temporally offset heartbeat. The sublime connectivity between human and the *fungi mycelium*—the largest organism in the world—was recognized by jury as an intelligent and poetic artwork that aims to create an awareness of lost interconnections between humans and other species that humanistic nature-culture dichotomy has arrogantly considered primitive.

PSX Consultancy · Pei-Ying Lin, Špela Petrič, Dimitrios Stamatis, Jasmina Weiss
A team of designers, artists and scientists conceived the *Plant Sex Consultancy* agency, which aims to help plants with their reproductive efforts. Since many of decorative plants' existence is possible only in artificial conditions pollinating by trial and error, the PSX project proposes plant-centered

sex toys designed for plants, enabling plants to enjoy successful reproduction. Although the reproductive augmentations conceived through this project are critically discursive objects rather than pragmatic design solutions, the jury recognized the witty intelligence of how the authors question the validity and the ethics of the cultural imposition on nature and explore sexuality in its trans-biotic manifestations. Despite its speculative design, the project has a critical message as well. The exploration of plant-centered design aims to highlight the human attitude of convenience, use, fascination, necessity and ignorance towards the plant realm with strange and quirky reflections that inform the existing perception of plants. Moreover, despite irreconcilable differences it encourages the possibility of a respectful awareness of the other, whether it is vegetal, alien or female.

ReBioGeneSys – Origins of Life
Adam W. Brown, Robert Root-Bernstein

The jury agreed that *ReBioGeneSys–Origins of Life* has all the elements to be classified in the Hybrid Arts category–it is an equal collaboration between an artist and a scientist and the aesthetics are dependent on the scientific equipment necessary to make the piece work properly. The artist / scientist team boldly present us with the question that has haunted humanity–the origins of life. They do this not by a metaphor or speculation as is usual in the arts, but by an active experiment that embodies this ultimate question. The art installation is a system / sculpture that combines chemistry, alchemy, conservation and computation to autonomously create extreme minimal ecosystems capable of autopoetic evolution. This ecosystem is theoretically capable of forming the self-organizing chemistries necessary to produce semi-living molecules and possibly even protocells. By employing all the theories of the origin of life, they actually produce "nature" in its most basic form, using all necessary conditions including desiccation, hydration, freezing, day and night cycles, exposure to UV light and electrical energy. The installation evolves continuously, since in the process some of the matter is destroyed, forcing evolutionary processes and natural selection.

Satelliten · Quadrature

Work by Quadrature questions the invisible machines in the sky by building an autonomous system that traces passing satellites onto physical maps. Around one thousand operational satellites orbit the Earth–visible only when they are at the perfect angle to reflect the sun. *Satelliten* is an exquisitely built machine that creates a temporal window revealing the seemingly invisible machines populating the skies. As the satellites pass over the specified longitude and latitude, the autonomous machine draws the path of the moving object in a 10 sq.cm square on a map. With an orbital period of 90 to 130 minutes for each satellite, the apparatus carves their way across the map, drawing over the artifactual ground.

Stranger Visions · Heather Dewey-Hagborg

Drawing on dystopia of biological surveillance and the political, social and legal challenges of pervasive everyday genetic profiling, Heather Dewey-Hagborg fuses the current trend towards hands-on amateur and DIY biotechnology with speculative renderings of what she has coined "forensic DNA phenotyping": for *Stranger Visions*, the artist collects "evidence" such as cigarettes, chewing gum or stray hair, and then analyzes genetic data to imagine what an anonymous stranger might look like, based on the extrapolation of bio-informatically correlated traits such as gender, skin, eye or hair color, and finally "giving a face" to the virtual and highly fragile data bodies. The jury detected a powerful tension in the artist's strategy to combine rapid prototyping of hyper-realistic portraits with the genre of detective stories, so as to subvert contemporary CSA fantasies and the biotechnologically updated belief in mechanical objectivity produced by apparatuses. In her work, biohacking in turn then implies the continuing need to develop systems of counter-surveillance.

This Tape Will Self-Destruct
Diego Trujillo Pisanty

In the light of an impending new Cold War and universal surveillance that we all are subject to, Pisanty's destructive machine could almost be regarded as a useful tool. The jury appreciates the artwork's sarcasm and topicality as much as its seemingly simple but effective construction. But the fascination for the absurd machine and its quick sequence of printing and destruction might prevent anyone from taking a look at the actual documents produced by the printer. Pisanty has selected images and texts from Cold War fiction, film and television programs and manually curated extracts that relate to previously revised contemporary secret documents. As such, *This Tape Will Self-Destruct* is a "machine fiction" made real in order to confront us with the fact that until now we citizens have only a vague understanding of the amount of data that is collected and of the level of international collaboration to obtain and interpret it.

Vanitas Machine · Verena Friedrich

The *Vanitas Machine* installation addresses the desire for eternal life and the potential of life-prolonging measures and creates a contemporary analogy to the endeavor to prolong the human lifespan with the help of science and technology. Based on a candle that uses the technical intervention of a flame sensor to control the quantity of oxygen in the glass chamber, it burns down ever so slowly. As one of the classical symbols of *vanitas*, a burning candle recalls the futility of the moment, the transience of human life and the certainty of the end of all existence. In view of the fact that the cosmetic industry is heavily abusing the meme of slowing oxidation in order to prolong the beauty of our bodies, the artistic strategy of stripping down the process of oxidation brings us an uncanny perspective on material ageing and the inevitability that the cosmetic industry blatantly denies.

Welt-Klimakonferenz
Rimini Protokoll

For more than a decade, Rimini Protokoll have been exploring and merging performance, intervention and theater formats, aiming to reduce the distance between the performers and the members of the audience. With their new work, *Welt-Klimakonferenz,* they have staged a simulation of a world climate summit, condensed to a three-hour participatory play. The project is outstanding on many levels—its dimension, complexity and topicality—and is to be regarded as another successful experiment by Rimini Protokoll to challenge its participants to take on a set of beliefs, values and interests, and hence to examine their own political position. While the jury did not question the project's general relevance and quality, it discussed whether it met the requirements of Prix Ars Electronica, not having a strong technology element. In awarding the project with an Honorary Mention the jury acknowledges the project's uniqueness, high level of immersiveness and particular hybridity between real life and theater, art and politics.

Plantas Autofotosintéticas

Gilberto Esparza

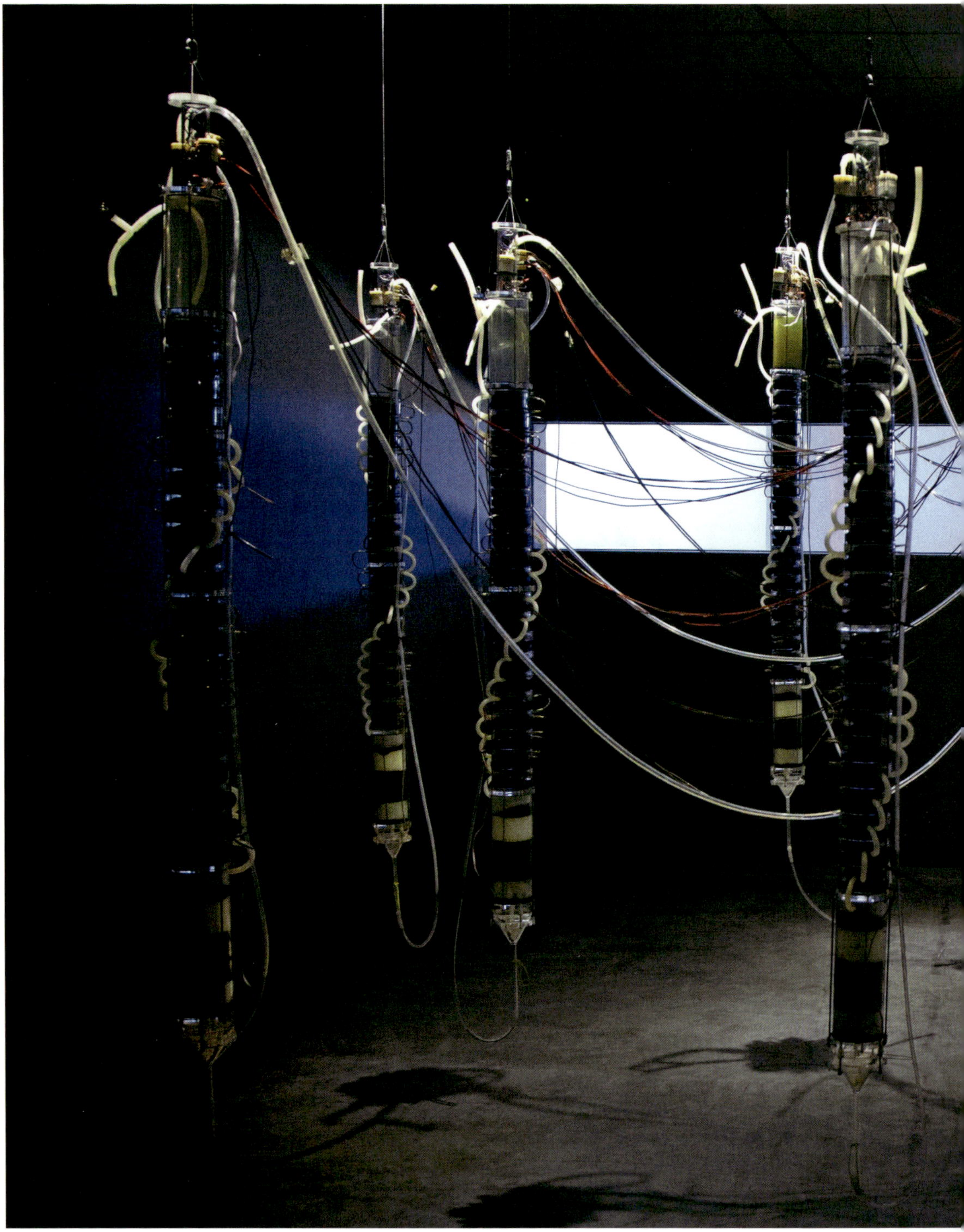

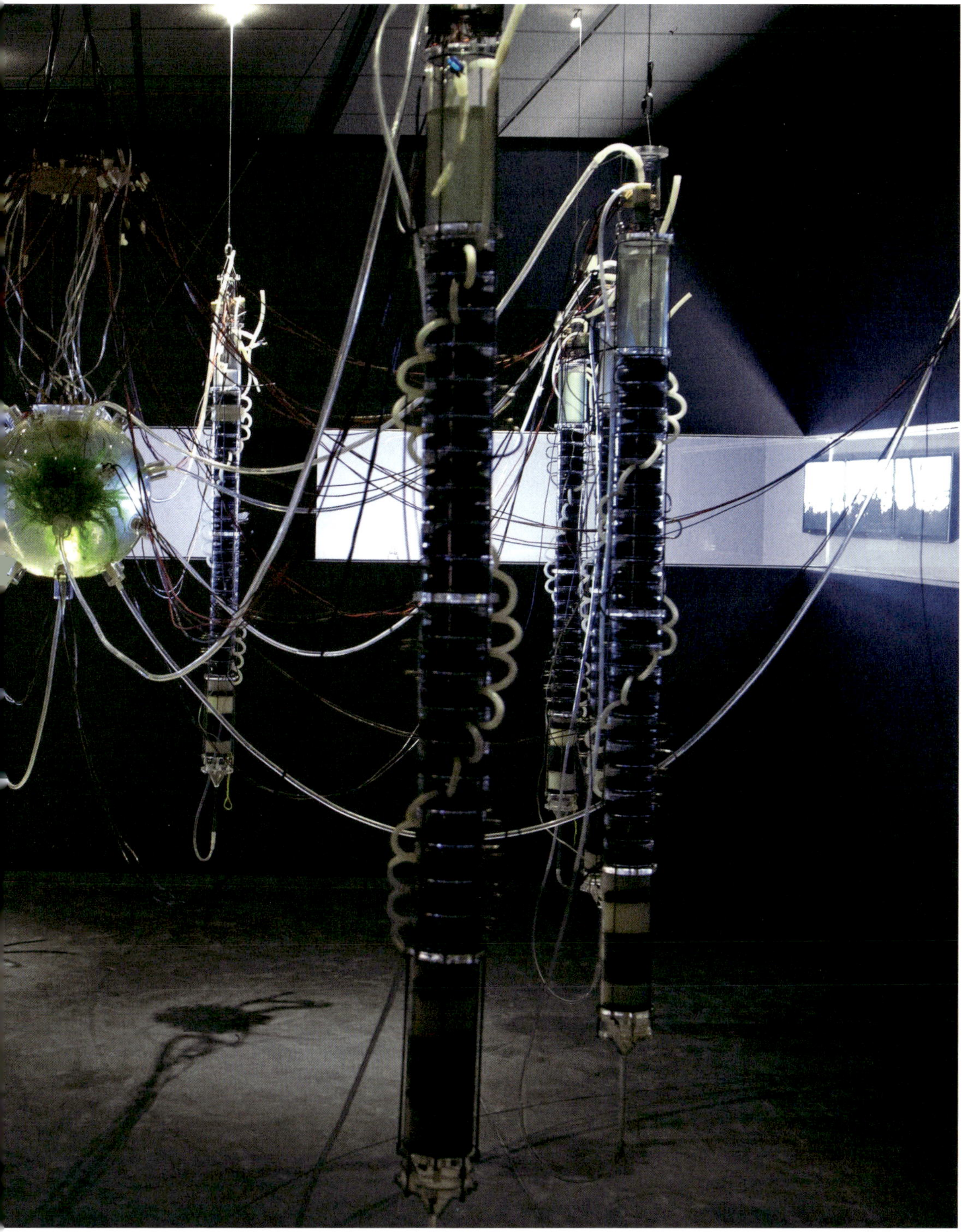

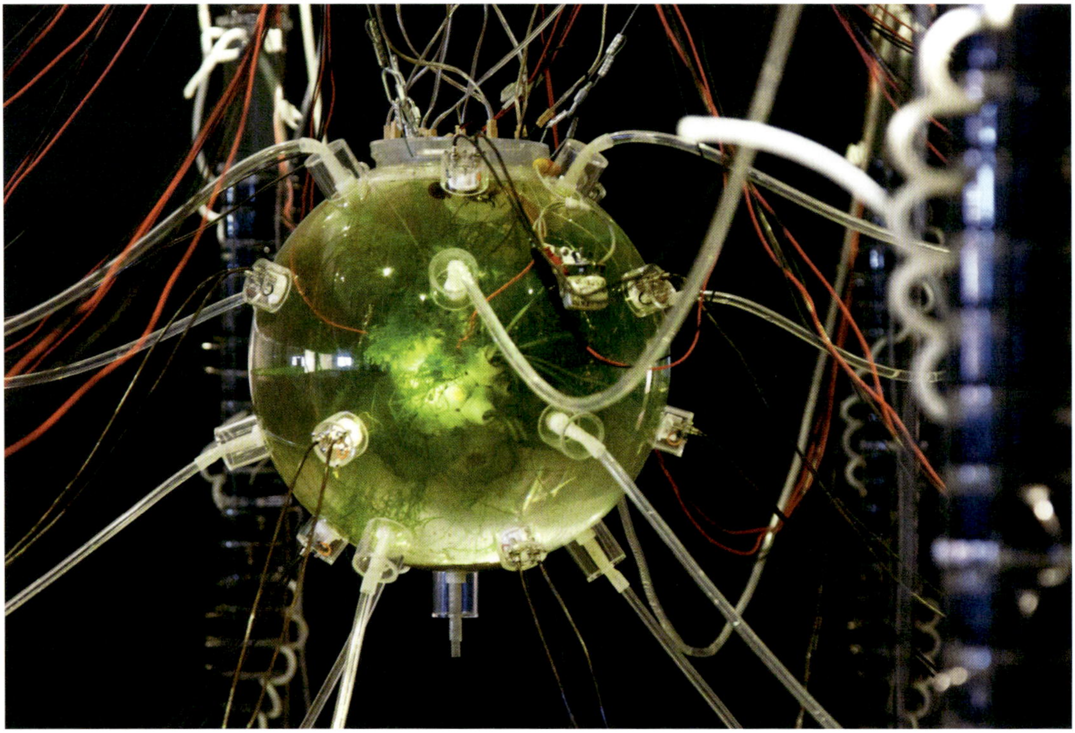

This symbiotic system re-imagines the management of sewage in order to salvage its potential as a source of energy. It is made up of a set of modular microbial fuel cells for the development of colonies of bacteria whose metabolism produces electricity and improves water quality. The modules create a hydraulic network that feeds bio-filtered water into the central container, creating an optimal environment where producer species and consumer species from different trophic levels (protozoa, crustaceans, micro algae, and aquatic plants) can achieve homeostatic equilibrium. The electricity produced by the bacteria is released as bursts of luminous energy, enabling photosynthesis by the plants living in the central container, which thereby complete their metabolic processes. When the organic material present in the microbial cells has been entirely consumed, an electronic monitoring network is responsible for pumping the byproducts generated by the species in the nuclear ecosystem out into the modular cells, restoring the cycle.

Plantas autofotosintéticas (autophotosynthetic plants) is the result of an inquiry arising from a question about the present-day society's relationship with water, which has prioritized its economic value and utility. Human settlements get their water from rivers, lakes, groundwater, through major engineering works that extract it and incorporate it into a cycle of use and disposal, taking little account of the huge network of vital relationships involved. Today many large Latin American cities use their rivers as sewers. The most important rivers are almost dead, breaking the balance of entire ecosystems, also affecting rural settlements along their course. This project raises the need to reestablish connections and reconfigure our relationship with water in a symbiotic way.

Plantas autofotosintéticas feed mainly on urban waste water. This organism is a symbiotic, self-regulating system that seeks to preserve life. It uses the energy available in the waste water to generate light, photosynthesize and improve water quality.

It consists of a set of bio-cells or microbial fuel cells interconnected to form a hydraulic network. Growing inside the cells are colonies of bacteria that live in urban waste water either from rivers or drainage systems that serve as means of disposal.
Microbial fuel-cell modules function as a digestive system. The waste water enters through the top of the modules and falls through the cells by gravity. Anaerobic bacteria are responsible for metabolizing organic matter, producing bio-filtered water and electricity. In short, its metabolism produces oxidative reactions releasing electrons, which are captured and concentrated in a capacitor to produce flashes of light. The water and light resulting from this process are used by the central container: the nucleus, where an optimal environment is created for producers and consumers species from different trophic levels (protozoa, crustaceans, algae and aquatic plants) achieving a homeostatic balance. The electricity produced by the bacteria is released as bursts of light energy, which allows the plants living in the nucleus to photosynthesize. The plants transform light and micronutrients into biomass as feed for consumers. Finally, the nervous system is an electronic network responsible for monitoring energy and water cycles. It is like a rudimentary brain that connects and regulates the other two systems, i.e. the nucleus and the cell modules, fulfilling three functions. The first is responsible for registering electrical activity in each module's microbial cells. The second controls the pumping of the nutrient-rich waste water. The third leads the bio-filtered water from modules to the nucleus.
The *Autophotosynthetic plants* installation is accompanied by a monitoring center with maps showing points where water has come from, and a series of voltmeters to measure levels of electricity generated by each module. In this table there is also an instrument that translates the light activity of nucleus and the biological activity generated in the modules into sound. The waste water feeding the *plantas autofotosintéticas* comes from different parts of a city, with each site having different pollution levels according to the context. The level of pollution is expressed by the light intensity that feeds the nucleus. This work refers to the type of pollutants generated in a city and salvages the potential of contaminated water as an energy source. The research presents a model of a self-regenerative water system which could be applied to cities.

A collaborative text by Gilberto Esparza, Constanza Díaz Mc Gregor (biologist) and Diego Liedo Lavaniegos (electronics).

Supported by: Espacio Fundación Telefónica Lima, Fundación Telefónica Mexico

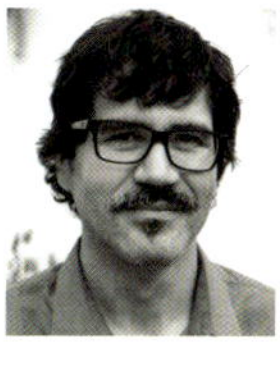
Brenda G Espinos

Gilberto Esparza (MX), born in 1975, is a Mexican artist whose work involves electronic and robotic means to investigate the impacts of technology in everyday life, social relationships, environment and urban structure. He currently conducts research projects on alternative energies. His practice employs recycling consumer technology and biotechnology experiments. In his projects he has collaborated research centers such as the Research Group in Chemical and Process Engineering at the University of Cartagena, Spain; Mechatronics Area of Cinvestav; Institute of Engineering, Juriquilla, UNAM; Digital Arts, University National Polytechnic Institute Guanajuato, Salamanca. Gilberto Esparza, graduated from the School of Fine Arts at the University of Guanajuato, Mexico and spent one year on exchange at the Faculty of Fine Arts of San Carlos in Valencia, Spain. As an artist he has participated in solo and group exhibitions in Mexico, the US, Canada, Brazil, Colombia, Peru, Ecuador, Argentina, Spain, Holland, Belgium, Slovenia and Dhoa. He received the award for Latin American Production at Life 09 and second prize at Life 13 Fundación Telefónica of Spain and a Honorary Mention at the Prix Ars Electronica. He currently is a member of the National System of Art Creators in Mexico.

ARTSAT1:Invader

ARTSAT: Art and Satellite Project

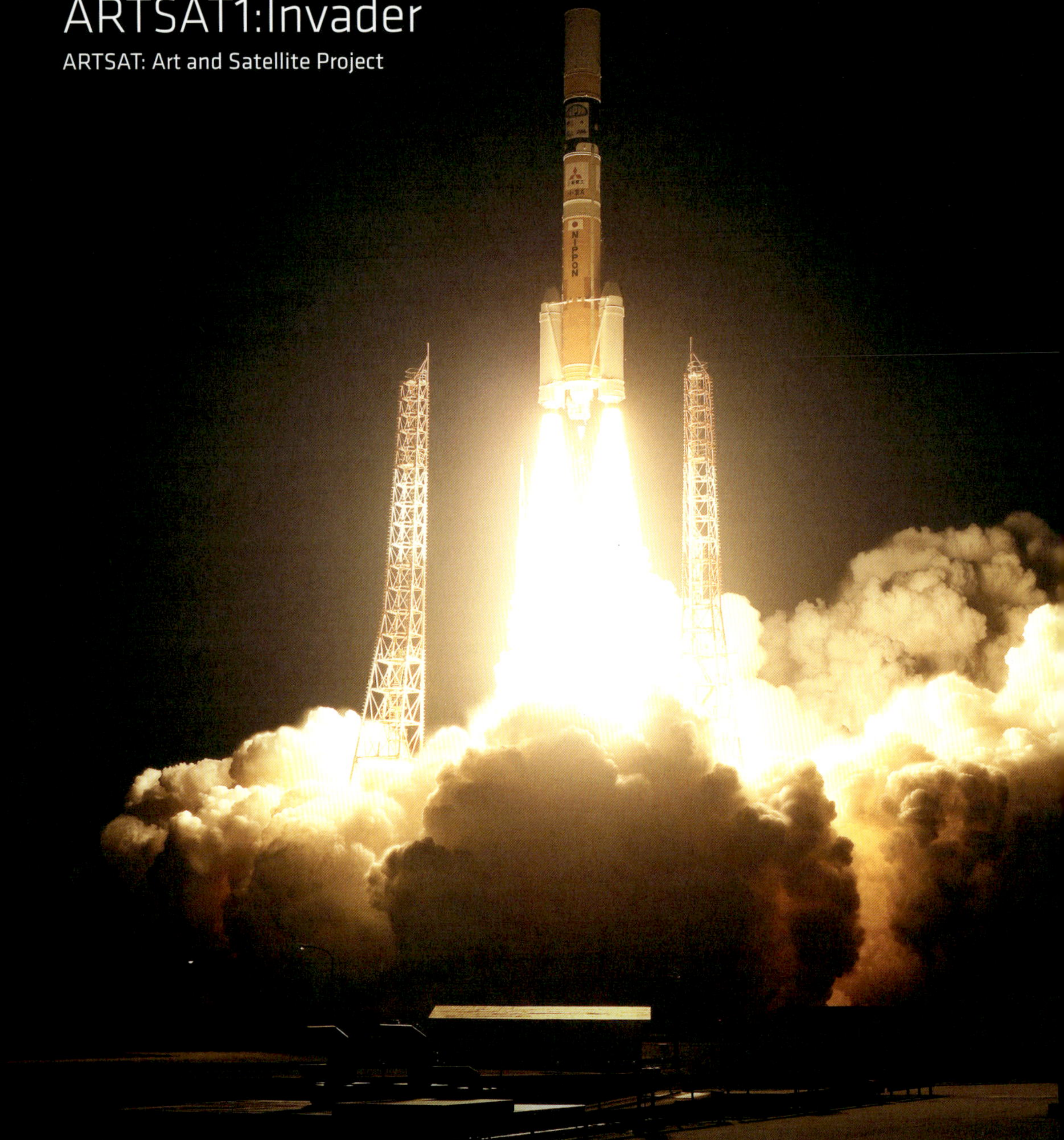

On February 28, 2014 (JST), the world's first art satellite, *ARTSAT1:Invader* was launched as a piggyback payload on the H-IIA F23 launch vehicle, and inserted into a non-sun-synchronous orbit at an altitude of 378 km and inclination of 65 degrees. *Invader,* a 10 cm cube 1U-CubeSat with a mass of 1.85 kg continued its steady operation on orbit, successfully performing an array of artistic missions by commands from the main ground station at Tama Art University. These missions included algorithmic generation and transmission of synthesized voice, music and poems, capturing and transmitting of image data and communicating with the ground through a chatbot program. *Invader* was also equipped with Morikawa, an on-board mission computer compatible with the Arduino open-source hardware platform, programmed with various functions reflecting today's maker/hacker culture such as in-orbit satellite operation and reprogramming via web browser.

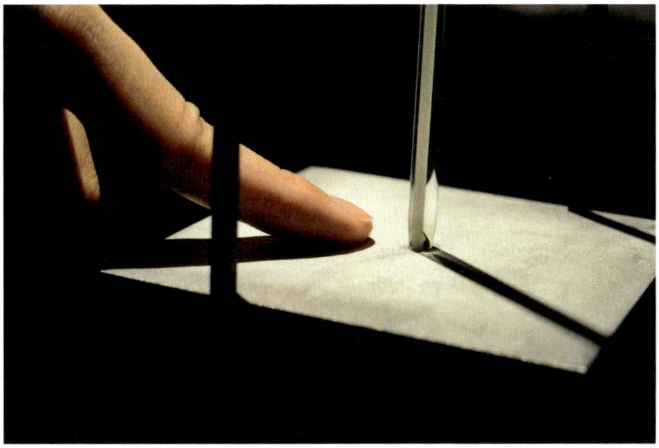

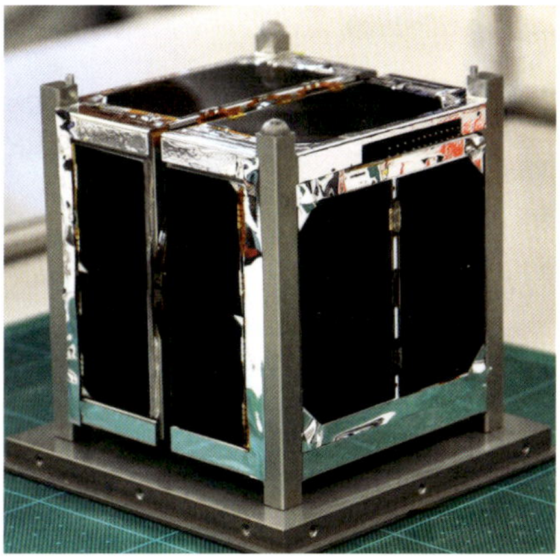

Invader extended its orbit for an additional two months and deorbited and re-entered the Earth's atmosphere for disintegration on September 2, 2014, 09:47 (JST). During the *Invader's* operation, The ARTSAT project took part in the "mission [SPACE×ART]—beyond Cosmologies" exhibition held at the Museum of Contemporary Art Tokyo from June 7 to August 31, 2014, realizing the world's first media installation using data from an operating satellite. In the installation, various elements and data from *Invader* are fragmented and decomposed so that visitors can reconstruct them according to their perception and imagination. It is a kind of circuit-style garden to appreciate ultra-small pieces of data from *Invader* in orbit. Trying to connect with the satellite by the irreplaceable ultra-small data is using the imagination to challenge the limits of the reality of digital data. It is an essential and indispensable experience for us on Earth in the age of big data.

Following *Invader,* the ARTSAT project designed and developed its second probe, the deep-space sculpture *ARTSAT2:Despatch. Despatch*—a 3D-printed, spiral (sculptural) form with an envelope area of approx. 50 cu. cm and a total mass of approx. 33 kg—was successfully launched as a piggyback payload on the H-IIA launch vehicle (main satellite: Hayabusa II) on December 3, 2014. *Despatch* is the world's first artwork to be inserted into deep-space orbit and marks the furthest distance of an artwork from the Earth. Its mission includes the transmission of "space-generated poems." *Despatch's* signal was successfully received from a distance of 4.7 million km (12 times the distance from the Moon), setting the new world distance record for a signal received by an amateur radio station. *Despatch* ended its operation on January 3, 2015, but it will continue semi-permanently to orbit the sun as a satellite.

A collaboration between Tama Art University and
The University of Tokyo

The **ARTSAT: Art and Satellite Project** (JP), which began in 2010, understands Earth-orbiting satellites and deep-space spacecrafts as "media that connect Earth with outer space." The project launched a miniaturized art satellite and an independently developed spacecraft to carry out experimental creative practices that utilize data transmitted from space, including interactive media art and sound/software art. The project, a collaboration between Tama Art University and the University of Tokyo, is run by members from various fields.

Teacup Tools

Agnes Meyer-Brandis

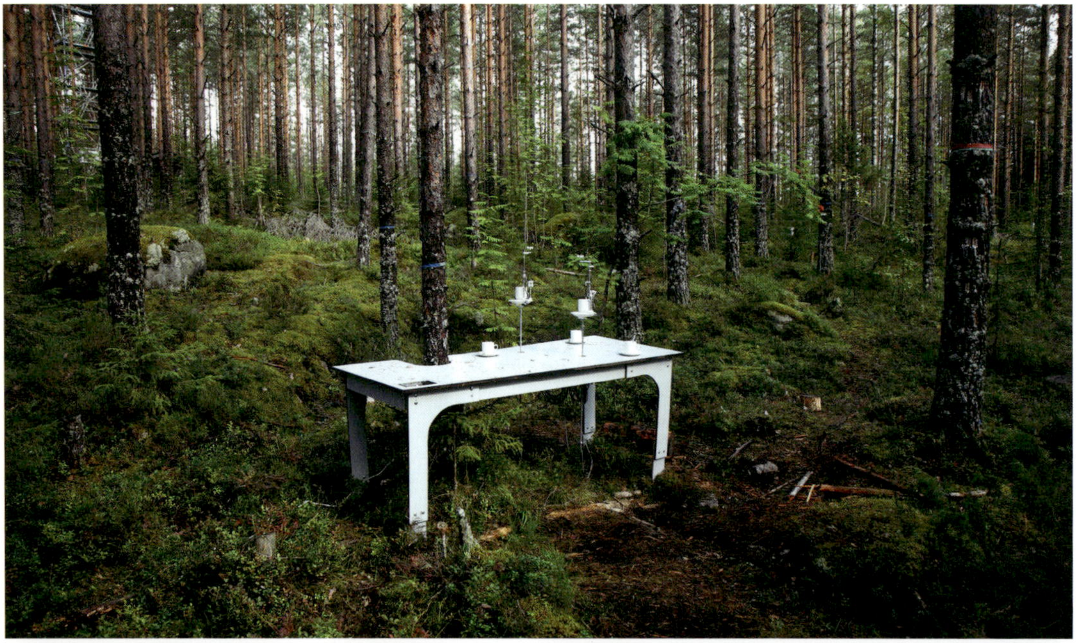

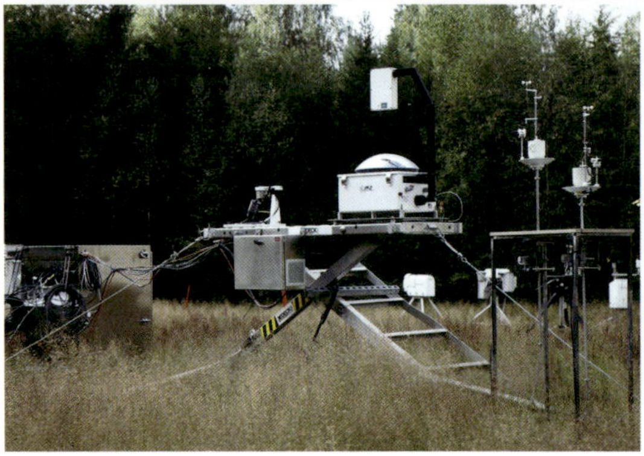

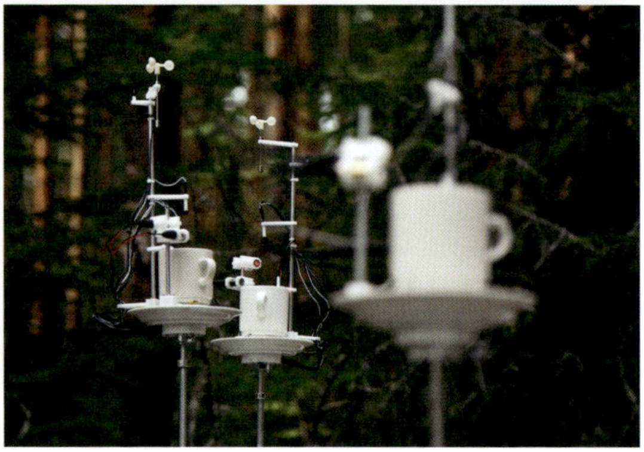

Teacup Tools is an array of cybernetic teacups, adapting themselves to the realm of climate-related sciences. The work appears as a multifunctional tool for the investigation of micro clouds above tea, for communication and for tea drinking. The tea and its clouds are made from anything falling from the sky: aerosols*, residues, rain and data computation. It is literally boiled by the calculations of the massive amount of collected data. The sculptures have a nomadic quality. Like parasites they can be found next to aerosol measurement stations, in parks, on streets, on roofs or in the neighborhood of research laboratories. The *Global Teacup Network* draws attention to the investigation of the invisible and borderless air and its aerosols*—tiny particles of organic and inorganic matter, with a major impact on cloud formation, crucial to weather and climate.

* Aerosol = solution of particles in air (ancient Greek *a-er* = air; Latin *solutus* = dissolved).

Background

Based on the observation that a tea does not give off steam in clean air as it lacks the aerosols, I developed a tool and method for instant aerosol visualization and communication. It started simply by *Having Tea with a Tree* and the invitation to scientists to do so as well. (TreeTeaTable Hyytiälä, 2013). The method grew into a cybernetic sculpture, which will develop into a *Global Teacup Network*. The first functioning *Teacup Tool* prototype was tested and installed at the SMEAR forest research station (Station for Measuring Ecosystem Atmosphere Relations) in Hyytiälä Finland. It was placed between aerosol collectors and other instruments to measure air quality and chamber measurements to measure emissions of trees, tree trunks, forest soil and leaves.

What Is a Teacup Tool?

The *Teacup Tool* is a multifunctional tool for the investigation of micro clouds above tea, for communication and for tea drinking. It consists of a table and machinery for raising two or more teacups individually. Various measuring instruments are built in and onto the tea cups, measuring the environment of the cup. The energy produced by these instruments heats the inside of the cups and brews tea from rainwater and the residues that have fallen into it. This tea produces a little cloud that contains the essence of the local air. The cloud again feeds back into the system as a subject of investigation by the tools connected to the cup. The teacups move up and down individually, according to certain aspects related to the collected data and environmental processes, dancing an endless choreography determined by raindrops and clouds, particles, measurements and tea drinking. Using a mobile phone one can log into the local *Teacup Tool* Wifi to look at the real-time data and curve written by the dancing teacups, listen to a *Data Tango*, and get more information on the *Global Teacup Network* and its climates.

The Destination

Based on this prototype the project aims at the development of a global network of *Teacup Tools*. These tools and tables would be set up at various places, near aerosol measurement stations, in parks, on streets, on roofs or in the neighborhood of research laboratories. The tea and its clouds will be made from whatever the environment provides. In a field of science where the things measured show up as digits that are subject to interpretation, the sculptures interrupt the routines and circumstances science is built on. Being placed among other machines that execute scientific tasks, the public can stumble upon these sculptures and wonder what this is about. Everybody can enjoy a tea, log in locally or globally and find out more about this strange network of dancing teacups and the climate they are built for and, last but not least, change the climate by interacting.

The project was developed at the SMEAR forest research station (Station for Measuring Ecosystem Atmosphere Relations) in Hyytiälä Finland, in the scope of the *Climate Whirl Project*, a collaboration between the Department of Forest Sciences, the Department of Physics (University of Helsinki), Simosol Oy and Capsula. Supported by Kone Foundation, University of Helsinki and Aalto Biofilia.

Thanks to: Hyytiälä Forest Station Team
Software/hardware: Ralf Baecker
Practical assistance: Kat Clear
TSI images: US Department of Energy Atmospheric Radiation Measurement Program (US DOE ARM Program)
Violin: Aino Korrensalo, Jens Brand, Elisa Halmeenmäki, Kourosh Kabiri, Janne Korhonen, Ulla Taipale, Ejia Juurola

Agnes Meyer-Brandis (DE), born in 1973, studied mineralogy for a year, then transferred to the Art Academy in Maastricht, the Düsseldorf Art Academy and the Cologne Media Art Academy. She comes from a background of both sculpture and new media art. Her work, awarded and exhibited worldwide, is at the experimental edge of art and science, exploring the zone between fact and fiction. Agnes Meyer-Brandis is the founder of the Forschungsfloss FFUR / Research Raft for Subterranean Reefology, a small institute whose chief aim is to explore and confirm subterranean phenomena and unknown life-forms. Since 2007 her focus of investigation has moved to higher altitude with its associated realities. She realized an artistic experiment in weightlessness in cooperation with the German Space Agency DLR. In 2011 she started breeding Moon Geese in Italy.

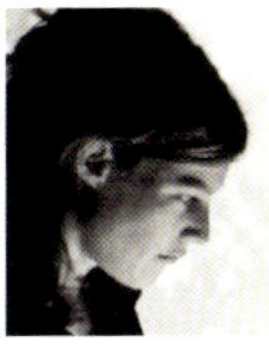

Drosophila *titanus*

Andy Gracie

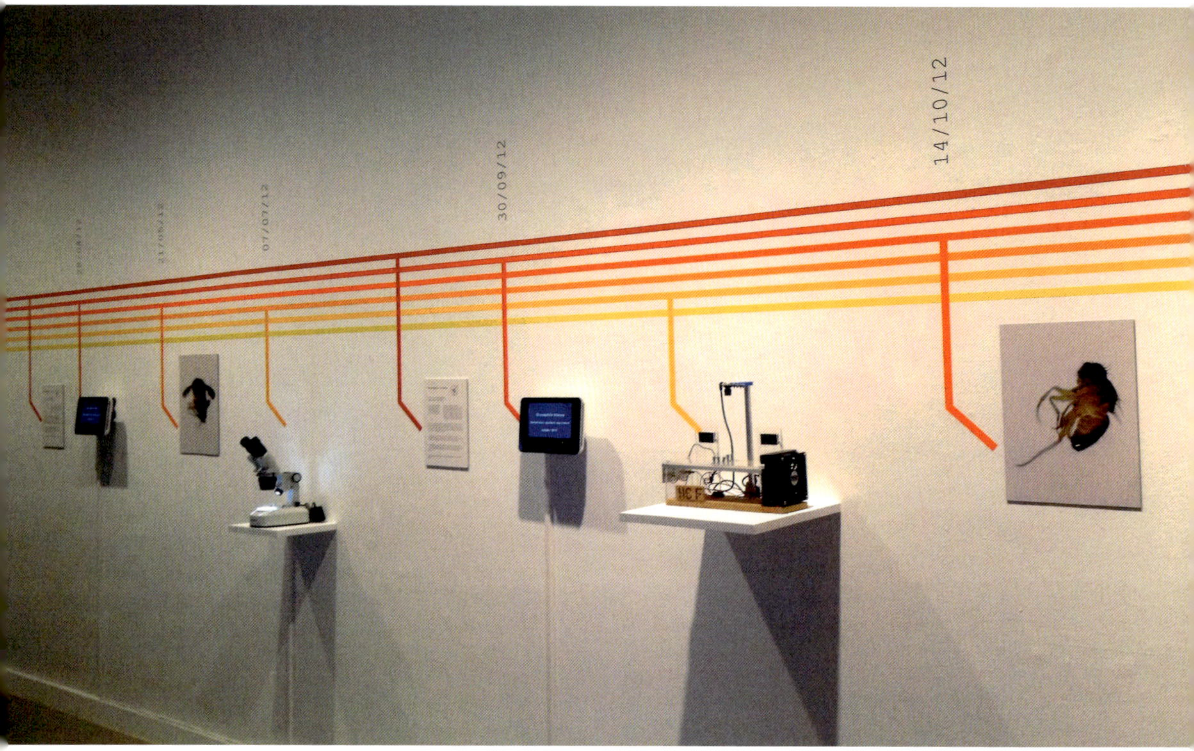

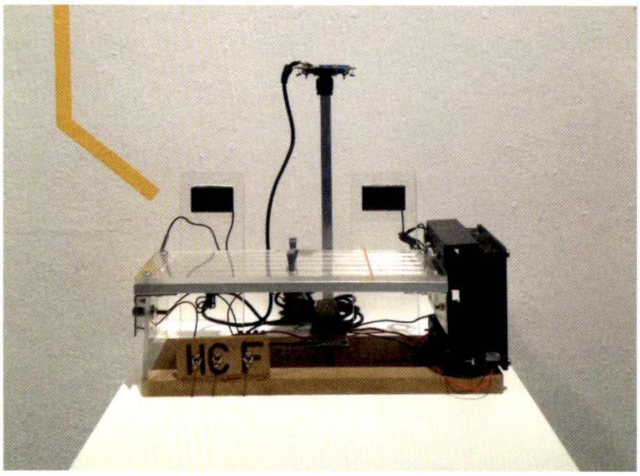

Drosophila titanus is an ongoing and long-term project which through a process of experimentation and artificial selection aims to breed a species of the fruit fly, drosophila, that would theoretically be capable of living on Saturn's largest moon, Titan. While being a virtually impossible project to complete "successfully", *Drosophila titanus* sites itself as a process within the ongoing discourse surrounding the complex relationships between art and science. By necessity the project needs to adhere to a rigorous scientific methodology and framework, however it endeavors to extract artistic metaphor, poetry and ambiguity from these apparent creative restrictions. The work embraces several interwoven narratives and concepts related to issues of species, artificially created organisms and the disquieting quest for biological perfection. Inherent in its discussion are darker issues such as Social Darwinism and its ultimate expression in eugenics. This search for biological perfection and the notion of the ideal genome are heavily implicated in the practice of artificial selection. Employing *Drosophila melanogaster* and Titan as metaphors for the human and Earth respectively, *Drosophila titanus* embraces the methodologies of experimentation, simulation and artificial selection to explore themes of species, biological perfection, perception and future life. Beyond the exploration of biological and evolutionary issues the project engages with biosemiotics in questioning the nature of reality and organic perception of environmental sensory signals. The work adopts the format of experiment as artistic investigation. *Drosophila titanus* uses the process of artificial selection on one original stock of *Drosophila melanogaster* with the vestigial wing phenotypical mutation. Through experiments replicating increased pressure, increasingly cold temperatures, atmospheric gas changes, circadian rhythms and so on, individual flies are selected for breeding the next generations. Thus over many generations the project specimens are pushed slowly towards adaptation and selective pressures and towards a possible speciation event. Perceived artificial stimuli allow the flies to become increasingly acclimatized to a set of environmental conditions alien to their "natural" domain. References to simulation theory, the notion of reality and biosemiotics are therefore implied. Close to the heart of the project experiment is the study of the relationship between genotype and phenotype, a relationship which is increasingly seen as being at the core of evolutionary biology. The complex relationships between genome and environment and how they become physically expressed as an organism seeks to adapt and survive form much of the scientific foundation of the ongoing exploration within this work. It is estimated that the project will require another 200 or 300 years to reach "completion."

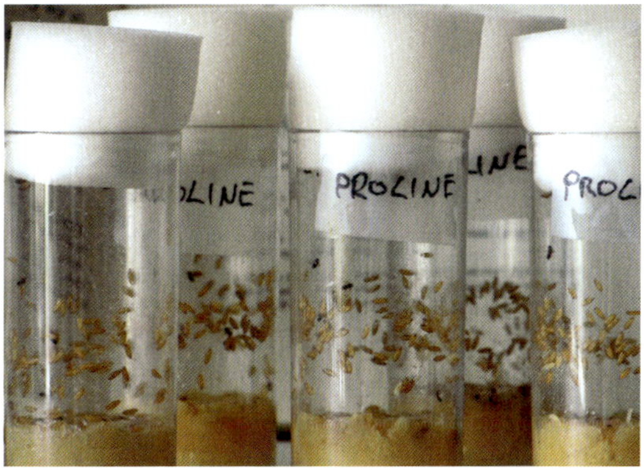

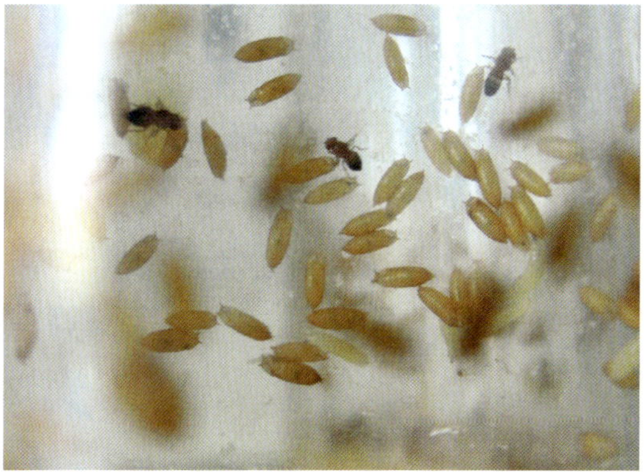

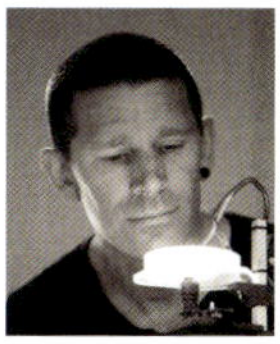

Andy Gracie (UK/ES) works across various disciplines including installation, robotics, sound, video and biological practice. Recently his work has involved studies and reactions to the science of astrobiology; notions of the origins of life coupled with a re-examination of its boundaries. His practice employs scientific theory and practice to question our relationships with environment and the notion of the "other" while simultaneously bringing into focus the very relationship between art and science. His work has been shown internationally and has included special commissions for new works.

Hare's Blood +
A transgenetic performance project

Klaus Spiess, Lucie Strecker

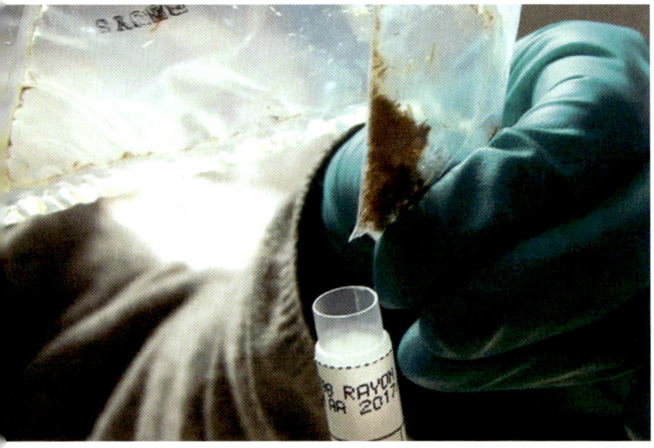

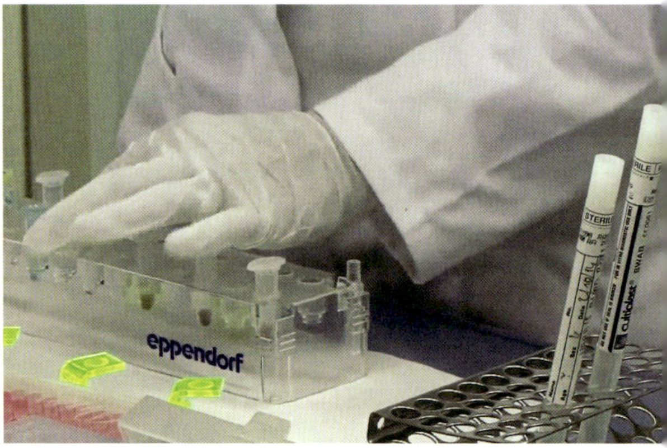

DNA presents a rather striking tension between the preservation of life and its disappearance, also found within a wide range of other areas such as religion, performance documentation or biobanking. However, DNA's capacity to preserve living matter is often understood as rather trivial naturalism disregarding many imaginary, narrative, performative and ontological contexts linked with it. We salvage DNA in order to compose mnemonic devices that diversify cultural memory. In our projects DNA stemming from biological relics of "knowing" animals which have been key figures in relevant scenarios within the arts, sciences, philosophy and genetics, i.e. the DNA from Beuys' hare, Freud's Chow-Chow, Derrida's cat, as well as from a laboratory worm. After having engineered a specifically responding synthetic gene from the relics' and a living host's DNA, we program interfaces which activate the synthetic gene as an ecopolitical agent. Beyond their historical routines, the synthetic genes now act as living money, as genetic timers, or as spoken microflora, which resist and subvert the commodification of the relic as well as its field of origin. In *Hare's Blood +* we questioned the exploding prices for artworks incorporating animal relics and recalled visions of a counter-economy as emphasized by Joseph Beuys. For Beuys, the hare's blood embodied a spiritual medium between life and death, capable of navigating between times and contexts. Beuys even explained pictures to a dead hare. For us the blood's intrinsic significance together with the multiple's reproducibility fulfilled the criteria of token money as well as DNA. For our project we opened one of the two hundred multiples in which Joseph Beuys had shrink-wrapped volatile hare's blood. Cooperating with molecular labs we inserted parts of the blood's catalase gene, which protects against stress and ageing, into living yeast cells, referencing the rhizomatic structures of fungi. We auctioned this transgenic Beuysian creature, which did not previously exist either in nature or in culture, at the Biofiction Festival in Vienna's Museum of Natural History. Through the expression of the Beuys' hares catalase gene, the programmed interface caused the size of the bids at auction to affect the growth of the yeast. When the actual bids in the room diverged too widely from the streamed livestock share prices, the protecting activity of the synthetic gene declined. Depending on their bids, the spectators saw the artwork aging or even decomposing, with their commercial interest governing its liveness. This ecospecies is capable of genetically processing data in time with Beuys' economic visions so as to negotiate its existence on the art

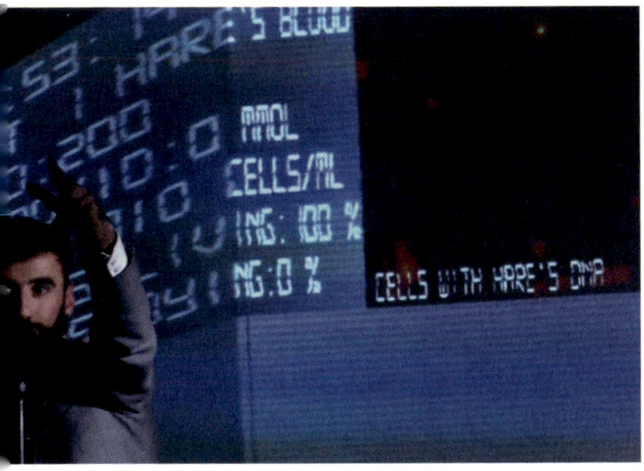

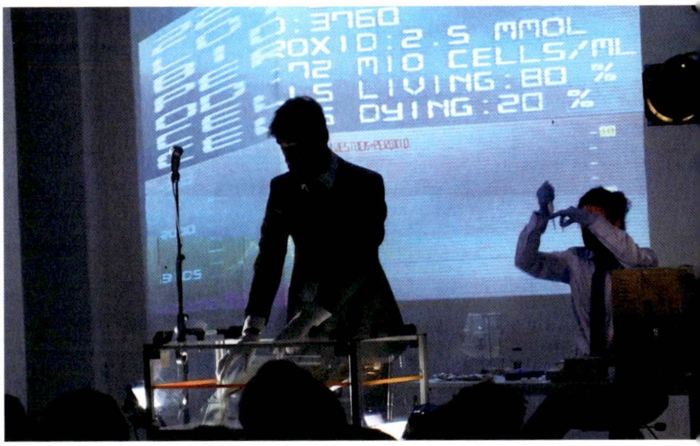

Camillo Meinhart

market. It is now neither merely an object of art nor a symbol for acting out animalism, but instead its genes have become informationally engaged in complex decisions about itself. When they transfer the historical connection between the animal's genes and its habitat to the connection between the synthetic gene and an immersive audience, the living recording devices reframe history and make the animal's past and its present mimic one another. This transference brings forward incomplete memory traces, advances parallel histories, and drafts speculative fictions. The relic thereby becomes an action, emerging from a combination of genetic discursive and immersive factors. Thus DNA engineering eventually becomes a non-trivial task of bringing the past back to life for an unpredictable future.

Co-Choreography: Costas Kekis
Performance: Evandro Pedroni, Raphaël Michon
Molecular Labs: DNA Consult Reinhard Nestelbacher; Department Cell Biology and Genetics, Salzburg University; Molecular Systematics, Museum of Natural History, Vienna
Supported by: Biofaction (EC-FP7 SYNENERGENE), Medical University Vienna

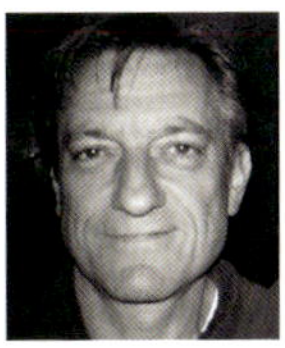

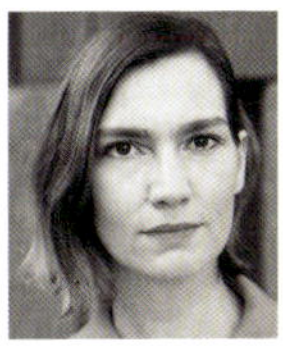

Thomas Draschan

For the last four years **Klaus Spiess** (AT) and **Lucie Strecker** (DE) have been developing hybrid and immersive art performances on the subject of biology and medicine. Klaus Spiess (AT) is a former endocrinologist, psychosomaticist, medical anthropologist and currently directs the Arts in Medicine Program at the Center for Public Health of the Vienna Medical University as an associate professor. Lucie Strecker (DE) is a performance artist, stage director and researcher. She has a diploma in fine arts from the Academy of the Arts, Berlin-Weissensee and graduated in stage directing at the Vienna University of Music and Performing Arts. Since 2012 she has been a Fellow of the Berlin University of the Arts, Postgraduate Forum for the Arts and the Sciences. Both have published numerous articles on performance research. Their works have been shown among others at performance houses such as the Tanzquartier Wien, the Museum of Natural History, and the 21er Haus, Vienna; Budascoop, Kortrijk; the House of World Cultures, Berlin, and Tate Modern, London. They have been working together with Philip Riera, Superamas, Ann Liv Young and Daniel Aschwanden

Light Barrier

Kimchi and Chips – Elliot Woods, Mimi Son

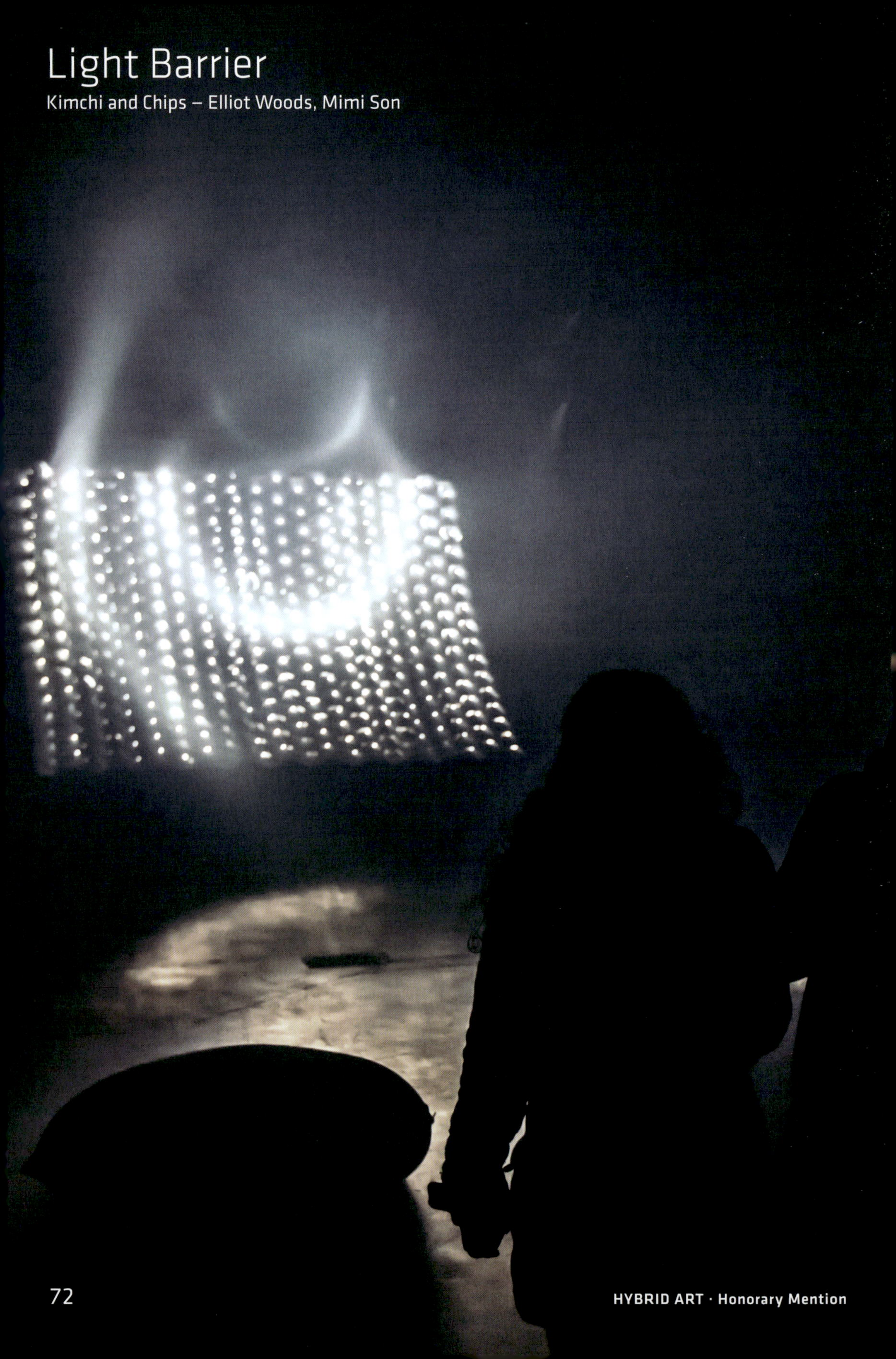

Light Barrier creates phantoms of light in the air, crossing millions of calibrated beams using a light field projection technique. The *Light Barrier* name references the theory of special relativity, which defined a new boundary between material and immaterial. It limits the actions of materials so they cannot move as fast as light, and by the famous mass-energy equivalence formula it denotes how matter and light can be exchanged. The physical-graphic sequence follows the story of a form. By passing through the *Light Barrier,* the digital form transcends the limits of its home reality and passes into a physical one. It explores the attributes of its physicality, while bringing something about its digital self into this new realm. Finally the physical form then passes through the *Light Barrier* again to pass into the next reality. The artists took inspiration from the impressionist painters. Their obsession with natural light led them to explore color and time through brush strokes, their hands became a tool encoded with their technique. The impressionists were responding to the invention of the camera, creating "viewer-less" images and finding new ways to capture the transient properties of physical reality. In parallel to this, Kimchi and Chips explore an obsession with digital light, encoding techniques into digital systems to create an image which exists without an implicit viewer. There is no image-plane, or "perspective window" as in paintings or screen-based works. Instead the image itself emerges from the plane of the canvas to create something material and transient in space. The floating graphic objects which it creates might be described as "holograms," somewhat different from other systems. It creates solid shapes made from condensed light, where the image is created by focusing light into locations in 3D space where it is scattered by fog.

Supported by:
STRP
British Council Russia
FutureEverything
Seoul Foundation for Arts and Culture
Nikola-Lenivets

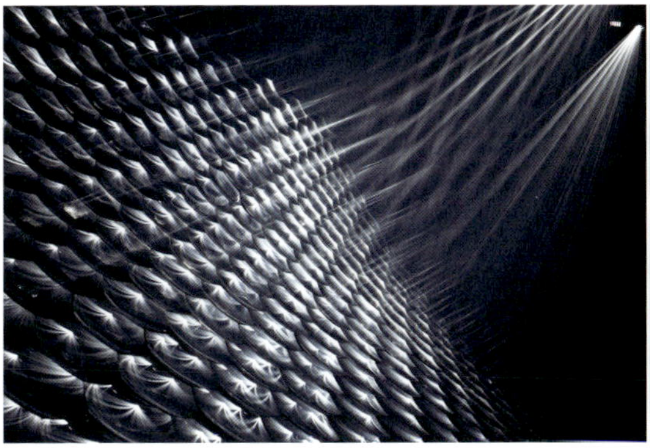

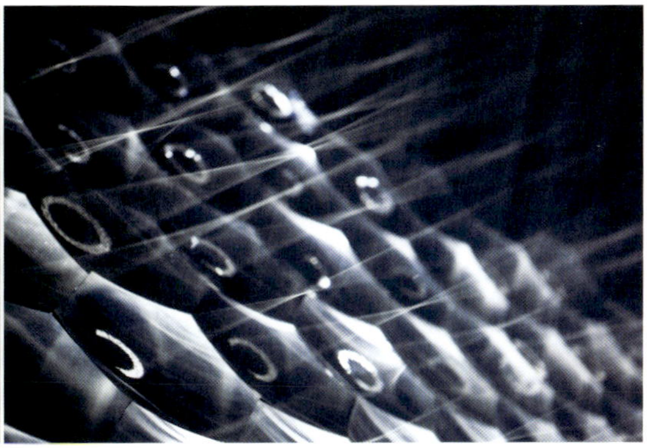

Kimchi and Chips is a Seoul-based art studio founded by **Elliot Woods** (UK) and **Mimi Son** (KR). They are known for discovering novel interactions involving people and media materials, discovering new technical and artistic paradigms. They formed in 2009 to combine the disciplines of code, form, material, concept and mechanism. They create installations and dialogs which have been exhibited on four continents. They create an emulsion of imagined reality within our physical world, in order to develop natural interactions between people, nature and the possibilities of the digital network.

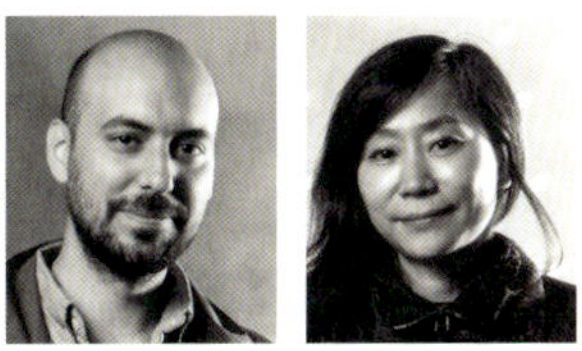

Mirage

Ralf Baecker

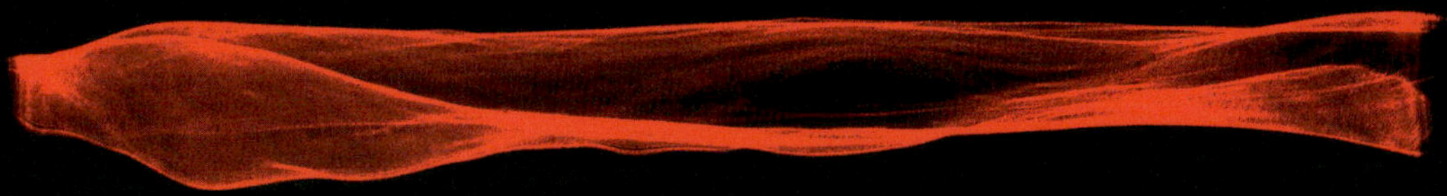

"When one understands the causes, all vanished images can easily be found again in the brain through the impression of the cause. This is the true art of memory."

René Descartes, Cogitationes privatae. in Frances Yates, The Art of Memory (1966), p. 373

Mirage is a projection apparatus that makes uses of principles from optics and artificial neural network research. *Mirage* generates a synthesized landscape based on its perception through a fluxgate magnetometer (Förster Sonde). It registers the magnetic field of the earth, which is dependent on the earth's geodynamo and its interactions with the activity of the sun, and feeds it into a unsupervised learning algorithm for analysis. At the same time the algorithm, is inspired by the principle of a Helmholz Machine, "dreams" variations of the previously analyzed signal. These variations are translated into a two-dimensional matrix that physically transforms a thin mirror sheet by 48 muscle wires. The surface of the mirror sheet changes in analogy to the system's state. A thin laser line is directed at the mirror surface at a acute angle to generate a landscape depth like projection on the wall. Through the constantly shifting signals the projection resembles a subliminal wandering through a landscape.

In 2013 Geoff Hinton, one of the leading researchers in the area of artificial neural networks and deep learning, joined Google to support them on various products that use AI and learning algorithms. He introduced back-propagation algorithms for training multi-layered neural networks. One of his contributions to the field of unsupervised learning algorithms is the Helmholtz Machine, a machine that uses the principle of a wake-sleep algorithm to consolidate its neural network. The algorithm is trained during the wake phase by its sensory input. In the sleep phase it cuts off its sensory input and feeds the network backwards with random patterns. On its input layer (retina) it generates versions of its previously perceived images of the world. I am speculating that the computers in the enormous Google data centers cut off their perception (search queries, user behavior, speech recognition, image data) once a day and go to "sleep." What do their "dreams" look like?

Supported by: LEAP Gallery, Berlin

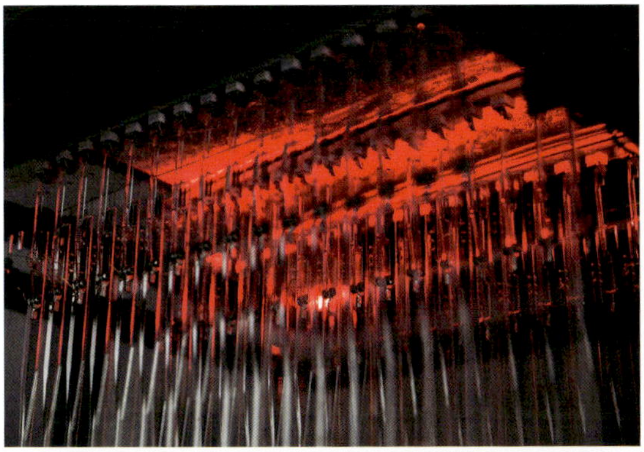

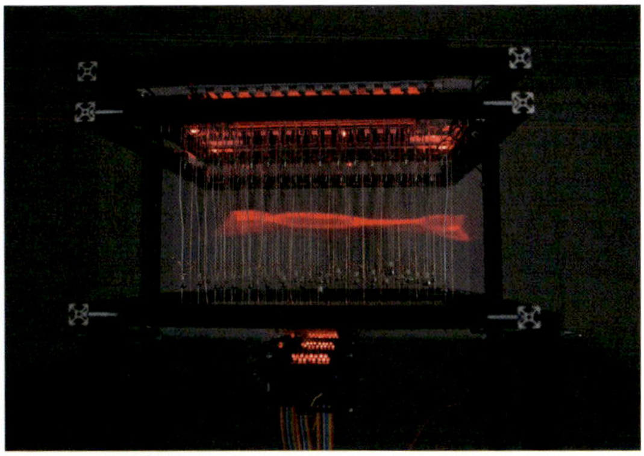

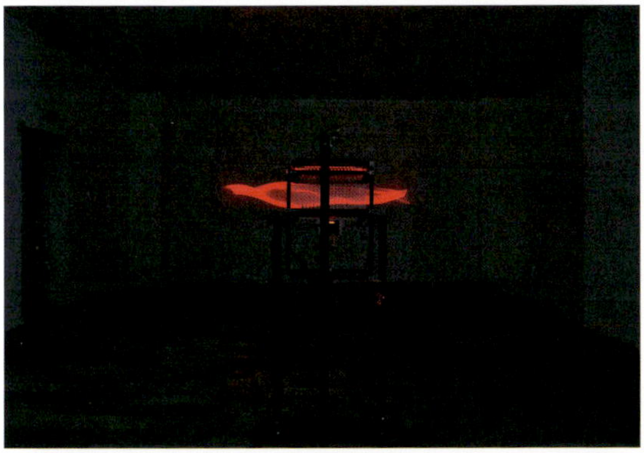

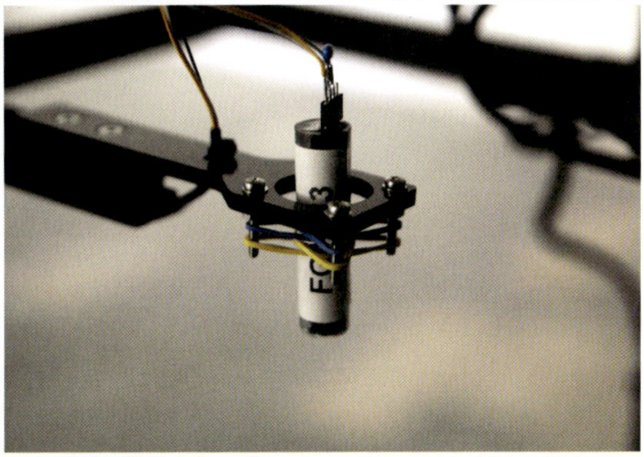

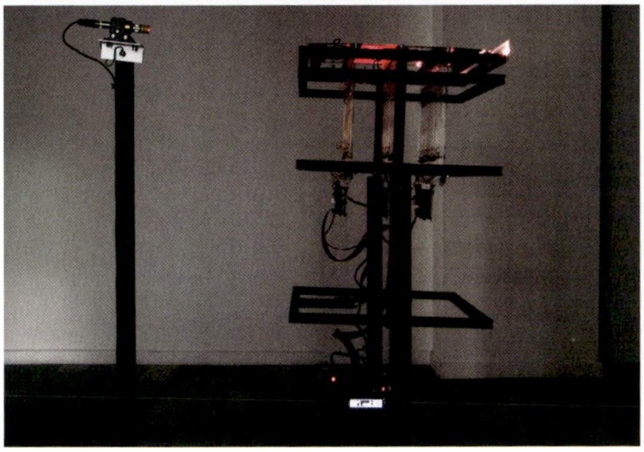

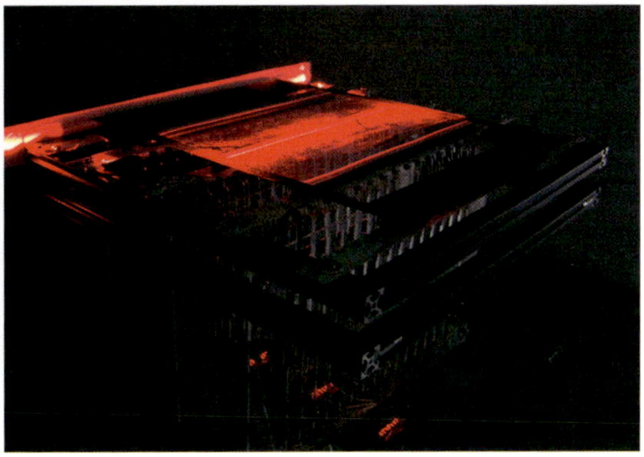

Ralf Baecker (DE), born in 1977 in Düsseldorf, is an artist with a background in computer science. Baecker builds systems and machines which explore the poetic potential of technology. His work focuses on the material scope of technology and its cultural construction. His projects have been exhibited internationally and were awarded an Honorary Mention at the Prix Ars Electronica (2012), and the second prize of the VIDA 14.0 Art & Artificial Life Award. In 2007, Baecker received a diploma from the Academy of Media Arts in Cologne, where he studied audiovisual media at the Media Art Department. He has worked as an artistic associate at the Media Department of the Bauhaus University in Weimar and since 2007 he has been working as an independent artist. Baecker teaches at the University of the Arts, Bremen, the College of fine Art, Kassel and ArzEZ in Arnhem. At present he is a fellow of the Graduate School of the University of the Arts in Berlin.

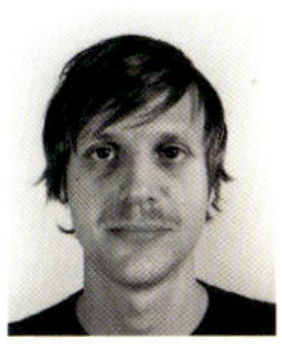

Myconnect

Saša Spačal, Mirjan Švagelj, Anil Podgornik

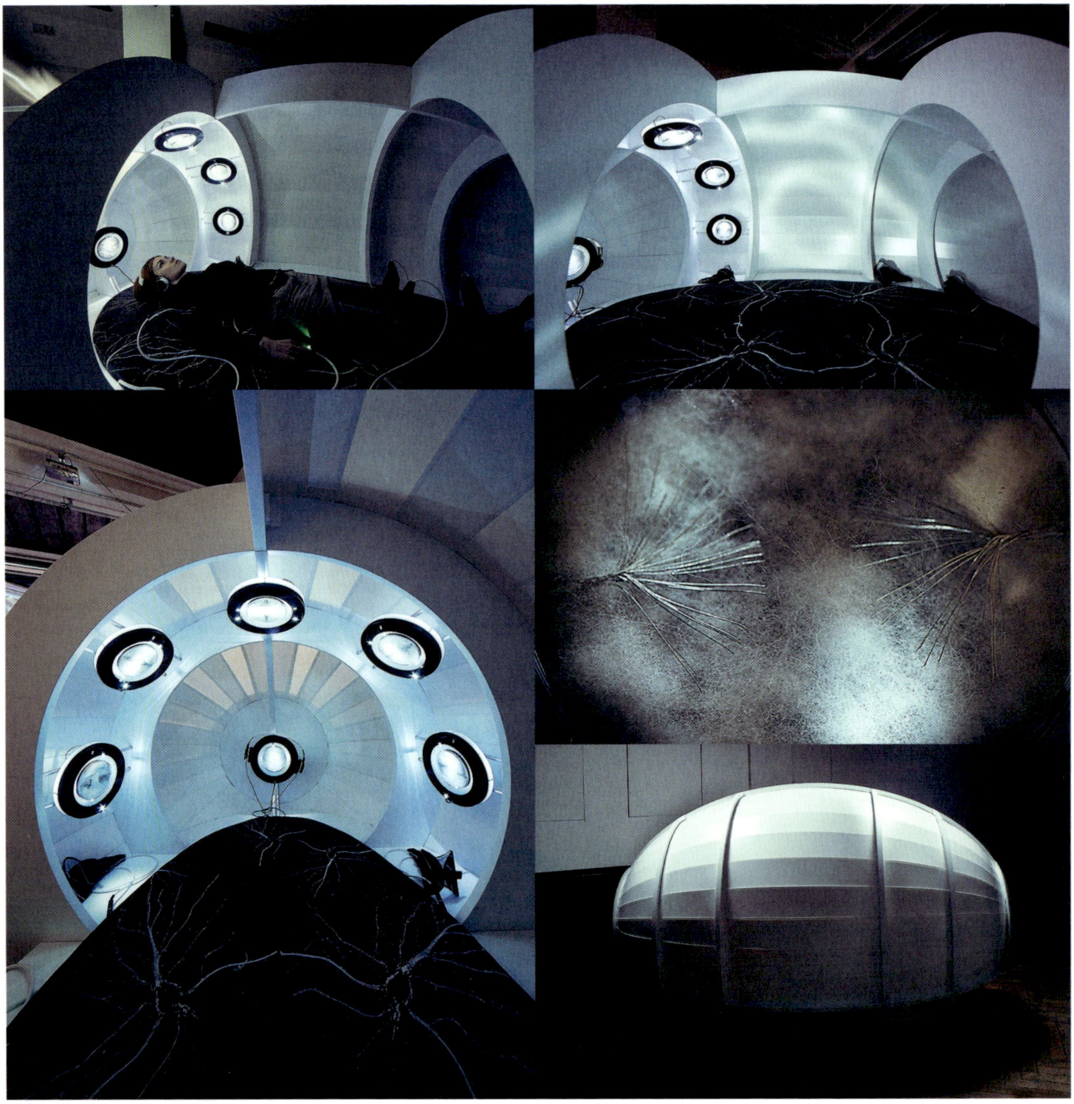

"For to connect is to affirm, and to affirm, to connect." – John Rajchman

Myconnect is an interspecies connector that emerged as an aspiration to enable human beings to transgress their own species and connect with another at a perceptive and physiological level. By entering the installation one joins with the otherness, another multiplicity i.e. the fungal mycelium. In the *Myconnect* capsule the nervous system of a person is integrated into a human-interface-mycelium biofeedback loop via their heartbeat. The mycelium's oscillations are produced by variable electrical resistance and correspond to the incoming temporally offset heartbeat. The hybrid sensation of electric resistance and pulse is then transferred back to the human body via sound, light and tactile sensory impulses. Transferred sensory experience indicates the notion of the dependence of perceivable reality on the sensory impulses in the environment. Such a symbiotic link highlights the integration of human beings in their multichannel network or their habitat. *Myconnect* is a symbiotic interspecies connector that questions the anthropocentric nature-human division. With its circuit of signals and impulses, generated and translated by biological and technological organisms, *Myconnect* performs an immersive experience of symbiotic interdependence. Through this experience the technological nature-human distinction can be seen as an arbitrary definition that serves particular biopolitical interests in human society, which can then be shamelessly wrapped in an ideology of utilitarianism and may conceal excessive exploitation. *Myconnect* creates an experience of connectedness, of unqualified immersion through the sensory system of the body. The experience of symbiosis in the *Myconnect* capsule is somewhat isolated, in the same way as microbiological cultures are isolated in a laboratory. In *Myconnect* symbiosis is purposefully separated from the environment in order to make it visible, audible and haptic for the visitor.

Myconnect can be seen as a neural connection, a sort of "tsaheylu" from the sci-fi film *Avatar.* In the Na'vi language, "tsaheylu" means a bond, a neural connection between two. The Na'vis connect to animals or plants that have neural whips or antennae, a strong, emotional, lifelong bond. With this bond the Na'vis extend and transcend their bodies. They become the environment, thus blurring the body-environment division. In the context of *Myconnect* such a neural connection, a "tsaheylu" is formed via a "mycosynapse," a two-way communication synapse that enables a constant symbiotic connection: one way leads from a heartbeat sensor to the fungal mycelium and the other from mycelium to the human body. As one of the vastest planetary organisms, which can outlive and repeatedly transform forests that grow above it, a mycelium seems a perfect network to plug into and experience oscillations of the electrical current flowing through it. A mycelium has multivalent connections through branching and nodal network allowing material to pass around it in all directions, it also forms biological interspecies connections—"mycorrhiza"—with the environment around it. In this way the mycelium is able to accommodate flows, principally of water and nutrients, around its structure. In this mutually beneficial association the fungus is provided with relatively constant and direct access to carbohydrates while the plant gains the benefits of the mycelium's higher absorptive capacity of water and mineral nutrients. In similar way *Myconnect* is an extension of fungi and human beings by enabling an experience of symbiosis.

Production: Kapelica Gallery
Supported by: the Ministry of Culture of the Republic of Slovenia, Municipality of Ljubljana–Department for Culture and ŠOU–Ljubljana

Saša Spačal (SI) is a media artist with background in humanities who is currently working at the intersection of living systems research, media and sound art. Her work focuses primarily on the post-human state, in which human beings exist and act as one of many elements in the ecosystem. Portfolio: www.agapea.si. **Mirjan Švagelj**, PhD (SI) is a doctor of biomedicine currently working for a biotech research and development company. He finished his doctoral studies at the University of Ljubljana in the field of medicinal mushrooms. **Anil Podgornik** (SI) is a DIY enthusiast with passion for electronics, mechanics and physics.

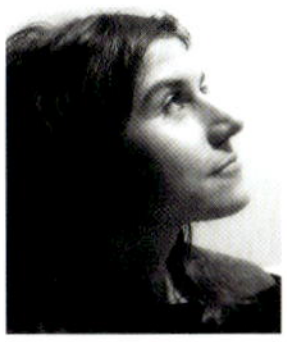
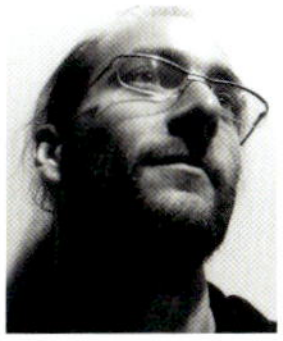
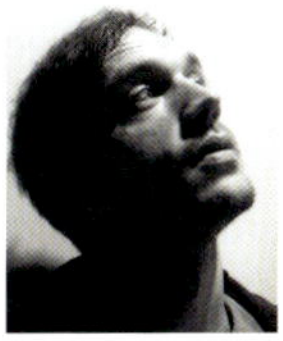

PSX Consultancy

Pei-Ying Lin, Špela Petrič, Dimitrios Stamatis, Jasmina Weiss

The *PSX Consultancy* project conceives augmentations for vegetal species to enhance the given client's natural reproductive processes. In other words, we make sex toys for plants. Misleadingly quirky, the *PSX Consultancy* is a project investigating the changing paradigm of the human/non-human relationship. Incorporating cultural frameworks through which we as humans understand ourselves and our environment—science, design and art—we improvise design tools that challenge our anthropocentric vantage point to think on the plants' behalf. The concepts produced by the interdisciplinary team of designers, artists and scientists are science-based, design-driven, irony-infused and playfully delivered. As the plant clients are silent about their necessities, we have relied on scientific knowledge of plant biology as well as design methodologies in the pursuit of thought-provoking, intelligible augmentations. What happens when artistic motivation appropriates human-centered design for use on plant clients? The result of the interdisciplinary approach is critically discursive objects posing as sex toys, inherently paradoxical and absurd, yet manifesting our "all means pos-

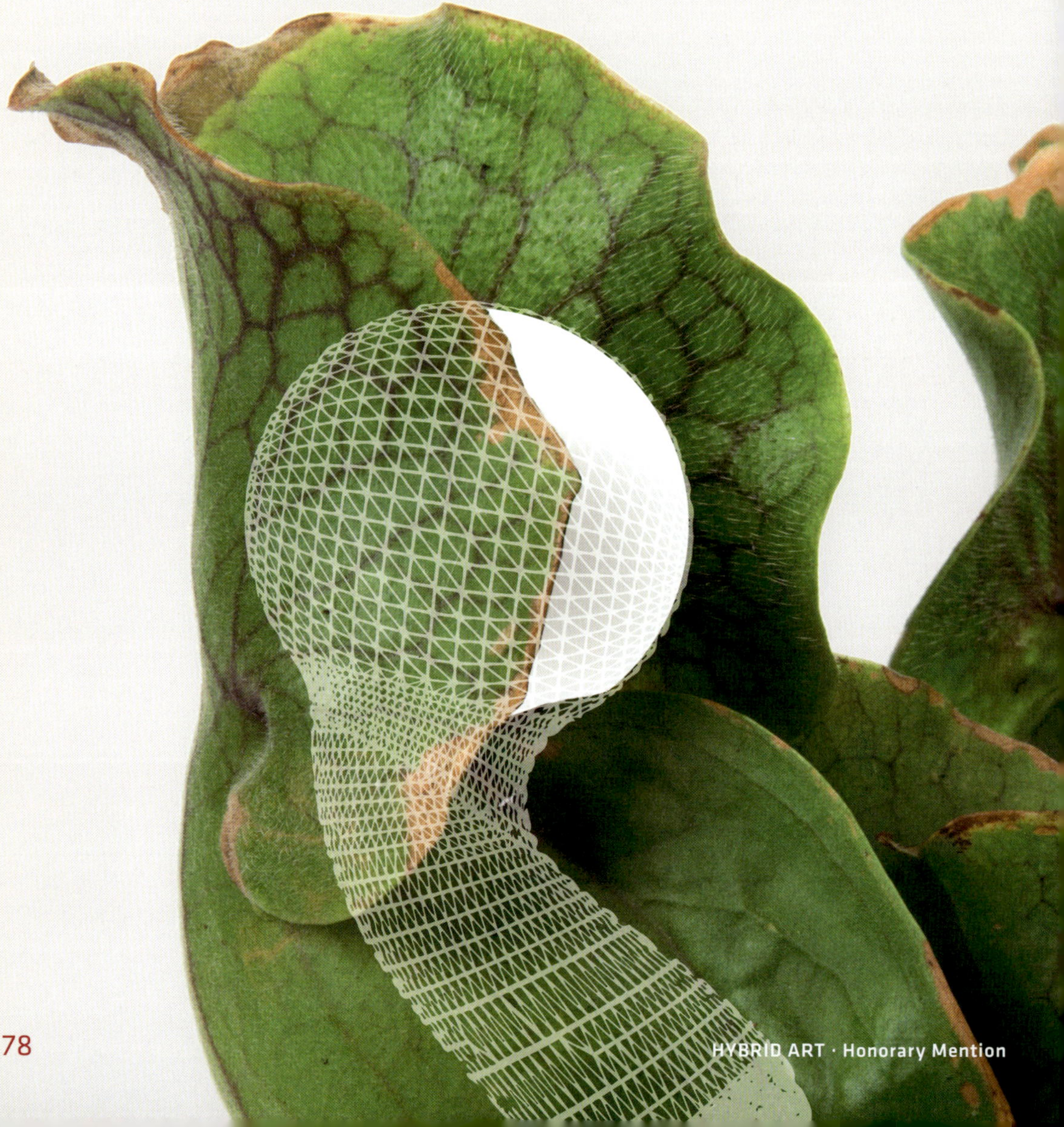

sible" attempt to truly understand the non-human. Through the hybrid exploration of the parallelism between plant and human reproductive strategies, we uncover the realm of bio-logic whilst provoking the ethical discourse connected to post-anthropocentrism. The motivation, client biology/requirements and bio-logic of the particular "sex toys" is explained in the attached booklet. The installation of 3D-printed proposals alongside the plant clients is only one of the outcomes of this process-based project. Equally important is the hands-on engagement of the public in the form of workshops and discussions across different cultural traditions, leading to an ever-expanding collection of plants and their sex toys while inviting the audience to explore the non-human experiences in their mind.

A collaborative project developed within the Designing Life topic at BIO50, the Biennial of Industrial Design 2014, Ljubljana, Slovenia.
Supported by: MAO, the Museum of Architecture and Design, Ljubljana; the Ministry of Culture of the Republic of Slovenia; the Ministry of Culture, Taiwan, RoC; National Culture and Arts Foundation, Taiwan, RoC

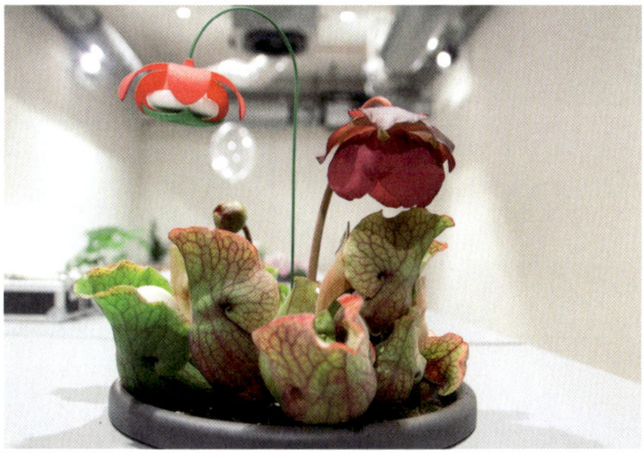

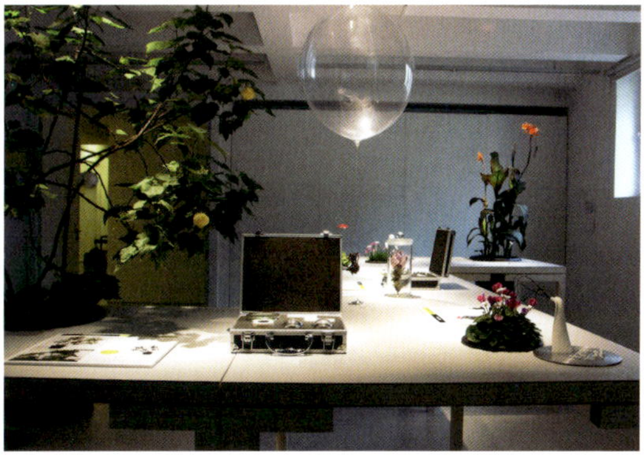

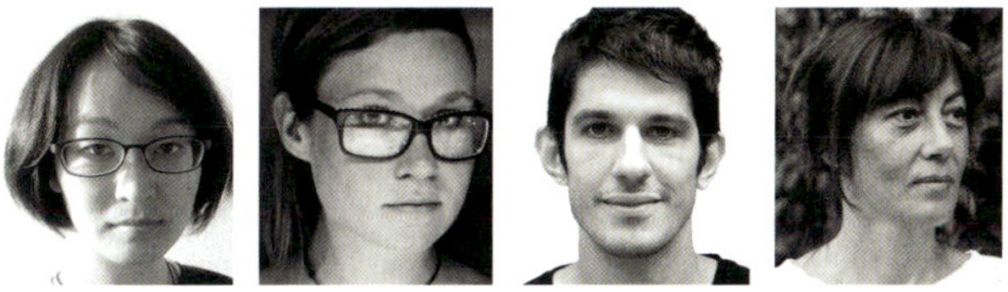

Pei-Ying Lin (TW), born in 1986, is an artist, designer and programmer with an MA in design interactions, Royal College of Art, and a BSc in life science, minor in computer science and cultural studies from National Tsing Hua University, Taiwan. Her main focus is on the combination of science and human society through artistic methods. She currently runs a Taiwanese BioArt community in Taiwan. **Špela Petrič** (SI), born in 1980, BSc, MA started her professional career as a scientific researcher in the field of biochemistry. Her interest in the context of knowledge production and its cultural impact motivated her to obtain a degree in transmedia at LUCA, Brussels. She has been working with living systems as an artist-researcher since 2011. Her artistic practice combines natural sciences, new media and performance. **Dimitrios Stamatis** (GR), born in 1983, is a designer with a formal background in product / graphic design. He has worked in Athens, London and Hangzhou designing products for a range of industries. Currently he works freelance (leavenlab.com), exploring how design can contribute as a catalyst for positive change. **Jasmina Weiss** (SI), born in 1963, is an interior designer and designer with formal background in architecture / design. She has worked in different fields connected with design, architecture and art. She has long been interested in different fields of science, culture, psychology, biology, ecology and environment.

ReBioGeneSys—Origins of Life

Adam W. Brown, Robert Root-Bernstein

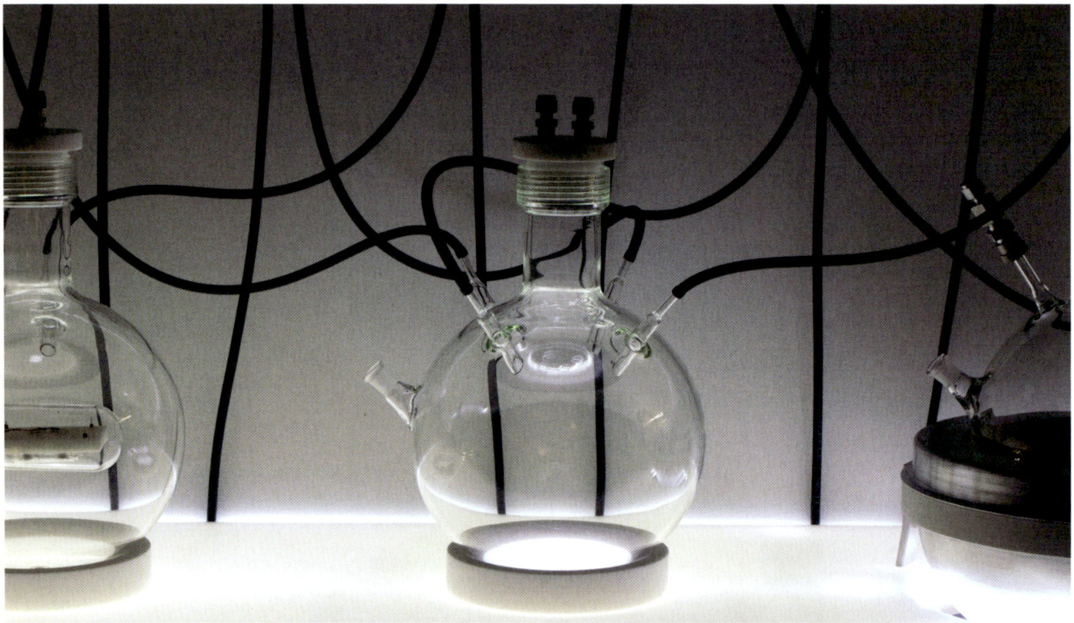

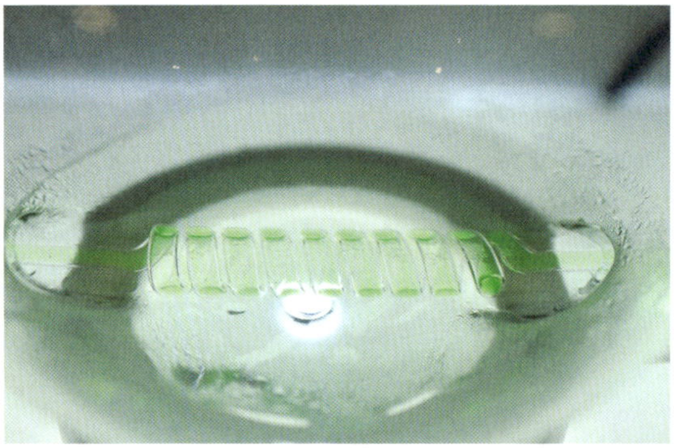

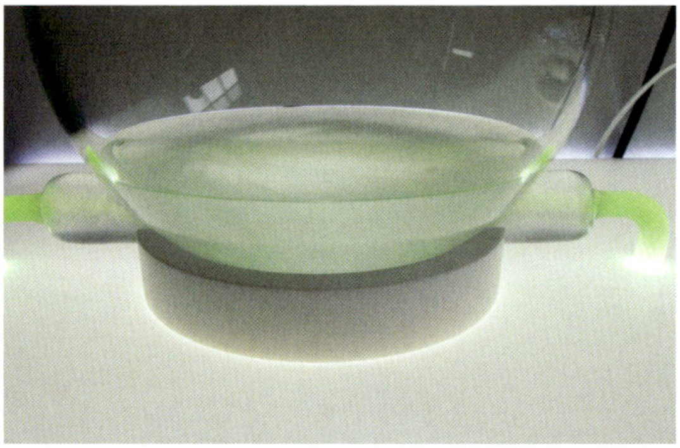

ReBioGeneSys—Origins of Life: a hybrid installation (process) that combines sculpture, chemistry, alchemy and conservation to create autonomous extreme minimal ecosystems capable of autopoetic evolution. *ReBioGeneSys* utilizes the processes and materials of science to ask fundamental questions about how all life seems to proceed from previous life and yet had to emerge from inorganic materials. Is life something special or is the possibility of life inherent in matter itself? Can the artist's approach to such questions help to resolve the conundrums that have stymied scientists? *ReBioGeneSys* is a fully functioning scientific experiment capable of being reconfigured into any real or imaginary world, be it Venus, Titan, our prebiotic Earth or Middle Earth. By combining all the scientific research on the origins of life in one set of integrated processes, *ReBioGeneSys* creates "mashed-up" extreme minimal ecosystems theoretically capable of forming the self-organizing chemistries necessary to produce semi-living molecules and perhaps even protocells. Artistically, *ReBioGeneSys* draws on the legacy of artists, such as the myth of Pygmalion and Jacques de Vaucanson's attempts to create "living" sculpture. But *ReBioGeneSys* is the first installation that actually does have the ability to

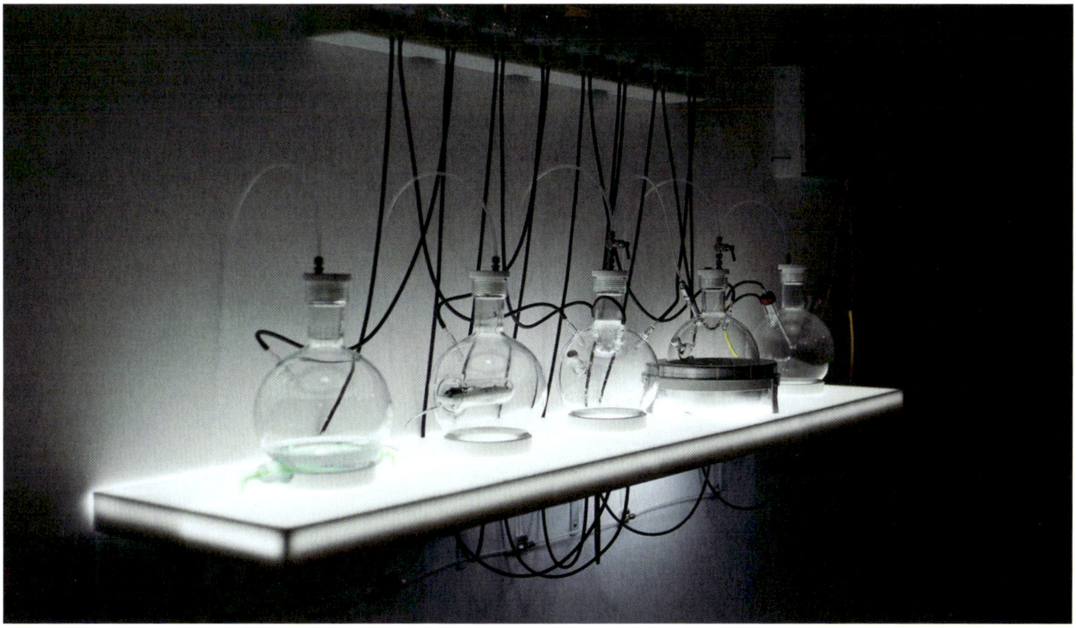

evolve itself. A system that can evolve by means of natural selection must incorporate a means of not only producing living matter, but also of selecting what is best adapted to that minimal ecosystem from the matter it produces. The evolution of *ReBioGeneSys* is inherent in its materiality and the processes it carries out, independent of the human beings that sculpted it, unaffected by the transience of the audiences that view it. An incarnation of new materialist philosophy that nonetheless is designed to produce a vitalistic outcome, *ReBioGeneSys* is an artifice designed not to mimic, but to produce nature itself through self-sustaining, ever-recursive autopoesis.

Automated control design: Barry Tigner
Supported by:
National Science Foundation
Michigan State University
Special Thanks:
The Physics and Astronomy Machine Shop, MSU
Scott Bankroff, Laboratory Glass, MSU

Adam Brown (US) is a conceptual artist whose work incorporates art and science hybrids including living and biological systems, robotics, molecular chemistry and emerging technologies. His art takes the form of installations, interactive objects, video, performance and photography. Brown's creative research is informed by a background in intermedia, an approach aiming at breaking down disciplinary boundaries and combining disparate fields of knowledge. Adam Brown is an associate professor in electronic art and intermedia at the Department of Art, Art History and Design at Michigan State University. **Bob Root-Bernstein** (US) is a professor of physiology and MacArthur Fellow at Michigan State University, USA. His laboratory research concerns the origins and evolution of metabolic control systems and autoimmune diseases. He also explores the intersections of arts and sciences through historical, philosophical and experimental studies. He is an editor of *Leonardo: The Journal of the International Society for Art, Science and Technology*, and the author of four books including *Sparks of Genius*, a study of the ways in which artists and scientist think alike.

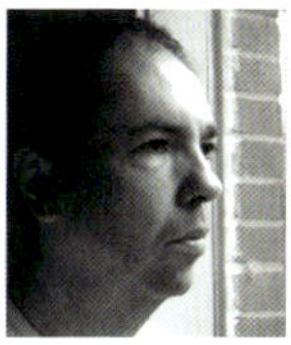

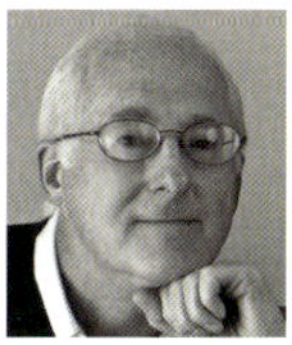

Satelliten

Quadrature

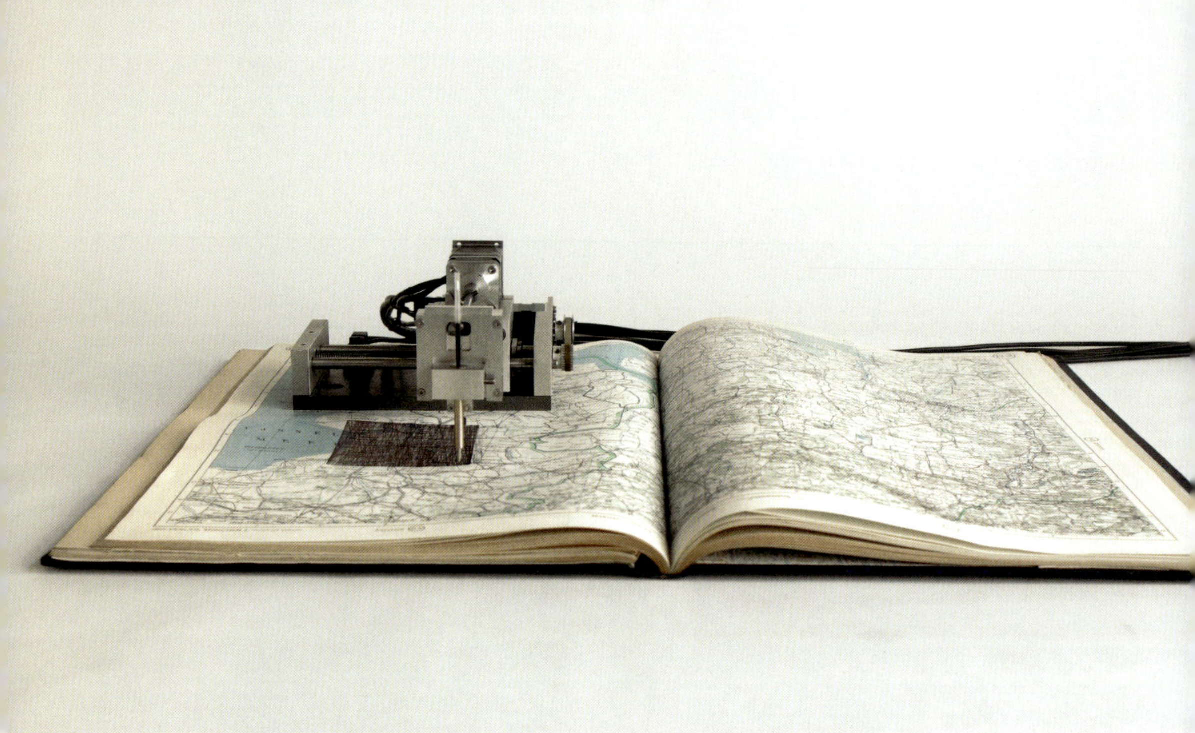

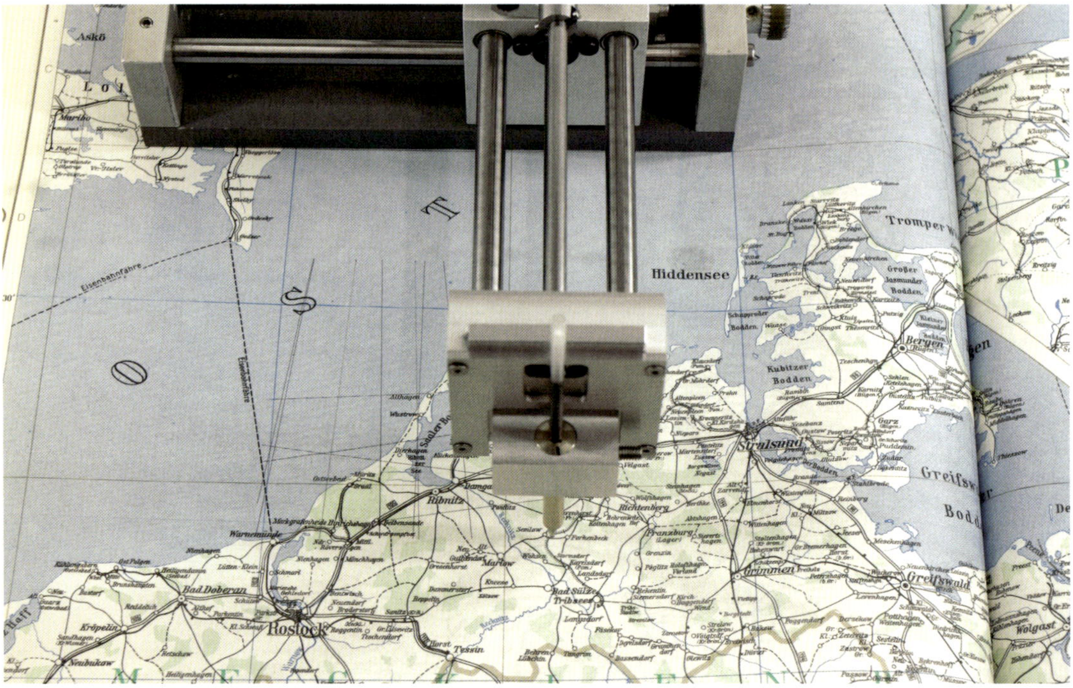

http://quadrature.co/
http://quadrature.co/work/satelliten/

Satellites are used for almost all modern achievements, from communication or navigation systems to environmental monitoring and military purposes. By now there are approximately 3,000 satellites in orbit, about 1,000 of which are still operating. The majority of these objects orbit our planet at heights of 200 km to 2,000 km, with an orbital period of 90 to 130 minutes. Despite their overall application, we hardly notice their existence. They are only rarely visible form Earth, when they are at the perfect angle to reflect the sun. As Kyle Vanhemert of *WIRED* has pointed out, however, for most of us, the only connecting link is in the form of a tiny dot in an online map on a screen showing our GPS location. We hardly ever decode the symbol and think about what it actually implies: satellites, in space. All necessary data about the positions and paths of satellites is available to the public, however, as it is crucial for determining free spots for new satellites for example. Accessing this information through a database maintained by the US Air Force, allows the drawing machine *Satelliten* to keep a record of the sheer number of satellite flyovers in regard to its own location. In a square of approximately 10 sq. cm, the machine traces their lines in real time until the distant object leaves our horizon again. *Satelliten* uses its own position coordinates as a starting point and old paper maps of the area as a base for its drawings. The output generated will vary depending on the location. In most western areas, the machine will detect satellites every few minutes. Only in remote regions, where there is less satellite activity, will it remain quiet for longer periods. For a long time, maps and atlas pages were one of the only sources for geographical knowledge. Now the paths of the satellites start to form on top of the familiar neighborhoods, thus relating the normally invisible traffic to our usual habitat. But as time passes the lines of the satellites will obliterate the well-known streets and cities, destroying not only the information the map originally contained but also the marks left by the preceding satellites. The new layer of human civilization covers the old one in an irreversible act of overwriting. In the long run only a black square will be left, it is the remains of this rather parasitic machine: a temporal window to the sky, showing the seemingly arbitrary but highly structured activities in lower earth orbit.

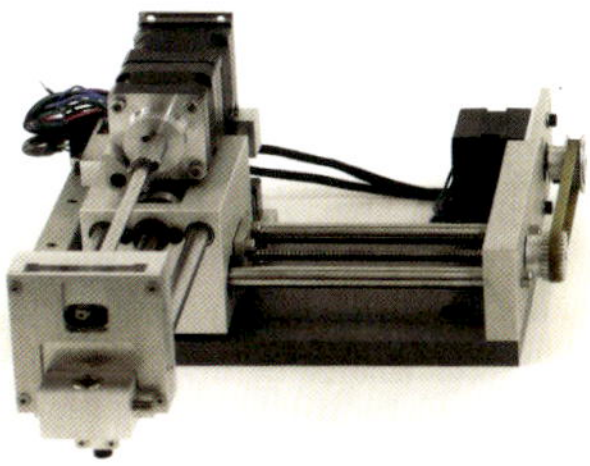

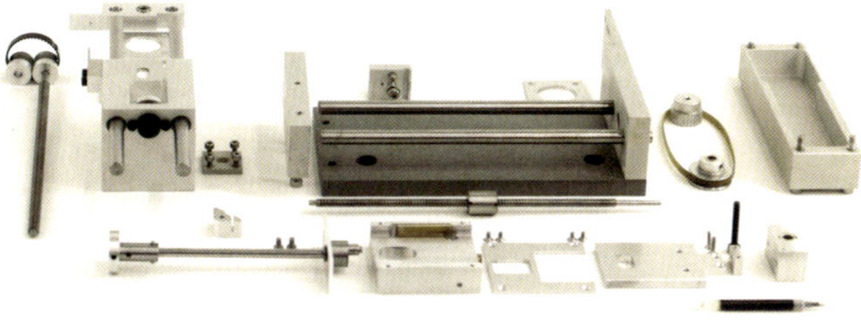

Quadrature (DE) is a collective for arts, light and robotics founded in 2012. With their works they try to challenge the usual perception of machinery and the ubiquitous expectation of its presumed functionality. The emphasis of Quadrature's works is on the intersection of the physical and digital worlds, of object and code. The three members of Quadrature, **Jan Bernstein** (DE), **Juliane Götz** (DE) and **Sebastian Neitsch** (DE), work and live Berlin. They all share a love of machines and outer space.

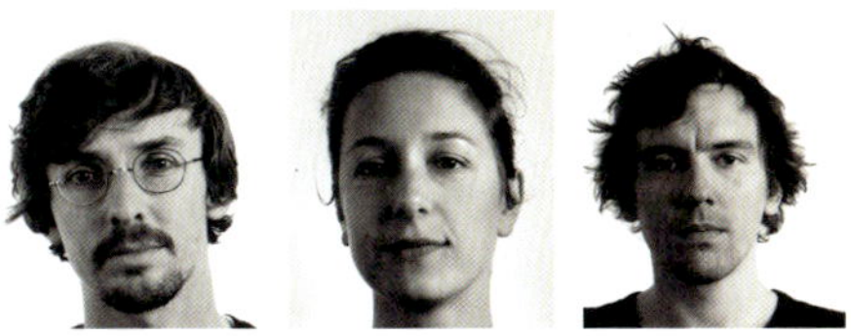

Stranger Visions

Heather Dewey-Hagborg

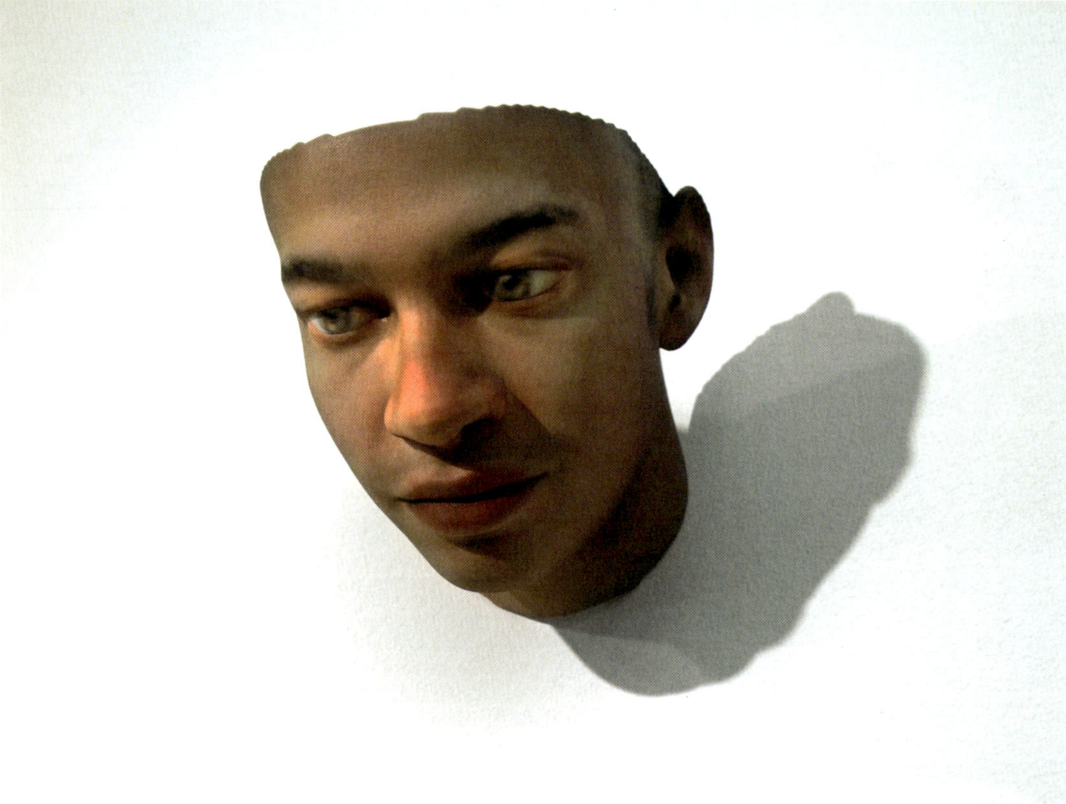

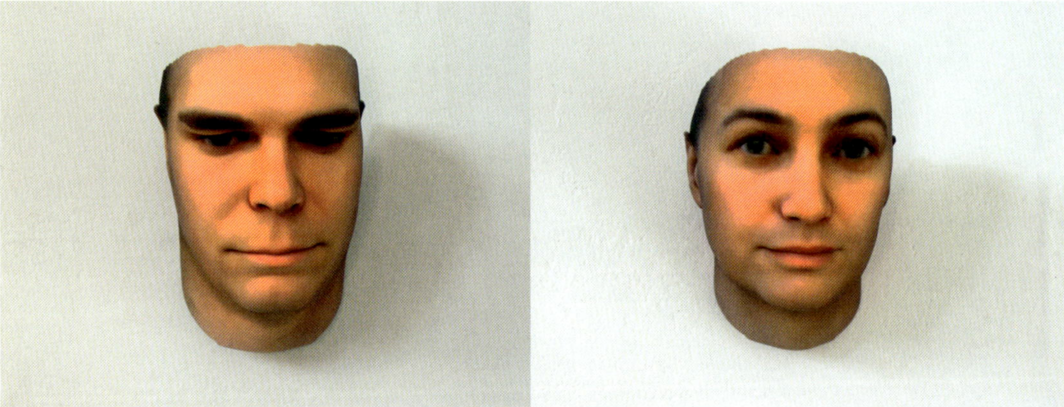

In my artwork *Stranger Visions* I create portrait sculptures from analyses of genetic material collected in public spaces. Working with artifacts that strangers unwittingly leave behind, this work demonstrates the possible future of forensic DNA phenotyping (determining appearance from DNA), and points to the emerging privacy issues related to the increasing accessibility and decreasing costs of biotechnology. Much of my work begins with a question. In past works I have asked questions about language, AI, creativity and machines. The question behind *Stranger Visions* came to me as I was sitting in a therapy session, ostensibly with the purpose of introspecting and reflecting on myself. Staring at a generic print on the wall, I noticed that the glass covering the print was cracked and in that crack was lodged a single hair. I became fascinated by this hair. Who did it belong to? What did they look like? How did they act? What did they think about? How much could I find out about a person from a single hair? I became entranced by this question of what I could learn about a person from a carelessly shed hair—like a detective story unfolding before me. On my way home that afternoon I began to notice all these genetic artifacts, all these *clues,* littered on the sidewalks, subway benches and streets. It occurred to me that if I could extract DNA from these kinds of items, I would have a pretty good indication as to who left them. So I began collecting "samples"—traces of human DNA that I found on my travels. I brought the samples into a lab and performed DNA extraction. I amplify certain regions of the DNA using a technique called PCR—polymerase chain reaction. This allows me to study certain regions of the genome that tend to vary from person to person, known as SNPs or single nucleotide polymorphisms. I determine what allele is present for a particular SNP on each sample, and then feed this information into a custom-built computer program I wrote, which takes all these values that correlate with physical genetic traits and parameterizes a 3D model of a face to represent them. I export the model and send it to a rapid prototyping machine that prints the model in full-color 3D. It is important to remember that this is art, not the development of a new product or company. *Stranger Visions* is meant as a provocation, a confrontation of the viewer with the possibility that someone might be able to examine their DNA, inspect their identity, from detritus they didn't even notice that they had left behind. The point isn't that I know *everything* about a person from a piece of chewing gum, rather that I, an amateur, know as much as I do. And I can potentially find out a whole lot more.

Supported by: Eyebeam Art and Technology Center, Genspace, Rensselaer Polytechnic Institute
Music: Timothy Day

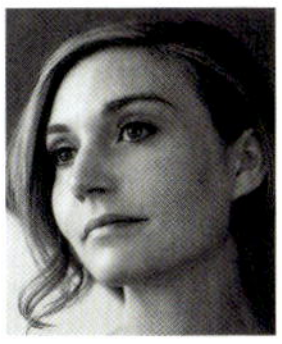

Heather Dewey-Hagborg (US) is a transdisciplinary artist and educator who is interested in art as research and critical inquiry. Heather has shown work internationally at events and venues including the Poland Mediations Biennale, Ars Electronica, Centre de Cultura Contemporània de Barcelona, the Science Gallery Dublin, PS1 MOMA, the New Museum, and Eyebeam Art and Technology Center in New York City. Her work has been widely discussed in the media, from the *New York Times* and the BBC to TED and *WIRED*.

This Tape Will Self-Destruct

Diego Trujillo Pisanty

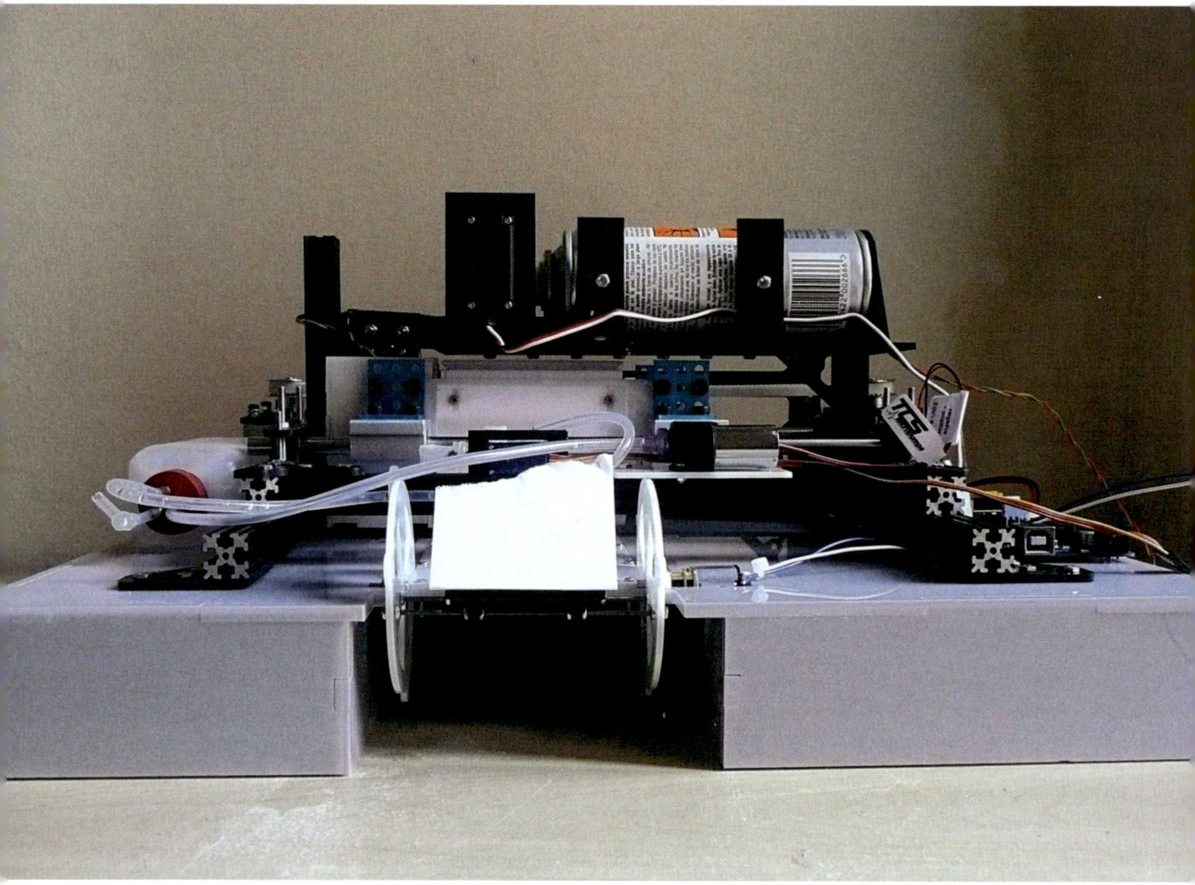

In July 2013 the BBC reported that the Federal Guard Service of the Russian Federation would revert from using computers to typewriters for the production of sensitive documents in order to prevent information leaks. The following January *The Guardian* newspaper released a video of its editors destroying the computer equipment that stored the National Security Agency (NSA) files provided by Edward Snowden. Wikileaks and the release of the NSA files will likely be part of this decade's history. However, the debate around governmental espionage and secrecy for the sake of national security seems more related to the Cold War era than to modern living. *This Tape Will Self-Destruct* explores the intersection between our present-day techno-political status and spy fictions from the Cold War. The project consists of an electronic device that produces self-destructing documents, a motif within the Cold War spy genre that has regained relevance in the context of digital communications and mass surveillance. The self-destructing documents created by the machine contain extracts from spy-themed films, television and literature produced during the Cold War, paired with excerpts from real, current day, leaked documents. The documents' contents were manually curated so that the contemporary leaked documents resonate with their fictional counterparts; matching the two extracts results in an amalgam that blurs present reality with past fiction. The machine prints each document in this emergent collection on thermal paper. Through a series of complicated electro-mechanical actions it is then treated with glycerol and potassium permanganate. Approximately one

http://trujillodiego.com/work/ttwsd.html

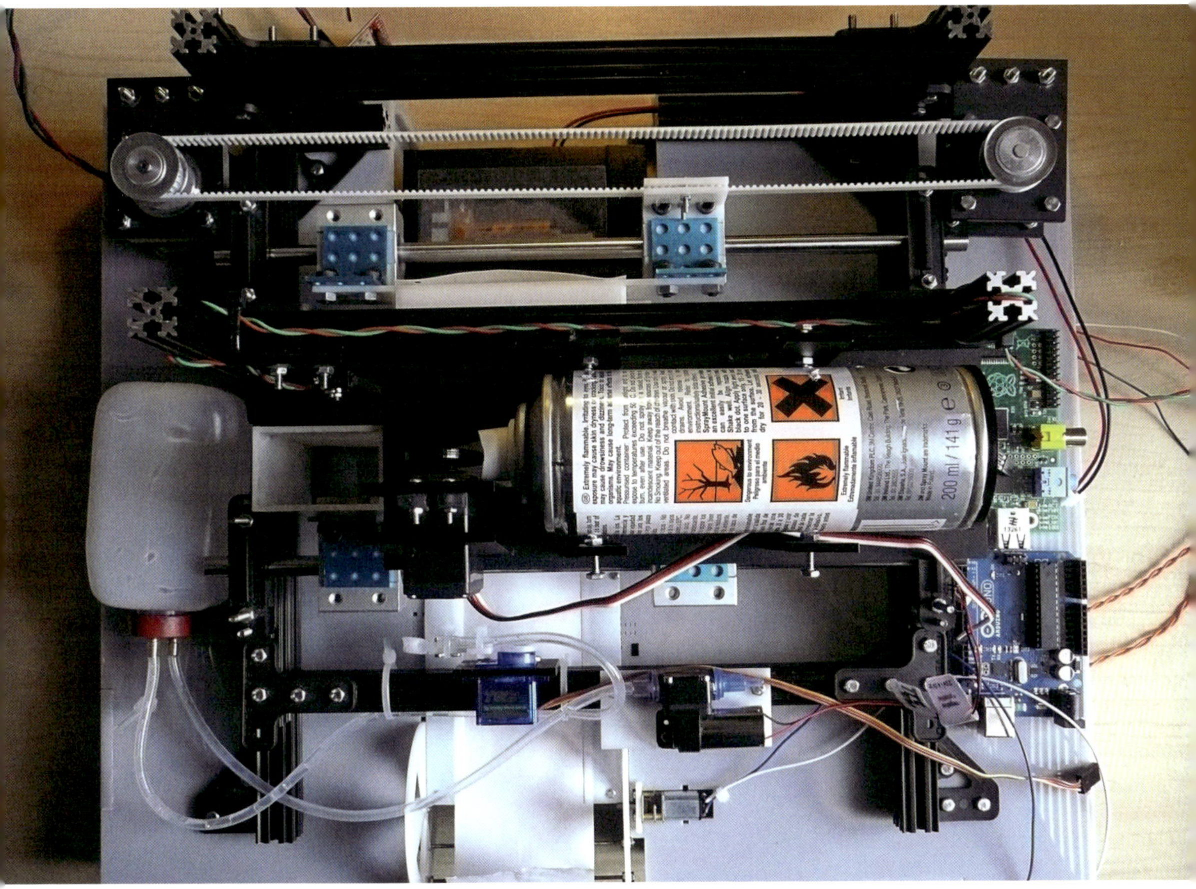

minute after the two chemicals mix they produce a strong exothermic reaction resulting in a fire that ignites the printed message, its content forever gone as the flames consume and blacken the paper. The printer and the documents it produces raise questions on the current value of secrecy and the role it plays in aspiring transparent democracies. It also makes us consider the rhetoric in political fictions that can lay the groundwork help ideologies establish themselves.

Supported by: Fondo Nacional para la Cultura y las Artes (FONCA)
Thanks to: Antonio Arango, Juan Manuel Escalante, Santiago Itzcoatl, Arturo Alvarez

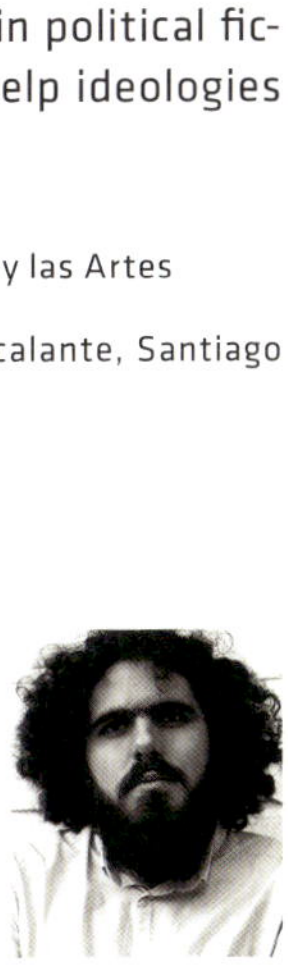

Diego Trujillo Pisanty (MX), born 1986 in Mexico City, where he studied a short degree in photography and a BSc in biology. His degree thesis on computer-simulated evolution spurred an interest in digital arts, which that led him to take an MA in design interactions at the Royal College of Art in London, from where he graduated in 2012. Diego's background has provided him with a broad set of skills, material knowledge and theory, which he integrates into his work characterized by an exploration of technology as a materialization of human complexity. He currently works in Culture Lab at Newcastle University, where he will remain until September 2015. Diego recently concluded a Young Creators' fellowship from the Mexican Fund for Culture and Arts (FONCA) to develop *This Tape Will Self-Destruct.*

Vanitas Machine

Verena Friedrich

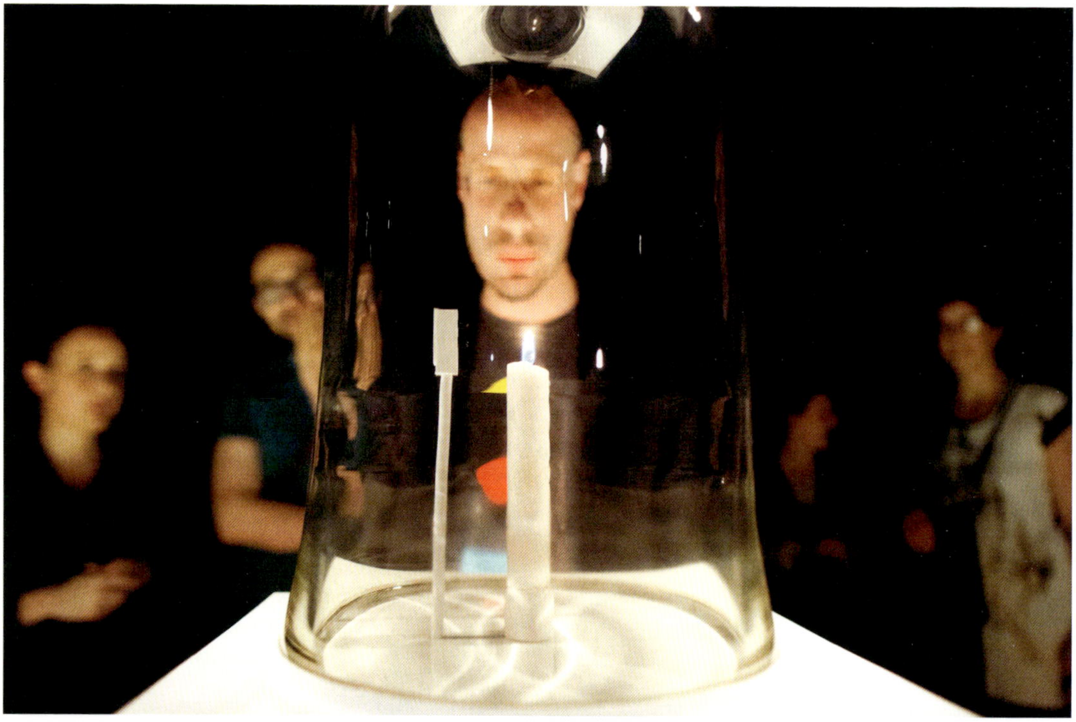

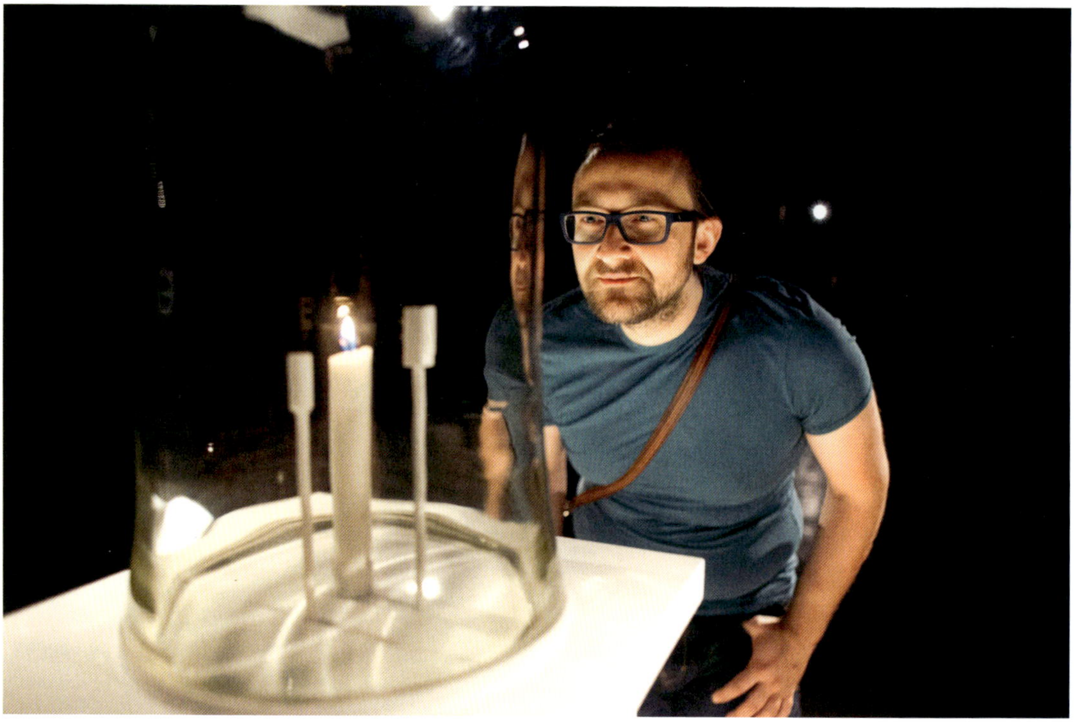

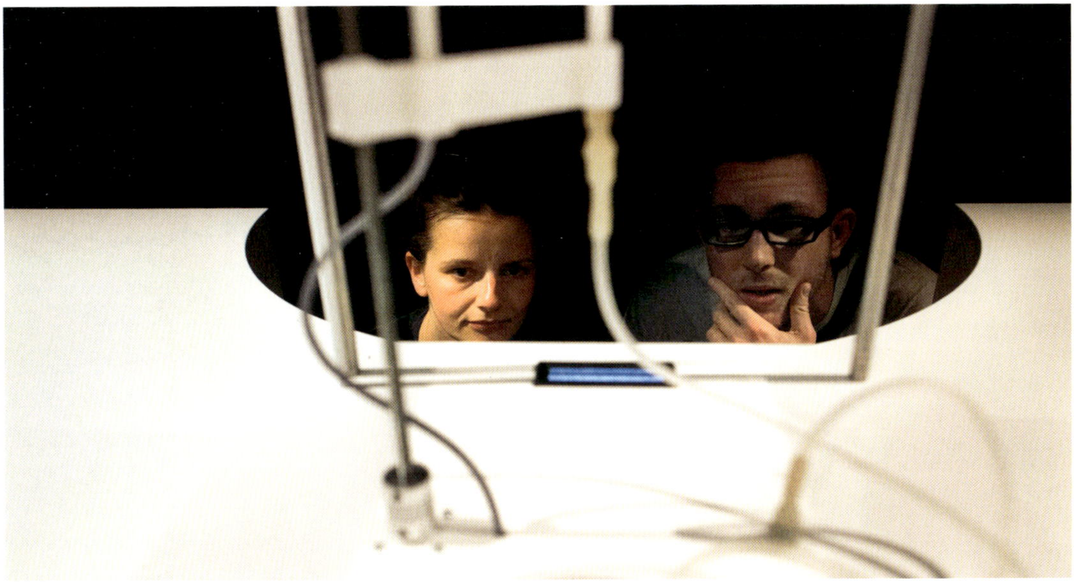

The *Vanitas Machine* addresses the desire for eternal life and the potential of life-prolonging measures. Based on a candle which—by technical intervention—burns down very slowly, the *Vanitas Machine* creates a contemporary analogy to the effort to prolong the human lifespan with the help of science and technology. As one of the classical *vanitas* symbols, a burning candle recalls the futility of the moment, the transience of human life and the certainty of the end of all existence. But is this end really still inevitable? In the course of the last two centuries, average human life expectancy has increased significantly in the industrialized countries. Moreover, in the context of scientific research the biological causes of ageing are being explored. Numerous theories of ageing have already been developed, pointing both towards physiological as well as environmental factors. One of the first was the "rate-of-living theory," which claims that the lifespan of organisms is reciprocally related to energy turnover and therefore connected to calorie intake, oxygen consumption and heart rate: the higher the metabolic rate, the shorter the lifespan of the organism. In *Vanitas Machine,* a candle is placed at the center of an experimental setup. Similar to the human breathing process, a burning candle consumes oxygen and produces carbon dioxide and water. The higher the oxygen and energy turnover, the shorter the burning time of the candle. The *Vanitas Machine* has been specifically developed to keep a candle "alive" under controlled conditions. By protecting it from environmental factors and by precisely regulating the oxygen supply the "metabolism" of the candle and thus its "lifespan" can be influenced.

Supported by the Academy of Media Arts Cologne; researched and developed at the Atelier Transmedialer Raum and the Lab3—Laboratory for Experimental Computer Science, KHM

Verena Friedrich (DE) studied at the Academy of Media Arts Cologne and the University of Art and Design Offenbach. Her projects have been presented internationally and have, for example, received the International Media Award for Science and Art from ZKM Karlsruhe, a special mention in the VIDA 13.2 Awards and the Young Artist Award of the State of North-Rhine Westphalia. Besides creating installations in which organic and electronic media come into play she is interested in direct interaction with scientists and engineers and the hands-on work in the bioscientific laboratory. In recent years, she has had residencies at SymbioticA Australia and the Max Planck Institute for Biology of Ageing in Cologne.

Welt-Klimakonferenz

Rimini Protokoll (Haug / Kaegi / Wetzel)

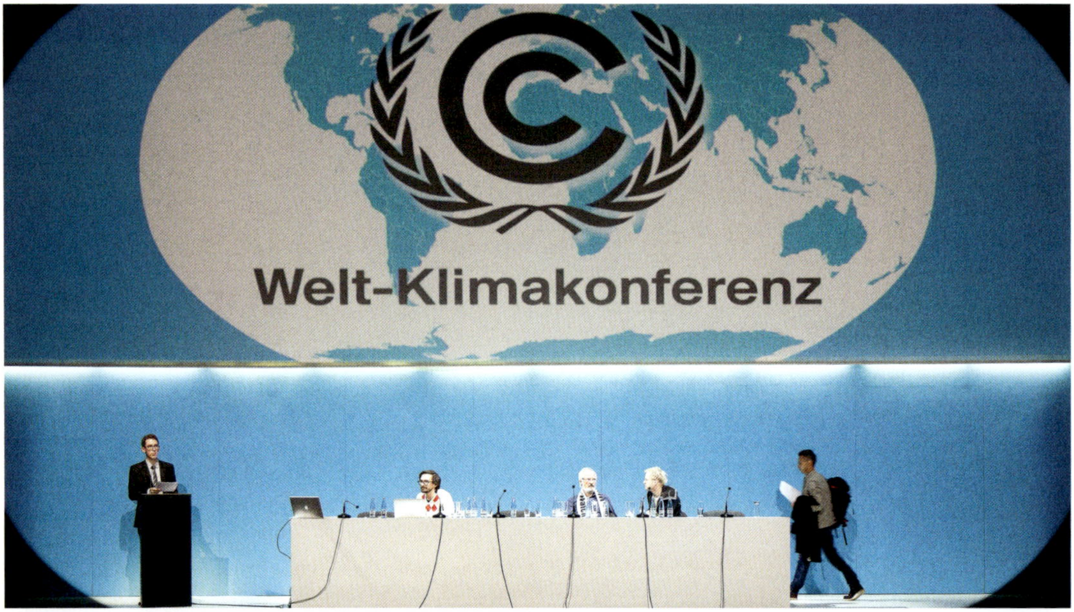

Benno Tobler

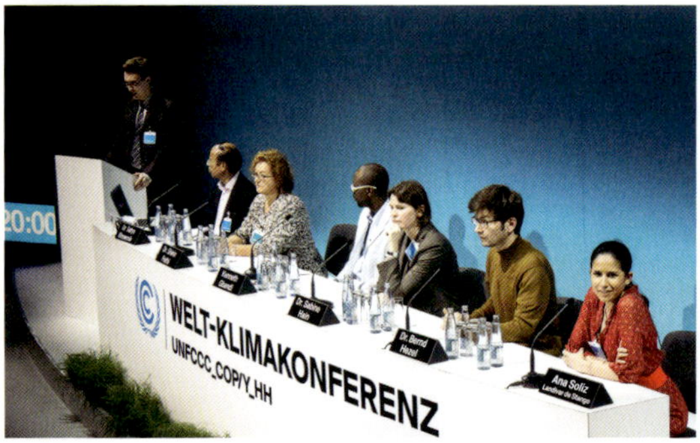

Melina Wagner

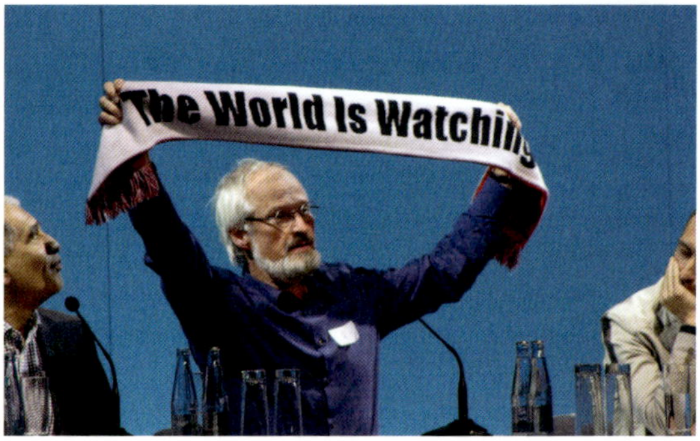

Dennis Kossowski

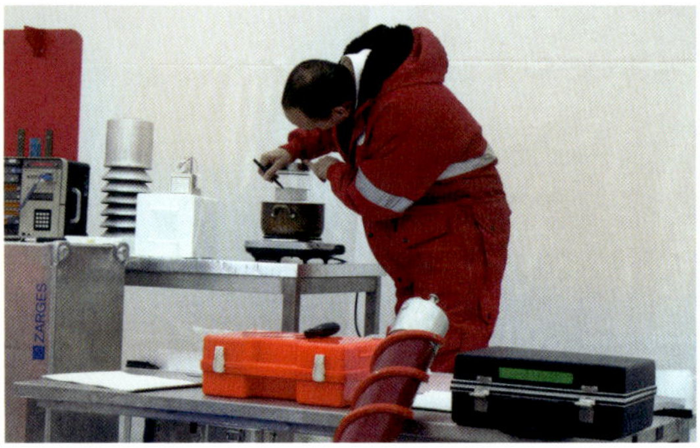

Lima Shengelia

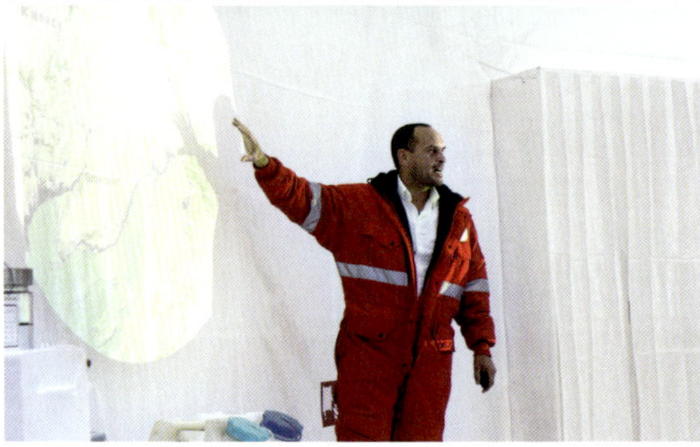

Melina Wagner

In this theatrical re-enactment of one of the most important formats of contemporary political and scientific discourse, the 650 audience members are invited to represent the 196 delegations of the original "conferences of the parties." Three or four spectators form a (randomly gathered) delegation and during the three-hour-performance are asked to make a decision for the country they represent

www.schauspielhaus.de/de_DE/repertoire/welt_klimakonferenz.1011591
www.rimini-protokoll.de

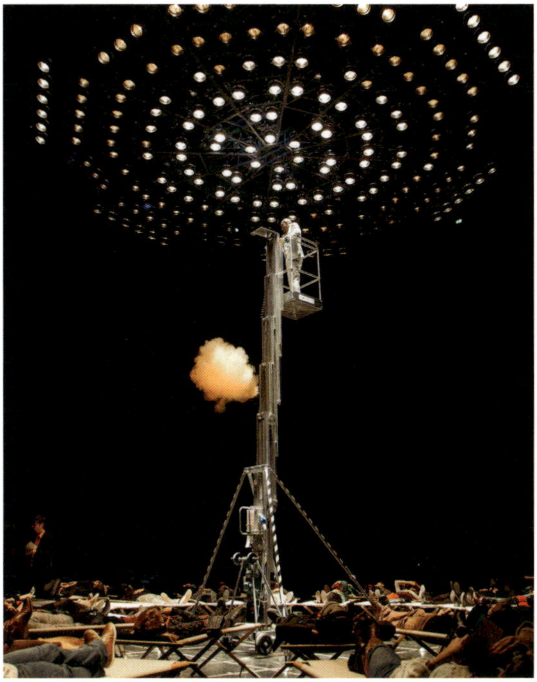

Benno Tobler

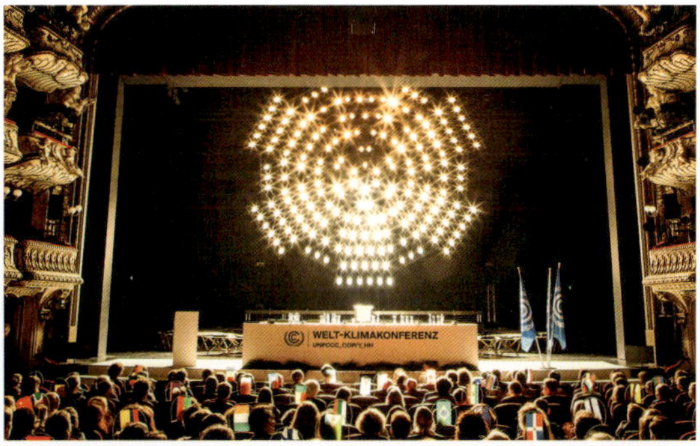

Benno Tobler

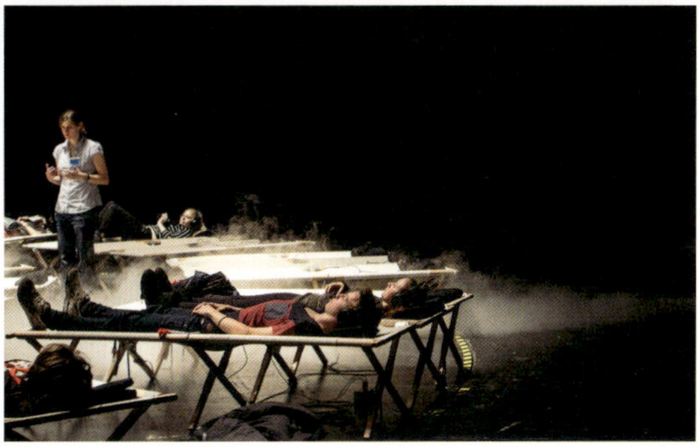

Visarut Namsiripongphan

about the level of CO_2-reduction and a financial contribution to the Green Climate Fund. At the end of the performance, the obligations and contributions gathered are presented and evaluated live in the theater. Eighteen real and well-known climate researchers, politicians, businessmen and representatives of NGOs lead the spectator-delegations through the diverse topics of climate conferences. The 650 "delegates" are split into groups of 60 people, they move through different scenarios and briefings, which prepare them to act as delegates of the 196 nations. Taking on the position of a country and a region that is very different from their own, the audience experiences a shift of perspective. The talks, briefings and negotiations the spectator-delegates are involved in create a dynamic exchange with the experts and between themselves—together they are all performers in this theatrical world climate conference. The performance is linked to events in the "real world" via Skype, experts from the real world conferences in Lima, and this year in Paris, communicate with the people in the theater and create a complex interactive and multimedia performance.

Stage: Dominic Huber
Dramaturgy: Imanuel Schipper, Jörg Bochow
Video: Hanna Linn Wiegel
Scientific Advisor: Florian Rauser
A project by:
Deutsches Schauspielhaus Hamburg / Rimini Protokoll
In collaboration with Max-Planck-Institut für Meteorologie, Germanwatch, Potsdam-Institut für Klimafolgenforschung, Alfred-Wegener-Institut
Supported by: Norddeutsche Stiftung für Umwelt und Entwicklung aus Erträgen der Lotterie »BINGO! Die Umweltlotterie«, Greenpeace Energy and klimaretter.info

Rimini Protokoll (DE)—Since 2000 **Helgard Haug** (DE), **Stefan Kaegi** (CH) and **Daniel Wetzel** (DE) have formed an author-director team. Their works in the theater, radio plays, film and installations are created in constellations of twosomes, threesomes and solos. Since 2002 all their works have been subsumed and announced under the Rimini Protokoll label. Their work focuses on the further development of theater in order to facilitate unusual perspectives on our reality. 2001 the Rimini Protokoll's total artwork was awarded the Silver Lion of the 41st Venice Theater Biennale.

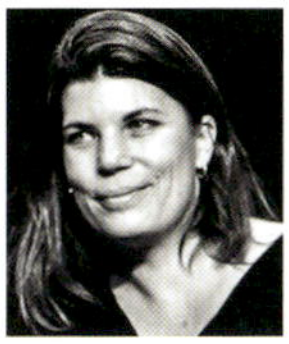

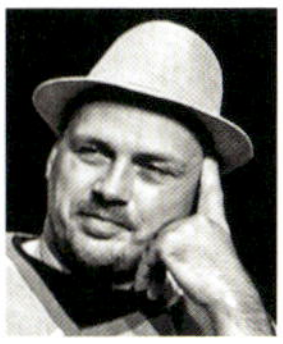

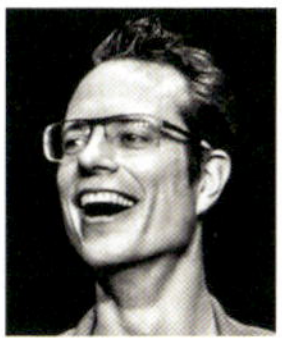

Digital Musics &

Sound Art

From Nature to Sound, from Technology to Art: the Complexity and Beauty of Modern Expressions

Seppo Gründler, Sergey Kasich, Christina Kubisch, Valeria Rueda, Naohiro Ukawa

This year the jury experienced wide diversity inside the category of Digital Musics & Sound Art. The use of very different media made it very hard to compare the various pieces.
The jury comes from very different backgrounds, cultures and generations. Nevertheless, after the first selections, the decisions were very clear. We noticed a narrower range of countries of origin of the submitting artists, so we would like to encourage people from outside the London-Tokyo-New-York axis to apply in future.
A surprise was that the winning piece was transferred from the Hybrid Arts category to our jury, and this again shows the increasing integration of the different disciplines. We would like to state that putting music and sound art into one category is a point for further discussion.
The quality of the first three projects was nearly equal, so it was hard to decide, but in the end the choice was unanimous.

Golden Nica

Chijikinkutsu · Nelo Akamatsu

Suikinkutsu, one of the decorations for Japanese gardens in the Edo period, is mechanized to reflect the sound of water dripping into an underground hole, for practical use for instance in agriculture or effluent treatment. *Chijikinkutsu* is a coinage combining *suikinkutsu* and *chijiki:* geomagnetism. With Akamatsu's theme on "formalization of invisibles", this work creates a subtle sound using copper wire and a sewing needle in a glass of water. In addition, he succeeds at a point where he merges a Western idea on physics with the view of nature in the traditional Japanese garden. This work encompasses what we can see and what we cannot see in our consciousness both in ordinary life and the psychological world. There is also a resonance with a variety of philosophies, as with the idea of the heart sutra: "Form is emptiness, and emptiness is form", Paul Klee's theory of form production, and William Gilbert's theory of magnetism. Capturing a magnetic field in an industrial glass, its appearance shows an essence of the cosmos. This work could be a pole of an ambient installation that has been part Japanese aesthetics for over 400 years since the Edo era.

Awards of Distinction

Drumming is an Elastic Concept · Josef Klammer

Musicianship, intelligent use of technique and the aesthetic quality of the physical performance of the piece *Drumming is an Elastic Concept* by Josef Klammer were the main criteria for selecting this piece. We see and hear the essence of a long and ongoing work and research with drums, combining analog and digital aids. The fascination is created by the mixture of the visible and the hidden origins of the sounds and the intensity of artists playing. The performance has a clear dramaturgic line, also showing that this music was developed alongside technical and aesthetic developments in improvised and electronic music. Humor has an important role, but is never too stretched. Besides the musical dimension the piece also deals with the spatial dimension of a performer on stage, connecting different means of generating and processing sound with the appropriate embodiment in the stage performance. *Drumming is an Elastic Concept* delivers a state-of-the-art discourse on playing and improvising live with electronics.

UNDER WAY · Douglas Henderson

UNDER WAY by Douglas Henderson, is a sound installation which works with a limited amount of material but expands in acoustic, visual and site-specific ways through its very special narrative quality. Only one speaker, situated in a self-constructed structure by the artist, associates the compass of a ship with a moving horizon. Henderson uses sound and light to locate the viewer on board a ship. The historical navigation instrument which is recreated and reinterpreted by very basic and simple materials now fulfills an artistic purpose. The light movements are completely under the control of the soundtrack, which is a real masterpiece of composition and therefore was much appreciated by the jury. Viewers find themselves on the high seas, not only visually but also acoustically. The illusion of traveling through space gives the public the possibility of individual associations and memories. The jury was impressed by the knowledge of acoustic processes as well as the original and expert use of materials. A small sculpture opens up not only a sound but also a visual horizon. The work makes evident that ideas about the importance of technological material and ideas about what simplicity means have to be rethought. They should not be seen as opposites but can join in many different combinations. It is the artistic idea and realization which in the end defines the result of the artwork.

Honorary Mentions

::vtol:: oil · Dmitry Morozov

::vtol:: oil is an interactive sound installation based on anti-consumerism and anti-possession ideas. The material objects of physical possession, provided by visitors, are transformed into immaterial sound for a listening experience in a form of printed CDs, which are given away. More than 1,000 CDs were recorded during first exhibition. The jury was particularly fascinated by the idea and conception of this work and was impressed by a quality of its documentation. At the same time the work, nominated for the sound-related category, had an obvious lack of music or sound extracts to judge, which of course cannot be a point of serious criticism for the project, when beauty and innovation is mostly in the conceptual and technical solution. Another discussable point is the not so obvious ambiguity of the concept itself. The "anti-consumerism" piece replaces physical objects, which were made by corporations and sold as commodities, not just with sound but with CDs, covered with the name of the artist—a physical artifact to own, tagged with a label—which in a way places the artist on the same level as the object of his criticism. But this is usually a quality of a good artwork—to create a discussion. The jury is pleased to award an Honorary Mention to *::vtol:: oil* in order to encourage further exploration.

bell · Soichiro Mihara

Soichiro Mihara's small sound sculpture looks fragile and emits only a faint sound. It was inspired by ancient Japanese wind chimes, which were intended to guard against evil that people could not perceive. Today there are a lot of unknown dangers that cannot normally be seen or heard. We need sensors and special equipment, which is often only accessible to those who create the unknown dangers. The small glass bell sounds when it detects radiation in the area it is positioned. Our hearing is our the most acute sense of perception we have. It is more refined than our sense of sight, but it is nowadays very often neglected. A subtle but intense sound warns us—against what? What is really happening around us? Owing to the Fukushima catastrophe the jury considered the work to be highly political, but at the same time aesthetically very beautiful—a combination that is hard to find in contemporary art—and a work which not only heightens our awareness but forces us to reflect about our environment.

BLACK BAT—a study of smashes—and maybe some splashes... · Hanna Hartman

Having developed her very own language the Swedish sound artist and composer Hanna Hartman creates compositions that are exclusively made up of her own field recordings. The composer knows all the technologies of a sound recordist but she uses the material in a non-documentary or descriptive way. Her sounds are taken out of their original context and mixed together in strange and often ironic constellations. Hanna Hartmann seeks to reveal hidden correspondences between familiar and unfamiliar sounds. Her piece is based on the idea of "pressure" as a force against something that opposes it. The unusual and imaginative combinations of recordings make her piece special and outstanding in the context of composing with field recordings.

To think of the immersion of this piece in an environment such as Berghain and hearing this through their sound system gives magnificent results. This would be an almost out-of-body experience, feeling submerged in a space of chaos, noise and aural eccentricity, implosive sounds with a strong character create this piece. The jury was captivated by the static immersion and emotional arousal of such implosive sounds and is looking forward to seeing and listening to all these beautiful pieces, which all offer the possibility of complete immersion in a very special audiovisual space.

Die letzten 25 Jahre in No. 1 Hits der deutschen Jahrescharts dargestellt durch Karlheinz Stockhausens Studie 2 5x. · Hannes Seidl
Hannes Seidl can easily deal ironically with the composing process, because he is one of the young composers of new music who knows his craft very well. The piece *(The last 25 years in No. 1 hits on the German year-end charts as represented by Karlheinz Stockhausen's Studie 2 5 times)* is what it says, the score of Karlheinz Stockhausens *Studie II,* but used to go in fast-forward mode through the last 25 years of the German pop-music charts. Two opposite genres are established: popular music and the austere avant-garde of the fifties. The charts provide the sound of society, the mainstream, where thinking about hierarchy, structure, time etc. is connected to the so-called new music. The composition was outstanding owing to its many layers, playing with different genres and asking very important questions about copyright and original in the cultural and media context.

Duty · Michaela Davies
Duty by Michaela Davies tells a story about traditional musicianship, society and control. Technology is used only where absolutely necessary. The fact that it has to be performed live, that the performers have to follow the electrical impulse of a machine, the reduction to very simple instruments and reducing the musicians to extended non-artificial limbs shows the politically and socially relevant aspect of the piece. In addition we get an aesthetically pleasing performance with bells and an audience watching people being tortured (only a little), thus also referring to famous experiments. *Duty* shows that you can make a political statement without connections to agitprop, playing with contemporary genres and situations, crossing the border between music, performance and dramatic arts, but being grounded in a deeply musical culture.

Electromechanical Modular · Gijs Gieskes
Netherlands-based artist and engineer Gijs Gieskes provided not an art-piece, but a surprising solution to expanding the sound palette of modular synthesizer systems. The author suggests using mechanical sound sources integrated into electronic circuits with standardized parameters for modular synths. In this way the long-term ideas of experimental music—based on live electronics and pick-up techniques (as starting probably from John Cage and others)—are now placed into a modern frame of the community-driven obsession for building electronic instruments. The project mixes today's zeitgeist of electronic music with historical practice of it in a strange and unexpected way. To prove his concept, the artist developed several working prototypes of the electromechanical modules in a very popular Eurorack format, completely mergeable with systems like Doepfer and others. The jury found this concept interesting and reframing, and with an Honorary Mention would like to encourage Gijs Gieskes to further studies.

littleBits x Korg Synth Kit
Paul Rothman, littleBits Electronics Inc.
"If you can't open it you don't own it" is a standing phrase in the contemporary DIY scene. *Synth Kit* shows, that big companies are also jumping on the bandwagon of open-source end-community-driven development. Matador, Fischertechnik or even LxGO, you name it, deliver the metaphor of this little sound-tinkering set. Their open-source approach is also well hidden (you have to dig deep in the website for blueprints, source code etc.). Being well connected to a whole ecosphere of sound-tinkering tools, the intention to empower people to understand the making of electronic sounds and to create in an easy consumable format, is honorable. These ideas can become viral and encourage kids to engage early in sound and electronics.

Otomo Yoshihide: Between Music and Art · Otomo Yoshihide, NTT InterCommunication Center [ICC]
Otomo Yoshihide, who has developed his musical activities in various fields such as noise/improvisation, cinema and pop music, has also been exploring visual art. This work is an installation presented at the Between Music and Art exhibition in Japan, which interconnects the expressions of music and art in different ways. In addition, this exhibition was named after a discourse by Hisanori Gotada, who had passed away in 2013. In the main artwork, *Quartets,* randomly reflects eight musicians on a surface of the white cube in silhouette. With improvised music by Jim O'Rourke, Karie Kahimi, Otomo Yoshihide and others, it creates a perpetual random operation. Wood, iron, and liquid, which make a live resonance along with their music, are also reflected in this box of space. In *Guitar Solos 1,* pieces of sound with around 100 guitar solos are

randomly played by sixteen speakers, which elevates its staircase to a space of sonic experience. Although, as here in Ars Electronica, categorization in media art is highly advanced, its boundary is still ambiguous. This work seeks a future vision for a new expression of "music and art".

Rawr! A Study in Sonic Skulls
Courtney Brown, Sharif Razzaque

In recent years, the voices of historical personages such as Leonardo da Vinci or Ryoma Sakamoro have been recreated by the development of voice technology. This research method has also been applied to dinosaurs. Based on the data from a skeleton, the voice of the dinosaur is synthesized through the estimation on a vibration of the vocal cords. Although those technologies are used in the dinosaur movies with 3D CG, it was just a digital file. However, this work takes a sound of the corythosaurus from the late Mesozoic era of the Cretaceous period, from disembodied simulation into physical existence. In this performance, the audiences give voice to the dinosaur by blowing into a mouthpiece, producing a resonating sound through the hadrosaur's life-size nasal cavities and skull. Through the voice, the compression of the lungs, and the vibration of the skulls, they can experience the sound made by the dinosaur's vocal cords live. *Rawr!* establishes a new layer in the arena of speech synthesis, as an interactive sound installation or an instrument to play a voice of the dinosaurs. It will be one of the important works with the contexts in Nigerian talking drum, which elevated a speech sound to its instrument several hundred years before, and the vocoder in 1930.

Soft Revolvers · Myriam Bleau

The visual aesthetic of this project truly captures the spectacle of light and movement. Although this is a musical piece, the light and the motion is actually still one of its most interesting and breathtaking features. Living in a world where we are constantly interacting with machinery and controlling devices, this approach has a new standpoint. When it comes to design in MIDI controllers and remote devices, it is a visual delight while serving a complex and intrinsic functional need. We feel this brings a new playground of experimentation to the intersection of art and technology. While covering basic and complex needs and showcasing beauty and artistic expression with every single move and note, Myriam's movement becomes the piece itself, one of many expressions entwined, almost creating a completely new way of interacting with controllers. Our fascination with light reaches new heights. Around beams of light that trigger complex musical patterns in real time are thought-provoking light transducers that capture a vast array of emotions with every single move and touch.

Tipping Point · Kathy Hinde

The artwork by Kathy Hinde is hybrid and at the same time technically intelligent and aesthetically and musically graceful. One of those thought-provoking works that create immersive impression with efficient combination of light, kinetics, conception and mesmerizing sound. The glass vessels filled with water are balanced by mechanics and a computer algorithm, which listens to the microphone feedback produced by the acoustic qualities of the vessels themselves. The always slightly changing sound pattern gorgeously builds spatial microtonal patterns at some very precious moments gathering into tonal chords. Then comes the "tipping point"—when chords slightly move into atonality, accompanied by movements of mechanics and light. The "tipping point" is a metaphor the artist uses to talk about balance in general and balance of human use of water sources of planet Earth as a particular problem. The jury was very impressed by the artistic, technical and musical quality of the piece. We also would like to appreciate the ecologically critical idea at the basis of the conception. The jury is delighted to support Kathy with an Honorary Mention.

Zeitraum · Gerhard Eckel, University of Music and Performing Arts Graz

Zeitraum by Gerhard Eckel is one of the rare pieces submitted at the intersection between art and science. Its aesthetic quality is only perceivable on site, giving the actual listener a central role. Questioning the essence of the perception of music, the sound being made purely by technology, the installation negotiates with the audience on the question whether this is music, art or a scientific experiment. It also shows the role of contemporary composers and musicians being part artist and part engineer, the music being time-based but also deeply connected to the space it is performed within. This piece shows one of the possible implementations of contemporary sound installations and/or music.

Chijikinkutsu

Nelo Akamatsu

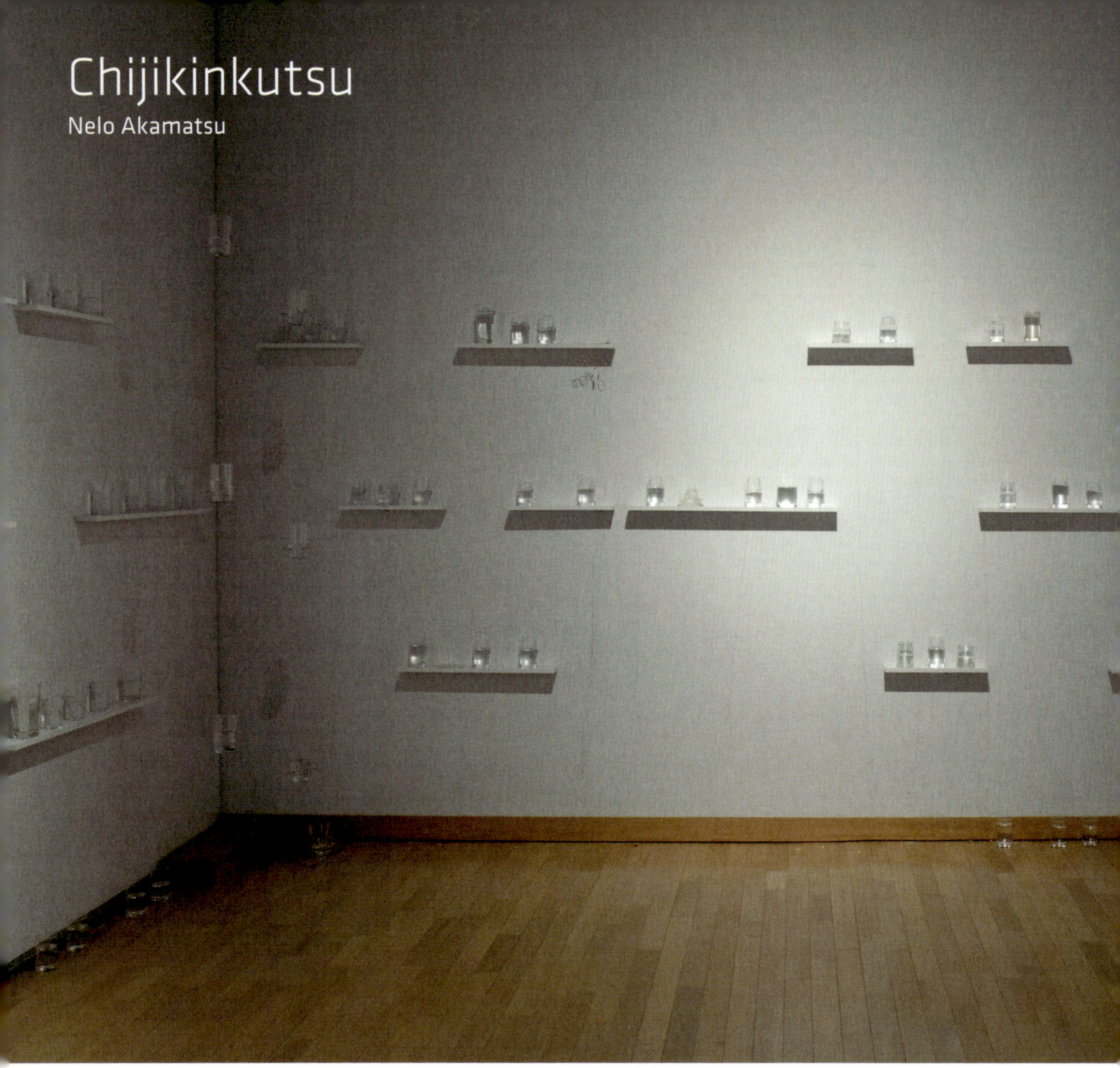

Chijikinkutsu is a coinage especially created for the title of this work by combining two Japanese words: "chijiki" and "suikinkutsu".
Chijiki means geomagnetism: terrestrial magnetic properties that have always existed and affect everything on earth, though it cannot be perceived by the human senses. Nevertheless, since long before age of discovery, people navigated with the help of compasses using geomagnetism. In recent years, various devices that utilize geomagnetism have even been incorporated in smartphones. On the other hand, some scientific research reports that the behavior of migratory birds, bees and some kinds of bacteria, as well as the cause of beautiful aurora, are all related to geomagnetism. The 16th-century English physicist William Gilbert even described geomagnetism as being like a life-form. However, modern physics has not yet completely unearthed what causes it. A "suikinkutsu" is a sound installation for Japanese traditional gardens, invented in the Edo period. The sounds of drops of water falling through an inverted earthenware pot buried under a stone washbasin resonate through hollow bamboo tubes. Since ancient times, the Japanese have been sensitive to perceiving nature as it is, from the sound of the wind through pine trees or singing of insects. Suikinkutsu was developed with this kind of delicate sense. While I was working on this work, I happened to visit my favorite temple, in the middle of a secluded mountain

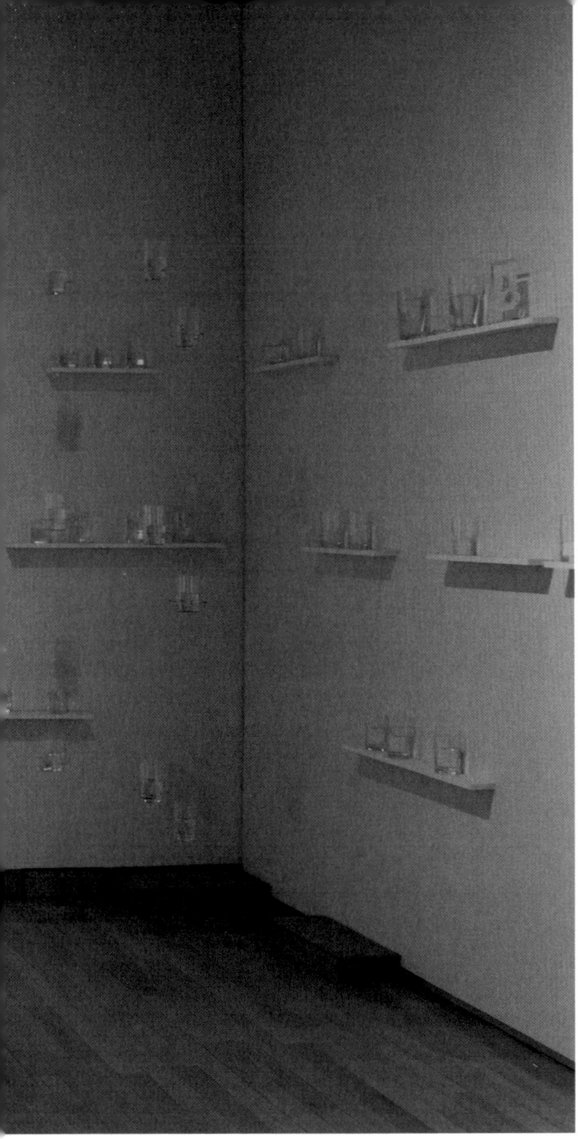

in Kyoto. The temple has an excellent garden with a big white pine tree spreading its branches in incredible shapes. In a small corner of this garden, was a "suikinkutsu". And when I carefully listened to the profound sound from underground, I noticed that my work coincidentally sounded similar to the "suikinkutsu". And afterwards, that awareness helped to polish the concept. The concept of the work *Chijikinkutsu* is not derived from the experimentalism of science and technology on which media arts rely, nor from the architectonic theory of western music on which some sound arts are based. While utilizing the action of geomagnetism, which is normally treated as a subject of science, this sound installation expands the subtle sounds of "suikinkutsu" in the context of the Japanese perspective on nature. *Chijikinkutsu* is made using water, sewing needles, glass tumblers and coils of copper wire. The needles floating on the water in the tumblers are magnetized in advance, so they are affected by geomagnetism and turn themselves in a north-south direction. When electricity is supplied to the coil attached to the outside of the tumblers it creates a temporary magnetic field that draws the needle to the coil. And the faint sound of the needle hitting the glass resonates in the space all around. A MIDI is used to control the system. A DTM sequencer app running on an iPAD sends MIDI data signals to the controllers which were especially designed for the work, and they distribute serial data to each port, switching the electric current to the coils. I did not include many elements in the work, but aimed to create a minimalist expression like a painting with a large unpainted margin. I can use the example of the sense of taste to explain this. Until the late 20th century, it was thought there were only four tastes—sweet, sour, salty and bitter—that made up the complex of human tastes. However, there proved to be the fifth category, corresponding to the flavor of glutamates. This is the pleasant savory taste also known as umami, which is the most important element in Japanese cuisine. Instead of mixing many flavors to make a thick taste, the Japanese like to bring out the best of umami from the ingredients themselves by adding the minimum appropriate seasoning. In other words, their approach to taste is the pursuit of purity. Getting back to my work, I did not add unnecessary elements such as many colors, LED lights, amplified sound etc., so that the acoustic sounds would stand out and viewers could concentrate on listening to them. Then some of them might notice that geomagnetism is affecting the movement of the needles. A round surface of water in the glass with a floating magnetized needle reminds me somewhat of a tiny earth with its geomagnetism. The fainter the sounds of the glass, the more keenly viewers' sensibility will be sharpened. In the meantime, they realize that the sounds are not coming from outside their bodies, but already exist inside their mind.

Concept, space design, hardware development, sound-sequence programming: Nelo Akamatsu

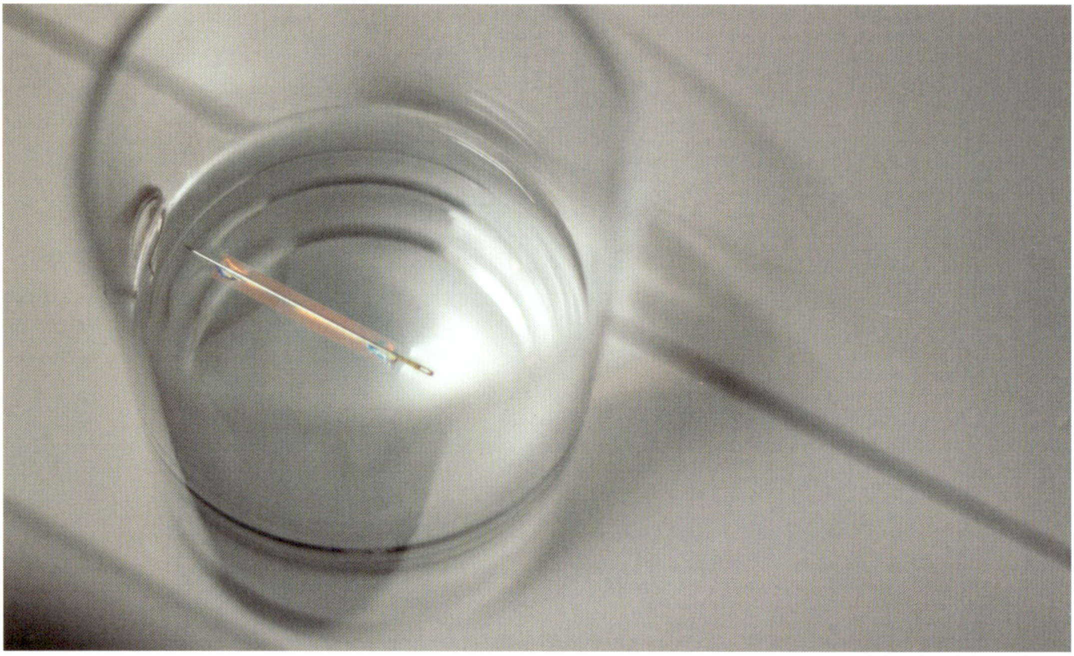

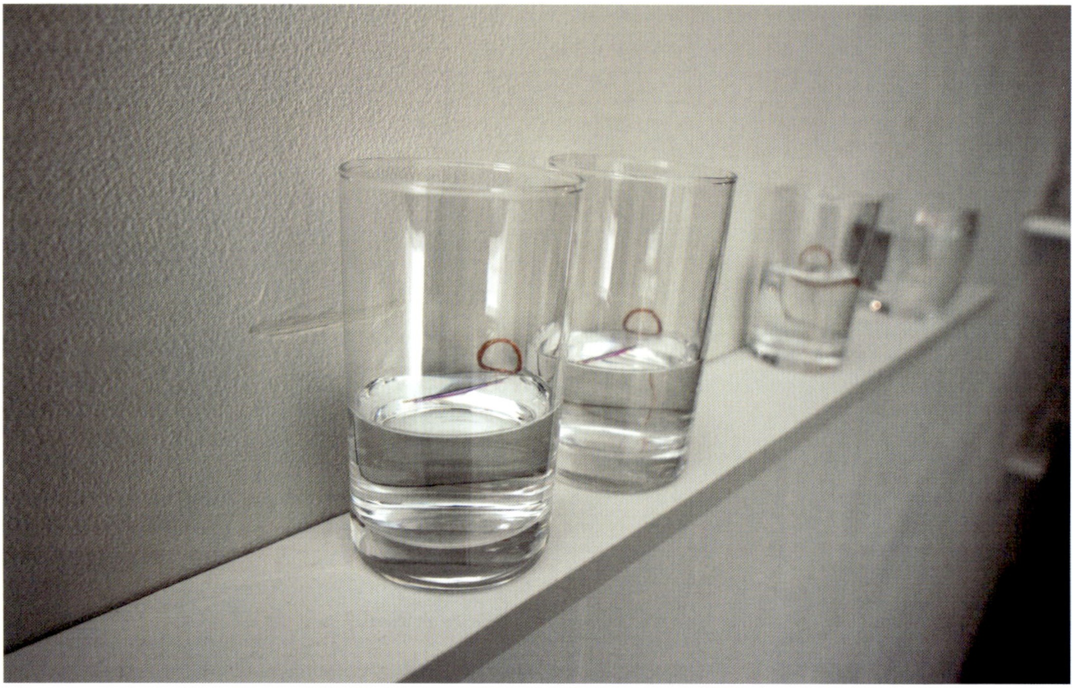

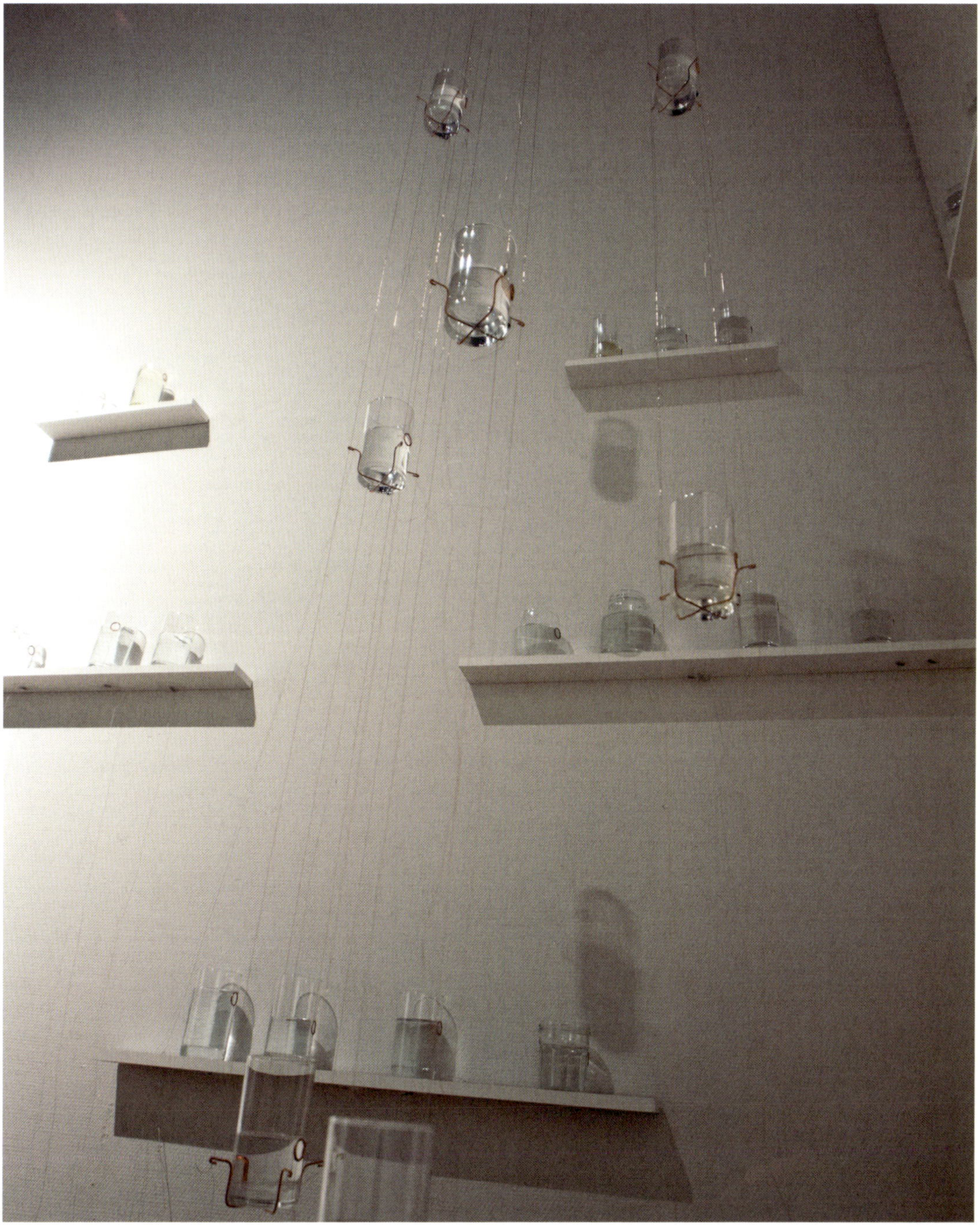

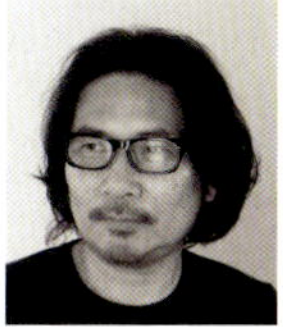

Nelo Akamatsu (JP) creates art works across several media such as installations with electric devices, event installations, video installations, sculptures, paintings and photos. He has an MFA from the Department of Intermedia Art of Tokyo National University of Fine Arts and Music in 2005. Main exhibitions: Taro Okamoto Award of Contemporary Art (prize 2004, 2014), joint exhibition at Bauhaus University in Weimar (2004), joint exhibition at Yokoham BankArt (2008), solo exhibition at the Italian Embassy in Tokyo (2009)

Drumming is an Elastic Concept
Staged solo concert for percussion and electronics

Josef Klammer

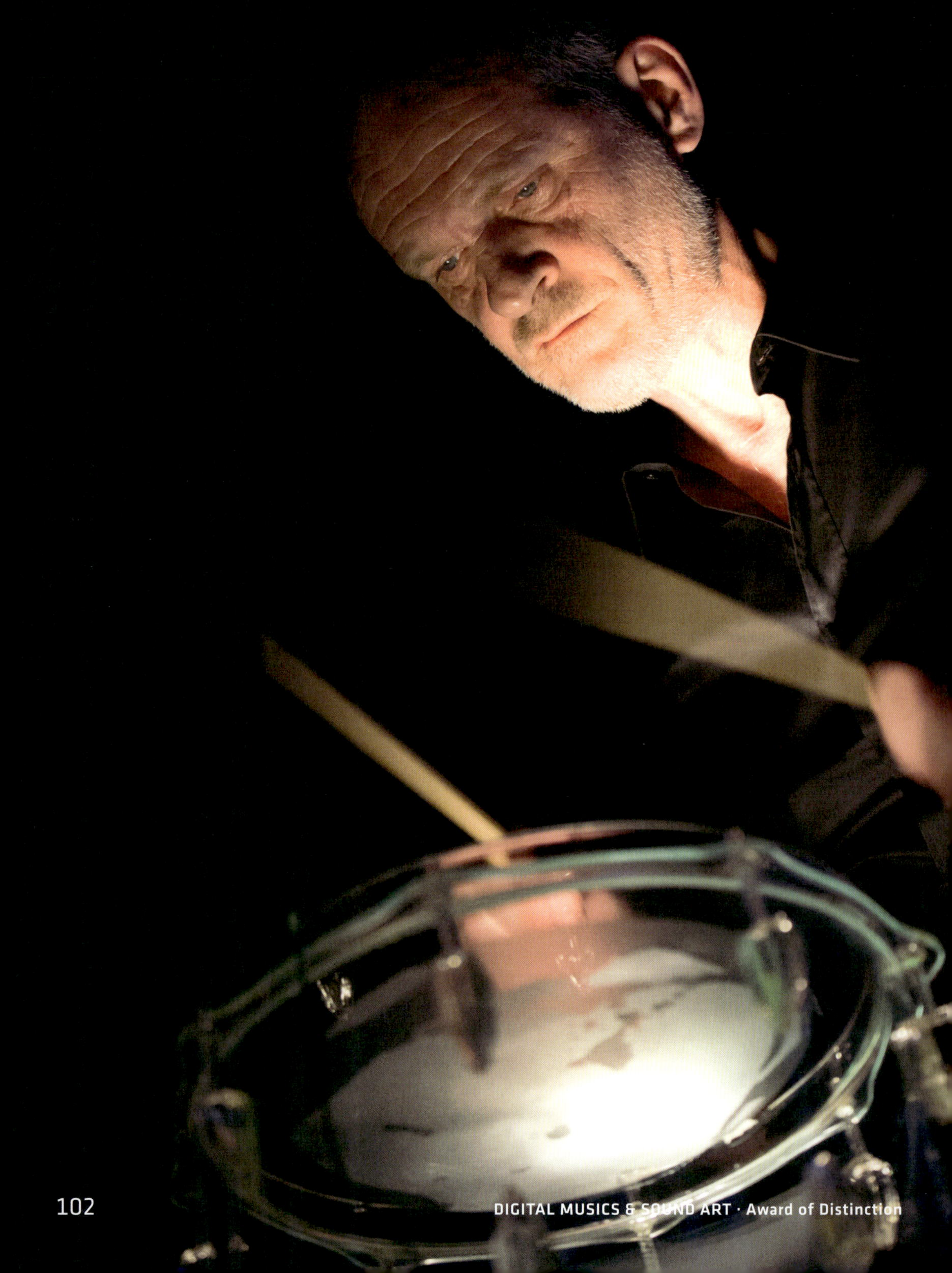

Since the mid-1980s Josef Klammer has been continuously working as a musician and media musician on the tonal enhancement of his instrumentarium, and on the exploration and transformation of media-immanent music potentials. His first full-length solo program, *Trommeln ist ein Dehnbarer Begriff (Drumming is an Elastic Concept),* is an anthology of his intensive efforts and their realization under the direction (scenic design) of Ernst M. Binder. The project's title is based on the Kunstradio program *Membran,* which Klammer created live on the Austrian national radio station Ö1 in 2008. Instead of the usual plastic drumheads, Klammer used latex skins. As a result, the drumbeats were slowed down and stretched, until only the "breathing" of the drum was audible. Thus the title not only stands for the visual illustration of a process, but also as a metaphor for the adaptation and enhancement of the instruments using analog and digital aids.

Concept, music, controller, percussion: Josef Klammer
Scenic design: Ernst M. Binder
Light design and sound engineering: Geari Schreilechner
A co-production with dramagraz
Supported by the Styrian State Government, the City of Graz, SKE Fund
Thanks to: Liquid Music and Werkstadt Graz

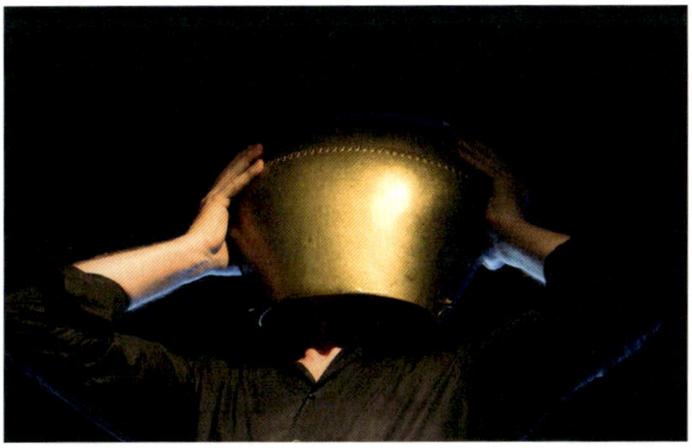

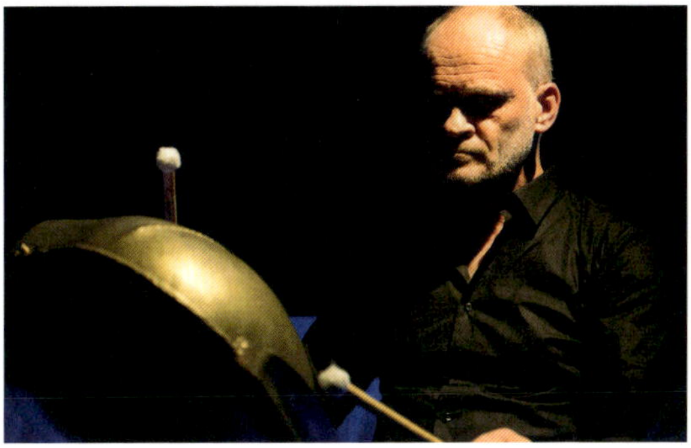

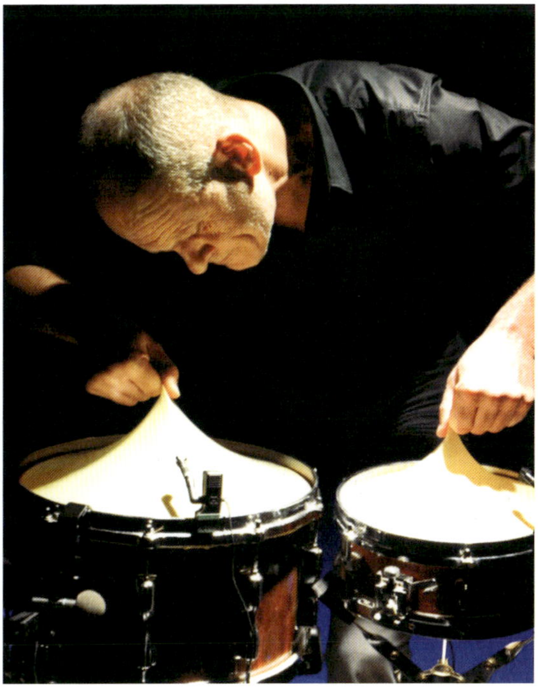

Josef Klammer (AT), born 1958 in Lienz, is a musician and media artist. Initially he worked as a photographer, then studied drums at Music University Graz. Since the mid-80s Klammer has worked continuously developing his instruments and sound whilst maintaining his involvement in research and the transformation of media-immanent music potentials. He has participated in numerous exhibitions, concerts and festivals all over the world, as well as numerous and regular concerts and recordings with a wide variety of ensembles playing new improvised electronic and experimental music. He is a curator for various festivals and initiatives, music projects and workshops at schools. In 1994 he received the award for computer music from the Austrian Ministry of Art and Science.

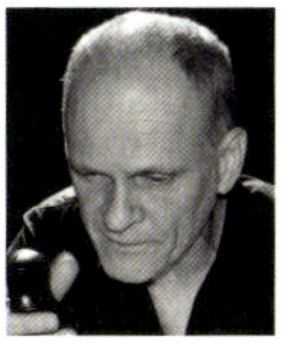

UNDER WAY

Douglas Henderson

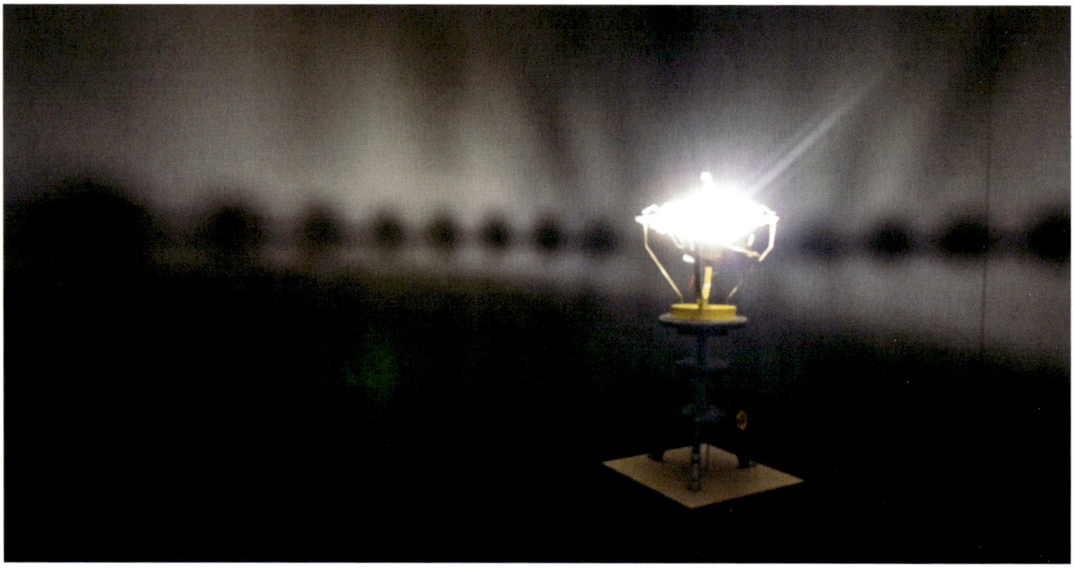

UNDER WAY metaphorically transposes the building which houses it into a ship at sea, and sets those who encounter it free on a voyage to uncharted shores. The intervention uses a series of epistemological inversions to create the perceptual conditions that allow the "ship" to set sail. It installs a moving horizon, with its ocean and stars, into the space, suggesting to the visitor that it is in fact the building which is moving. The instrument of this horizon is an illuminated, kinetic loudspeaker assembly, inspired by marine chronometers and compasses, the essential instruments of navigation. In the days of square-rigged sailing ships, both chronometer and compass were suspended in intricate baskets of gimbaled rings, so that as the ship moved, they would remain static, enhancing accuracy. Here I invert not only the building, moving its horizon to its interior, but also the chronometer, so that it continually tilts on its gimbals and drives the motions of a horizon projected onto the walls. The reimagined compass, no longer a silent introverted guide, projects an altered reality into the entire space. The physical installation consists of a 12" loudspeaker mounted on gimbals so that it can move freely on two axes. Movement is initiated entirely by the soundtrack playing from it, via a small wire pressing on its membrane. A mirrored film floats on top of the membrane, and it is surrounded by a fixed ring of multi-element LED spotlights, directed inward, forming a continuous though highly variegated shadow line around the walls of the room, thus creating the horizon. Then,

https://vimeo.com/88984132
www.douglashenderson.org

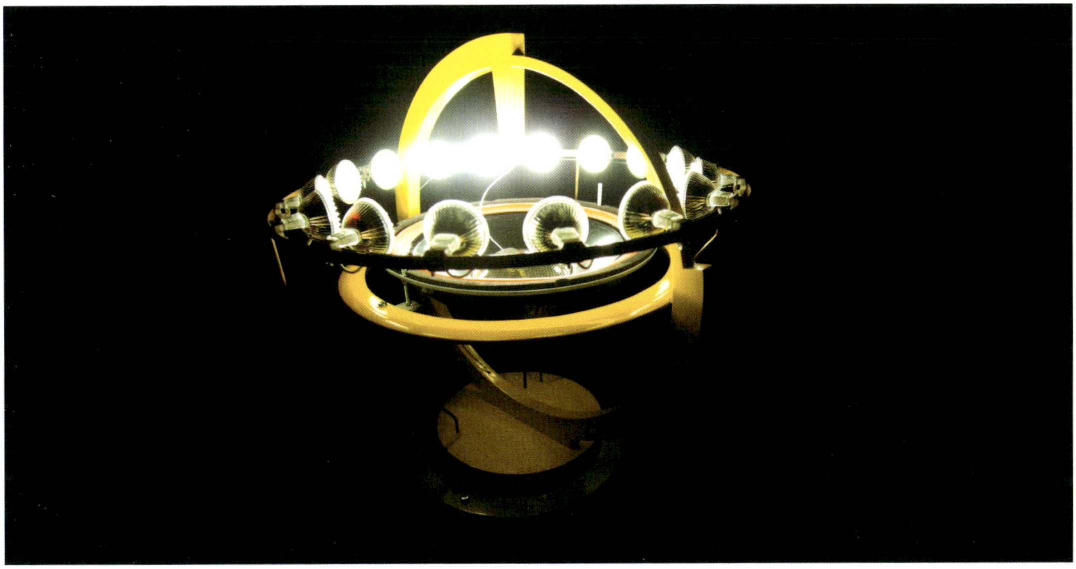

as the speaker moves so does the horizon, with a rich, undulating wave. The mylar ring also reflects the lights upward, projecting a celestial map overhead, rocking with the motion of the ship. At the center of the installation is a five-channel electroacoustic composition which addresses several layers of compositional imperative: its low-frequency components must drive the motion of the speaker, while steady tone material is used to initiate standing waves in the room. Because the speaker is constantly reoriented, these waves and nodes are constantly varying, and, combined with reflections from the walls as well as noticeable Doppler effects, they develop a highly complex and changing sonic architecture. This part of the composition is derived from recordings made from inside a bottle which was thrown into the sea. The resonance of the bottle provides a singular tone, while the actions of the water develop a narrative. The fluttering of large sail cloths, a kind of macro-rhythm, is heard from four speakers concealed in the base. These sounds were mixed using complex phase and frequency shifts as well as convolution, so that they seem to emanate from the walls and the floor, not from the central instrument. And thus a final inversion: the sounds of the ship's sails become the waves upon which it navigates, while the sound of the sea steers it from above.

Wood, brass, LEDs, loudspeakers, carbon fiber, mylar, linen.
165 cm x 45 cm x 45 cm. 5-channel audio, 20-minute loop

Originally created for the Skulpturenmuseum Glaskasten Marl/ European Soundart Award (prize winner), with assistance from Freundeskreis Habakuk

Douglas Henderson (US) is a sound artist whose work spans all aspects of the medium, from electroacoustic sound compositions to sculptural works and installations. He harnesses the energies of sound both as a sensual medium and as a culturally charged fabric of social implication. He is particularly interested in the dialog between sound and visual art, and the intricacies of expression that become possible as new, hybrid art forms develop. Among his awards are the 2013 Deutscher Klangkunst-Preis, a 2012 Gigaherz Prize for electroacoustic music, a 2008 Rockefeller Foundation MAP Award, and a 2007 guest of the DAAD Berliner Kuenstlerprogramm.

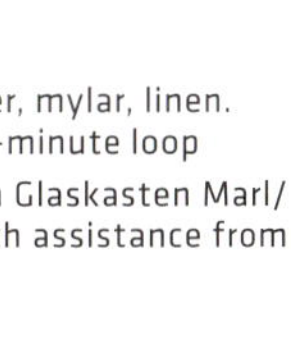

David C. Scher

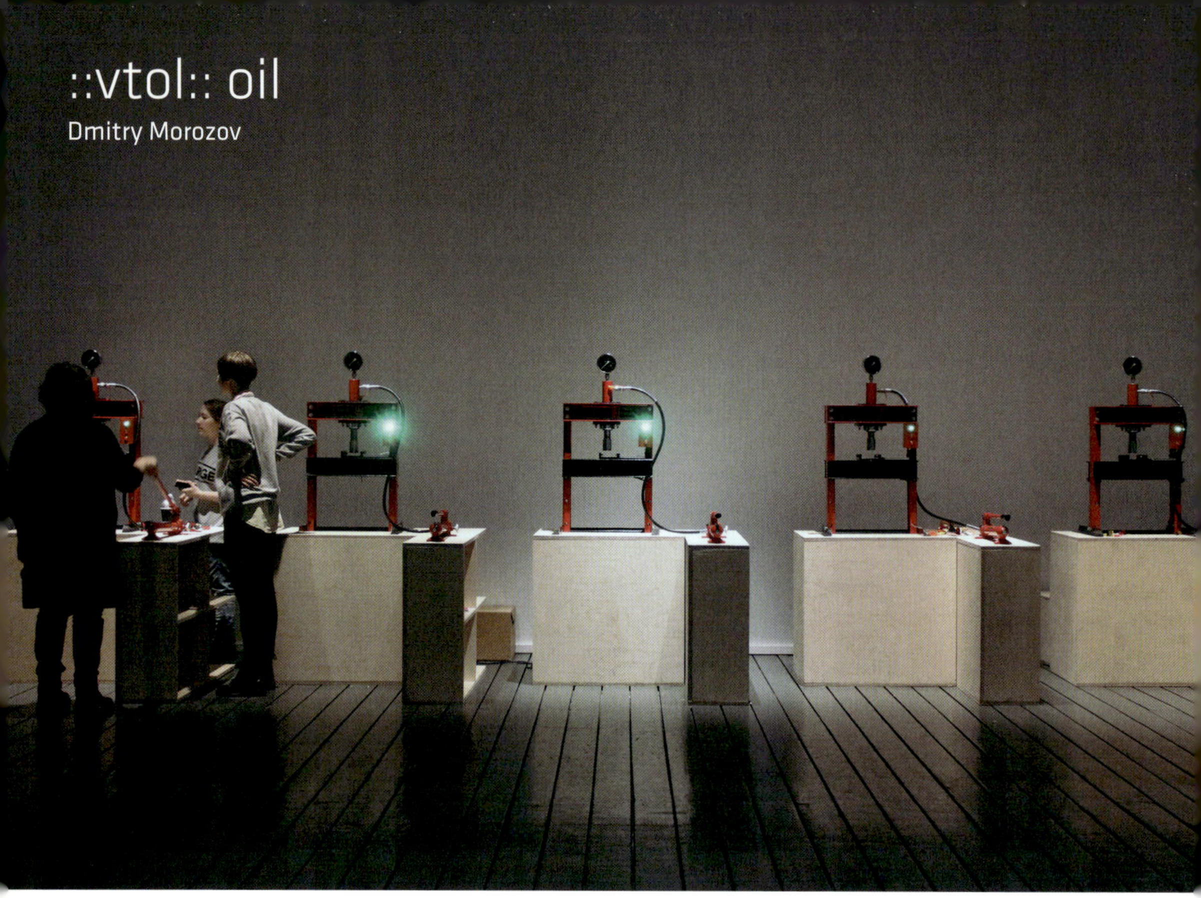

::vtol:: oil

Dmitry Morozov

The main idea of this project is to present exhibition visitors with the chance to destroy any object they might happen have on their person, in order to transform it into a unique sound production. The installation consists of five hydraulic presses, capable of crushing practically any object (a mobile phone, a pair of glasses, headphones or whatever). In the process of destruction, a special microphone records the sounds made as the object undergoes deformation, and in just a few minutes, a computer algorithm transforms them into a 20-minute album. The project is intended to provoke visitors into spontaneously ridding themselves of material consumer objects in order to create their own individual work of art via deprivation, divestment and destruction. Sound has been taken as the chief medium here with good reason, since sound art is perhaps the least material and most abstract of all genres in art. The technological aesthetic involved constitutes an ironic attempt to turn the process of art production into a technological process, but the result, unlike that of mass production, demonstrates a contrary phenomenon—this is a work involving programming and code in the context of generative art, with the potential to broaden the range of instruments at art's disposal. At the end of the process, the sound production is automatically recorded on an audio CD and given to the participant, completing the process of exchange. 1,574 disks were recorded during the first show.

Hardware: x5 Arduino Uno, microphone and preamp, 10-ton hydraulic press, Apple Mac Mini plus Apple CD drive
Software: Pure Data, Max/Msp, Applescript

Commission by the Garage Museum of Contemporary Art, Moscow, 2014. Special thanks to Cyrille Henry, Valentina Osokina, Nikolai Zheludovich

http://vtol.cc
http://vtol.cc/filter/works/oil
https://vimeo.com/117032507

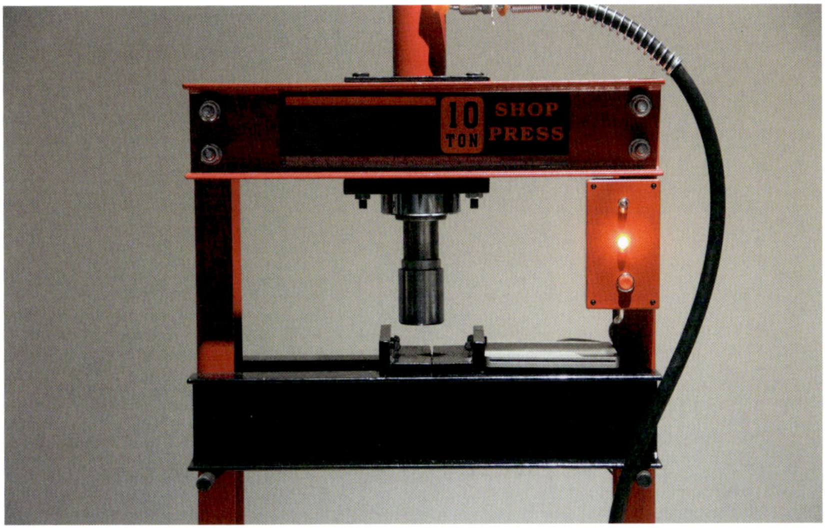

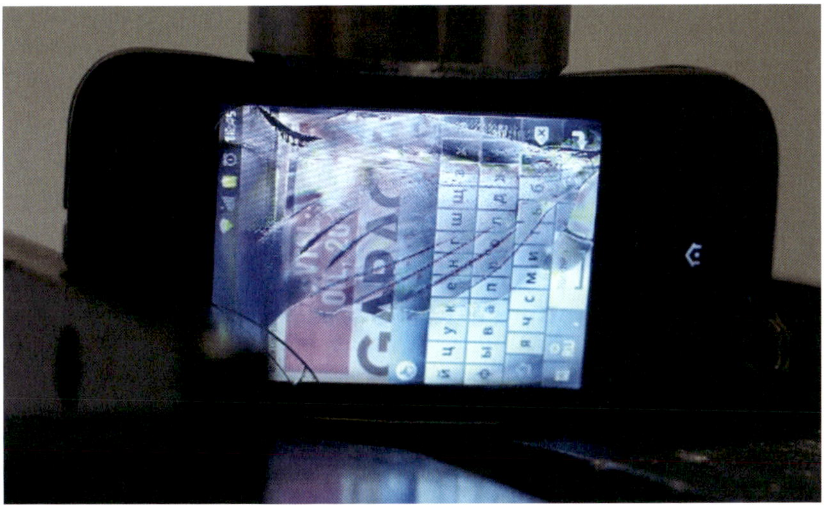

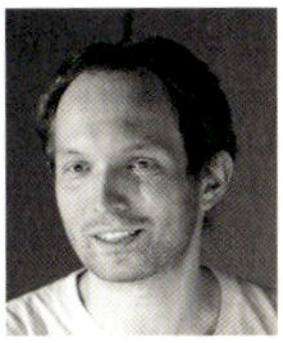

Dmitry Morozov (RU), is a Moscow media artist, musician and engineer of strange-sounding mechanisms. In the mid 00s Dmitry started actively using his DIY and circuit-bent instruments for his own music projects, as well as making instruments for other musicians and media artists. He is the first batch producer of music and video synthesizers in the post-Soviet area. Besides making music and instruments, Dmitry creates audiovisual art installations and promotes circuit bending and DIY electronics in Russia through lectures and workshops.

bell

Soichiro Mihara

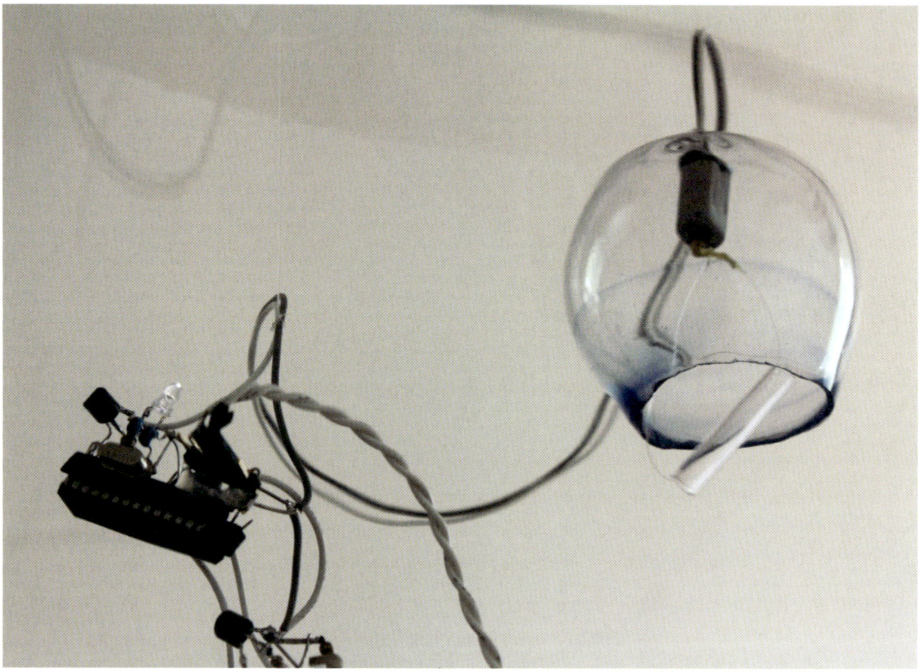

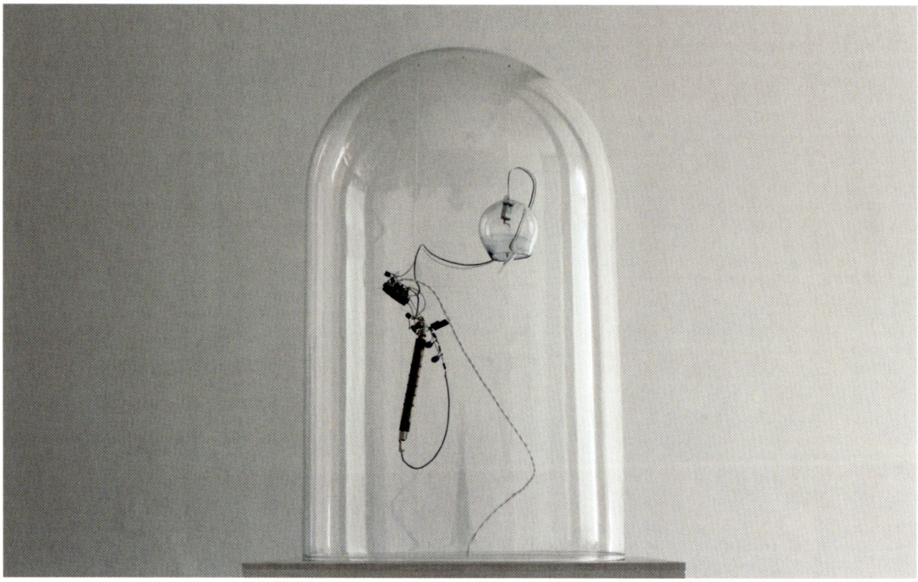

After the disaster I am conscious of listening to a presence that we cannot perceive.
The sound comes from a glass bell, triggered by a radiation sensor in the art work.

Have you heard this sound before?

It is the sound of a wind chime, called a *furin* in Japan.
It is said that the *furin* originated in ancient times.

Chimes were placed on the edge of a territory
in order to sense and to enable us to avoid an evil that we cannot perceive.
It seems science has developed now, so there cannot be a concept of the good and evil in this sound.

But once I understood this context, I felt this was now the approach to this radiation sound signal.

A glass dome keeps out wind and also shuts out the sound.
It is still chiming as a reminder of radioactive waste disposal.

In 2011 I started a project themed around blank spaces, investigating the relationship between technology and blanks that brings society into existence. The artwork is the second part of an ongoing blank project. We always receive certain amount of natural radiation. Rays pass through the artwork, space, and our body in all directions once every four to twelve seconds. Hearing is the most acute perception with which to sense radiation, as it is highly sensitive to its uncertain orientation and random cycles. If art requires questioning, then the significance of the sound needs a balance between the need for tone and a critical eye. In the process of struggling with many sound materials, I came across a Japanese wind bell. The concept of evil fascinates me more than the origin of sound aesthetics. It exists not only in Japan, from our cultural roots, but also from China and Asia to Ancient Rome. I also believe the attraction of a gentle but solemn sound is ubiquitous. Though it seems science has now gone beyond this, I still like to hear within this context. It is common sense that a concept of good and evil does not exist in nature or technology. So has evil been completely cleared away now? This is what I want to consider with the enclosed tiny chime.

Soichiro Mihara (JP), born in 1980 in Tokyo. He currently works in Kyoto, presenting systems as open art works that question the relationship between technology and society. He started the *blank* project in 2011, when eastern Japan was hit by an earthquake. He has exhibited his award-winning projects at international venues such as Kunstquartier Kreuzberg Bethanian, Berlin, 2013 *(The world filled with blanks);* Sapporo International Art Festival, Japan, 2014; ZKM, Germany, 2012 *(Soundart–Sound as a Medium of Art);* NTTICC, Japan, 2012 *(Open Space);* Museum of Contemporary Art Roskilde, Denmark, 2011 *(Simple Interactions–Sound Art from Japan);* ISEA2010 RUHR, 2010, Kunstverein Dortmund, and many more.

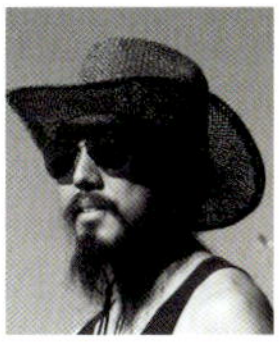

BLACK BAT a study of smashes—and maybe some splashes...

Hanna Hartman

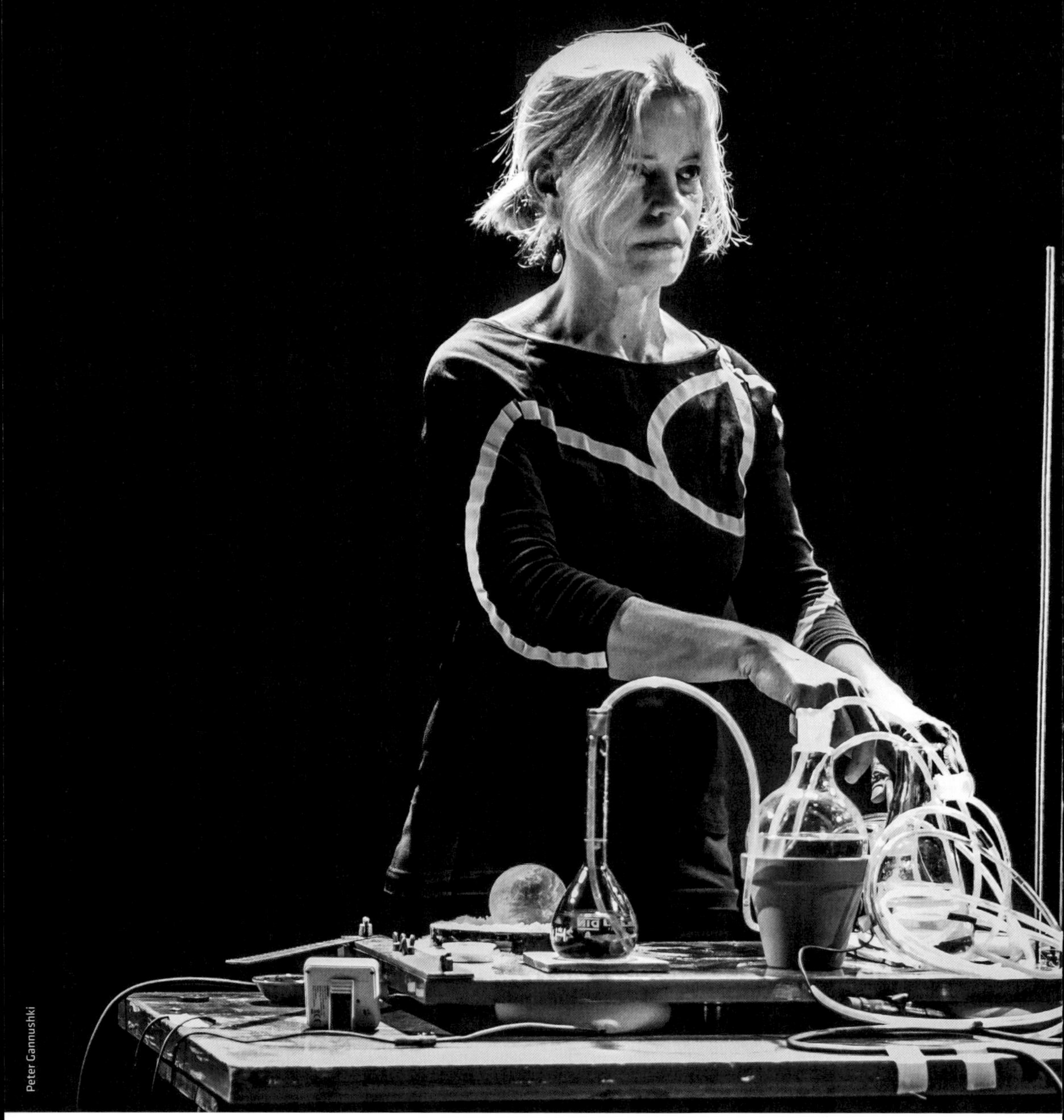

Peter Gannushki

This is a stereo piece made for the big speakers in Berghain, the number one club in Berlin, where it was first performed in 2014 at Art's Birthday by Deutschlandradio Kultur.

Composed by Hanna Hartman. With recordings of Theo Nabicht on bass clarinet. Commissioned by Marcus Gammel, Deutschlandradio Kultur and Mirella Weingarten, Schlossmediale Werdenberg.

Hanna Hartman (SE) is a Swedish composer, sound artist and performer living in Berlin. She studied literature and theater history at the Universities of Uppsala and Stockholm, radio and interactive art at the Dramatiska Institutet and electroacoustic music at EMS in Stockholm. Since the early 1990s she has composed works for radio, electroacoustic music and has created sound installations and given numerous performances all over Europe. Her many awards and grants include the Karl Sczuka Prize (2005), the Phonurgia Nova Prize (2006), a Villa Aurora grant (2010) and the Rosenberg Prize (2011). In 2007 and 2008 she was Composer-in-Residence for Swedish Radio.

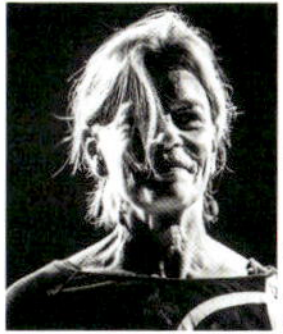

Peter Gannushki

Die letzten 25 Jahre in No. 1 Hits der deutschen Jahrescharts dargestellt durch Karlheinz Stockhausens Studie 2 5x.

Hannes Seidl

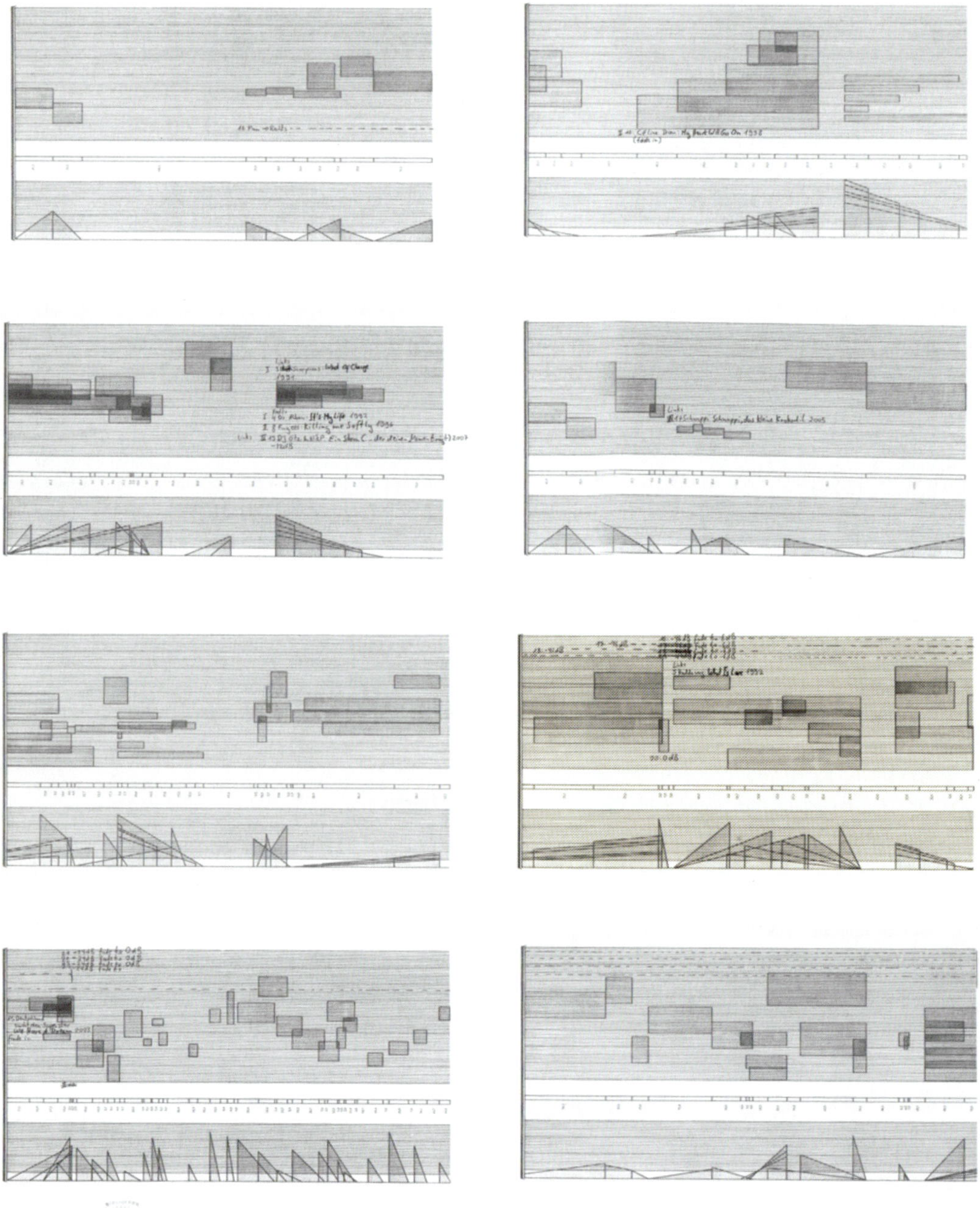

http://www.hannesseidl.de
https://vimeo.com/108558792

Though still little known to non-professionals, Karlheinz Stockhausen's *Studie II* is one of the 20th century's most influential pieces of early avant-garde electronic music. In *Die letzten 25 Jahre ...* its idea of a musical restart by inventing everything from scratch—from musical instruments, scale, horizontal and vertical proportions to the formal and structural elements—is contrasted with late 20th-century recycling and sampling culture. *Studie II* is organized like an instrumental composition consisting of a score that defines musical values to be played by an instrument, in this case sine-tone generators. For *Die letzten 25 Jahre ...* the score remains basically unchanged, while the sine-tone generators have been replaced by a sampler fed with 25 German number one hits from 1989 to 2013: the score reads through 25 years of pop history. In this way two opposing ideas of music-making collide, each read through the other: the post-war avant-garde music from Germany on the one hand, strictly avoiding tonality, beat or loop patterns and strictly distancing itself from popular music. On the other hand music as an industrial product, valued by its sales volume. While the rapid tour of musical pop history reassembles the sound of a society, of its mainstream, *Studie II* seems to represent a radical approach to music as a utopian project. But Stockhausen's *Studie II* has become a historical piece of music as well; it can be replayed and recycled itself and become a part of sampling aesthetics even though its approach was opposed to it. To realize *Die letzten 25 Jahre ...* a slightly modified MAXMSP patch by Georg Hajdu was used to trigger the samples through a real-time version of Stockhausen's score. The numbers five and two play a central role within Stockhausen's work itself (five-part chords, a scale consisting of steps multiplied by the 25th root of two, sections of five). For *Die letzten 25 Jahre ...* they are intensified: Stockhausen's score is played five times in a five-part canon. Every run through represents five years of number-one hits. The occasion was also the 25th anniversary of the Mousonturm Frankfurt. This piece can be performed live or played back as a five-channel stereo version.

The realization is based on: Karlheinz Stockhausen's: *Studie II*, Stockhausen Verlag 1954
It uses a modified version of the real-time MAX MSP patch by Georg Hajdu.
Download: http://georghajdu.de/6-2/studie-ii/

Samples used from: David Hasselhoff: *Looking for Freedom*, Matthias Reim: *Verdammt ich lieb' dich*, Scorpions: *Wind Of Change*, Dr. Alban: *It's My Life*, Haddaway: *What Is Love*, Mariah Carey: *Without You*, Vangelis: *Conquest Of Paradise*, Los del Rio: *Macarena*, Sarah Brightman & Andrea Bocelli: *Time To Say Goodbye*, Celine Dion: *My Heart Will Go On*, Lou Bega: *Mambo No. 5*, Anton feat. DJ Ötzi: *Anton aus Tirol*, No Angels: *Daylight In Your Eyes*, Las Ketchup: *The Ketchup Song (Asereje)*, Deutschland sucht den Superstar: *We Have A Dream*, O-Zone: *Dragostea din tei*, *Schnappi: Schnappi, das kleine Krokodil*, GoLeo VI pres.Bob Sinclair feat. Gary Nesta Pine: *Love Generation*, DJ Ötzi & Nik P.: *Ein Stern (der deinen Namen trägt)*, Timbaland pres. One Republic: *Apologize*, Lady Gaga: *Pokerface*, Israel "Iz" Kamakawiwo'ole: *Over The Rainbow / What A Wonderful World*, Jennifer Lopez feat. Pitbull: *On The Floor*, Michel Telo: *Ai Se Eu Te Pego*, Avicii: *Wake Me Up*.

Hannes Seidl (DE) is a German composer and sound artist. His works include sound installations, music theatre, short films and concert music. Born 1977, he studied composition with Nicolas A. Huber and Beat Furrer. He has received scholarships and prizes including the Darmstadt Summer Courses, Akademie der Künste Berlin and the DAAD and Best Experimental Film (together with Daniel Kötter) at the Bolzano Short Film Festival. His compositions have been performed at numerous festivals such as Maerzmusik Berlin, Ultima Oslo, steirischer herbst and Warshaw Autumn. Since 2008 he has been working intensively with video artist Daniel Kötter. Hannes Seidl lives in Frankfurt/Main.

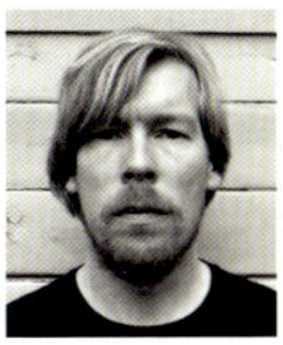

Norman Thoere

Duty

Michaela Davies

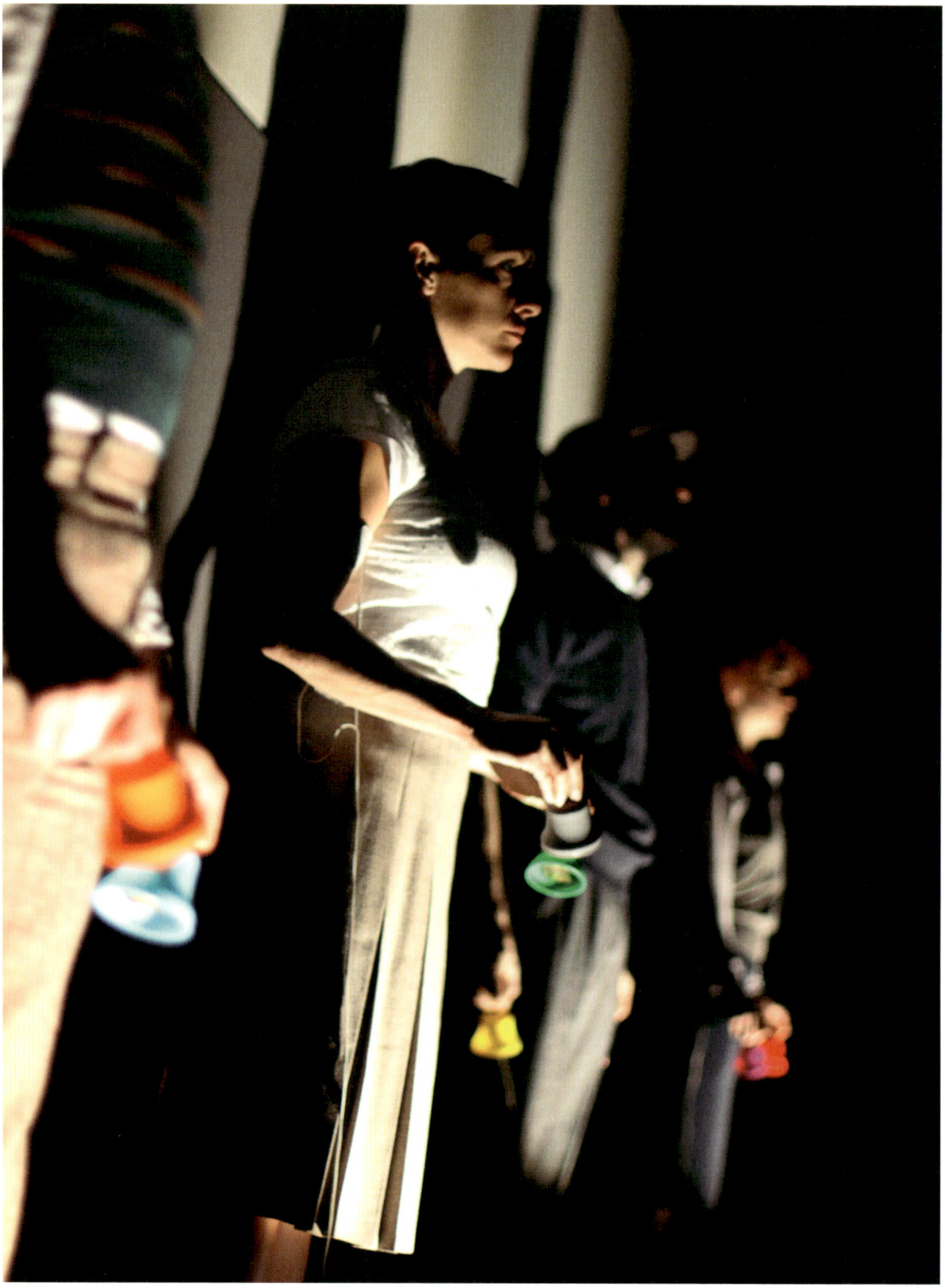

http://www.michaeladavies.net/duty.html
http://www.michaeladavies.net

Duty explores sonic possibilities and human limits, harnessing the bodily convulsions produced by electrical impulses to control seven performers in a work composed in one octave for fourteen handbells. The title of the work refers both to the movement of a bell and the imposition of physical obligations—or duties—upon the performers. The work creates a distributed system where the artist/composer executes motor actions in the performers via electric muscle stimulation (EMS). A composition converted to MIDI triggers two custom-built EMS devices, which deliver electrical impulses to specific points on the performers' arms via electrodes attached to their skin, causing their muscles to contract and generating pre-determined involuntary movements at changing velocities. Variations in voltage, frequency and pulse width dictate different muscular responses in the performers, ranging from unnatural jolts to abnormally fast movements. *Duty* uses the induction of involuntary movement to explore the way physical (and psychological) constraint can determine a musical outcome and extend sonic possibilities. Expanding the potential of the human body beyond conscious control, the use of electric muscle stimulation enables experimentation with complex rhythmic structures and fast movements that the performers would be unable to achieve of their own volition. Overriding the messages that the central nervous system sends to the muscles to control action achieves one of the primary aims of mid-20th century experimental music practice. Disrupting a performer's physical agency in the creation of sound achieves the kind of Cage-ian "non-intention" previously sought by experimentalists, which aimed to free the performer from the shackles of his or her own preferences and habitual actions. The application of EMS to musical performance provides a novel way to explore the interface between technology and live performance, and raises interesting questions regarding creative agency in the creation of music. The transmogrification of the performers' body as an input/output device literalizes aspects of musical performance, where musicians frequently describe feeling like conduits or transcribers of a creation that is not their own. A perverse take on Schoenberg's (1911) claim that "art is born not of 'I can' but of 'I must'," *Duty* explores the liminal space between didactic execution and free interpretation inherent in all musical performance. In a broader sense, *Duty* questions assumptions about agency and free will both in musical performance and everyday contexts. An enquiry into the nature of agency within systems where cognition is distributed across people, objects and environment through technologies of connection, *Duty* explores what happens when embodied experience and sense of agency is disrupted or extended. As the performers engage in this strange but not entirely unfamiliar negotiation they create a distorted reflection of the struggle for control that occurs both in and beyond the context of musical performance.

Commissioned for Sonic Social, curated by Performance Space at the Museum of Contemporary Art Australia, 2014.
Performers: Claire Conroy, Nick Rayment, Matte Rochford, Reuben Alexander, Jodi Clark, Louise Maloney, Mark Cauvin
Hardware development: John Hirsch, Richard Allen

Michaela Davies (AU), her cross-disciplinary practice is informed by an interest in the role of agency both in and beyond the context of musical performance. Using electric muscle stimulation and other methods to obstruct and extend human capabilities, her work has been presented at venues and festivals including the Museum of Contemporary Art Australia, Institute for Cultural Enquiry (Berlin), Experimental Intermedia (New York), ISEA (Sydney), Mona Foma Festival (Hobart), and Sonica Festival (UK). Davies has a PhD in psychology and was recently awarded a Creative Australia Fellowship from Australia Council for the Arts.

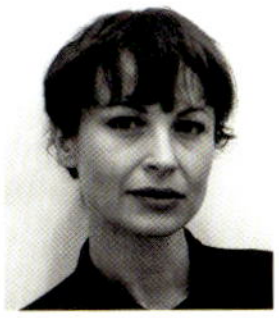

Electromechanical Modular

Gijs Gieskes

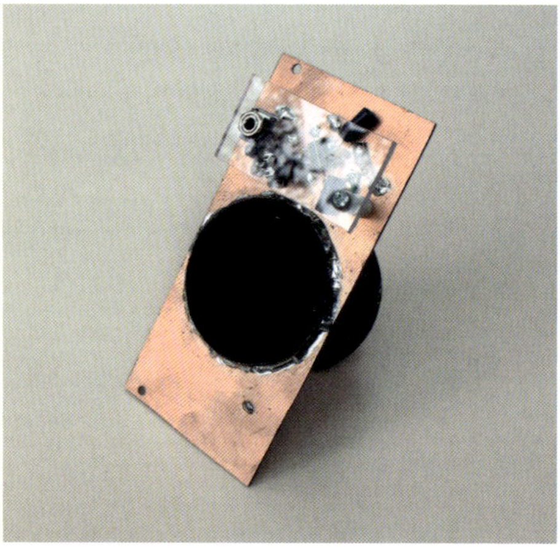

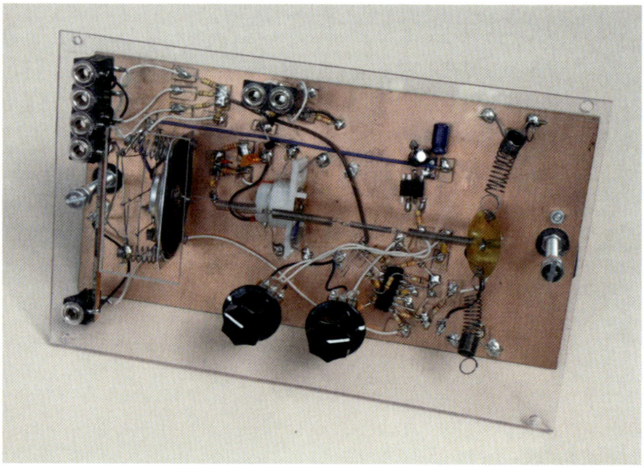

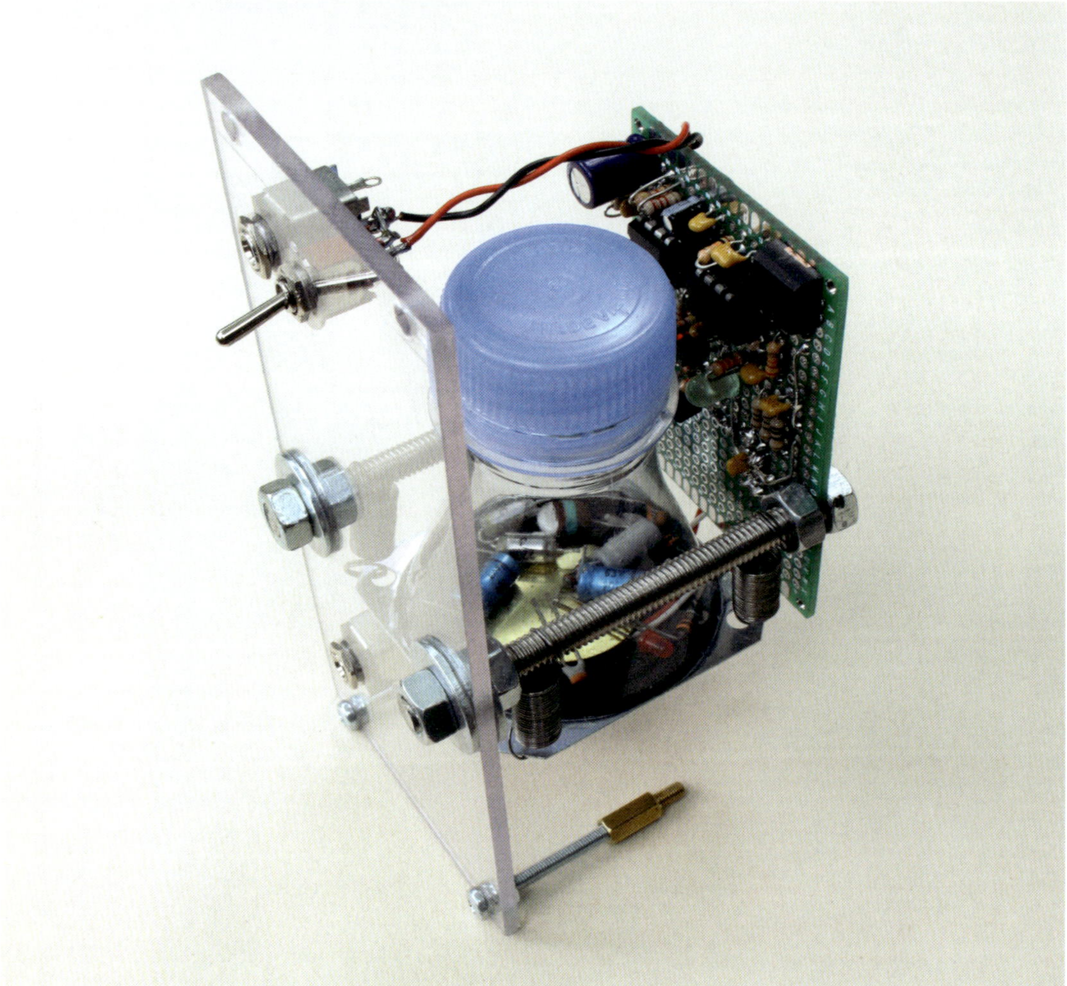

http://gieskes.nl/undefined/eurorack/
http://gieskes.nl/eurorack/?file=vu-perc
http://gieskes.nl/eurorack/?file=vco-fan

The idea for this project comes from one of the first things I made with electronics, a mechanical sequencer. When I made the *Seq1* and *5-volt sequencer* I hardly knew anything about electronics, I made it mechanical because it was the only way I knew how to build it. And I also liked the idea that the sounds would never be the same: every time a sound is played back it will be a little different, just like an acoustic instrument. I based the sequencer on the TR-808, because that was the drum computer I had. So after learning a lot about electronics over the last ten years (learning from the internet and tinkering) I decided to go back to the start and make an improved version with the knowledge I had gained—resulting in the *electromechanical modular* (in Eurorack specifications). All modules are made as small as possible, just like in electronics where everything is made as small as possible to fit as much functionality as possible into a small space. This should also result in the most elegant and aesthetic solution. The *modular* will produce sound mainly by mechanical movements, for instance parts hitting things, and by measuring movements with different types of sensor. For instance, the sensors used are piezo elements, which transform small movements into sounds. The *modular* uses the Eurorack standard, which influences the size of the modules, the voltage levels, the connectors and the power consumption. Motors usually use more power than modules without moving parts. So sometimes an external power supply is used for an individual module.

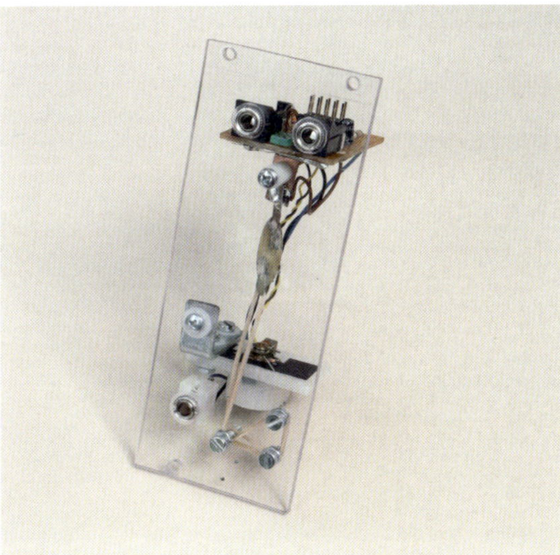

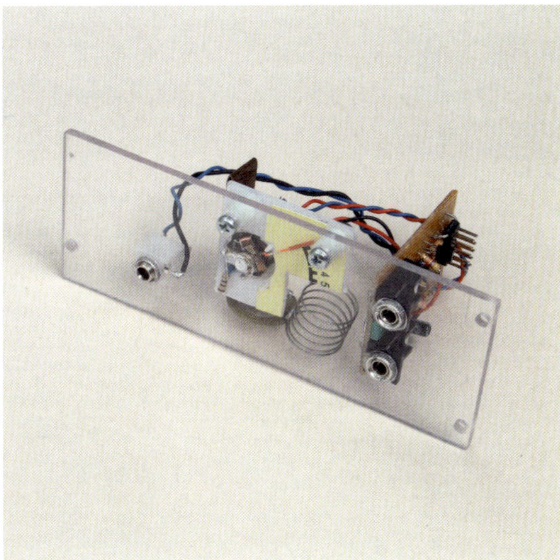

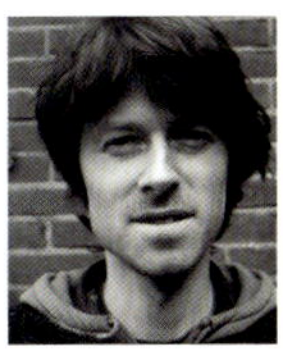

Gijs Gieskes (NL), my education was as an industrial designer and artist at the Design Academy Eindhoven and the Icelandic Art Academy. I started making instruments around 1998, for audio or visual use but mostly for audio. When I needed an instrument I found out how to build it and then built it myself. Usually I used the instruments for a few performances and then I built a new device. After a while I started making more instruments for other people, leaving me less and less time to use my own instruments.

littleBits x Korg Synth Kit

Paul Rothman, littleBits Electronics Inc

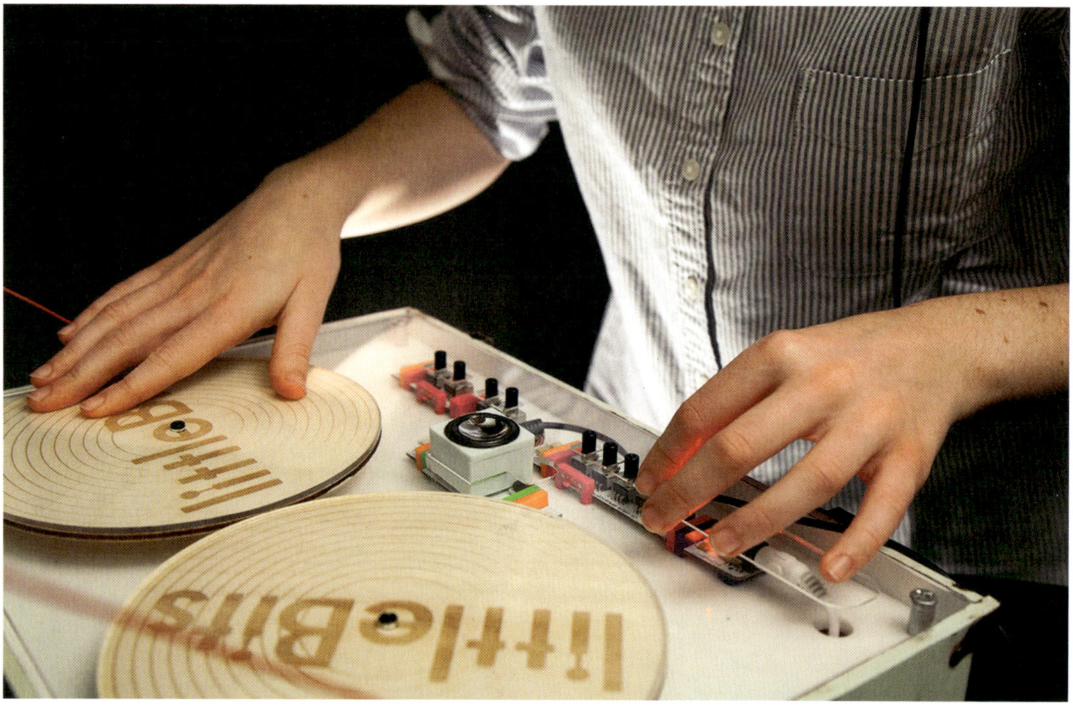

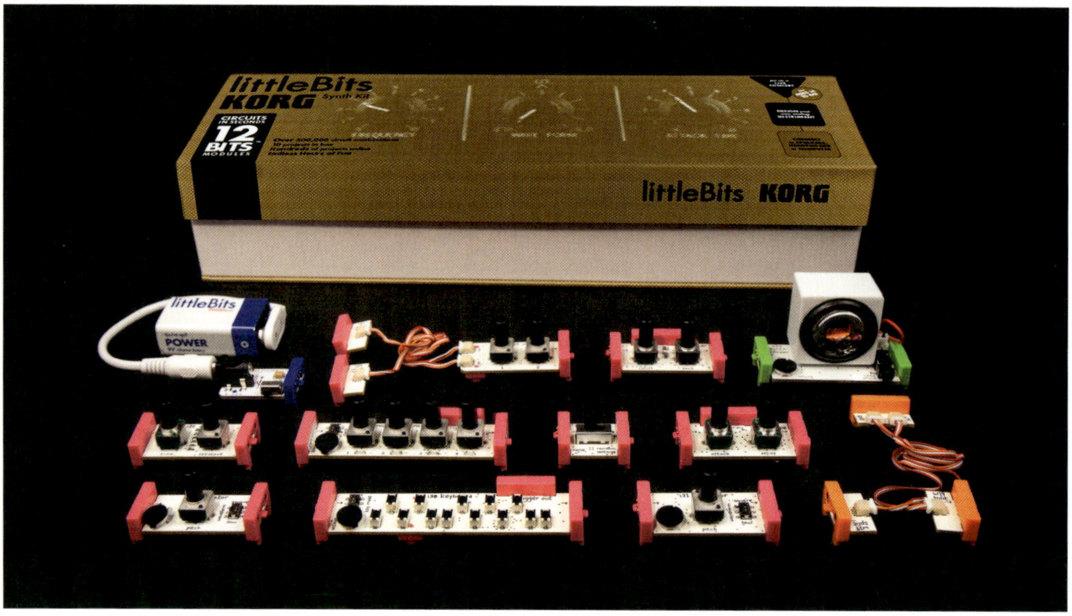

Music, like making, is universal. No matter how far you travel across distance or time, you will find people creating. This act of creating—sounds, objects, ideas—is a constant that connects us all. Taking our goal of putting the power of electronics into the hands of everyone, littleBits partnered with Korg, the world-renowned electronic instrument company, to combine music and making to provide an experience that has never been seen before. Now anyone can dream up new sounds or songs and make them a reality as fast as their mind will allow. We think this could be the start of a new chapter in the history of music technology. The *Synth Kit* is a collaboration between two seemingly different companies that share very similar ideals and principles. We embarked on creating a kit that would behave as a modular analog synthesizer but was simple enough to be accessible to anyone. Additionally, the kit would integrate with all of the other littleBits modules, allowing the user to add various kinds of light, motion and sensors to projects expanding the realm of possibility into the visual and mechanical world. The *Synth Kit* extends our mission to democratize electronics and break down complex technologies so anyone can use electronics to learn, build and invent. We started by imagining the different modules that might be included, and picked the ones that would offer the most complete and varied experience. The *Synth Kit* includes an assortment of twelve electronic Bits that snap together with magnets to create circuits like those used in Korg's famous analog synthesizers (like the MS-20). The modules include power, oscillators, filter, keyboard, micro sequencer, envelope, delay, mix, split, random and speaker. These combine to teach the fundamentals of sound synthesis and allow for nearly endless experimentation. The *Synth Kit* also includes a project booklet outlining step-by-step instructions for ten projects, as well as a brief history of synthesis and the science of sound. Since the release of the *Synth Kit,* we have seen recordings and performances from across the globe (even from a twenty-piece *Synth Kit* orchestra). The *Synth Kit* is designed for musicians, hobbyists and music lovers with an interest in making new sounds and building their own infinitely customizable and expandable analog modular instrument.

Paul Rothman, littleBits Electronics Inc.
Geof Lipman, littleBits Electronics Inc.
Ayah Bdeir, littleBits Electronics Inc.
Tadahiko Sakamaki, Korg Inc.
Tatsuya Takahashi, Korg Inc.
Engineers and Designers at littleBits Electronics Inc.
Engineers and Designers at Korg Inc.

littleBits (US) is a New-York-City-based startup that builds a library of electronic modules that snap together with magnets to let anyone build, create, prototype and invent—no soldering, wiring or programming required. The company's goal is to democratize hardware the way software and printing have been democratized. The littleBits mission is to break down complex technologies and put the power of electronics in the hands of everyone. **Korg** (JP). Since it was founded in 1963, Korg's goal has been to create new experiences in music and performance. Korg is resolved to continue to create innovative and uncompromising instruments which maintain the high quality that inspires professional artists and creators, and yet are approachable enough for anyone to play. The musical instruments Korg will deliver are reflections of the ideas and values of the many artists and users who continue to love Korg products—now and into the future.

Otomo Yoshihide: Between Music and Art

Otomo Yoshihide, NTT InterCommunication Center [ICC]

Otomo Yoshihide is active as a musician in a broad range of musical fields from improvised to popular, and works on soundtracks for cinema and TV among many other things. At the same time, he has so far created and exhibited installation pieces and numerous other works in the realm of art, which have been featured in various exhibitions at museums and galleries. The exhibition *Otomo Yoshihide: Between Music and Art* coupled *quartets*, a commissioned work made in 2008 at the Yamaguchi Center for Arts and Media (YCAM), with a new sound installation, *guitar solos 1*, created for this exhibition. The general theme is "between music and art." Music and art as two different types of artistic expression have up to this point developed individually in both institutional and methodical terms, so we can say that they have been operating within totally different systems regarding production techniques and markets. There are differences between both in several respects, such as the relationship between creator and audience, methods of distributing and presenting works etc. Against this backdrop, various creative activities characterized by mutual intervention between music and art have emerged since the 1960s. The results of such endeavors have been referred to as "intermedia," "performance" or "sound art," which later, with the development of environments enabling the utilization of various media, led to the establishment of "media art" and other forms of expression described as "interdisciplinary." While expanding the traditional definitions and interpretations of artistic genres, such endeavors have at once blurred the boundaries that once existed between them. This is exactly what has made it possible for artists like Otomo to create works that are situated right in the middle, "between music and art." This exhibition focused on the dissimilarities between the originally different disciplines of music and art, with the aim of using several installations and various related events to define what exists "between" these two systems.

Exhibited Works

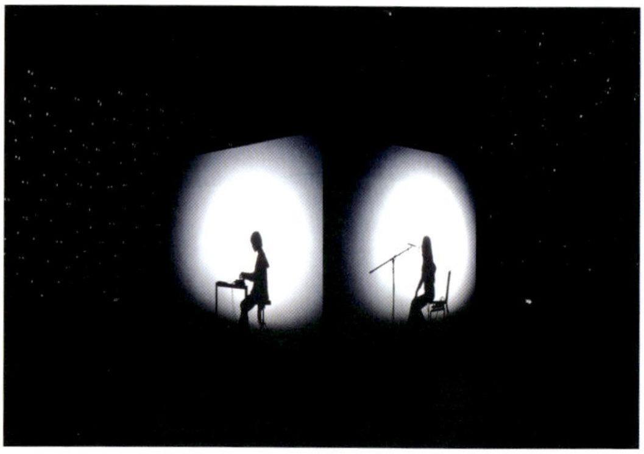

quartets 2008 (commissioned by YCAM)
Otomo Yoshihide, Yuki Kimura, Benedict Drew, Norimichi Hirakawa, Ko Ishikawa, Yoshimitsu Ichiraku, Jim O'Rourke, Karie Kahimi, Sachiko M, Axel Dörner, Martin Brandlmayr
Co-developed with YCAM InterLab

Silhouettes of musicians are projected onto each side of a white cube installed in the center of the exhibition space, while the musicians' music is audible from the inside of the cube. Both silhouettes and music are recordings of the eight musicians' individual performances. The temporal arrangement for each sequence is controlled by a computer program to create a continuous "ensemble" performance in which the individual performances interact and mix with each other. At the same time, images showing details of objects made of wood, iron, liquids and other materials are projected onto screens on each of the exhibition space's four walls, immediately opposite the sides of the cube. These images pulsate/flow into the music performed by the silhouettes on the cube. As visitors cannot look at the projections on the four sides of the cube and the surrounding walls all at once, they can never view the entire piece, even though they can hear the ensemble of all the musicians performing at the same time.

Direction, sound composition: Otomo Yoshihide; Art direction (cube screen): Yuki Kimura; Video, objects (outer screen): Benedict Drew; Algorithm design, programming, system: Norimichi Hirakawa; Recording, Mixing: Takayuki Ito, YCAM; Shooting: Richi Owaki, YCAM; Shooting assistant (cube screen): Soichiro Murata; Technical support: Satoshi Hama; Guitar, Turntable: Otomo Yoshihide; Voice: Karie Kahimi; Synthesizer, Guitar: Jim O'Rourke; Sho: Ko Ishikawa; Percussion: Yoshimitsu Ichiraku; Trumpet: Axel Dörner; Drums and Percussion: Martin Brandlmayr; Sinewaves: Sachiko M; Curator for original works: Kazunao Abe, YCAM

http://www.ntticc.or.jp/Archive/2014/Between_Music_and_Art/index.html
http://otomo.ycam.jp/contents_en/quartets/index.html

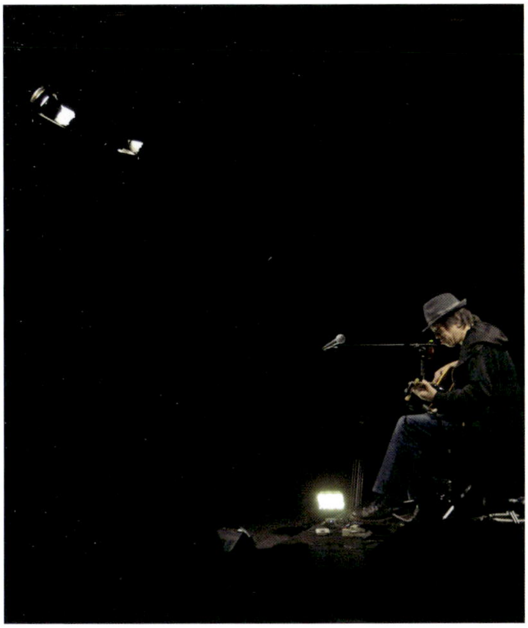

guitar solos 1 2014
Otomo Yoshihide

Sound installation on the stairway up to Gallery A. Sixteen speakers are placed on either side of the stairs. Otomo's pre-recorded guitar sounds are played back randomly from each speaker, whereas the visitor can never hear all the sounds together. The work is to be appreciated while passing by, stopping at some point, or walking up and down the stairway.

Programming, System: Akihiko Matsumoto
Cooperation: Fostex

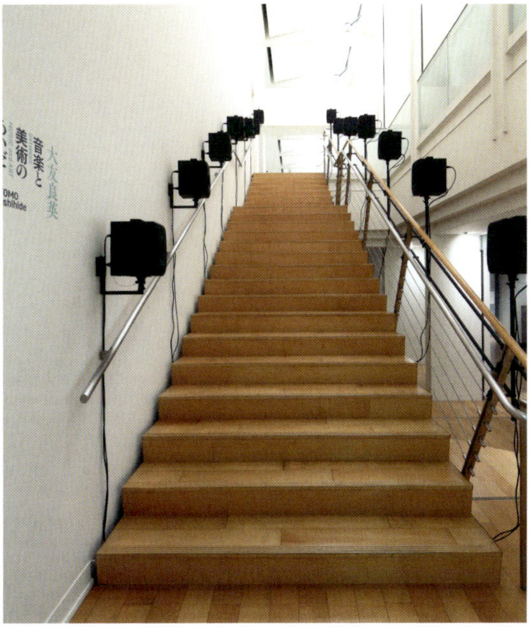

Between Music and Art

On display are questionnaire responses from musicians, artists, critics, curators and other individuals working in the fields of music and art, alongside essays related to *Between Music and Art.*

Contributors: Kazunao Abe, Christophe Charles, Richard Chartier, DJ Sniff / Takuro Mitzuta, Yukio Fujimoto, Yosuke Fujita, Haco, Shuta Hasunuma, Holly Herndon, Norimichi Hirakawa, Kanta Horio, Atsuhiro Ito, Soichiro Mihara, Yuko Mohri, Rie Nakajima, Carsten Nicolai, David Novak, Aki Onda, Tetsuya Ozaki, Hankil Ryu, Sachiko M, Ryuichi Sakamoto, Atsushi Sasaki, Akio Suzuki, David Toop, Toshiya Tsunoda, Tetsuya Umeda, Ei Wada, Tomoko Yabumae, Lyota Yagi, Fuyuki Yamakawa, Seiichi Yamamoto, Taro Yasuno, Tadashi Yonago, Hisanori Gogota

Curator: Minoru Hatanaka, NTT InterCommunication Center [ICC]
Organizer: NTT InterCommunication Center [ICC]
Cooperation: YCAM – Yamaguchi Center for Arts and Media
Production cooperation: Sachiko M

Otomo Yoshihide (JP) born 1959 in Yokohama is a guitarist / turntablist / composer / film-score composer / producer. He is engaged in the independent creation of various types of music, ranging from improvised and "noise" styles to pop music, recently focusing on collaborations with a variety of people as a core element, and is at the same time also noted for his music workshops for handicapped children, and participatory projects such as the *Project Fukushima!* His endeavors have won numerous international awards. **NTT InterCommunication Center [ICC]** (JP) is an innovative cultural facility in Tokyo Opera City Tower in Nishi-Shinjuku, Tokyo, which was established on April 19, 1997, in commemoration of the 100th anniversary of telephone service in Japan (1990).

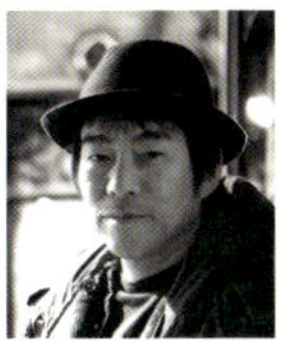

Rawr! A Study in Sonic Skulls

Courtney Brown, Sharif Razzaque

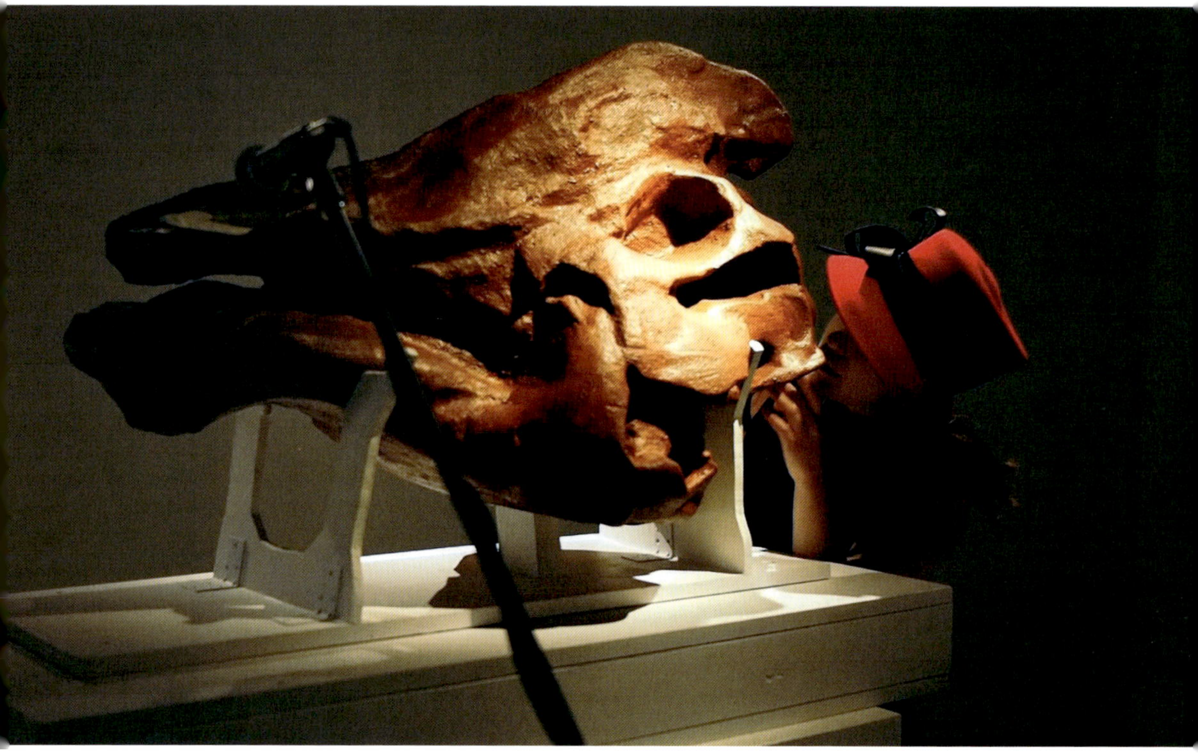

This work is an interactive sound installation and musical instrument based on imagining the sounds of a lambeosaurine hadrosaur, duck-billed dinosaurs known for their large head crests, which researchers hypothesize were resonators for vocal calls. We use scientific research as a starting point to create a means of sound production and a resonator, using a 3D model obtained from computed topology (CT) scans of a corythosaurus skull, and an endocast of its crest and nasal passages. Users give voice to the dinosaur by blowing into a mouthpiece, exciting a larynx mechanism and resonating the sound through the hadrosaur's full-scale nasal cavities and skull. Through the controlled exhalation of their breath, users get to know the dinosaur and how the compression of the lungs leads to a roar or a whisper. Our intention is to lift dinosaur sound from disembodied simulation into physical being. Gallery visitors and performers complete this process by blowing into the installation, momentarily becoming the dinosaur. Uniquely, this instrument offers an embodied, experiential window into the distant past. For example, it takes an effort to get the skull to roar. It is not easy. Our lungs are human-sized, a fraction of those of the corythosaurus. Through this effort, we can feel the enormity. We no longer need to see it to understand it. We know it in our gasping for breath. It exists in the relation between our diaphragm, the roar and the sputter. Accordingly, our design requires users to use their own breath. This action activates the larynx mechanism, resonating through the corythosaurus's nasal cavities and crest. The roar is not synthesized. It is the consequence of physical processes produced by the breath, mediated by the construction and materials of the skull and larynx. Vibrations flow back into the lungs and become part of the experience. The interaction is rich in complexity because of the physicality of its design.

https://vimeo.com/78323032
http://www.courtney-brown.net

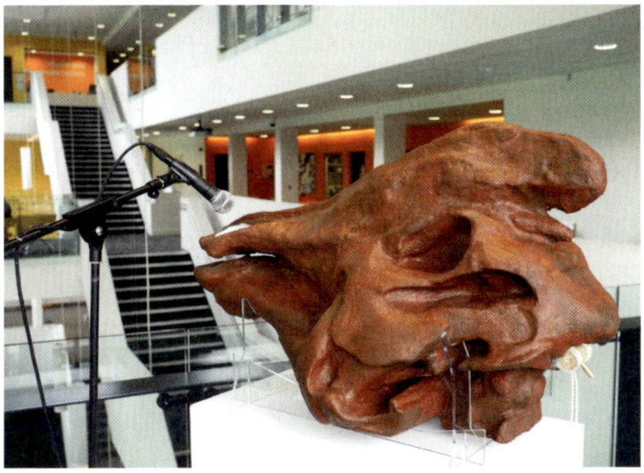

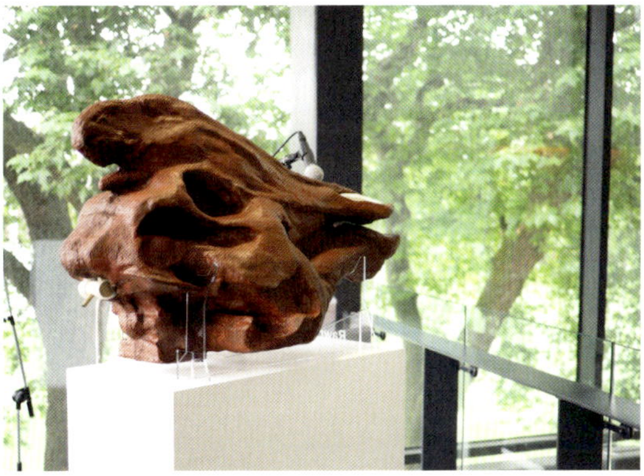

Composer, music researcher, engineer, sculptor: Courtney Brown
Engineer, digital fabrication: Sharif Razzaque
Digital fabrication and advice (nasal passages): Carlo Sammarco
Advisor: Garth Paine
3D model of a hadrosaur skull: Lawrence Witmer
Funding: Arizona State University GPSA
Support and assistance: Brent Brimhall, Gordon Bergfors, Sallye Coyle

Courtney Brown (US) is an interactive sound artist, composer, Argentine tango dancer, and software developer. She is a doctoral candidate in Interdisciplinary Digital Media and Performance at Arizona State University, and a former Fulbright Fellow, composing interactive Argentine tangos in Buenos Aires. She is also a graduate of Dartmouth's Electro acoustic Music Master's Program. **Sharif Razzaque** (US) is an inventor, designer, and computer scientist. He has a PhD from UNC-Chapel Hill, in collaboration with Univ. College London and HIT Lab at Univ. Washington in Seattle. As InnerOptic Inc.'s CTO, he develops surgical devices with 3D virtual interfaces. Ultimately, his work is about understanding human perception and using this to create compelling and effective experiences and tools.

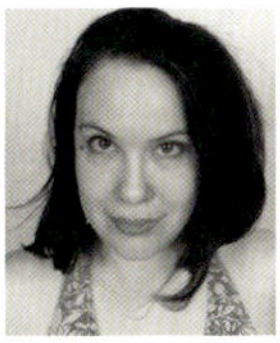

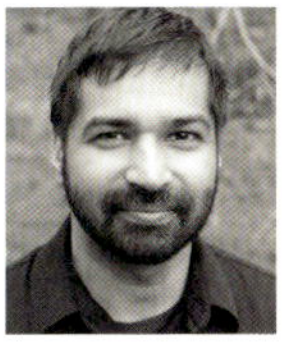

Soft Revolvers

Myriam Bleau

Soft Revolvers is a music performance for four clear acrylic spinning tops designed and built by the artist. Each top, 25 cm in diameter, is associated with an "instrument" in an electronic music composition. The tops are equipped with gyroscopes and accelerometers that communicate wirelessly with a computer. The motion data collected (speed, unsteadiness at the end of a spin, acceleration spikes in case of collisions) informs musical algorithms and controls custom sequencers designed in Pure Data. LEDs inside the tops illuminate the body of the objects in a precise counterpoint to the music, creating stunning spinning halos. With their large circular spinning bodies and their role as music-playing devices, the spinning-top interfaces strongly evoke turntables and hip hop culture. Some of the mappings between gestures and sound have been borrowed directly from the bimodal behavior of turntables: at slow speeds the sounds produced can remind of scratch solos, with the characteristic unstable pitch variations. At full speed, the spinning tops act like normal turntables playing vinyls, in this case playing pre-composed material. Familiar objects, in this case spinning tops, engage audience members in a particularly intricate manner, awakening subconscious physical memories of their lived experience with those objects in terms of behavioral expectations, function and symbolic connotations. The public can anticipate the physical rules that will guide the performance and thus actively participate in the tension and release dynamics at play in *Soft Revolvers*.

Composition, performance, technical design, fabrication: Myriam Bleau

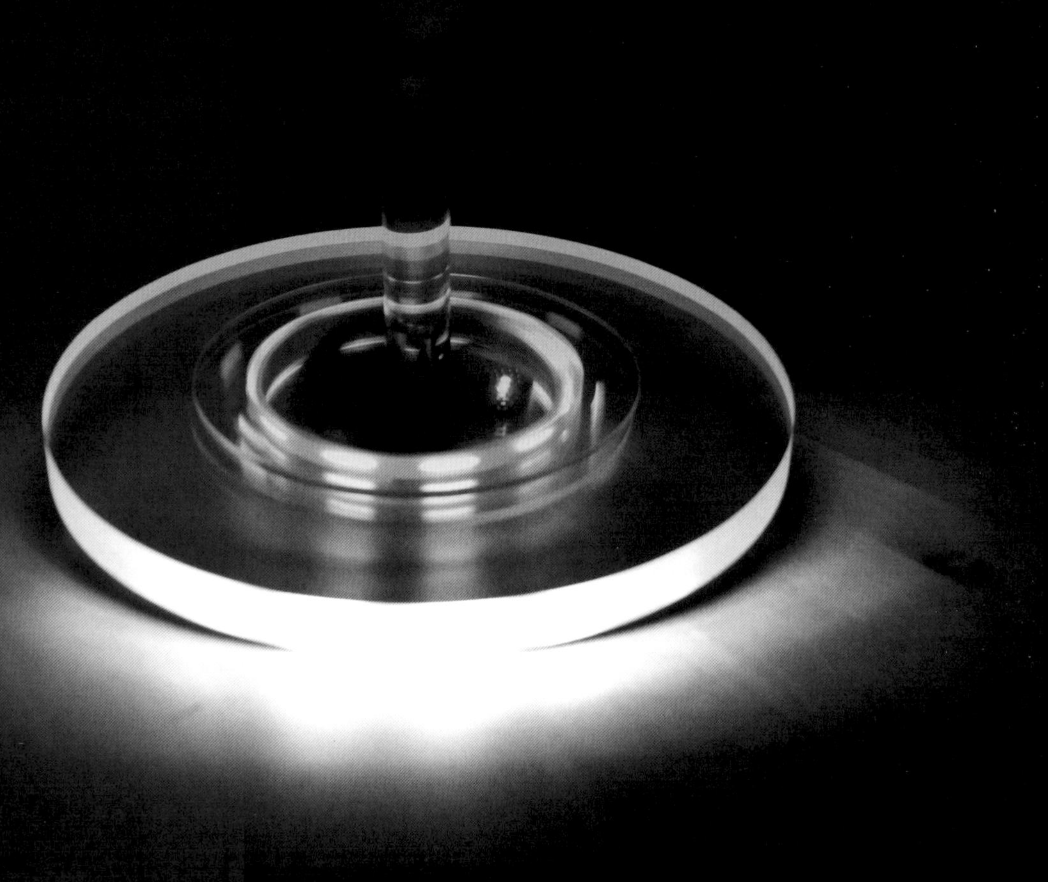

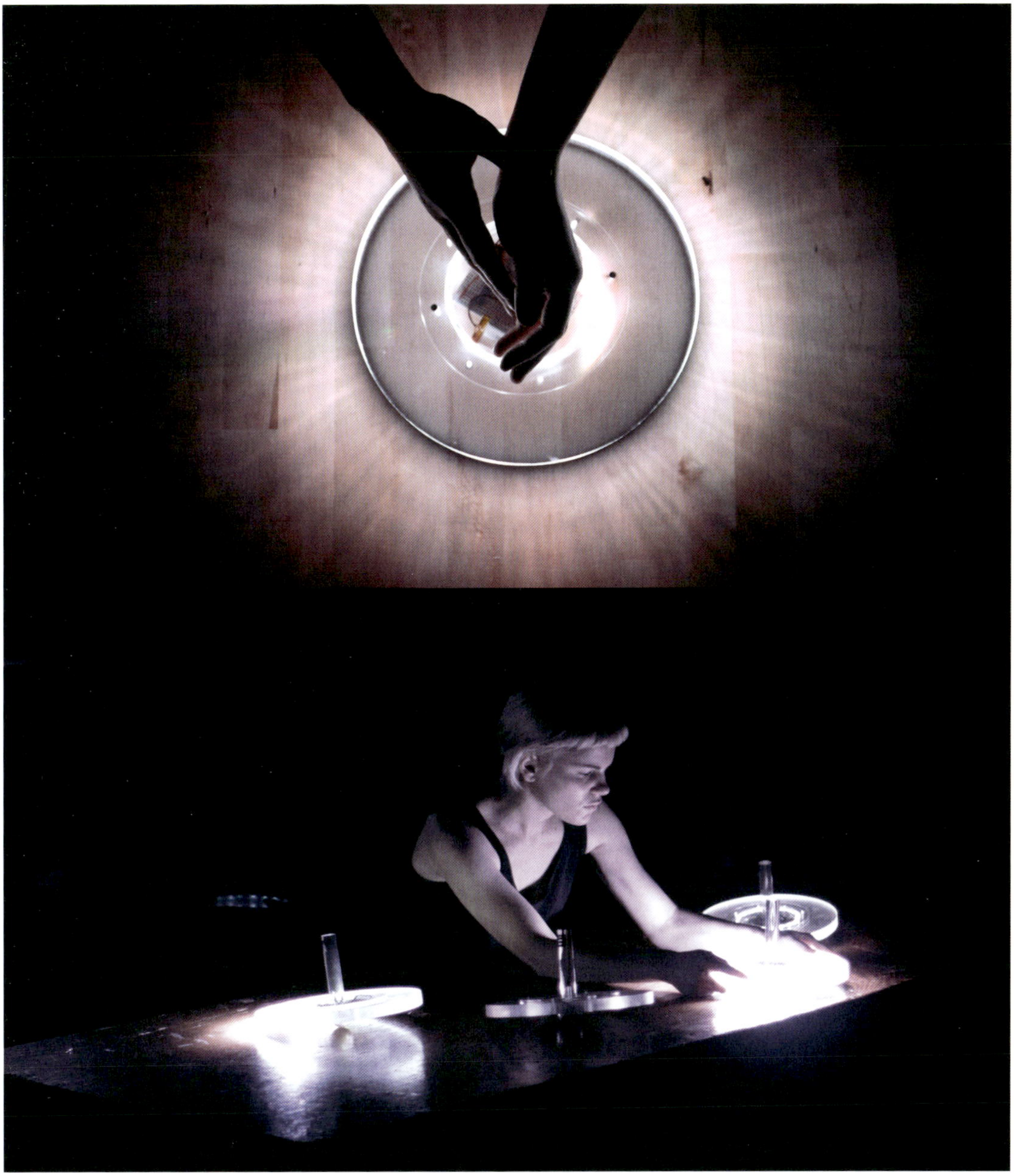

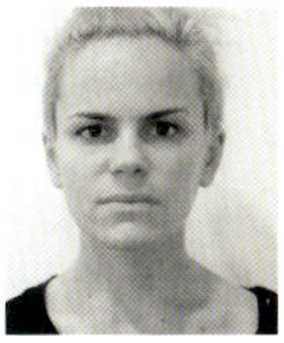

Myriam Bleau (CA) is a composer, digital artist and performer based in Montreal. Exploring the limits between musical performance and digital arts, she creates audiovisual systems that go beyond the screen, such as sound installations and performance-specific musical interfaces. Her presence on the popular music scene influences her hybrid electronic practice that integrates hip hop, techno, experimental and pop elements. Her work has been presented across Canada, in the US and in Europe in festivals such as Transmediale, Elektra & Akousma.

Tipping Point

Kathy Hinde

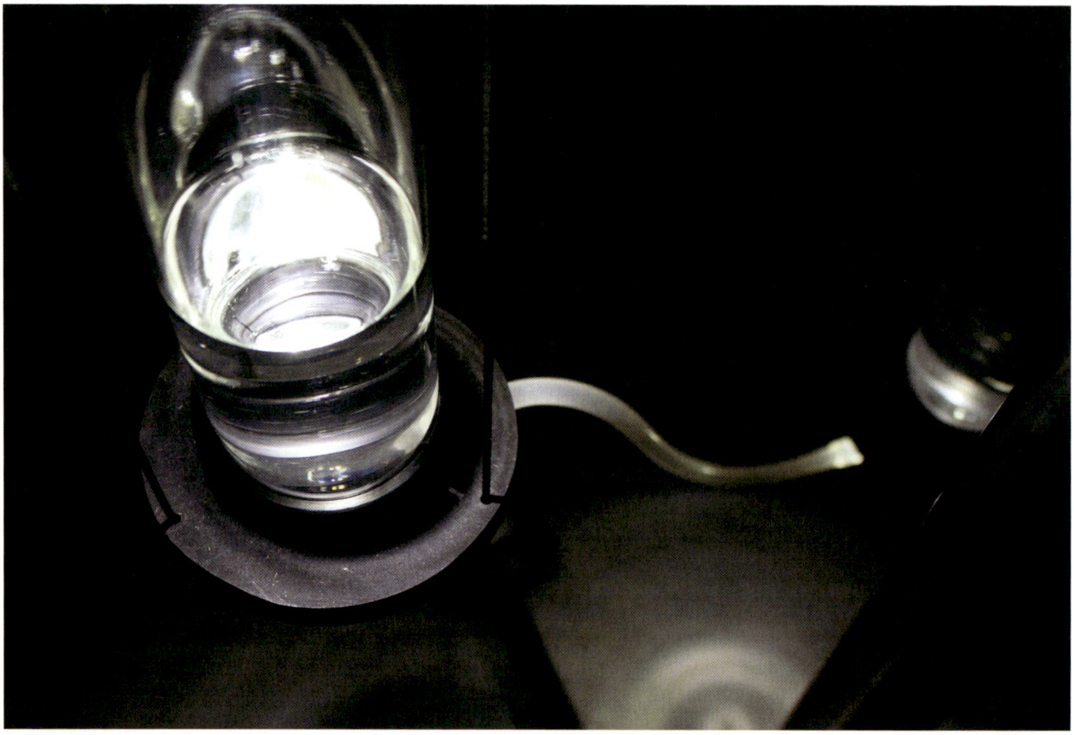

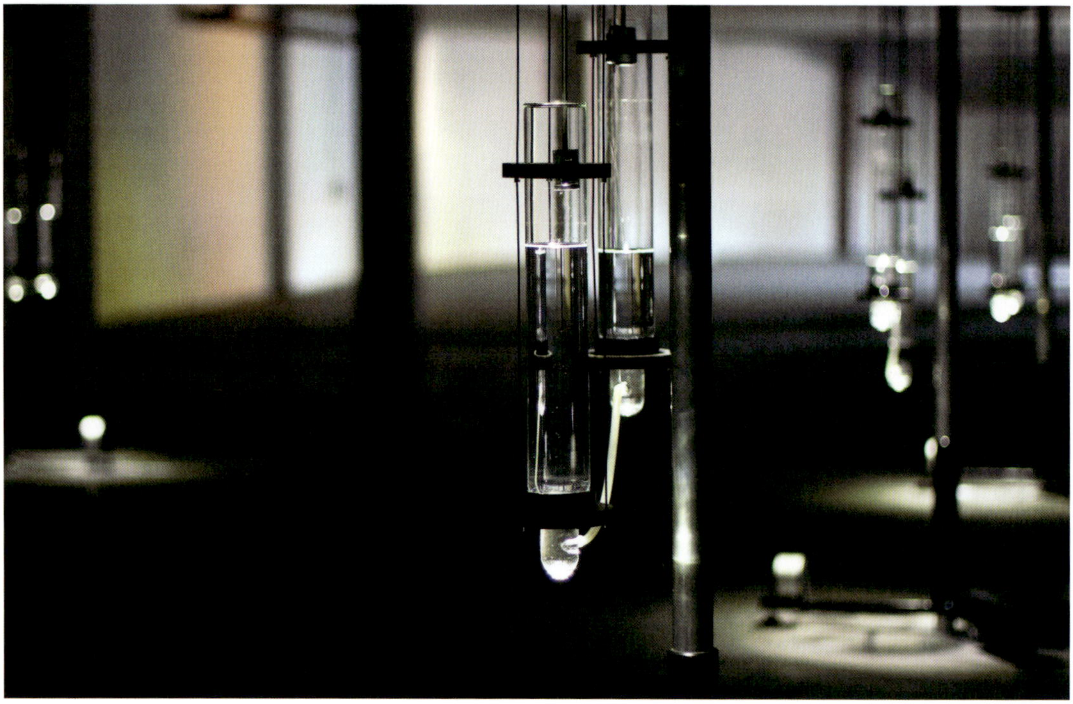

Tipping Point invites us to consider our relationship with water and the need to balance how we use the world's water resources. The installation is created using a delicate combination of glass, water, audio feedback and lighting. Twelve glass vessels are arranged in pairs and suspended from mechanical arms that slowly tip from left to right. Each pair of vessels is connected, which allows a shared body of water to flow from one to the other. This causes the relative water levels to shift inside each glass vessel. As one fills, the other empties. They are intricately linked and need to keep re-balancing and adjusting so neither overflows or completely empties. Sound tones are produced live via a microphone that feeds back inside each glass vessel. As the water levels change, this audio feedback is tuned to different pitches based on the resonant frequency of the remaining space inside each glass vessel. Software keeps the audio feedback in balance at its "tipping point", by listening to the volume and adjusting the microphone gain to maintain a tone, but preventing it continually increasing in volume. Consequently, the sound tends to flicker slightly and fluctuate in volume. This phenomenon is accentuated by LED lights that illuminate each vessel, with their brightness being determined in relation to the volume of each vessel's resonating sound. The number of glass tubes that are resonating varies. When all twelve vessels are resonating, a layered, choral texture is created, whereas a solo or duet reveals the plaintive rising and falling scales. This system is controlled by generative software so the sequences and patterns created will not repeat. *Tipping Point* forms both a sculptural sound installation and the basis of a live performance. Kathy Hinde performs *Tipping Point* live by manually controlling all the parameters of the installation. She then further sculpts the sounds through various guitar pedals, which in turn affects how the audio feedback behaves inside the vessels.

Composition, concept, design, construction, electronics:
Kathy Hinde
Handblown glass vessels: John Rowden
Software programming: Matthew Olden
Specialized parts: University of Bristol,
School of Physics Mechanical and Glass Workshop
A Cryptic commission for Sonica. Supported by PRS for Music Foundation, The Britten-Pears Foundation, The Esmée Fairbairn Foundation, The Hinrichsen Foundation and Cove Park

Kathy Hinde (UK). Her artwork and music grows from a partnership between nature and technology expressed through audiovisual installations and performances that combine sound, sculpture, image and light. She often uses open scores, graphic scores and chance procedures to create a framework from which an artwork can emerge and evolve. Kathy frequently works in collaboration with other creative practitioners and professionals from different disciplines in order to enrich and challenge her creative process. She has shown work across Europe, Scandinavia, China, Pakistan, the USA, Colombia and Brazil. Kathy is an Associate Artist with the producing art house Cryptic in Glasgow, Scotland.

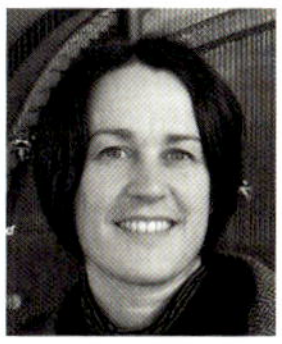

JoeClarke

Zeitraum

Gerhard Eckel, University of Music and Performing Arts Graz

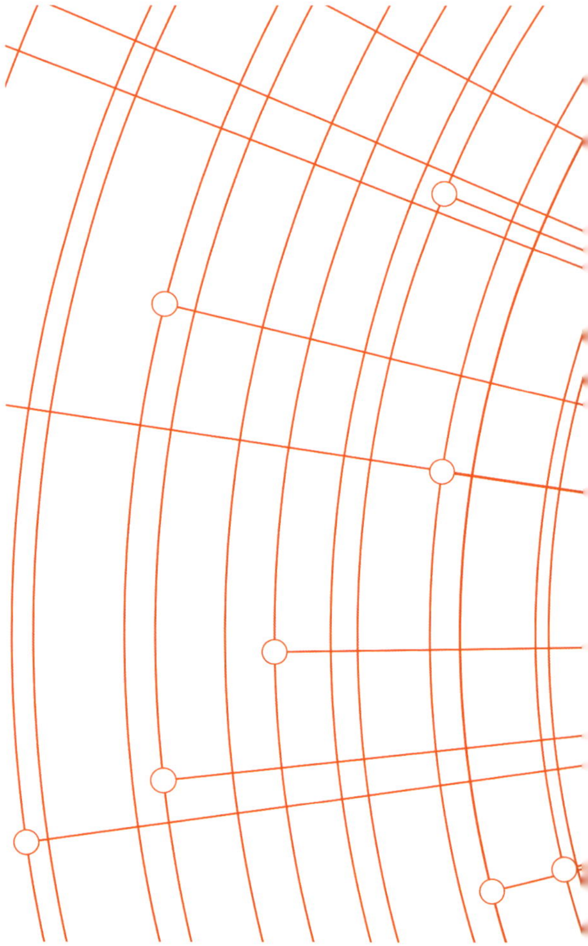

Zeitraum (German for "timespan", literally "time space") is a sound environment exposing the interrelation of time and space in acoustic communication. The environment is composed of many identical sound sources dispersed irregularly in a large space, playing an aleatoric ostinato of percussive sounds. When listened to from a particular location (the sweet spot), the pattern is perceived as an accented but isochronous pulse. The ostinato is structured so that the sounds from all sources arrive at the sweet spot with the same delay, compensating for the differences in propagation time. As one moves away from the sweet spot, the regular pulse becomes increasingly distorted as the distances to all sound sources change and with them the propagation delays from the sources to the listener. What starts as almost imperceptible deviations and passes through various areas with different kinds of grooves, ends up in a rhythmically completely disrupted and apparently chaotic sequence of events when listened to far from the sweet spot. By moving about the space, the audience explores a space literally made out of time, a time space—a bewildering experience enacted through one's movement, revealing the always baffling relativity of observation. Although the time lag between lightning and thunder is a well-known phenomenon—being evidence of sound's relatively slow propagation speed of about 1,200 km/h, which is about 870,000 times slower than the speed of light—it is surprising to experience that this fundamental condition of acoustic communication can completely disrupt the rhythmical integrity of a regular but spatialized musical structure. *Zeitraum* reveals what skilled musicians unconsciously compensate for when playing together over bigger distances: the fact that sound takes a considerable amount of time to reach our ears—considerable with respect to rhythmical structures in music and already occurring in smaller concert halls. It also reveals the ear as a high-precision measuring instrument for time intervals. Once synced on a pulse, it can distinguish very small deviations from an expected next beat. Such deviations may be experienced as a pleasant groove or an irritating irregularity depending on the context and listening habits. Most of these aspects may remain unconscious to the listener, which will not lessen the pleasure of exploring how the time-space keeps

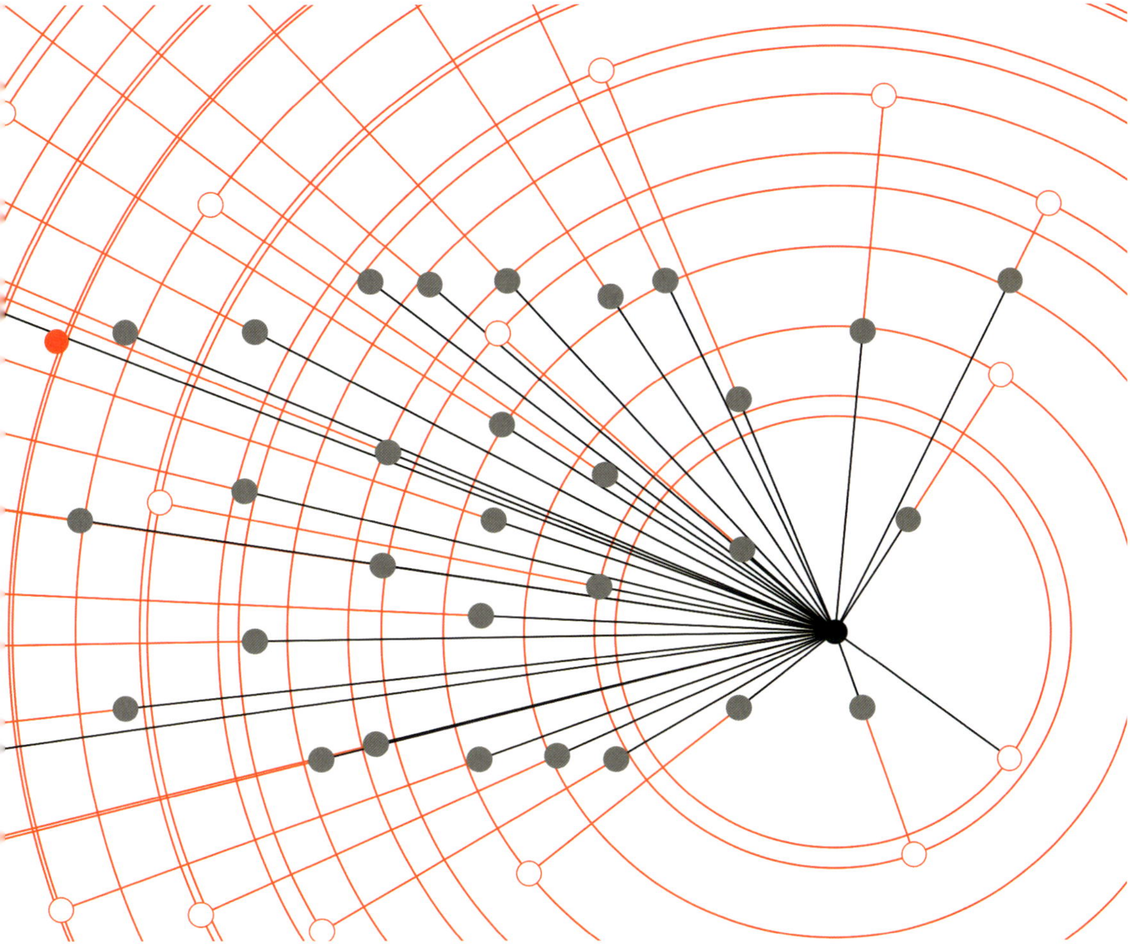

transforming the ostinato. Thus the environment offers both a rich aesthetic experience and much to reflect upon for those inclined to do so. The latter is particularly supported by the sound design, which permits verbal communication among the audience. Neither does speaking interfere with the work nor do the percussive sounds impede spontaneous conversations among the listeners while collectively exploring the work. Hence, besides establishing a time-space, *Zeitraum* also creates a social space, enabling the audience to deepen their experience and understanding through communication.

Gerhard Eckel (AT) is an artist using sound to explore ways of world making. He aims to articulate the aesthetic and epistemic dimensions of art, understanding artistic experience as a compound of action, perception and reflection. His works are the results of research processes drawing on the practice and theory of music composition, sound art, choreography and dance, installation art, interaction design and digital instrument making. Gerhard Eckel is a professor of computer music and multimedia at the University of Music and Performing Arts Graz in Austria. He also serves as affiliate professor at the KTH Royal Institute of Technology and as visiting professor at the Royal College of Music in Stockholm.

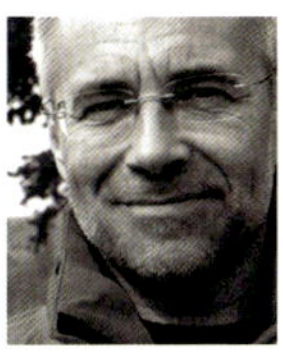

Marion Schwebel

Visionary Pioneers

of Media Art

Visionary Pioneers of Media Art

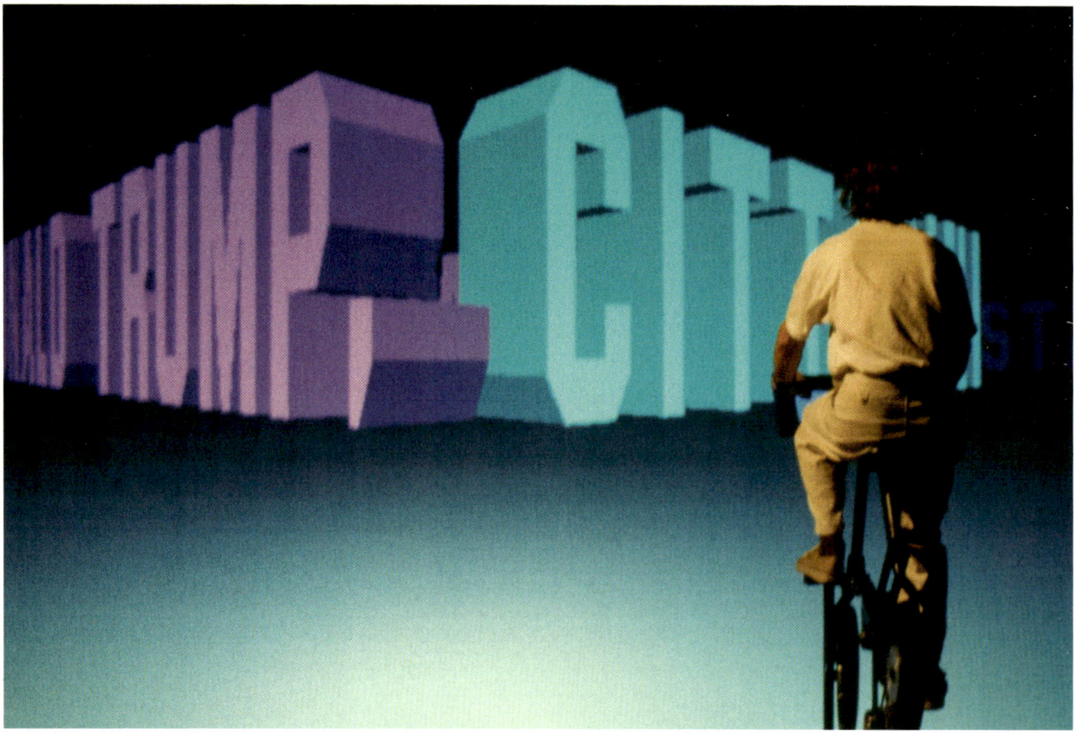

Launched last year, the new category is dedicated to recognizing and celebrating the men and women whose artistic, technological and social achievements have decisively influenced and advanced the development of new artistic directions.
What began as a technological revolution has since developed into a new cultural and social reality with its own specific forms of communication, cultural techniques and artistic expressions, the roots of which extend far back into the past and lead us to encounters with extraordinary personalities—the visionary pioneers of media art. Thus, in many respects, these men and women established the foundation of media art as we know it today. In order to give them the recognition commensurate with their accomplishments, we have created the new prize: the Prix Ars Electronica's Golden Nica for Visionary Pioneers of Media Art.
One goal of this prize is also to generate more awareness about the history of media art in general, so the first edition in 2014 was accompanied by a lively discussion about possible criteria, because of course it is quite difficult to compare artists from so many different genres and backgrounds. Another point of discussion was the geographical background and the fact that by far the most nominations were for artists from within the usual triangle of Europe, North America and Japan, and that such a prize should pay particular attention to media art pioneers who are not so well known or come from other parts of the world. That is why this year we decided to change the procedure of the prize slightly and to ask an international team of experts to come up with the nominations and especially to look into the lesser-known areas. Each of the experts had a special geographical focus. The experts we asked for nominations were:

- Erkki Huhtamo: Europe, North America, Australia
- Machiko Kusahara: Japan, East Asia
- Andrey Smirnov: Russia, countries of the former USSR, South East Europe
- Barbara London: North America, Australia, Europe
- José-Carlos Mariátegui: Latin America
- Marcus Neustetter: Africa
- Monica Narula: India, South East Asia

This group of experts did a wonderful job, with excellent nominations, and with the detailed descriptions of the nominees and their work they made a strong contribution to filling in some gaps in media-art history as well.
The decision-making process to select the recipient of this very special award was again put in the hands of all previous recipients of a Golden Nica since the Prix Ars Electronica's inception in 1987—a distinguished community of consummate artists and visionaries in their own right. Each of them had one vote to select the final winner.
The carefully selected nominations by our international expert committee were an excellent and challenging basis for the voting process. Excellent because all the nominees are really great artists and each of them would of course more than deserve such an award themselves. But it was also challenging, because quite a few of the nominees were pretty much unknown to many of us, despite the important work they have been doing for such a long time. There was some discussion and critique about this situation and we received many recommendations, for which we are more than grateful. These inspiring recommendations will do much to help us improve the process in the future.
There are of course various ways to structure such an award and still we have to say that we are very pleased with the process and the outcome of this year. It was not to be expected that some of the not so well-known artists would immediately win first place, but it is already an important step to have their names and work on the radar now.
The second edition of this new award has been successfully completed thanks to the wonderful participation and support of the decision-making group of artists.
Seventeen artists were nominated, 71 votes were cast, and with 19 votes Jeffrey Shaw was selected as the recipient of the Golden Nica for Visionary Pioneers of Media Art 2015. Congratulations to Jeffrey Shaw and to all the other nominated artists.

Jeffrey Shaw—Visionary Pioneer of Media Art 2015

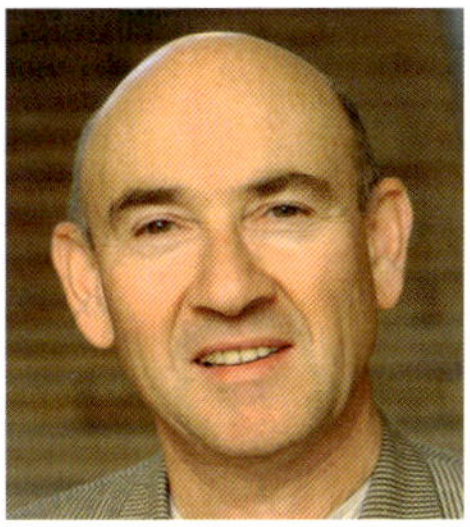

Jeffrey Shaw was born in 1944 in Melbourne, Australia. From 1962 to 1966, Shaw studied architecture and art history at the University of Melbourne, and sculpture at the Brera Academy in Milan and at the St. Martins School of Art in London. Shaw was co-founder of the Eventstructure Research Group in Amsterdam (1969-1979), and founding director of the ZKM Institute for Visual Media Karlsruhe (1991-2002). At the ZKM he conceived and ran a seminal artistic research program that included the ArtIntAct series of digital publications, the MultiMediale series of international media art exhibitions, and over one hundred artist-in-residence projects. In 1995, Shaw was appointed Professor of Media Art at the State University of Design, Media and Arts (HfG), Karlsruhe, Germany. In 2003 Jeffrey Shaw was awarded the prestigious Australian Research Council Federation Fellowship and returned to Australia to co-found and direct the UNSW iCinema Centre for Interactive Cinema Research in Sydney from 2003-2009. In 2009 Shaw joined City University of Hong Kong as Chair Professor of Media Art and Dean of the School of Creative Media (SCM). In 2014 Shaw received an honorary doctorate in creative media from the Multimedia University, Malaysia, and was appointed visiting professor at the Central Academy of Fine Art in Beijing, and visiting professor at the Institute for Global Health Innovation, Imperial College, London. In recognition of his major international impact on the field, Shaw has won several awards for his new media projects and publications, including the Ars Electronica Honorable Mention for Interactive Art, Linz, Austria, 1989; the Immagine Elettronica Prize, Ferrara, Italy, 1990; the Oribe Award, Gifu, Japan, 2005 and the Lifetime Achievement Award, Society of Art and Technology, Montreal, Canada, 2014.
(Source: Jeffrey Shaw)

Jeffrey Shaw—Pioneering the New Media Experience

Anne-Marie Duguet

Jeffrey Shaw is a pioneer in the field of new media in numerous respects. The breadth of his influence is due not only to the experimental and radically anticipatory character of what he has produced, it is also the outcome of the context of the research work he has carried out since the early 1990s at several institutions. Equally important were the positions he held at ZKM—Center for Art and Media Karlsruhe and the UNSW iCinema (Sydney) and now holds at the CityU School of Creative Media in Hong Kong. He was thus able to conceive ambitious projects that did not have to conform to either the exigencies of a market or the criteria of legitimation of contemporary art, and were also not subject to economic constraints. His initiatives nurtured an attitude towards creativity and research that enabled him to encounter technology in a way that was free of prejudice and yet still permitted him to maintain a critical eye with respect to the utilization of this technology and its limitations. It is also to this formidable dynamism that one must pay tribute today.

The singularity of Jeffrey Shaw's oeuvre already manifested itself in his first animated film and continues to do so today in his virtual environments—namely, the constant dialectic between the explicit appropriation of languages, techniques and models of representation derived from many different cultural traditions and the exploration of those new territories that technologies have opened up to him.

His first works—produced in the context of the intellectual, cultural and political ferment of the 1960s and 70s—manifest the principle paradigm shifts of contemporary art: refocusing attention towards the *dispositif* of representation and the prevailing conditions within which this representation is experienced; the involvement of the spectator in accordance with multiple perceptual, mental and behavioral modalities; the insistence on the process and the context of the work; the consideration given to history and memory; the interest in the heterogeneity of language; the collaboration among artists working in different disciplines; and, finally, the experimentation with alternative settings for art.

What emerged in particular over the course of these years is an artistic personality that gradually garnered recognition as an inventor of systems as well as a producer of specific technical and conceptual constellations that would later be referred to as *dispositifs.*

There is neither representation nor experience outside of a *dispositif.* In fact, it is the very condition of their possibility. Artistic installations, above all those of experimental cinema and video, have had the task of analyzing what constitutes the foundations of the dominant mode of representation since the Renaissance. It is not cinema or painting or the photo that is submitted to a meticulous re-examination but rather it is the entire ensemble of mythic and non-mythic *dispositifs* that is brought into consideration, from Plato's cave to Brunelleschi's tavoletta, from the camera obscura to Dürer's perspectival gateway, from panoramas to contemporary surveillance systems. The entire history of representations is rehearsed every time in these theaters of seeing, whose heuristic function thus becomes quite clear.

This critical, analytical and reflexive dimension of the installation has been essential to Jeffrey Shaw's oeuvre. In recombining various elements of the cinematic *dispositif* so as to allow unique configurations to develop out of them, as well as by coupling that *dispositif* of representation with other ones, the artist has repeatedly exposed the limits of the standard regulations of traditional cinema. Multiple screens, environmental projections, interactive scenes—the image is exceeded in every one of its dimensions, even at the level of its fullest and most complete nature.

The question of time has heavily impinged on artistic theory and practice since the 1960s. It has emerged not only as a recurrent theme but also as a constituent parameter of the very nature of an artwork. Performances, environments, events, installations have an exploratory duration, they are eminently contingent, closely tied to the specificity of a site or a context, and often dependent on the direct intervention of the audience. They necessarily incorporate chance and accident.

With these early works, Shaw began to conceive of

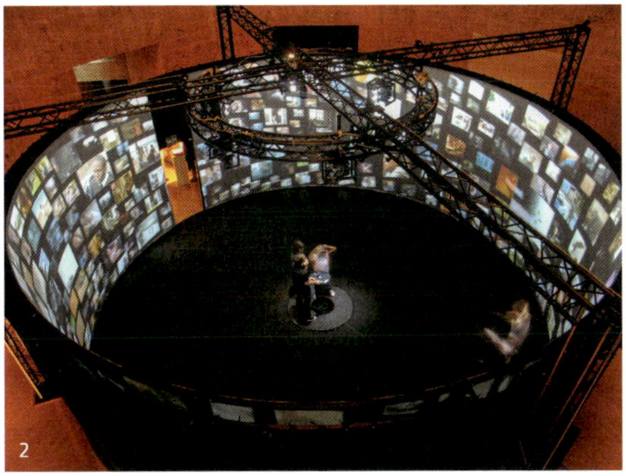

2

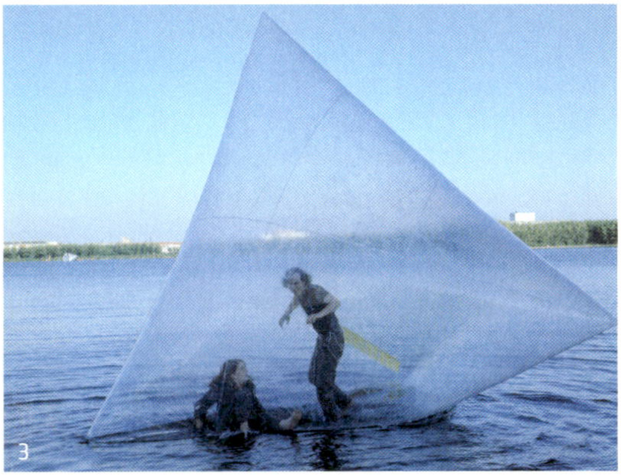

3

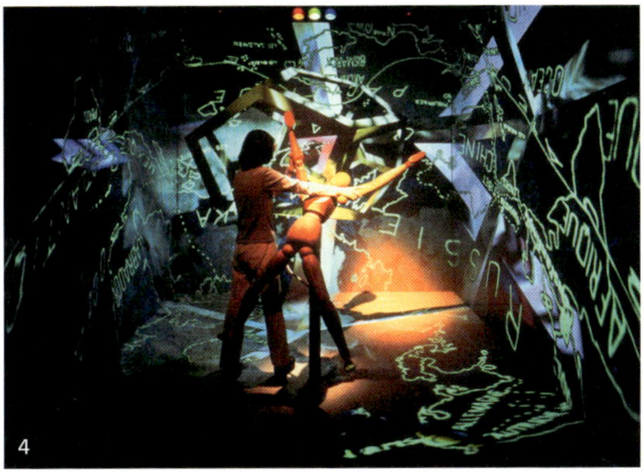

4

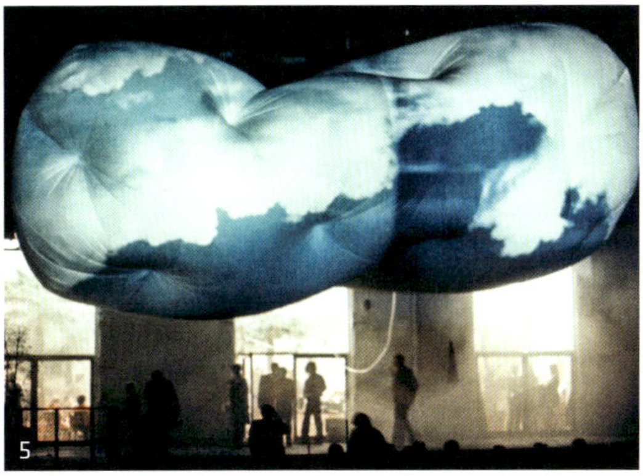

5

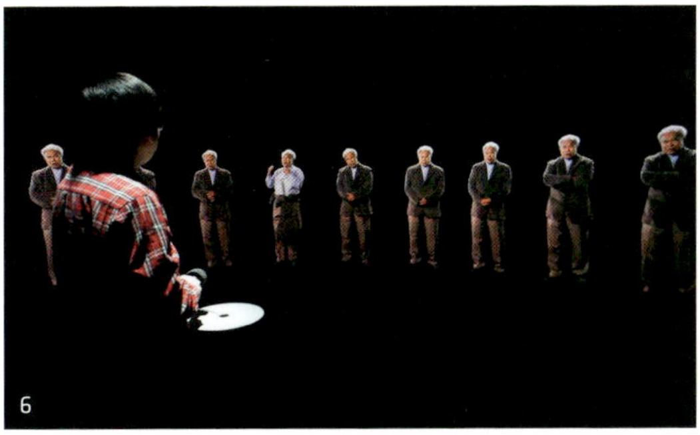

6

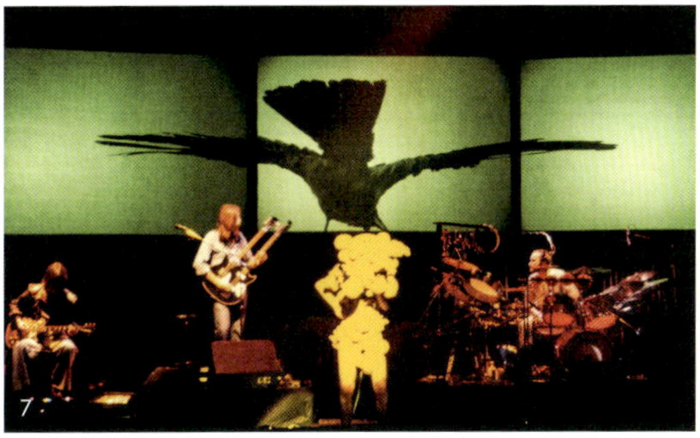

7

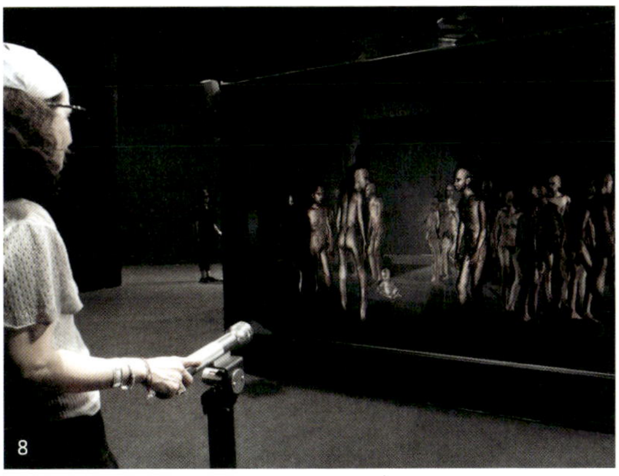

8

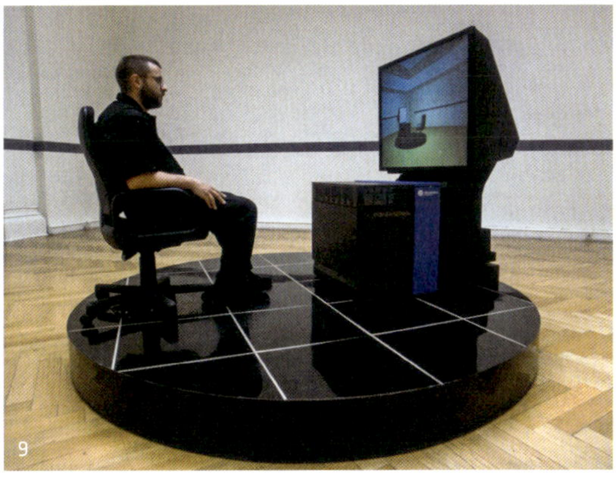

9

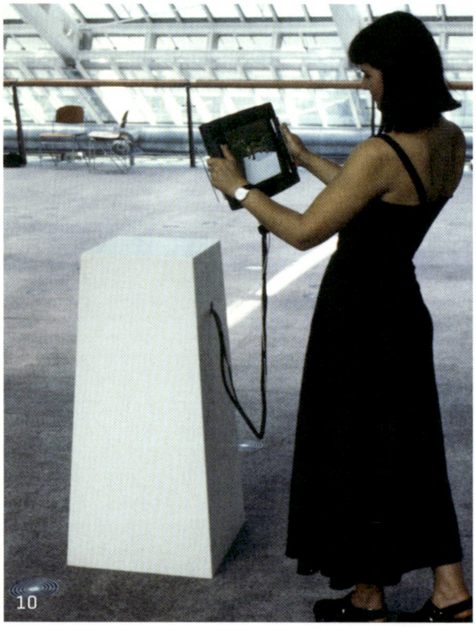
10

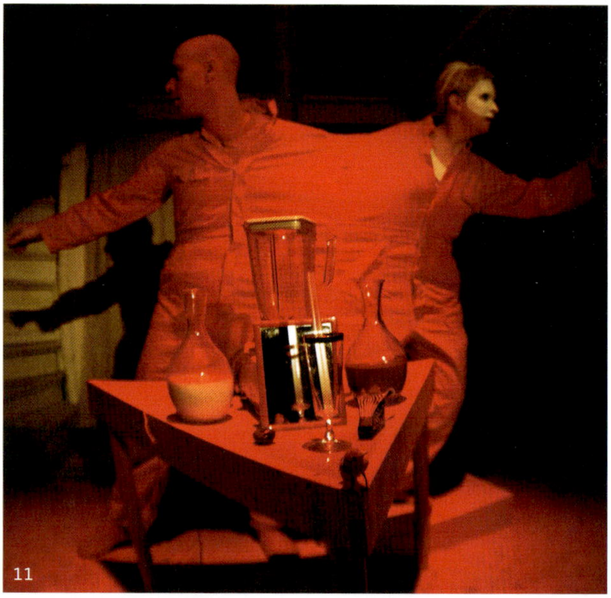
11

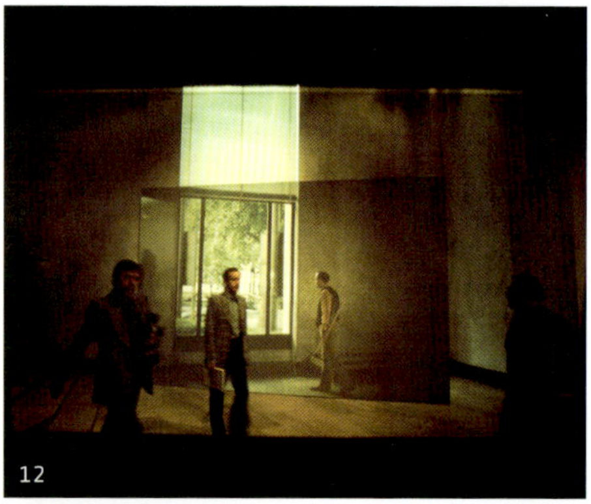
12

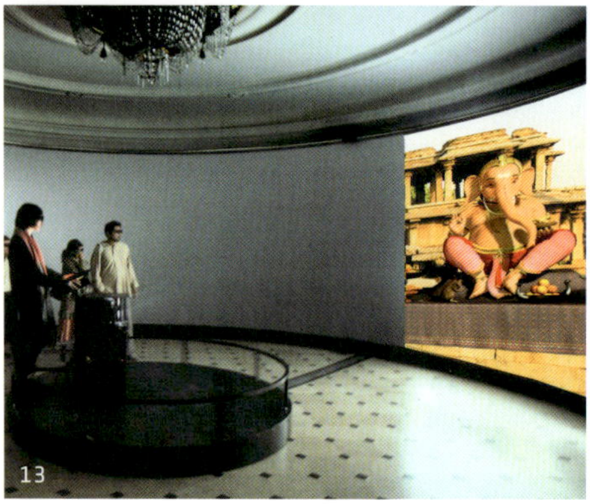
13

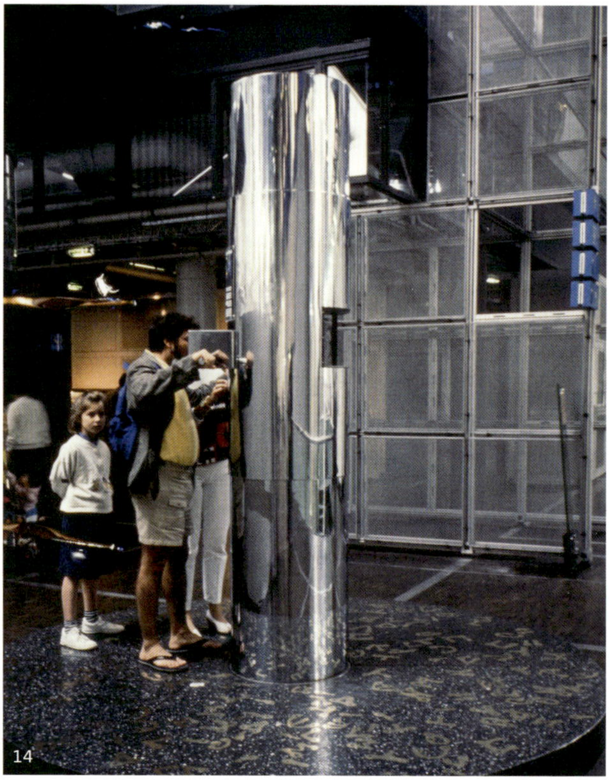
14

an artwork as an "event structure" (a notion developed by John Latham),[I] a field of complex interactions composed of simultaneous events, each having its own duration (a performance act, the running time of a film, various physical phenomena).
Shaw then appropriated highly diverse techniques and elements, preferably fluid, evanescent, malleable, and inconsistent: water, fire, air, neon, polyethylene, pneumatic devices, pyrotechnics, films, photos, lasers etc. What counted was their ability "to physically embody the immaterial," which still remains an issue and above all an interrogation at the heart of Shaw's research.

Exceeding Architecture / Expanding Cinema

By adopting the principle of inflatable structures, Shaw exceeded the limits of architecture and proposed a soft architecture that is transformable, mobile, ephemeral and receptive to intermediate states. This concept was later developed further in *Utopia Triumphans* (2002). From a vocabulary of architectonic forms that pervade one another and protrude into a virtual space, a structure is permanently auto-generated in accordance with certain algorithms.
The critical and highly provocative approach of the Eventstructure Research Group (with whom Shaw produced his first pieces in 1967) entailed not only conceiving architecture as spatially fluid but also making it practicable. Pyramids, pavilions and domes became playful spaces able to produce unusual sensations for all visitors.
Right from the start, Shaw's artistic practice addressed a broad audience, not merely that of art galleries. The desire to avoid making art a separate activity, to connect it to everyday life, prompted him to seek out new exhibition contexts such as a street, a facade or a canal. *Neon Wave Sculpture* (1979) was a kinetic light sculpture placed high on the side wall of a building. A luminous wave traveled through the neon tubes, describing a programmed pattern that was determined according to the speed of the wind. The artwork was thus rendered "sensitive" to natural phenomena and was open to chance factors (a key parameter in Cage-influenced experimentation of the day) including public intervention.
One important aspect of such pieces is the often collective nature of their production. The early 1960s saw increasing collaboration between artists from different fields. The Experiments in Art and Technology group (E.A.T.) for instance, was designed to spur encounters between artists, technicians and scientists. Such cooperation stemmed not only from the very nature of pieces that entailed complex technical and computational systems requiring specific skills, but also from a conception of artistic practice as ongoing work, activity, process and experimentation that escape the control of a single artist. Art was no longer a question of a sole creator's subjectivity. This attitude has been a driving force behind Jeffrey Shaw's output; he has always collaborated with several programmers as well as with writers, composers, artists and art historians.[II]
As much as architecture, Shaw appropriated cinema to re-work its constituent principles. With his first installation, *Emergence of Continuous Forms* (1966), he inaugurates a series of "expanded cinema environments", expanded in space by projecting his film onto a series of semi-transparent screens set up over the length of the gallery, as well as by the intervention of visitors who could modify one screen by inflating it.
The question of the screen—be it three-dimensional and borderless or a viewing window—has been central to Shaw's thinking; he subjected it to a multitude of trials, steadily challenging its specific qualities: paper screens are torn, smoke screens dissipate etc. The image printed on the film strip is no longer the main center of interest, rather it is the uncertain status of the projected image, the image-in-formation. Film projection itself thus becomes a performance. Shaw declared, "all my works are a discourse, in one way or another, with the cinematic image, and with the possibility to violate the boundary of the cinematic frame—to allow the image to physically burst out towards the viewer, or allow the viewer to virtually enter the image."[III] Two "performance events" produced in the Netherlands in 1967, *Corpocinema* and *MovieMovie,* sum up his exploration of this notion of expansion. The "corpocinematic concept" also meant giving body to film, endowing it with volume, the third dimension that it lacked.
It was not the arrival of digital simulation and the resulting possibilities of specifically interactive modes that prompted Jeffrey Shaw to interrogate the relationship between spectator and artwork. His environments, events and installations, although the ones not employing computer technology, necessarily implied and defined procedures of involvement that went beyond simple levels of contemplation, identification or interpretation. What

clearly emerged then was the idea of the audience's responsibility, that its presence as well as a deliberate intervention was an integral part of the overall process.

A retrospective look raises one point of particular interest, namely the way in which Shaw immediately generated experimental fields and experiential "occasions" that involved the human body in playful, poetic actions, and that were, in a way, precursors to the perceptual situation now offered to travelers in virtual worlds. Impressions of immersion, floating and suspension were all effects engendered at the time by provocative concepts like Shaw's "soft responsive architecture." They belong to an initial group of experiments on the notion of environment as organic space.

Anticipating Augmented Reality

Well before the use of computers, *Viewpoint* (1975) provides a good example of Shaw's systematic investigation into the nature of virtual images and of the potential of installations that he began to explore for exposing representational processes.

This work powerfully inaugurated the total dependence between the image and its spectator, as in a mirror situation. An image was no longer given, could not pre-exist its actualization—here, its perception by a spectator. The point of view became the very site and condition of visibility. In several other pieces, such as *The Golden Calf*, *The Virtual Museum* or the series of *Place*, the construction of optical illusion was dependent on the perfect coincidence of the spot from where the photograph or video was shot, the source of the image projected (or displayed on a screen) and the position of the observer.

The radicalization of the process of virtualizing images inevitably led to the complete abolition of the screen. Thus right from the late 1970s Shaw began developing a "see-through virtual reality system" based on stereoscopic principles. His optical device (a forerunner of the head-mounted display HMD and BOOM) coupled a semi-transparent mirror with a computer screen onto which two wire-frame images of a cube were displayed. The spectator could observe the basic rotation of the cube projected onto the room, integrated with the other elements of the space. In this *Virtual Projection Installation* (1978) the original function of the "screen" had completely evolved toward a "viewing system" but it was henceforth in the hands of the spectator.

With *Points of View* (1983), the image became an environment to be activated and transformed. Once the spectator enters the scene, representation lost its autonomy and become a theater of operations.

Virtual Totality and the Panoramic Impulse

For the interactive sculpture *Inventer La Terre* (1986), Shaw developed another viewing device comprising a small video monitor and a periscope installed in a column with an opening in the middle through which the spectator looked at the exhibition space. By rotating the column, the viewer selected various sites to explore within a virtual panorama; floating travelogue images of the selected site then appeared superimposed onto the exhibition space. Tales, signs and symbols taken from ancient times and cultures on various continents, expressed the multiplicity of representations of the world, constituting what Shaw calls a kind of "museum within the museum." This work, meanwhile, crystallized a major notion within his own oeuvre, namely "virtual totality," based on the twin principles of the viewing window and the panorama.

Since *Diadrama* (1974) devised for a theatrical stage, Shaw developed his work on environmental immersive projection through various *dispositifs*, based on a sphere or a cylinder, exploiting the model of the panorama. *Place—A User's Manual* (1995) combines and reinterprets two key elements of the 19th-century panoramas: the circular screen and the central observation platform. The image is projected onto the screen from a small rotating platform where the visitor stands, providing a privileged point of observation. Since the image covers only one third of the screen, the observer can generate a total view of the panorama solely through time and a continuous sweep. The spectator's memory and capacity for anticipation are required to complete the environment. The dialectic between global and fragmented view, already present in several of Shaw's pieces, becomes all the more striking in *Place—A User's Manual* insofar as total vision is precisely what the panorama promises. But while the viewer gains the control of exploration and the feeling of power it confers, he has to deal with a constant negotiation between manipulation and contemplation.

Cultural Heritage

The television screen of *Revolution* (1990), which fully assumed the metaphor of a "window on the world", displayed the vast visual memory of revo-

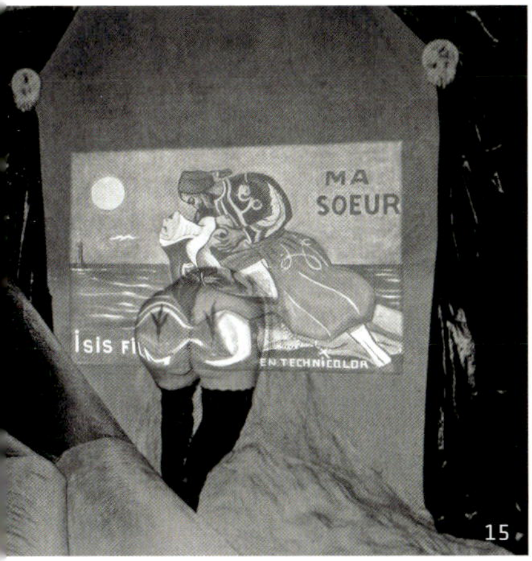

15

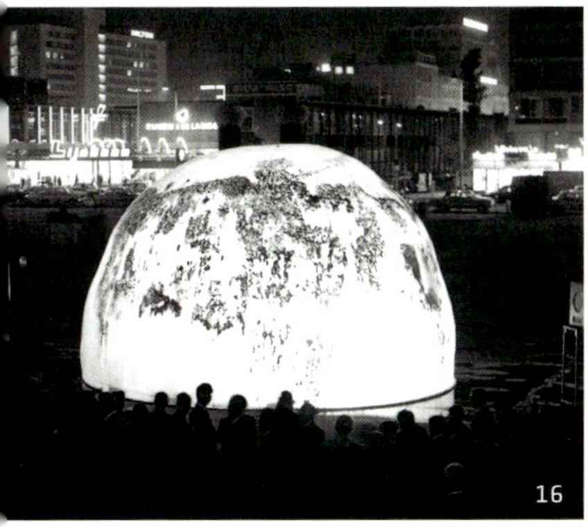

16

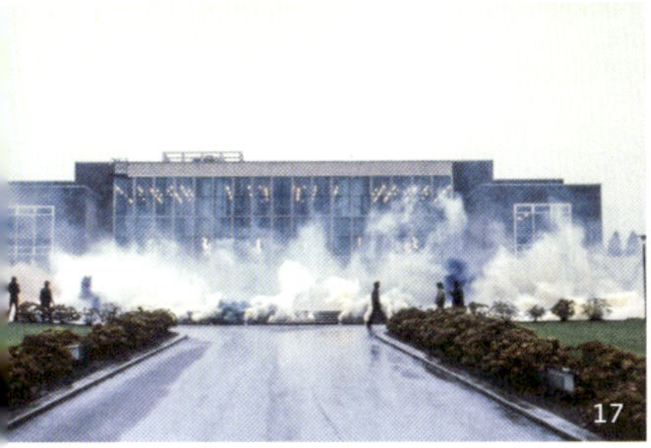

17

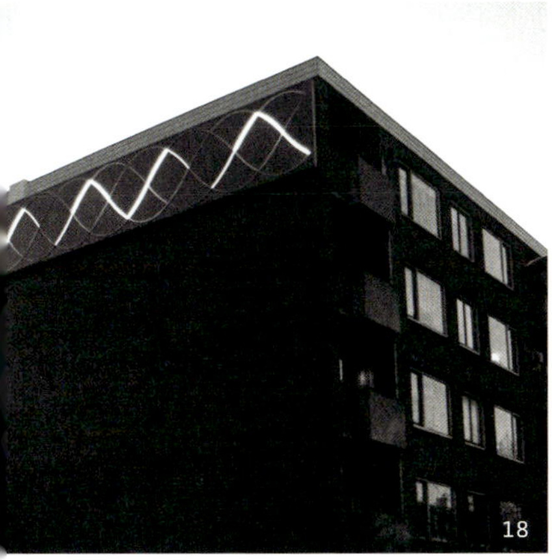

18

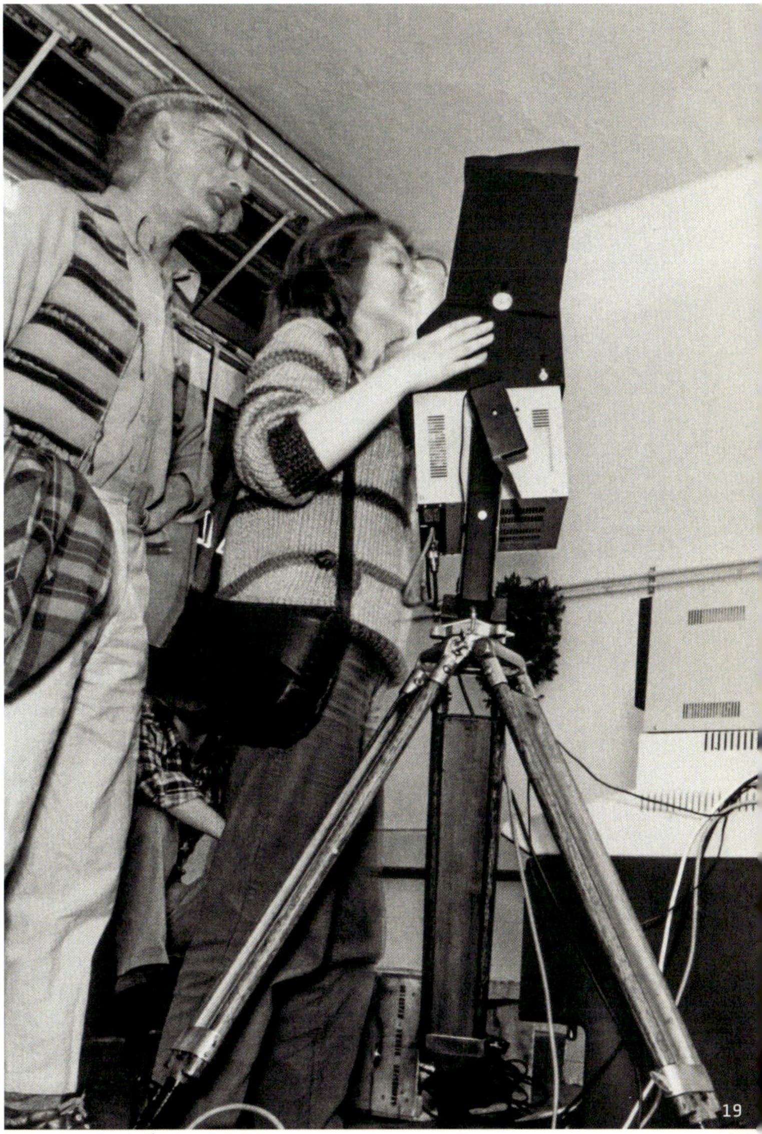

19

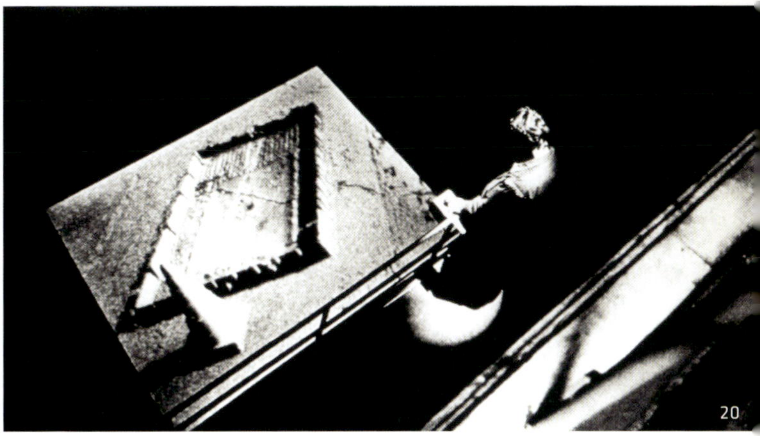

20

lutions since 1789. Visitors were invited to turn the wheel of history and access a series of images constituting humanity's collective memory.

In more recent works *Place–Hampi* (2006) or *Pure Land–Inside the Magao Grottoes at Dunhuang* (2012), both in collaboration with Sarah Kenderline, Shaw pursues research on World Heritage sites by exploiting these two similar environmental systems: the panorama as re-worked in the *Place* series, and the AVIE,[IV] a stereoscopic interactive visualization and audio environment. With a cylinder twice as high as *Place*, it is the most immersive system conceived by Shaw, to be explored with polarizing glasses, which eliminate the distance to the scene and isolate the viewer from the actual environment. The realism of the experience is reinforced by the 1:1 scale of high-resolution photography and the surrounding sound system.

Photography fixes the memory of an architectural grouping. However, the myth escapes any capture and its "documentation" can only be the actualization of an imaginary representation. By activating the high-resolution panoramas of the archeological site of Vijayanagara in Hampi, one comes across beings that are not photographic but animated representations. Digital characters inhabit these spaces as "living" gods and mythical figures from the *Ramayana*, bringing to life an ancestral collective memory, evoking contemporary beliefs about the creation of the site.

Pure Land is another "theater of memory" in which the visitor can explore one painting of the Caves of the Thousand Buddhas with a device simulating a torch light, or a magnifying glass to look into details. Here 3D animations are also called on, giving poetic and historical information such as ritual dances or musical instruments of the time.

With this undeniable way of preserving an exceptional heritage two main issues are at stake. First, a methodological bet: getting back closer to the project of the historical panoramas with advanced technology, it provides a persuasive surrogate kinesthetic experience of a site, based on immersion and narrative to stimulate the imagination and desire for discovery. Secondly, the multi-layered interpretation of the site history and of its various cultural elements, this "augmented memory" resulting partly from reconstitutions, question the "document" as a given trace speaking by itself. As Michel Foucault stress in *The Archaeology of Knowledge*, the primary task of history now in relation to the document is: "to work on it from within and to develop it [...] trying to define within the documentary material itself unities, totalities, series, relations."[V]

Discontinuity and Simultaneity in Narrative Structures

Different forms of narrative are at work in most of Shaw's installations: autonomous micro-narratives in *Viewpoints* which the spectator can access in no particular or predetermined order, or narrative lines to follow/read in the calculated streets and 3D architectural texts of *Legible City*. Parallel narrations respond to the multiplicity of points of view, often in the mode of a fragment, without links but with passages and with possible leaps from the one to the other. Meanings are largely produced by the spectator from a virtually discontinuous linearity. Beyond the text itself, it is the very conception of potential pathways—the manner in which the text/image "happens"—that enables a reader to develop his/her own branching rhizomes.

The "theater of signs" of the first Shaw works has given place to scenes performed by actors as in *Eavesdrop* (2004) or *The Infinite Line* (2014) with the poet Edwin Tumboo. Nevertheless a very singular narrative engagement between users and virtual characters is at stake in *UNMAKEABLELOVE* (2008), in collaboration with Sarah Kenderline. Computer-generated human bodies[VI] perform, with a paradoxically autonomous obsessive behavior in a prison-like space. Inspired by *The Lost Ones* by Samuel Beckett, there is no text but a complex *dispositif* based on a surveillance system of the other and of the self simultaneously. The visitors, outside a hexagonal construction, the Re-Actor, referring to the model of the Kaiser panorama, peer into this virtual cage with probing torch lights replacing the windows of the Panopticon and surveillance cameras.

What makes Shaw's approach so innovative does not so much lie in his exploration of some of the most advanced techniques available, as it does in his invention of interfaces. As the executor of transactions between the virtual and real, the interface is necessarily at the heart of his research. Inseparable from the whole *dispositif*, it is part of a whole web of metaphors. Shaw creates architectures/interfaces that respond both together to the conceptual requirements of a particular project, and to the perceptual conditions of these new works that the virtual environments are, repeatedly, inventing other ways of seeing and experiencing a work.

The text includes excerpts from Anne-Marie Duguet's essay published in: Duguet, A-M., Klotz, H., Weibel, P. (1997). *Jeffrey Shaw–A User's Manual: From Expanded Cinema to Virtual Reality*, Ostfildern: Hatje Cantz.

I John Latham, artist, taught film at Saint Martins School of Art, London, where Shaw studied in 1966.

II Collaborators include: software developers–Larry Abel, Gideon May, Adolf Mathias, Bernd Lintermann, Matt McGinity, Leith Chan; writers–Dirk Groeneveld, David Pledger; composers–Harry de Wit, Les Stuck, Paul Doornbusch, Torsten Belschner; artists–John Latham, Tjebbe van Tijen, Theo Botschuijver, Agnes Hegedues, Dennis Del Favero, Bernd Lintermann, Saburo Teshigawara, Peter Weibel, The Wooster Group, Jean Michel Bruyere, Sarah Kenderdine.

III Jeffrey Shaw in discussion with Ueno Toshiya: "We are Materialists, We Employ Science and Technology to Concretize the Virtual," in *Media Passage*, ed. InterCommunication Center, Tokyo, 1993, p. 53.

IV AVIE (Advanced Visualisation and Interaction Environment) collaboration Jeffrey Shaw, Dennis Del Favero, Matthew McGinity, Ardrian Hardjono, Volker Kuchelmeister. UNSW iCinema Centre, Sydney. AVIE is "a cylindrical silver projection screen 4 meters high and 10 meters in diameter. It has a set of 5 high-resolution digital video projectors that together project an active 3D 1000 x 8000 pixel stereoscopic picture over the entire 360-degree surface of the screen." (cf *www.epidemic.net)*

V Michel Foucault, *The Archaeology of Knowledge*, Pantheon Books, New York, 1972, p.6-7 Trans. A.M. Sheridan Smith

VI "The obsessive behaviours of these inhabitants have been motion captured, computationally animated and then rendered in real-time using a game engine and A-Life and algorithms." (Shaw and Kenderline's description)

Anne-Marie Duguet (FR) is Professor Emeritus at University of Paris1 Pantheon-Sorbonne. She is the author of books such as *Vidéo, la mémoire au poing* (1981), *Jean-Christophe Averty* (1991), *Déjouer l'image. Créations électroniques et numériques* (2002). Art critic and curator: Jean-Christophe Averty (Espace Electra, Paris 1991); Thierry Kuntzel. (Jeu de Paume, Paris, 1993); Smile Machines (Akademie der Kunst, Berlin, 2006); co-curator of Artifices Biennale, Saint-Denis, (1994, 1996). Director of the multimedia series *anarchive* (Muntadas, Snow, Kuntzel, Otth, Nakaya, Fujihata).

Photos

1 *The Legible City*, 1989-91, *Artec*, Nagoya, Japan Co-author: Dirk Groeneveld; Application software: Gideon May; Contruction: Huib Nelissen, Photo: Jeffrey Shaw

2 *T_Visionarium;* 2006, Scientia, UNSW, Sydney, Australia Co-authors: Dennis Del Favero, Neil Brown, Matthew McGinity, Peter Weibel; Application software: Matthew McGinity; Construction: Huib Nelissen; Photo: iCinema UNSW

3 *Waterwalk;* 1969, Sloterplas, Amsterdam, Netherlands Co-authors: Theo Botschuijver, Sean Wellesley-Miller (Eventstructure Research Group); Photo: Pieter Boersma

4 *conFiguring the CAVE;* 1997, NTT Intercommunication Centre, Tokyo, Japan; Co-authors: Ágnes Hegedûs, Bernd Lintermann, Les Stuck (sound); Application software: Bernd Lintermann; Photo: ICC Tokyo

5 *Cloud (of daytime sky at night)*; 1970, Stedelijk Museum, Amsterdam, Netherlands; Projection mapped air-structure; Co-authors: Theo Botschuijver, Sean Wellesley-Miller (Evenstructure Research Group) Photo: Pieter Boersma

6 *The Infinite Line;* 2014, Chronus Art Centre, Shanghai, China; Co-authors: Sarah Kenderdine, Edwin Nadason Thumboo; Application software: Leith Chan Photo: Jeffrey Shaw

7 *The Lamb Lies Down on Broadway;* 1975, Genesis World Tour; Projections, laser and inflatables performance Co-author: Theo Botschuiver; Photo: Evenstructure Research Group

8 *unmakeablelove;* 2008, *eArts/eLandscapes*, Shanghai, China, curated by Richard Castelli; Co-author: Sarah Kenderdine; Mixed reality installation; Application software: Scot Ashton, Yossi Landesman, Conor O'Kane; Construction: Huib Nelissen; Photo: Jeffrey Shaw

9 *The Virtual Museum;* 1991, *Das Belebte Bild*, Art Frankfurt, Frankfurt, Germany, curated by Peter Weibel Mixed reality installation; Application software: Gideon May; Construction: Huib Nelissen; Photo: Jeffrey Shaw

10 *The Golden Calf;* 1994, *Ars Electronica*, Linz, Austria Augmented reality installation; Photo: Jeffrey Shaw Application software: Gideon May

11 *Once upon a time ... we lived happily ever after;* 1979, Gallery Bedaux, Amsterdam, Netherlands; Javaphile performance; Photo: Javaphile Productions Co-authors: Carlyle Reedy, Robert Hahn, John Munsey

12 *Viewpoint;* 1975, 9th Biennale de Paris, Musee d'Art Moderne, Paris, France; Augmented reality installation; Co-author: Theo Botschuijver; Photo: Eventstructure Research Group

13 *Place - Hampi;* 2006, *Lille 3000*, Lille, France, produced and curated by Richard Castelli; Co-authors: Sarah Kenderdine, Paul Doornbusch (sound), John Gollings (photography), Dr. L. Subramaniam (music) Application software: Adolf Mathias; Construction: Huib Nelissen; Photo: Sarah Kenderdine, Jeffrey Shaw

14 *Inventer la Terre;* 1986, Cité des Sciences et de l´Industrie, La Villette, Paris, France; Augmented reality installation; Co-author: Walter Maioli (sound); Photo: Jeffrey Shaw

15 *Disillusionary Hommage to Clovis Trouille;* 1966, Kasteelhoeve Beek En Donk, Netherlands; Expanded cinema installation; Co-author: Tjebbe van Tijen; Photo: Pieter Boersma

16 *Corpocinema;* 1967, *Sigma Projects*, Amsterdam, Rotterdam, Netherlands; Expanded cinema performance; Co-authors: Theo Botschuijver, Sean Wellesley-Miller, Tjebbe van Tijen

17 *Smokescreen;* 1969, Swansea Art Festival, University of Swansea, UK; Pyrotechnic performance; Co-author: Theo Botschuiver; Photo: Eventstructure Research Group

18 *Neon Waves;* 1979, Koopvardersplantsoen, Amsterdam, Netherlands; Interactive neon installation; Co-author: Theo Botschuijver; Photo: Eventstructure Research Group

19 *Virtual Sculpture;* 1981, Melkweg, Amsterdam, Netherlands; Augmented reality installation; Co-author: Theo Botschuijver; Application software: Larry Abel Photo: Pieter Boersma

20 *The Narrative Landscape;* 1985, Aorta, Amsterdam, Netherlands; Co-author: Dirk Groeneveld; Application software: Larry Abel; Photo: Jeffrey Shaw

u19–CREATE YOUR

WORLD

Inside & Between u19

Sirikit Amann, Conny Lee, Elisabeth Menasse-Wiesbauer, Peter Schernhuber, Erwin Wagenhofer

The Prix Ars Electronica's u19–CREATE YOUR WORLD category has been honoring excellent projects by young people in Austria annually since 1998. The u19 jury awards a Golden Nica grand prize, two Awards of Distinction, two Merchandise Prizes in the u10 and u14 sub-categories, and ten Honorary Mentions. In a preliminary round of judging, all the entries for prize consideration are divided up among the five jurors so that, in an initial viewing, each one can get a feel for the range and quality of the works. Then, at the jury sessions on site in the Ars Electronica Center, all the projects are discussed individually over the course of three-day deliberations until the list of outstanding candidates is gradually narrowed down to the final fifteen. These decisions are made on the basis of various criteria. How original or innovative is the project? Is the entrant's work characterized by independence and self-determination? Is the theme socio-politically relevant, does it express the zeitgeist, or make a statement about youth culture? To what extent is the work consistent with the title of the u19–CREATE YOUR WORLD category?

After all, "create your world" isn't just a slogan; it's actually the assignment in u19. Thus, we're calling upon young people to do nothing less than to create a world. But, then again, that's not exactly the case either: not just a world; their world. We want to single out for recognition youngsters who reflect on a world that reflects them—their wishes, their problems, their ideals and visions, and their humor. How is it possible to comply with the conditions of such a broadly defined assignment using the ways and means available? Needless to say, art always offers lots of options when it comes to creating worlds, giving them a makeover or a reinterpretation. A camera or a computer will do, or even a brush and paint if you like. And you can just as easily execute what you're after with a video installation or an actionist performance. Music, text, objects of stone, wood, plastic ... surely, it's unnecessary here to list all the channels art can flow through.

This year animation was the means of choice to create new worlds. The number of stop-motion films, video collages and other types of animated motion pictures submitted was especially high. But the quantity isn't the only thing that deserves mention; many of them were of extraordinary quality, which explains why six of the fifteen prizewinners are animation projects, including the recipient of the Golden Nica and both the u10 and u14 merchandise prizes. Working successfully in this medium calls for not only an artistic vision but also technical implementation skills. The projects singled out for honors impressed us for a variety of reasons—some with their imaginative design, others with touching or urgent content, and still others with creative use of the technical means at hand. So youngsters can take an artistic approach to creating their world; they can, of course, go about it technically too. After all, what's more characteristic of everyday life nowadays, not only of young people but of society as a whole, than technology? Communication, mobility, the environment, shopping, leisure—there's no sphere of life that isn't in the process of being reshaped by machines and thus can also be redesigned using technical means. And, once again this year that's precisely the mission that many u19 entrants have volunteered for. Young inventors thus take advantage of the latest high-tech devices, above all the possibilities that affordable microcontrollers and open-source technology open up. But there are also youngsters who aren't satisfied with what's available; they'd rather write their own software, build unprecedented equipment and find solutions to problems that others have simply learned to live with until now.

The subject of a strikingly large number of submissions was how human beings deal with communications and how we are increasingly losing the art of conversing with others because we spend so much time staring at our smart devices as if hypnotized. Many videos deal with and criticize this sorry state of affairs. Ecological matters like energy, sustainability and genetic engineering are on the minds of many youngsters who took part in u19 this year. The fact that the next generation's consciousness has been raised is certainly encouraging, but it also shows how concerned young people in Austria are about current facts and circumstances, a situation for which they are not to blame. They would have every right to be enraged or reproachful, but instead of recriminations they want to tackle this problem and solve it. They aim to enlighten, mobilize and improve, and this, once again, truly impressed the jury.

The diversity of the submissions, the topics they deal with and the genres that creators of all ages work in gave the jurors insights into how young people in Austria perceive their world right now. The submissions reflect the coming generation.

As previously mentioned, animation and film are the preferred means of expression for many; for a few, it's technical innovation. What, however, found favor among relatively few participants this year were, for example, photography and audio (like radio plays and broadcasts). Video games were few and far between, which is pretty puzzling considering all the talented young game developers out there. What the jury would also like to see more of in coming years are transdisciplinary works like installations and actionism in public places. And we once again encourage future participants to submit objects that they have made themselves by hand, such as sculptures, prototypes and models.

And we cannot omit praise for the many teachers in Austria whose support for their students in the context of Prix Ars Electronica goes far beyond the call of duty. In the final analysis, though, what counts for the u19 jury is what young people want to get across to us. That's the essence of selecting, from among all these important, interesting and relevant submissions, the fifteen recipients of an Honorary Mention, Award of Distinction, Merchandise Prize and a Golden Nica. This process is difficult, and the jurors, once again this year, took it seriously. After long deliberations we chose the following projects.

Golden Nica

Inside & Between · Gabriel Radwan

"A short film by Gabriel Radwan" is what it says in the opening credits of *Inside & Between.* Three minutes later, the viewer is left astounded by the entire universe the filmmaker has evoked in this animated work. Gabriel Radwan creates compressed images that speak volumes, poetry in its purest form. His brilliant use of motion pictures and sounds is both playful and sophisticated. His film derives its emotional force not from the narrative elements on the surface but rather from what's inside and between them.

Awards of Distinction

Are you worth it? · Sonja Aberl

This skillfully made montage of TV commercials and sequences that the filmmaker shot herself addresses the crises a girl has to deal with while going through puberty—self-doubt, thoughts of suicide, and a friendship that isn't one after all. 19-year-old Sonja Aberl's multifaceted film shows the extent of the pressure as well as the sense of fascination that are the outgrowths of omnipresent ideals of beauty. We were particularly impressed by this film's authenticity and emotional strength.

β-Book · Laurenz Birnbaum, Luca Eichler

β-Book is an eBook for the blind. These two young men developed both the software and the hardware themselves. Their project not only attests to their prodigious technical skills and creativity, it also makes a prototype for an extremely socially useful tool available, one that provides blind people with access to eBooks. Deserving of prominent mention is the fact that the duo completed this project independently, with no help from teachers or parents. This is a superb example of the application of new technologies in the service of barrier-free living, and of laudable commitment on behalf of a good cause.

u14 – Merchandise Prize

Waste or Treasure · Leonhard Trinkl

With its laid-back pace and eye-catching aesthetic, this animated work touches the viewer's soul. That's what makes it so unique. Not only does the plot have all necessary functional elements, but what also contributes to making it work so well are the many details (all of which you don't notice until you've seen this animated film a few times). And then there's the cast of characters and their exquisite wardrobe. And the set—which isn't just a space; it really gives the impression of being a place where real people live. The stills that the filmmaker submitted with his entry show how the set was constructed, and the documentation lays out the story behind the production. This work is a treasure upon which we are delighted to bestow the u14 Merchandise Prize.

u10 – Merchandise Prize

Space Pi Si · Class 3b, Zwi Perez Chajes School

Imagine that you've laid waste to a planet by squandering its resources and now you're ready to move on to the next one—one more time, in the spirit of subjecting everything to humankind's will. But upon arrival you encounter a native of the new planet who refuses to admit you, because he won't permit the destruction of his environment, and who holds a mirror up in front of you. These elementary school pupils produced a charming, imaginative screenplay. They drew and crafted objects to create a set that's coherent and bespeaks good cooperation among classmates. Even though the elements were produced by individuals, the sum total is the output of a crew. On the whole, that won us over and garnered them the u10 Merchandise Prize.

Honorary Mentions

Animatronic Arm · Gernot Keuschnig, Paul von Ahsen, Nino Wegleitner, Lukas Ziegelbauer

Many occupations entail handling dangerous machines or chemicals on a daily basis. This project's mission is to see to it that laborers no longer have to put their hands or their health at risk to do jobs like these. They can also be done by an animatronic arm operated by motion control via a glove and a Kinect camera. The developers have achieved an almost delay-free transmission of the operator's hand movements to the robotic arm, which can reduce job-related risks in many factories and other workplaces. The u19 jury wants to support this achievement in the form of an Honorary Mention.

ENERKEY—Wer hat den Schlüssel zur Energiewende? · Lukas Fankhauser, Fabio Gschweidl, Nicola Stampfer, Johannes Wallner

"There is nothing more powerful than an idea whose time has come." This quote from Mark Twain makes an appearance somewhere in the middle of *ENERKEY*, a 30-minute film produced to promote a world that's new, different and better. From start to finish, we feel the filmmakers' commitment to this cause. And they certainly do succeed in emboldening us to finally take the first step and to quit foisting off responsibility on others.
We see a plaque that reads "The future starts today" and historic footage of the groundbreaking ceremony for the Zwentendorf nuclear power plant, which, by the way, is finally delivering electricity today, though its from photovoltaic panels.

fruub · Moritz Böswirth, Kilian Hanappi, Marcel Kulhanek, Georg Tertsch, Marcus Wagner, Sebastian Weber

Fruub is an installation that deals with genetically modified foodstuffs. The aim of those who propagate them is to better appeal to consumers without regard to consequences for the health of human beings or the ecosystem. The installation presents a fictitious fruit that has been genetically manipulated to make it cube-shaped and thereby easier to ship and store. The installation itself consists of a background made up of three screens, in front of which are rotating cubes and a three-dimensional model of a head, on which the presentation is displayed by projection mapping. This work takes a critical approach to a highly controversial subject, does so on a high technical level, and not without an occasional wink of the eye.

Geschwüre der Wissenschaft
David Nimmervoll, Michael Traxler

In *Abscesses of Science* two young game developers have applied their creative talents to the point & click adventure genre and developed a game that need not shy away from comparison to what the industry's big boys are turning out. Humorous and quirky, this is a pastime for players who like pondering puzzles and enjoy a good laugh. Earth has stopped rotating on its axis, and we're playing the scientists who can save the world—if we can only manage not to lock ourselves out of the lab. As the game continues, our objective is to reopen the locked door and get back inside. Particularly impressive are the game's sets and protagonists, which the developers themselves drew using the Paint program. For the jurors, it was delight at first sight, but the proof of the pudding was in the playing, which is what ultimately opened the door to an Honorary Mention.

Loopex–Konstruktion eines Filament Extruders
Alexander Brenner, Nicolas Groß, Matthias Thym
Here the tried-and-tested technique of DIY is applied to the latest technical advances. How to use what's available and give old stuff a new lease on life is the main matter at hand for this crew of up-and-coming engineers. Their Loopex melts down granulate derived from recycled PET bottles and extrudes the filament that is the raw material for 3D printers. Their technically savvy invention packs industrial design into a slick-looking shell.

Mach was Handfestes · Katja Haller, Hannah Hradec, Ivan Lastric, Ahmed Parmaksiz, Bogdan Vieru
In the TV commercial *Make Something Tangible* for learning a craft, young people show how cool it is to receive well-grounded practical training. Certain clichés are turned round and poked fun at in a very charming way. The most excellent feature of this film is that its dialog is the language of young people and the "acting style" of the cast is totally naturalistic. It's refreshing, witty and well-made—and really convinces you to sign up for an apprenticeship! The crew is certainly justifiably proud of this film.

Screenrunner · Class 8c, BORG Bad Leonfelden
Screenrunner shows how you can use a cell-phone's touchscreen both as a video display as well as an object to tell a story in a very witty and original way. The filmmakers have come up with quite a playful approach to the medium of animated film and developed a very refreshing style out of it. *Screenrunner* doesn't require editing or dialog to keep its dramatic arc going strong to the very end.

Unknown Forms of Face · Dominik Koller
It's a fallacy to assume that facial recognition software can really recognize people. Instead, what it does is translate human beings into mathematical terms—that is, physiognomy as a numbers game, the face as a collage of paler and darker dots, as an arrangement of light, shadow and distance. Comparing individual digitized portraits with one another is actually what makes this so-called recognition possible. Technically speaking, this is nothing more than a search for sets of mathematical values with an extremely high degree of correspondence. Proceeding on the basis of these considerations, Dominik Koller programmed an algorithm that, amid all the optically chaotic, hectic digital noise, seeks faces and does indeed find some. Or at least it believes it does—for instance, the dark spots that are recognized as eyes by *Unknown Forms of Face*. Koller's project can be understood as a tale about life in the Digital Age and, at the same time, read as a commentary on the information-based society and pervasive surveillance in it.

Wenn uns der Zwerghamster zu Unrecht beschuldigt · Sebastiano Develli, Elias Gäbler, Lorenz Krischan, Julia Moser, Nikolaus Schoner, Eva-Maria Sprenger, Moritz Stark
The animated film *If the dwarf hamster wrongfully accuses us* was produced in a media workshop by 13-16-year-olds under the guidance of filmmaker Daniel Pöhacker and media artist Manfred Raggl. As its subject it takes the real-life habitats of these young people (their room, their family's apartment or house) and out of them creates a shared virtual space. This is where these young people's animated avatars meet and engage in interpersonal communication—about themselves, their spatial surroundings, the configuration of their coexistence, and their various needs. The animation's charm and appeal are the result of a shared visual language enunciated in rough drawings and the humorous depiction of the content.

Y-Rail Security · Maximilian Krexner, Thomas Lanik, Philipp Schrittwieser, Matthias Wotke
The history of modern technology and culture is mirrored by the history of the railroad. *Y-Rail Security* addresses a particular detail of this story—the points—and takes it to the next conceptual level. No longer do the tracks and points determine the direction of traffic flows; the rolling stock decides for itself. A vehicle using this system has least two guide rollers, each enclosing three-quarters of the diameter of a round rail. If the section of track divides, then the guidance system rotates by 90° and the vehicle veers off in the correct direction—a clever trick that the young inventors hope will yield benefits in the form of easier maintenance. An initial prototype underscores this project's feasibility.

Inside & Between

Gabriel Radwan

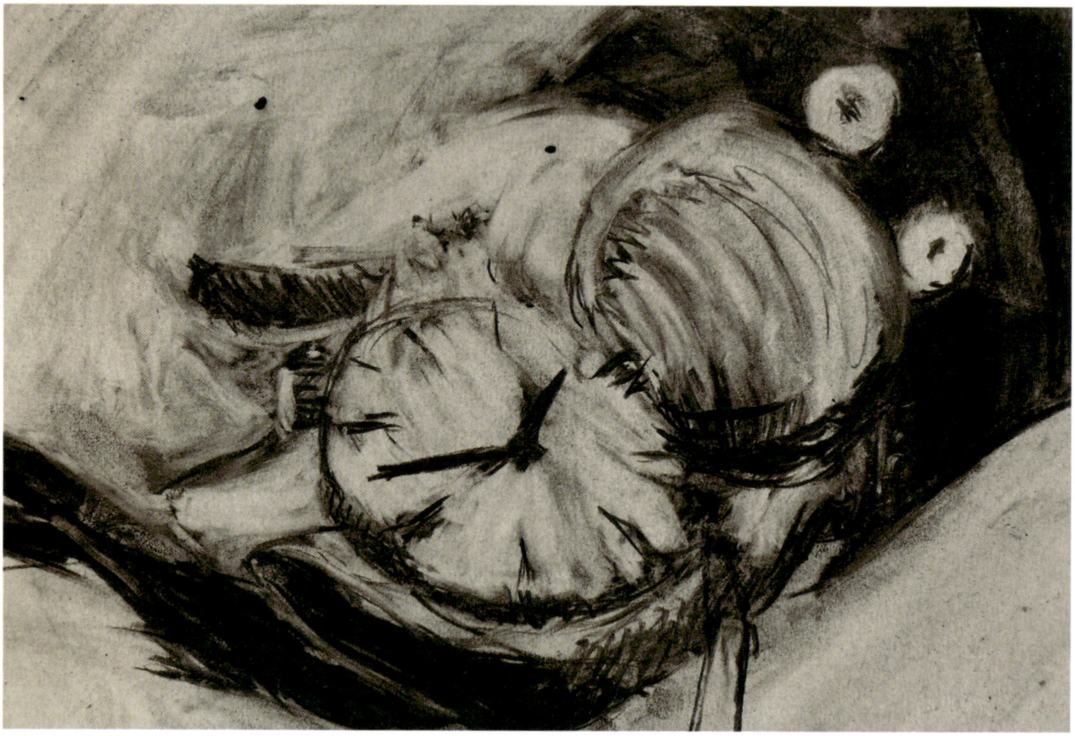

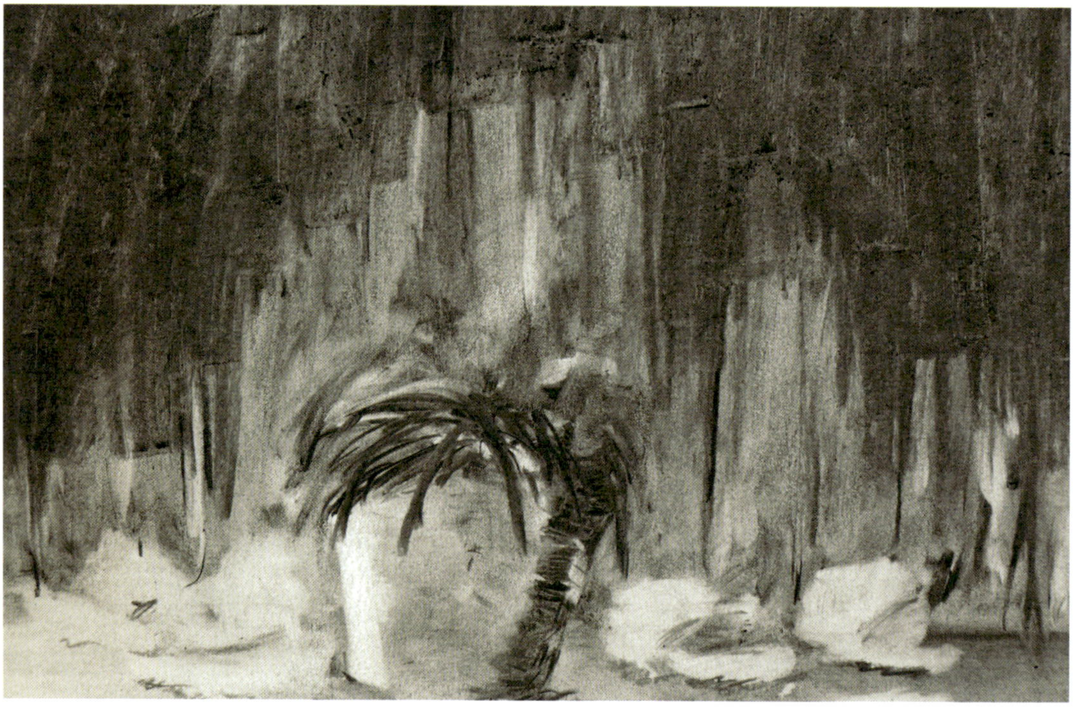

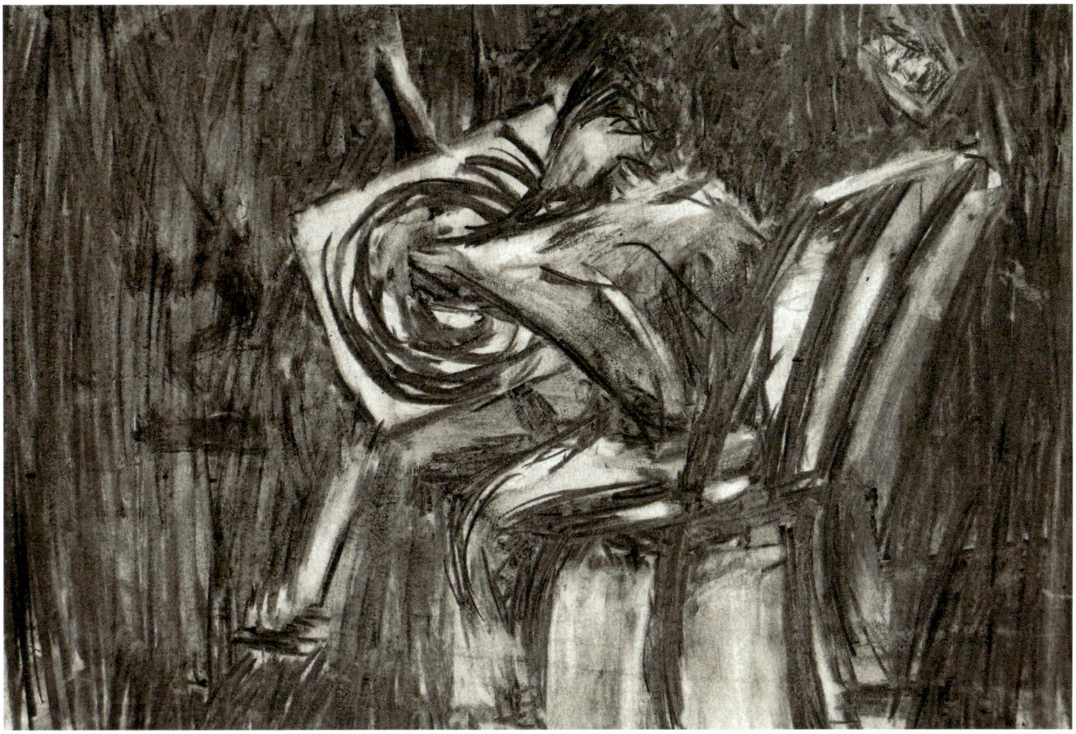

Now pay close attention: My film isn't a copy! It has certain similarities to works by William Kentridge, I freely admit that. He's shown many times that the combination of painting/drawing and film can produce a very special effect. Due to my love of motion pictures and the fact that I'm pretty good with charcoal pencils, I got the idea of shooting a stop-motion film. You have a lot of different possibilities when you have total control on paper over everything that's supposed to happen. To produce the images, I made drawings on sheets of paper and then used an eraser to create the lighting effects. After each modification that was to appear on screen, I took a photograph with a camera mounted on a tripod. But in contrast to Kentridge, the point of my work isn't to draw attention to social problems. Instead, it's an attempt to stimulate the imagination that's in all of us, and to get across my thought processes.

In a certain sense, my film's content didn't just materialize out of the blue. The idea for the plot came from (music and) lyrics by Roger Waters. As in the album *The Wall,* this is about a protagonist who gets lost in a self-created world in which he cuts himself off from the world outside. But in my film the artist isn't surrounded by a wall, he's shut up in the same room where everything started. So how did this come about? He just incessantly worked on painting his picture until I guess he just forgot about everything else—even time, which simply took leave of him. Who wouldn't have done the same?

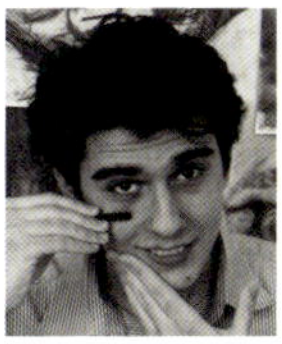

Gabriel Radwan, I was born and raised in Vienna, but most of what I learned came later. At the age of twelve, I moved to St. Georgen am Ybbsfelde in Lower Austria and attended a secondary school in Blindenmarkt with a strong music program. Music has always been an important part of my life, and maybe that comes across in my work. The same goes for art in general and the school I've attended—they've left their mark on me over the past five years.

Are you worth it?

Sonja Aberl

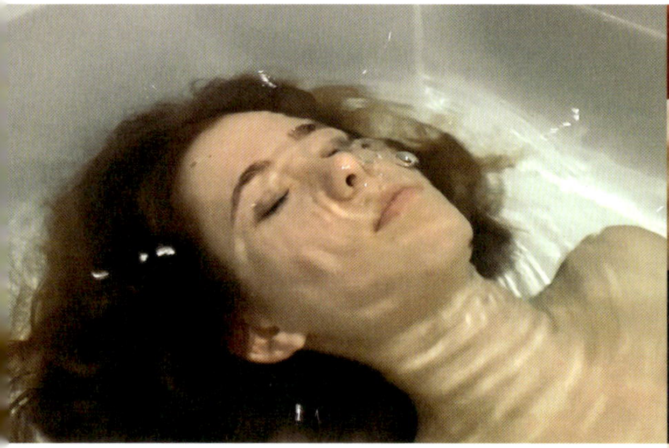

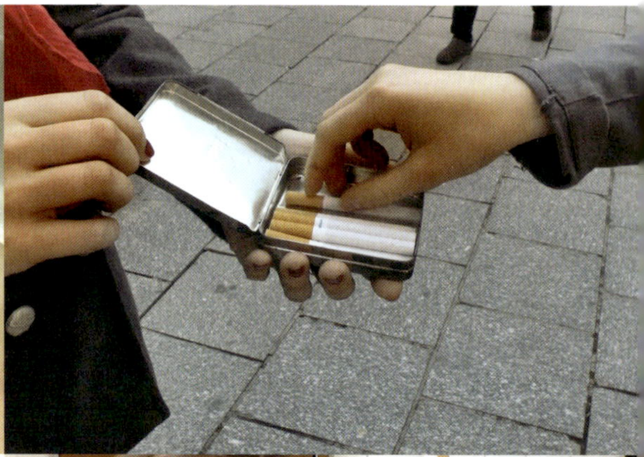

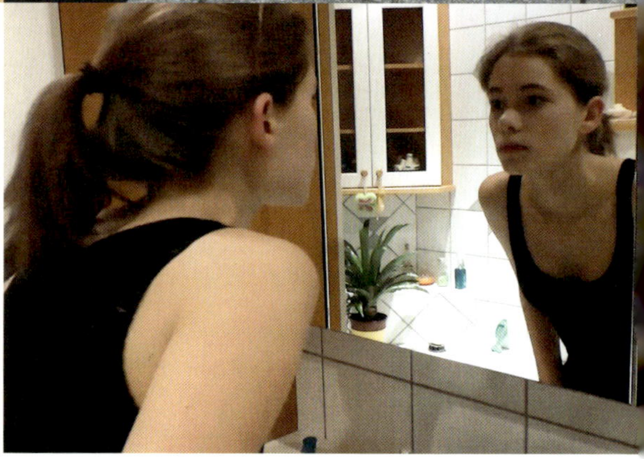

This world of ours in which advertising increasingly sets the tone puts many young people in particular under such pressure that it threatens to really mess them up. Lately the ad industry has succeeded in becoming such an essential part of everyday life that we don't even notice how much we're being manipulated on a daily basis anymore. This regrettable development is what I wanted to address in my project. *Are you worth it?* is about a young girl who's trying to get her bearings in the world and how, in doing so, she's influenced by the media and society. The protagonist is insecure and feels inadequate, so she tries to imitate her girlfriend and what she sees in advertising. She orients herself on trends and commercials for cosmetics. She turns into a dedicated follower of fashion, but it gets to be too much for her. My protagonist—I named her M.—stands for the young generation and thus all teenagers who seem so easy to manipulate. M. looks up to the models she sees in commercials and magazine ads and strives to be as beautiful as they are. At the same time she feels like she's overwhelmed by the omnipresence of the media, and she's unable to cope with that.

Between the scenes that I shot myself, I edited several sequences from commercials into my video to create a striking contrast between reality and advertising. The models in the ads seem strong and self-confident, looking at the viewers in a way that invites them to follow suit. The soundtrack of the video is made up exclusively of music used in commercials or corporate promotional videos.

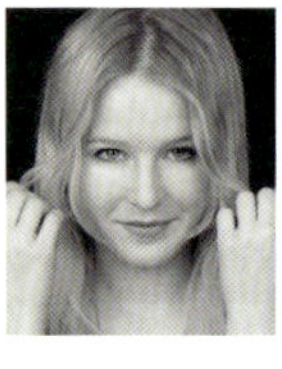

Sonja Aberl is a nineteen-year-old student at the HBLA—High School for Artistic Design—in Linz. She likes to work in the medium of video, taking predominantly critical looks at topical issues such as the media's influence on how people represent themselves and the ideals of beauty prevalent in this day and age.

β-Book

Laurenz Birnbaum, Luca Eichler

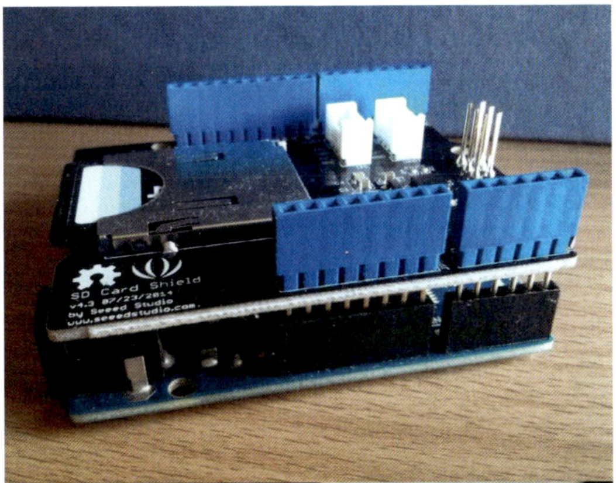

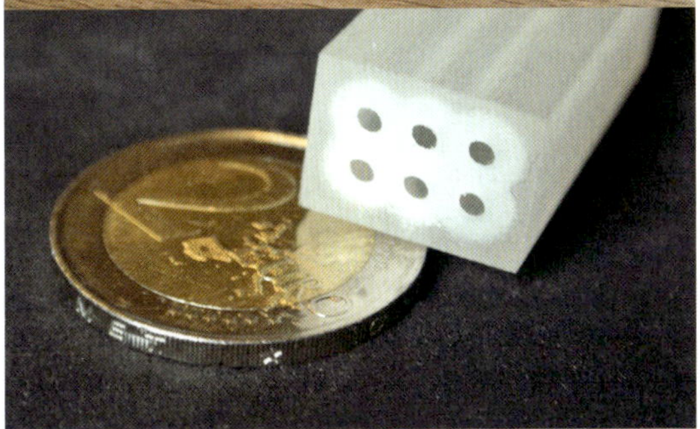

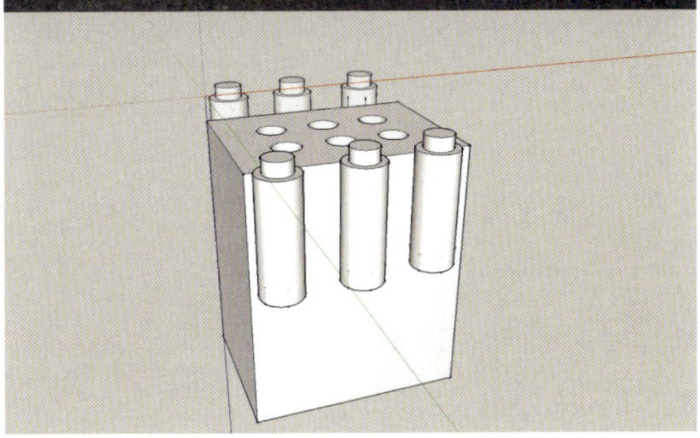

An eBook for the blind—it sounds weird but, since so few books are published in Braille, it can provide people who can't see with access to the world's literature in its entirety. The *β-Book* makes the entire book market available to the blind. Plus, an "eBook for the blind" has tremendous commercial potential, since consumer electronics for people with severely impaired vision is a pretty much nonexistent sector at present. Braille is a tactile writing system for the blind. Braille characters consist of tiny palpable bumps or raised dots. The number and arrangement of these dots distinguish one character from another. The *β-Book* is made up of two parts: a control console and a head. The head, a device about the size of an eraser, is fastened around the reader's index finger. It contains electromagnets that enable it to display Braille characters letter by letter. Its precision mechanism is the output of a 3D printer. A cable connects the head to the control console containing a rechargeable battery and the circuit board with a data storage unit onto which eBooks can be saved. The circuit board also controls the head's electromagnets.

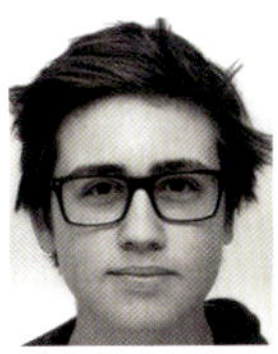

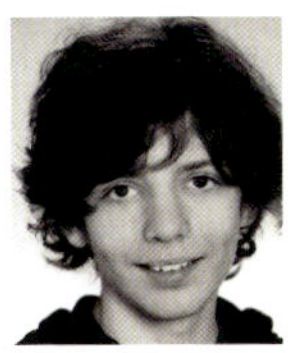

Laurenz Birnbaum is a fifteen-year-old high school student in Innsbruck. He came up with the *β-Book* idea in his capacity as student project group leader. Applying his passion for tinkering and invention, he worked out the basic plan for the project that later resulted in the current prototype. He assembled the hardware substructure, and also created the concept and design of the head. **Luca Eichler** is Laurenz's sixteen-year-old classmate. A programming enthusiast, he was invited by Laurenz to contribute the software to the *β-Book* project and offer advice on platform selection and hardware compatibility. Since he was already familiar with the Arduino platform and programming in Java, he suggested that Laurenz use that platform.

Space Pi Si

Class 3b, Zwi Perez Chajes School

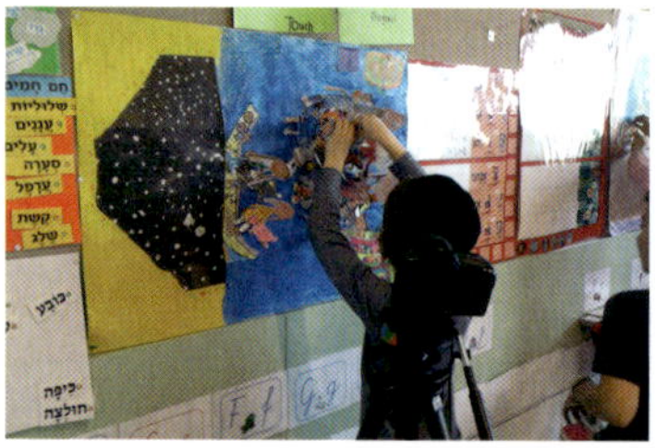
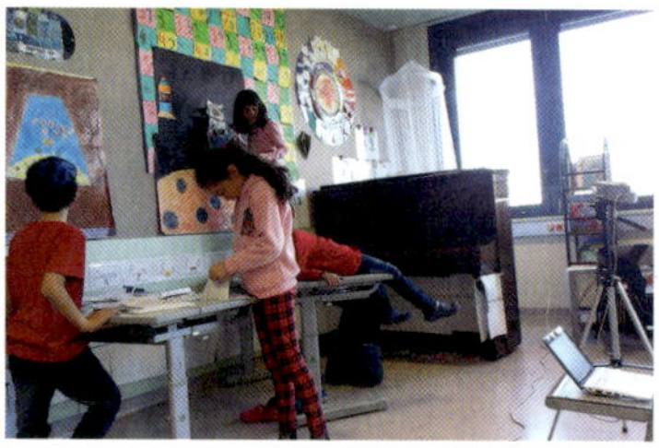
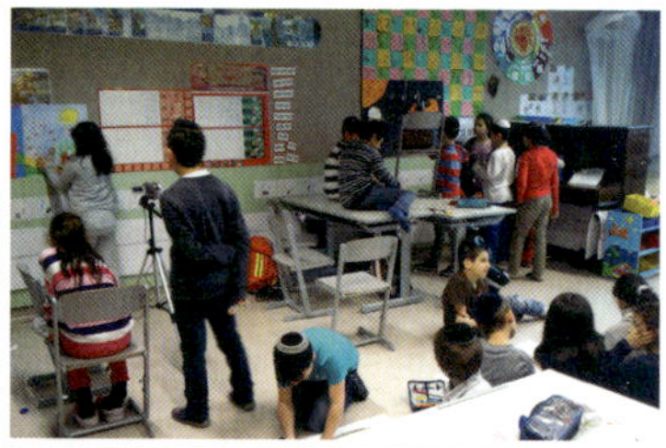
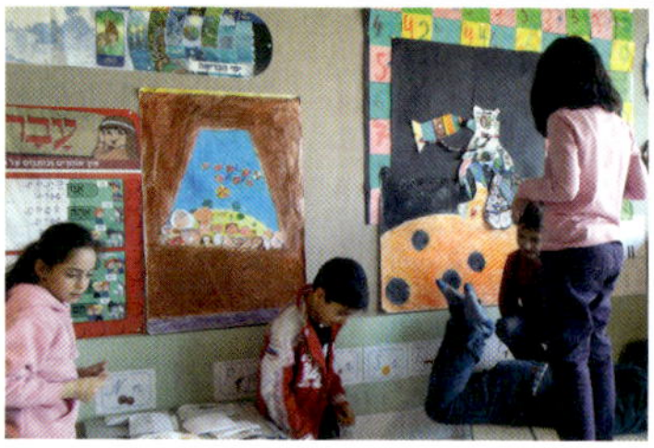
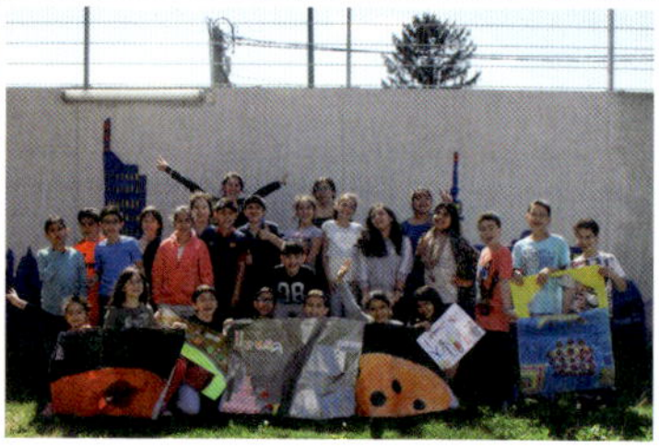
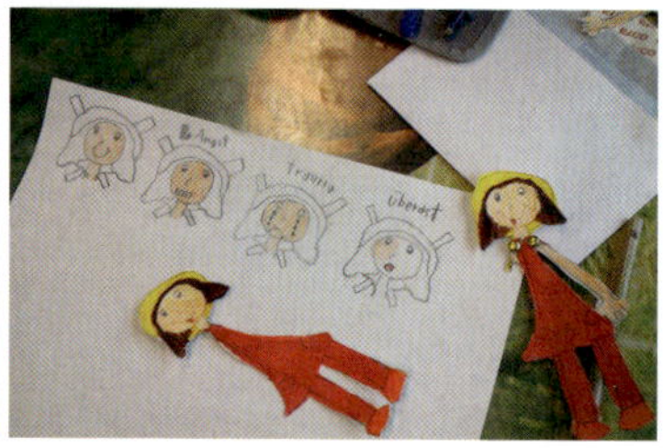

Class 3b focused on working with digital media last year. At first, we couldn't agree on a theme that we were all really satisfied with, but then, following extensive discussions, we came up with something everybody was excited about: outer space, the final frontier! We did a lot of research, asked puzzling questions, but many things nevertheless remained unexplained. That's why we decided to take things into our own hands: embark on an adventurous journey and check out outer space up-close-and-personal on our own terms. The first thing we needed was an exciting narrative to be played out over the course of our mission. So a few gifted authors got busy gathering ideas for our space trip and writing them up as a plot. Once we had recited, discussed, remixed and rewritten the various elements, we could finally take our patchwork plot and create a storyboard we could then use for orientation.

The next step was to make all the preparations to shoot the film. We did a lot of arts and crafts activities: painting, cutting and pasting, assembling, designing figures and making props. After many hours of work, we were ready to roll. It was Day 1 on the set. With computers, cameras and a special freeware program (Monkey Jam), we snapped our first pictures. Pictures? For a film? That's right, because to produce our film, we used a special technique called stop-motion. The object is moved in small increments between each picture, which creates the illusion of fluid movement when the series of spliced-together shots is played as a continuous sequence. The more pictures you take, the more fluid the scene appears to the viewers. Following a year of hard work in which we had to reshoot several scenes, make a lot of sound recordings, and compose the music and lyrics of a song for our soundtrack, on the final day of school we not only received our report cards, we also attended the premiere of our production. And I'll tell you this—it's amazing how much work, teamwork, differences of opinion, reconciliations, ideas and lots more stuff goes into such a short little film!

https://www.youtube.com/watch?v=kluouxrzQhw

The 22 pupils in **Class 3b** of the Zwi Perez Chajes School include thirteen bright boys and nine creative girls who used cameras and computers to give free rein to their imagination for a whole year: Jakov Ascherov, Noam Baybatchaev, Dana Cohen, Orel Dorel, Eden Fisher, David Hen, David Izhakow, Ben Katz, Sarah-Lee Kuyenov, Salomom Loss, Elinor Malaev, Lian Mamat, Ilan Minasian, Sean Morris, Benjamin Motaev, Efraim Natanov, Coral Sabag, Daniel Taviv, Livia Tultschinsky, Fabian Wurm, Naomi Yossef and Ashley Zvaniashvili.

Waste or Treasure

Leonhard Trinkl

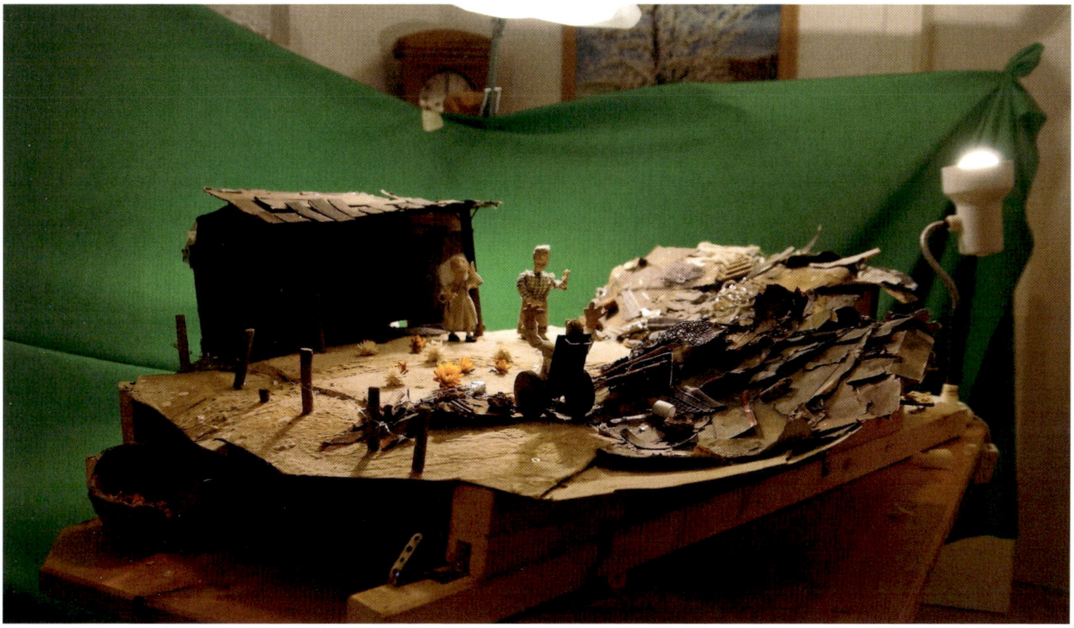

The new world that I've attempted to create cinematically is one in which people live amidst garbage. The slums they inhabit resemble South American *favelas*. They're built and furnished out of garbage, which means this new world is one we're already all too familiar with. Values such as helpfulness and modesty are supposed to be embodied by three protagonists. Life in the trash heap and a physical injury sustained by one of the protagonists—both perceived as disadvantages—are turned into positive advantages and thus made bearable by goal-oriented actions. And the great opportunities that this trashed landscape makes available aren't wasted. Garbage gets people going! The plasticine action figures have a wire endoskeleton so they can be conveniently manipulated. Cardboard and water-colors were my materials of choice in implementing my design concept. I also used chroma key compositing. The photos were taken with a cell-phone camera and a compact camera, and I finally used Pinnacle Studio 16 to put them together. I got interested in animated filmmaking while I was taking the stop-motion course taught by Prof. Derflinger at the high school I attend in Lambach.

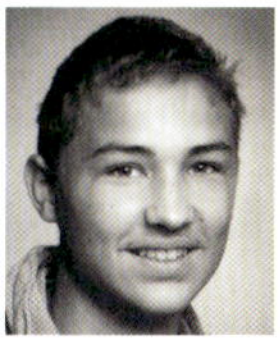

Leonhard Trinkl was born in 2000 in Wels and now lives in Gunskirchen, Upper Austria. He attended elementary school in Gunskirchen 2006–10; since 2010, he has been a student at the college preparatory school of the Benedictine Monastery in Lambach.

Animatronic Arm

Gernot Keuschnig, Paul von Ahsen, Nino Wegleitner, Lukas Ziegelbauer

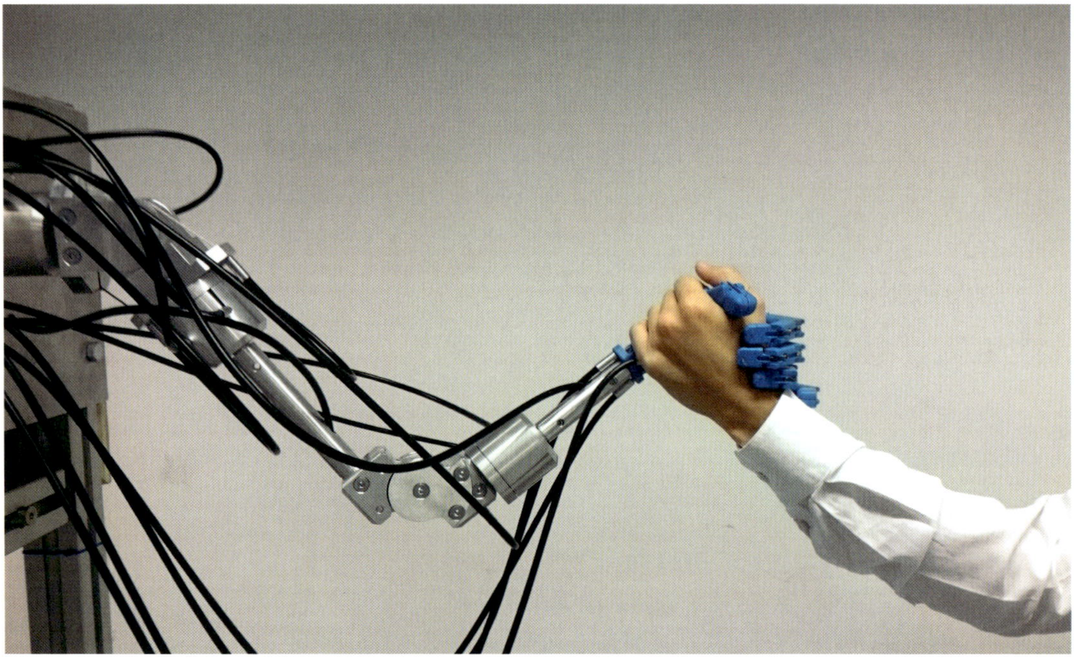

Over 100,000 people are injured at work in Austria every year. These accidents can not only result in dreadful suffering and financial losses for the victims personally, they also entail considerable costs for the economy and the public sector. The *Animatronic Arm* is a response to precisely this challenge. It's a mechanical arm that performs actions that would otherwise be the job of a human worker, who is now spared the need to enter a danger zone and whose risk of injury is thus minimized. Thanks to intuitive control of the arm via the 3D camera and an individually adjustable wired glove (data glove), the arm can be operated by anyone; no prior training or technical knowledge is required. The system registers motion data and sends it via wireless network to the mechanical arm, which mimics the operator's motions with minimal delay. The arm is powered by a hydraulic drive unit and moved by a cylinder and pulleys. Situating the drive components externally to the arm itself, the installation of specially constructed aluminum joints and the use of a mechanical hand produced by a 3D printer made it possible to keep the weight of the arm down and, in turn, achieve a quick reaction time and agility.

http://www.animatronica.at

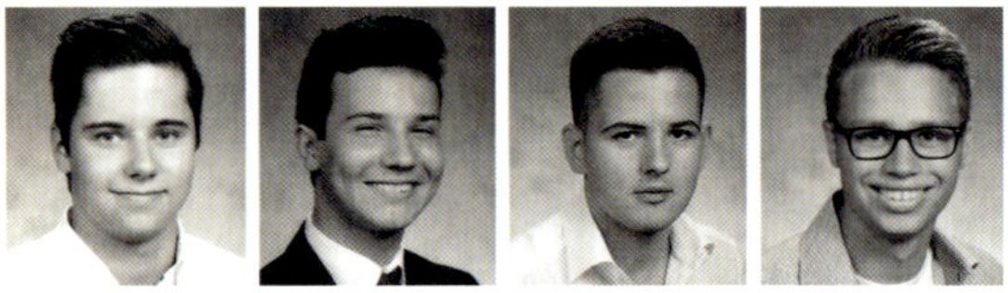

Gernot Keuschnig, Paul von Ahsen, Nino Wegleitner, Lukas Ziegelbauer are 18- and 19-year-old boys attending Rennweg Technical School in Vienna where, in addition to the usual academic subjects, they take courses in the three sub-fields of mechatronics: mechanical engineering, electronics and information technology. This wide-ranging technical background enabled them to carry out this entire project independently: construction, electronics and programming. The *Animatronic Arm* project was completed as part of their diploma.

ENERKEY – Wer hat den Schlüssel zur Energiewende?

Lukas Fankhauser, Fabio Gschweidl, Nicola Stampfer, Johannes Wallner

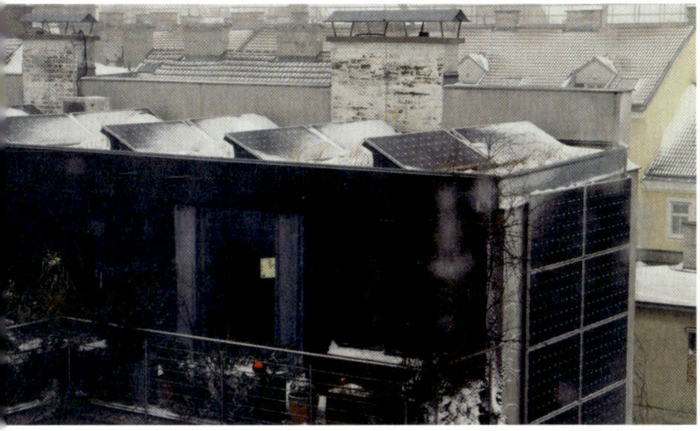

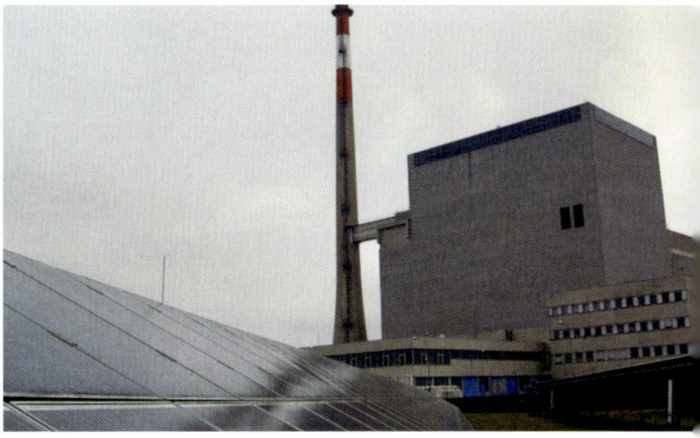

Humankind is dependent on fossil fuels and atomic power, the consequences of which are already evident. The climate is changing. Lately, consumers who've seen the light have been focusing on renewable energy sources. Many dream of satisfying their energy needs entirely from the power of the sun and the wind. Some of these people are pioneers who are already using these approaches to bring about the Energy Revolution–for instance, Wolfgang Löser, a farmer who maintains that he achieved energy self-sufficiency in 2002 and has been completely independent of fossil fuels and oil companies ever since. What has motivated such people to go through this transition? *ENERKEY–Who Has the Key to the Energy Revolution?* is a documentary that provides insights into the various possibilities for renewable forms of energy for Austrian households. Several individuals give accounts of their plans and the implementation of the ideas with which they aim to change how people acquire and use energy. Comedian/actor Roland Düringer has spent a lot of time confronting these issues and is well aware of the social changes that will be necessary in the future. How can an atomic power plant contribute to the Energy Revolution? In Zwentendorf, a solution seems to have been found. This documentary shows how people, the powers that be, and previously implemented initiatives can serve the best interests of nature, the climate and their own survival–always supported by the courage and the strength of individuals. In the words of Mahatma Gandhi: "You must be the change you wish to see in the world." The research leading up to this film began in October 2014. The first scene was shot the following month. The entire shoot took a total of six days over the next six months. It just so happened that many of the protagonists showed up spontaneously and agreed to participate. The editing was mostly done in the evening (after the filmmakers had done their homework). 170 hours of editing went into the finished film.

http://www.enerkey-film.at

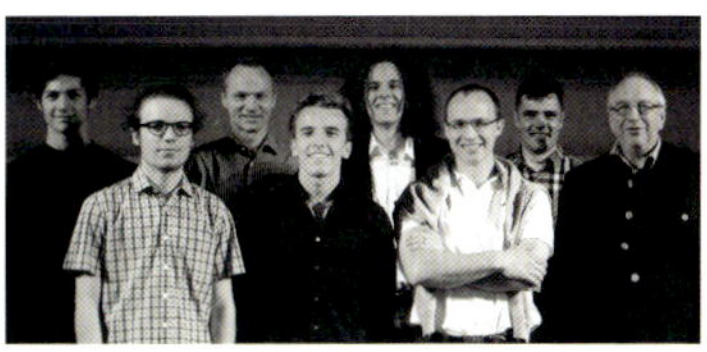

Lukas Fankhauser was born in 1997 and is currently on the multimedia course at the HTBLVA (High School for Graphic Arts) in Vienna. His main interests are the web, sound and photography. He does bodybuilding in his spare time. **Fabio Gschweidl** was born in 1997 and is currently on the multimedia course at the HTBLVA (High School for Graphic Arts) in Vienna. His main interest is film. Variety is the spice of his life, so he enjoys organizing diverse projects that bring together a wide range of people. His hobbies are reading and cooking. **Nicola Stampfer** was born in 1996. He enjoys watching documentaries and, for a few years now, making them too. In addition to his studies on the multimedia course at the HTBLVA (High School for Graphic Arts) in Vienna, he works as a cameraman, time-lapse photographer and film editor. He regards telling (true) stories with the camera as his mission in life. **Johannes Wallner** was born in 1996 and is currently on the multimedia course at the HTBLVA (High School for Graphic Arts). He is interested in various areas of multimedia. For him, the message is more important than the medium.

fruub

Moritz Böswirth, Kilian Hanappi, Marcel Kulhanek, Georg Tertsch,
Marcus Wagner, Sebastian Weber

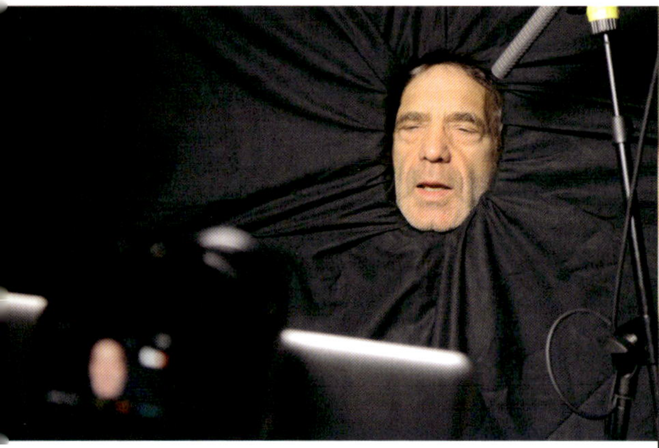

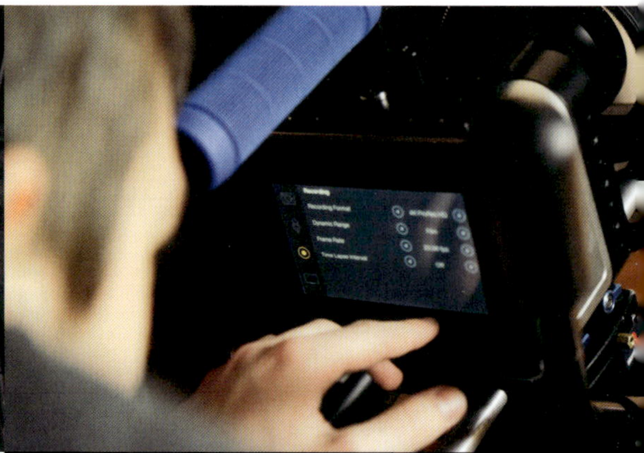

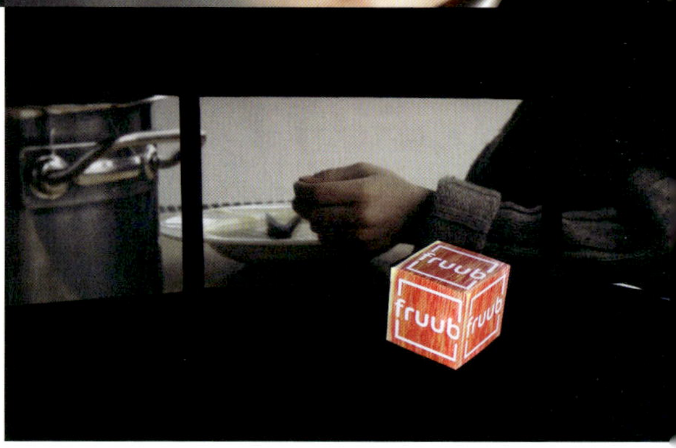

fruub is a multimedia installation that uses projection mapping to showcase a fictitious product. The installation consists of a cube, three screens and a Styrofoam mask onto which images are projected by two beamers. In concrete terms, *fruub* is about a fruit that has been genetically modified to perfectly satisfy consumer demands. It's cube-shaped so it can be efficiently stored using a minimum of space. It's a bite-size morsel that is seedless and doesn't have a peel—in fact, anything the least bit suggestive of natural fruit has been eliminated. *fruub* represents a revolution in the field of genetic engineering. The harbingers of this revolution have already reared their heads: seedless grapes, peeled fruit available at supermarkets, smoothies. Convenience is the main thing. Few people give any thought to sustainability. An innovative product calls for an innovative presentation. We want the launch of our branding campaign for this perfect new fruit to make as big a splash as possible. On one hand, the solution should be impressive; on the other hand, it should display a certain "future touch." The reason why we decided to go with projection mapping is that it enables us to make the depiction of our product as tangible as possible. Rotation and special effects are part of our effort to take maximum advantage of this technique. *fruub* is meant to represent a futuristic scenario that we regard as thoroughly realistic. The aim of this project is to make viewers aware of current developments in the field of genetic engineering and to raise the question of whether they are ethically tenable.

http://fruub.at

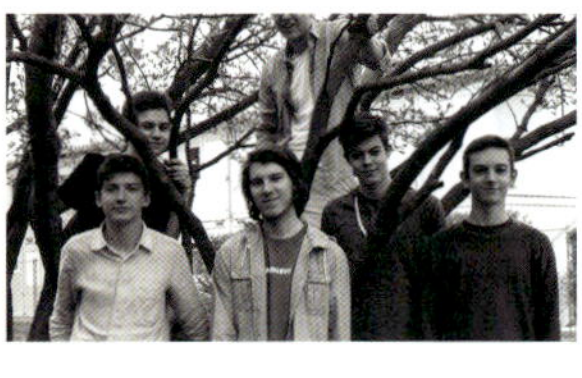

Moritz Böswirth, Kilian Hanappi, Marcel Kulhanek, Georg Tertsch, Marcus Wagner and **Sebastian Weber** are eighteen-year-old boys on the multimedia course at the HTBLVA (High School for Graphic Arts) in Vienna. Their diverse interests helped them meet the demands of this project.

Geschwüre der Wissenschaft

David Nimmervoll, Michael Traxler

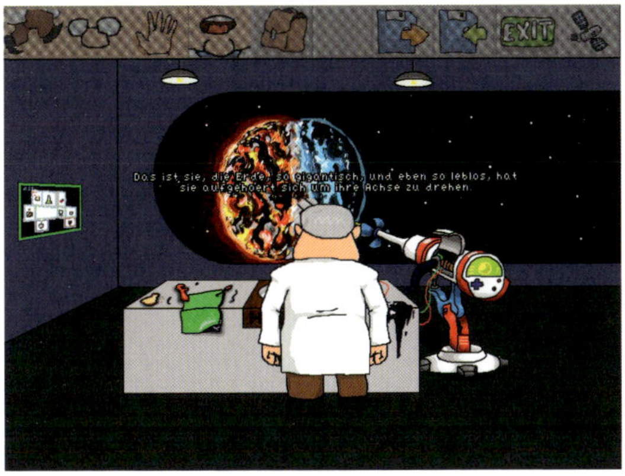

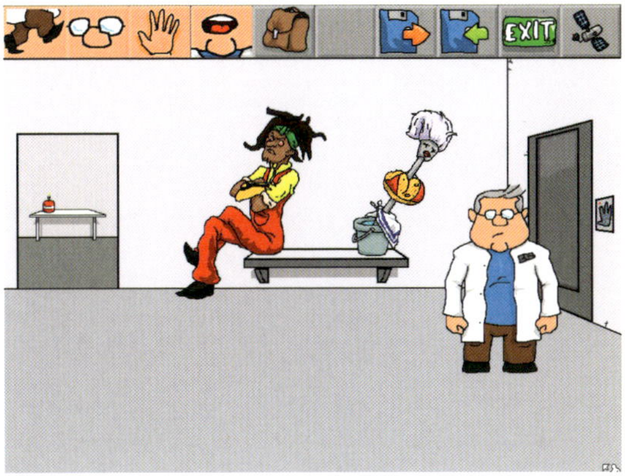

One day, when the Earth suddenly stopped rotating on its axis, Igun Grawladkov, a scientist aboard the Austrian Space Station, thought that his big chance had come. He would use a laser he had developed himself to get the planet spinning again and thus be celebrated as a hero by all humankind. Unfortunately, he is unable to complete his laser because a particular component is still missing, and he thus has to lower himself to ask for assistance from his colleagues, the "vile abscesses of science."

The game *Geschwüre der Wissenschaft* (Abscesses of Science) was produced with Adventure Game Studio, a free program that offers an easy way to get started developing games. The aim was to create a classic point & click adventure in the style of the old Lucas Arts and Sierra games. All the backgrounds as well as the figures on all the animation levels were drawn by mouse using the Microsoft Paint program, as were the interface and all menus. The featured element of a game session is witty dialog with the characters. They include a Rasta man on the custodial crew who is in love with his broom, a nutcase going through caffeine withdrawal, Bruno, Konan the Barbarian's big brother and messenger for a parcel service, and a rather stressed-out game designer who is constantly working on completing the huge dungeons in the cellar. The player has various options to take part in these dialogs, each of which steers the conversation in a different direction. Moving about the space station, Igun comes upon various items that he either takes possession of or inspects on the spot. Some of them can be combined to form new items, which in turn open up new paths in this ongoing, epic tale of the rescue of humankind. Michael Traxler and David Nimmervoll produced this project in conjunction with a high-school elective course in information technology. Their advisor was Wolfgang Hoffelner. Such elective courses offer students regular opportunities to deal intensively with a particular subject and dedicate their efforts to a project over an extended period.

http://www.borgplay.at/2014/06/7b-7c-adventure-games/

David Nimmervoll and **Michael Traxler** attended regular primary and intermediate schools before enrolling in BORG Bad Leonfelden, Upper Austria, where they are doing their high-school diplomas this year. Both young men discovered the fascinating world of video gaming at an early age. The sense of fascination they derive from it—discovering the unknown, achieving the impossible and experiencing the unbelievable—has been part of their programming ever since.

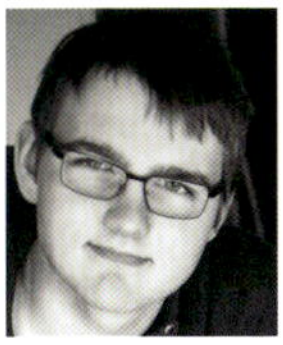

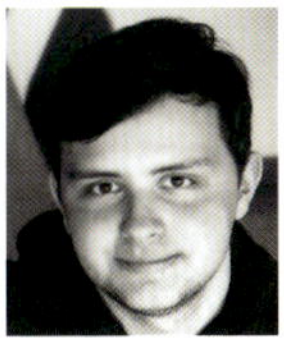

Loopex–Konstruktion eines Filament Extruders

Alexander Brenner, Nicolas Groß, Matthias Thym

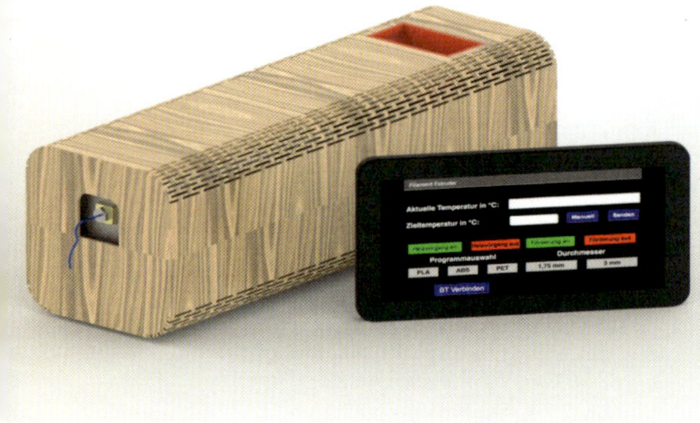

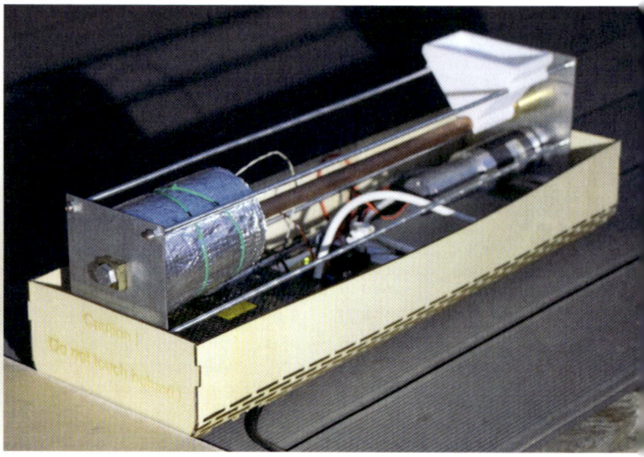

The evolution of 3D printing technology in recent years has unleashed a boom in this field. Now there are even a few 3D printers that are affordable for hobbyists. Besides the purchase price of the device itself, the major cost factor in 3D printing is the material, the filament. On the other hand, the filament's raw material in the form of plastic pellets is comparatively cheap, so producing your own filament can significantly reduce the operating cost of a 3D printer. This can be made using a filament extruder. As our high-school diploma project, we developed *Loopex*, a filament extruder in which the raw material is poured into an intake and then funneled into a heating compartment where the plastication takes place. The resulting homogenous, viscous mass is then pressurized and extruded through a nozzle. In order to achieve output that is usable by a 3D printer—a uniform filament with a diameter of 1.75 or 3 mm—this seemingly simple process has to be coordinated with utmost precision. Time permitting, we plan to expand our project, developing additional components and investigating whether the pellets we are currently using can be replaced by recycled material without diminishing the quality. If it turns out that high-quality filament can be produced using shredded plastic waste such as PET bottles, then *Loopex* would make a contribution to increased efficiency in the recycling of various plastics.

https://loopextruder.wordpress.com

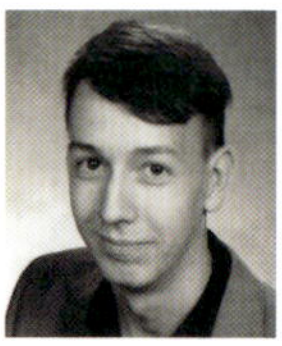

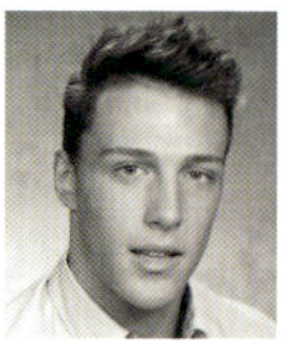

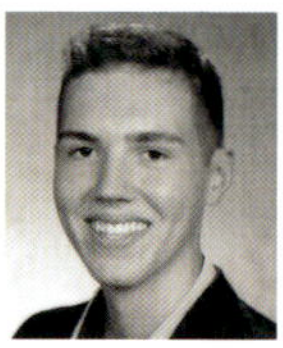

Alexander Brenner, Nicolas Groß, Matthias Thym. We were born in 1996 and are enrolled in the Mechatronics program at Rennweg Technical School in Vienna, from which we'll graduate this year. We formed our crew at the end of our fourth year. Since each of us already had experience working with 3D printing and this field is an important part of Rennweg's curriculum, we decided to pursue a project dealing with this rapidly developing technology.

Mach was Handfestes

Katja Haller, Hannah Hradec, Ivan Lastric, Ahmed Parmaksiz, Bogdan Vieru

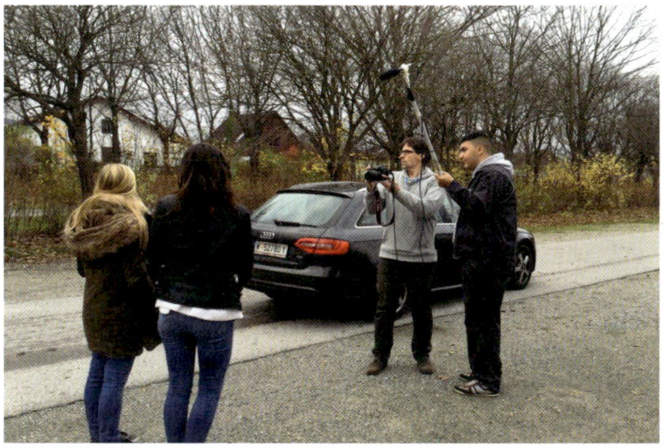

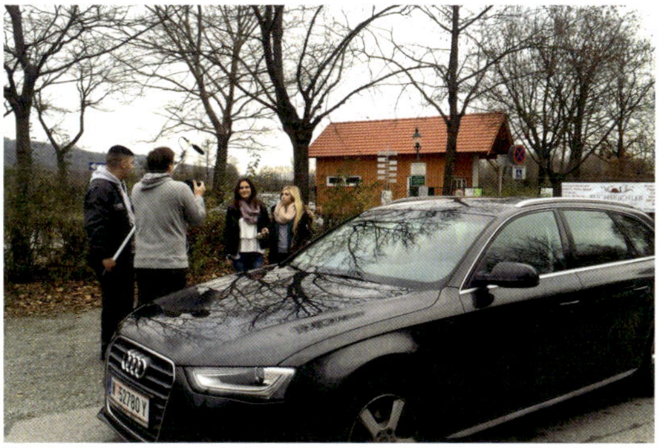

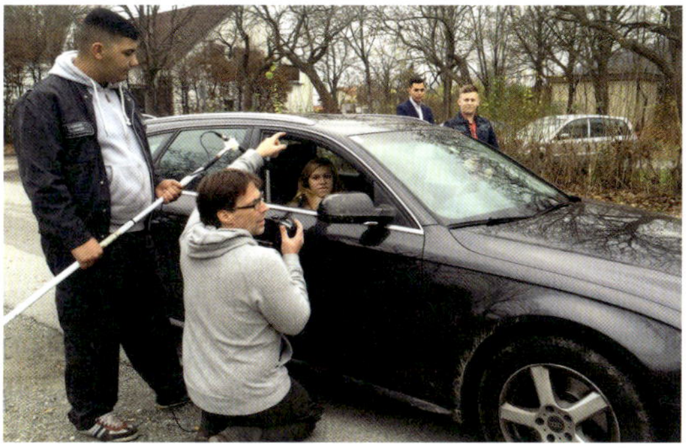

The idea behind our project *Mach was Handfestes* (Make Something Tangible) was that the way people think about apprenticeship is in desperate need of improvement. Apprenticeship's image has to get a facelift to make it more appealing to young people. And who can do that better than youngsters themselves? Who knows their job better than those who are learning and practicing it? Our clip is meant to be a promotional video for the job of motor vehicle technician. When we initially tried to get apprentices in various classes and groups interested in our project, the creative yield was rather meager—most groups' output was more or less simple posters. But suddenly, when the prospect of producing a commercial was raised, this initiative started to get some serious traction. Although we didn't have any concrete ideas yet, one thing had definitely emerged: in the competition to get girls, automotive apprentices somehow had to come out on top against boys pursuing other types of training. So the direction of the narrative arc was clear right from the start. At first the setting was supposed to be a car dealer's showroom with a workshop attached, but this concept was junked in favor of the one we ended up going with. Someone had the idea of switching roles—that is, the boys as the clueless and helpless ones and a female automotive apprentice as the heroine—but that turned into a non-starter because there just weren't enough girls who wanted to perform in front of the camera.

Due to bad weather and organizational problems on the day of the shoot, we had only about two hours to make our video. Plus the memory card didn't have enough capacity for multiple takes. We constantly had to delete previous scenes we had shot to make room on the card for the new ones. At the last minute, roles were reassigned, articles of clothing swapped, and everybody collaborated on rewriting a few plot details. All in all, at the end of this brief shoot and despite the chilly weather the intrepid members of the cast/crew were glad to have participated and proud of what they had done!

Katja Haller, Hannah Hradec, Ivan Lastric, Ahmed Parmaksiz and **Bogdan Vieru** are 1st and 2nd year students at Vienna's Vocational School for Automotive Technology, where they spend one day per week in conjunction with their apprenticeship. In this timeframe, they planned and implemented their project.

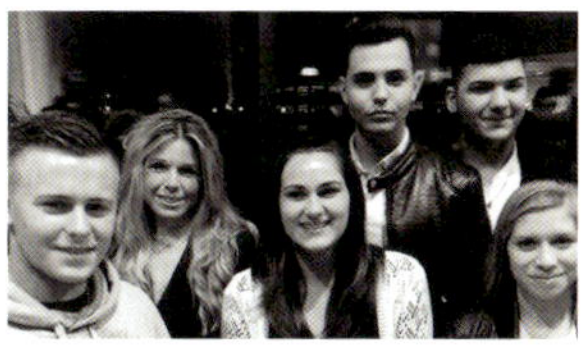

Screenrunner

Class 8c, BORG Bad Leonfelden

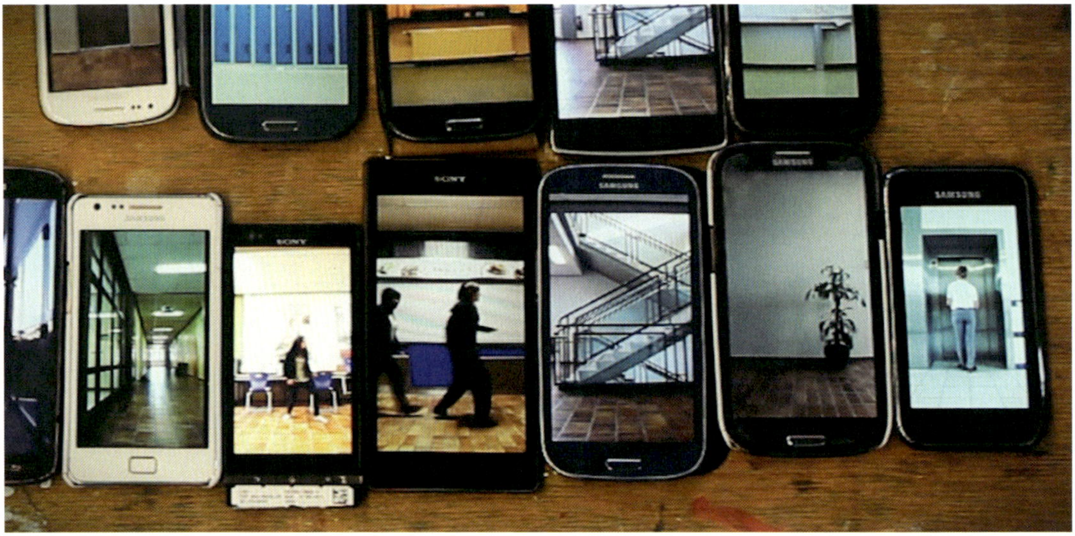

They're everywhere: picture screens! Wherever you look these days, you see a display. Now, there are even smartphones offering better picture quality than a TV monitor. And just about everybody has one. So using them as the basis of an art project seemed like a pretty doable idea. After a bit of brainstorming, we quickly agreed on a project concept. We wanted to try to make a figure walk out of one cell phone and into another. Our objective was to achieve a visually fluid transition from one device's display to the next. We began to think up a story and sketched the individual scenes on small sheets of paper meant to represent our smartphones. In this way we could rearrange, redraw or replace whatever we wanted. The next step was technical implementation. At this point, we didn't even know whether this was feasible or how well it would work. So, as a test, we shot two sequences at different locations in our school and tried to play them back side by side on a computer. We were delighted with the results. Motivated by our initial success, we began shooting the individual scenes. More than anything, the scenes in which several protagonists appear really put our patience to the test, since their timing when entering and exiting had to be perfect. At some points we had to adjust the video's speed in post-production to lengthen or shorten the pauses between scenes. Even the final recording of the entire sequence of events put a few stumbling blocks in our way—for instance, somebody's finger didn't fully depress the play button, or a cell-phone suddenly switched to standby mode. Nevertheless, we finally succeeded in executing and capturing one totally perfect sequence, and we now proudly present the finished product.

http://www.borgplay.at/2015/02/8c-screenrunner/

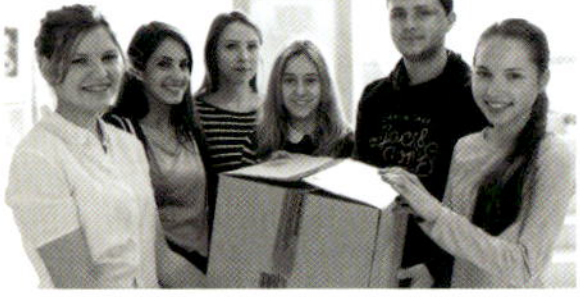

The members of Class 8c at **BORG Bad Leonfelden** are Theresa Awad, Anna Birngruber, Anja Burgstaller, Christina Engleder, Julia Gründlinger, Lucia Klecatzky, Hanna Pammer, Teresa Reisinger, Madelleine Roob and Michael Traxler. This project was produced by students taking a special media design course as part of the Media / Art program at BORG high school in Bad Leonfelden. Together with advisor Wolfgang Hoffelner, they regularly produce projects in a variety of multimedia disciplines. *http://www.borgplay.at*

Unknown Forms of Face

Dominik Koller

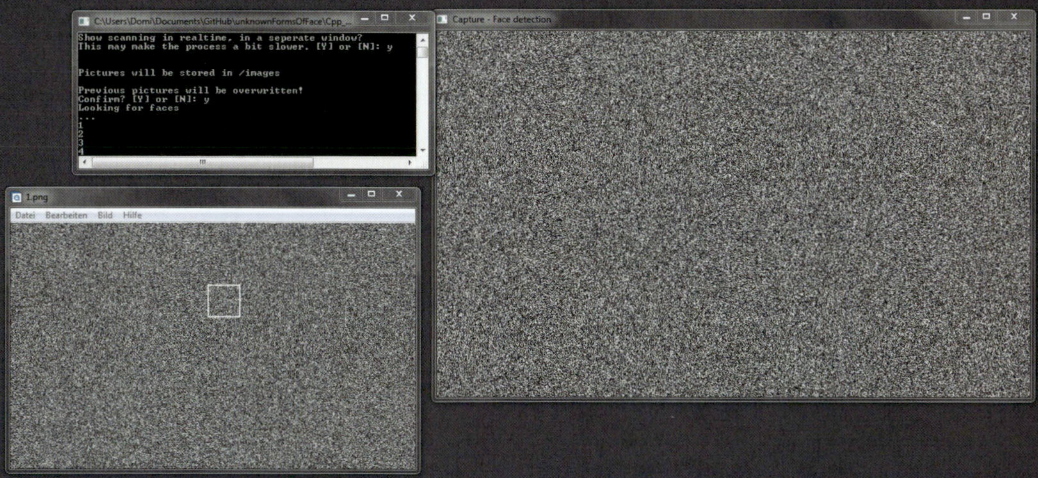

This work generates random image data and, by means of pattern recognition, will detect faces in these images. A random image—usually looking like static noise—could possibly display anything (including a portrait of you). It just isn't very likely that you are going to see anything recognizable at all. However, when creating a large number of these images, it becomes more likely that some of them contain information distinguishable by the human eye—faces, for example. Running a face-detection algorithm, those images are filtered out, and if you look (very) closely, you can see (human?) faces looking at you out of the gray randomness. I find this a very neat metaphor for—well, life, after all. Being very improbable, but possible, it does become likely to happen if there are enough chances—so goes the theory. You just have to look in the right places. This work not only displays the actual similarity of human sight and computational pattern recognition, it also plays on the idea of (random) information and its interpretation (as the arguably random data gains new meaning only by human interpretation) and the probability of (the origins of) life.

http://dominikkoller.net/UnknownFormsOfFace

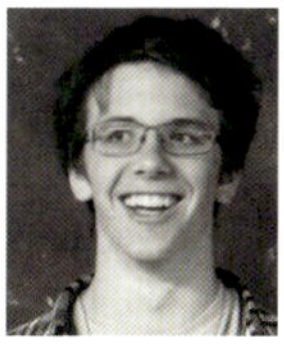

Dominik Koller is a student from Austria, passionate about innovation, technology and art. He likes to explore, create and realize experimental ideas, often with code. He was previously awarded a Golden Nica for his work *Visual:Drumset*. He has been able to gain professional experience at the studio Nexus Interactive Arts, London, and the vvvv Group, Berlin, and has given workshops at the NODE15 Forum for Digital Arts.

Wenn uns der Zwerghamster zu Unrecht beschuldigt

Sebastiano Develli, Elias Gäbler, Lorenz Krischan, Julia Moser, Nikolaus Schoner, Eva-Maria Sprenger, Moritz Stark

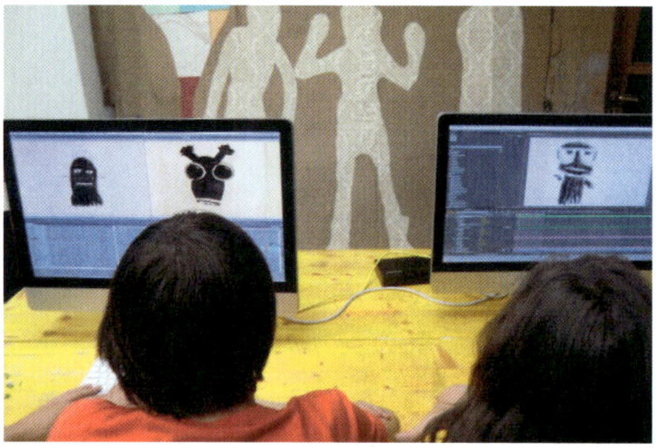

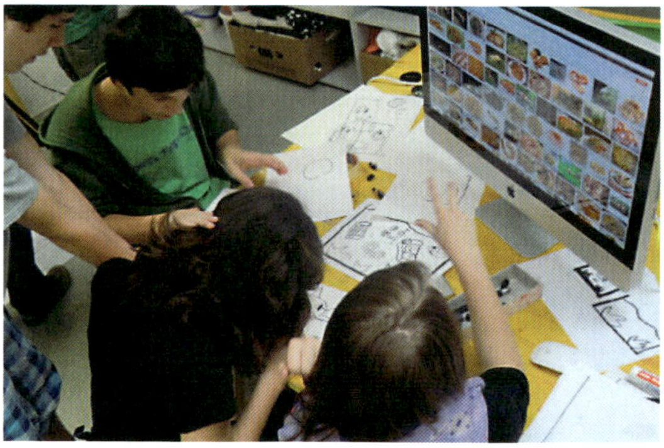

In our film we create a virtual world composed of elements of our real everyday lives. We developed a pictorial common parlance that we used as a means of communication, which offered us insights and provided us with access to new spaces for activities. Our own drawings, the thoughts set down on paper by a hand—that's us. *Wenn uns der Zwerghamster zu Unrecht beschuldigt* (If the dwarf hamster wrongfully accuses us), involves several elements. By narrative and image, a personal habitat is sketched, an analog avatar of oneself is created, and the virtual world is interwoven with the real one. We jointly create a picture that can tip into one world or the other at any time depending on point of view or intention, a theme that, in a technologized world—human/machine, domain of technology/realm of feeling—raises questions, seeks answers, creates possibilities and calls for taking stances. What creates identity? How can I understand and how can I be understood? Who am I and who are the others? What connects us? Where do I stop and where do the others begin? What is situated in between?

The media workshop at *bilding: Art & Architecture School for Children and Young People* was conducted by filmmaker Daniel Pöhacker and digital artist Manfred Raggl. The young participants were aged between thirteen and sixteen. The film was produced between March and June 2013. The group jointly developed the theme and content, both of which emerged over the course of this collaborative process as a result of the composition of the group (none of whom were previously acquainted) and their preferences as graphic artists. The plot, direction, camera, sound, editing, animation etc. were done as a team. We believe that this work applies to the topic "Designing the Future" where it's a matter of an individual's confrontation with himself/herself and with other people, with a person's own identity, the way strangers are and what they have in common, with one's own creativity and a collaborative process of production.

https://vimeo.com/channels/bilding
http://www.bilding.at

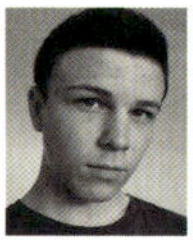 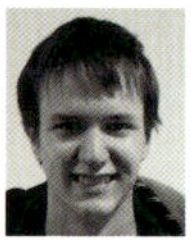 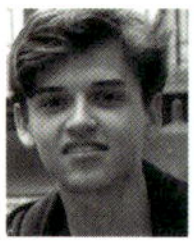 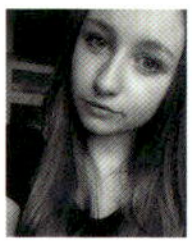 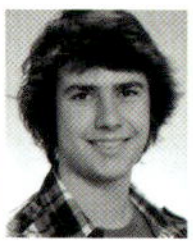 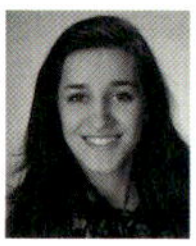 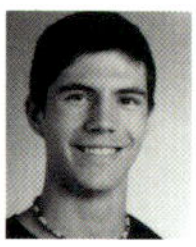

Sebastiano Develli, Elias Gäbler, Lorenz Krischan, Julia Moser, Nikolaus Schoner, Eva-Maria Sprenger, Moritz Stark attended the *bilding: Art & Architecture School for Children and Young People,* a unique facility in Innsbruck in which youngsters aged four to nineteen receive support in discovering and developing their creative interests, skills and talents.

Y-Rail Security

Maximilian Krexner, Thomas Lanik, Philipp Schrittwieser, Matthias Wotke

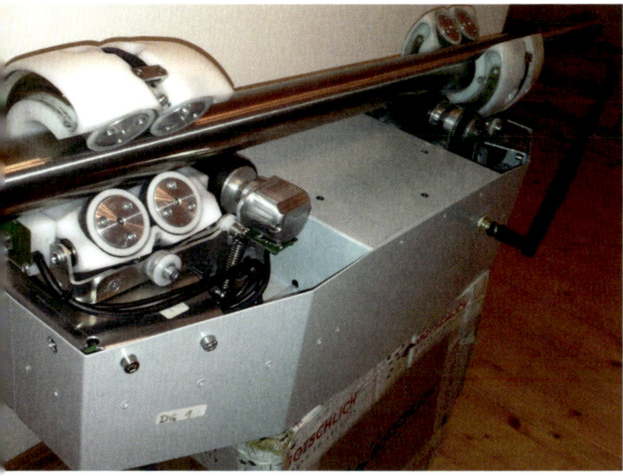

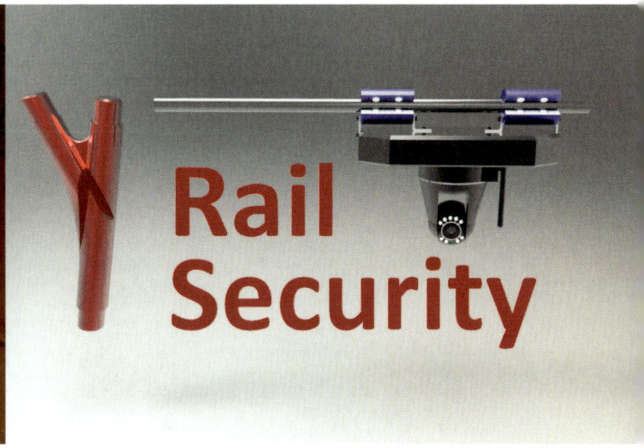

The aim of our *Y-Rail Security* project is to develop an alternative to conventional track-based transportation systems. The problem with traditional systems is that the points contain moving parts that cause problems in controlling the switching process and are also subject to wear and tear. That's why these dynamic components have to be replaced on a regular basis. In our diploma project, *Y-Rail Security,* we've developed a solution to the above-mentioned problems: a track concept that functions strictly with static points. That's also the source of our project's name—the track, from a bird's-eye view, resembles the shape of the letter Y. Its surface is scored with grooves that make it possible for the vehicle to either veer off or continue straight ahead. The movement is determined entirely by the guide profiles, which can practically determine their path on their own by simply rotating 90° in one direction or the other. This concept has numerous potential applications. Our system could be used for surveillance purposes at sprawling facilities such as Vienna International Airport or the voestalpine steel mill. *Y-Rail Security* is designed to move quickly, quietly and on command, and to do so loaded with various cameras or other surveillance equipment. Our vehicle could also be used to transport small objects in places like factories or Amazon warehouses. Our brightest prospect for the future, however, is transporting people. Our system could be set up in the airspace above current traffic arteries like a sort of rollercoaster and thereby constitute an innovative new public transit system. The stainless steel tubes used for the network of tracks are wear-resistant, functional regardless of weather conditions, tough and durable. A very hard, heavy-duty plastic has also been used for the points to make them wear-resistant. This makes *Y-Rail* an infrastructure investment with great future promise.

http://www.y-rail-security.at/

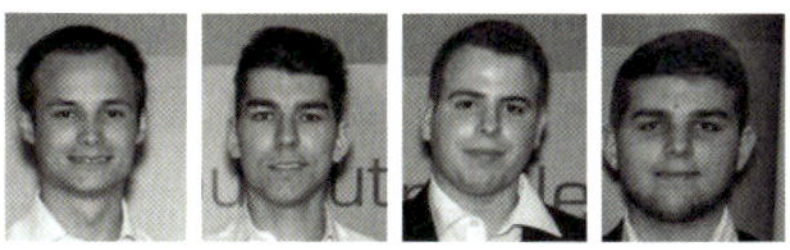

Y-Rail Security was the diploma project of four students at Rennweg Technical School. **Matthias Wotke** was primarily responsible for construction and directed the mechanical production; **Thomas Lanik** was in charge of electronics and helped out with production; **Maximilian Krexner**, as assistant project director, handled project management, the electronics and the finances; and **Philipp Schrittwieser** was project director and responsible for programming and marketing. Special thanks to our supervisor, Werner Reindorf, who knew how to help whenever problems arose.

[the next idea]
VOESTALPINE ART AND
TECHNOLOGY GRANT

Saving the Future

Yamina Aouina, Rikke Frisk, Horst Hörtner, Michael Sterrer-Ebenführer, Kazuhiko Washio

The aim of this art and technology grant is to honor new and extraordinarily promising ideas and to support the process of developing them further.
This year the jury observed that the submitted ideas were dedicated to the big challenges humankind is facing today. The issues addressed in the submissions ranged from medical care and food supply, to challenges related to waste, pollution and disasters. Similar to the broad range of submissions, the proposed solutions and strategies to contribute to these problems took various directions. Hence the jury members were confronted with smart engineering approaches as well as with DIY concepts, artistic installations and creative interventions. Consequently the challenge of this year's jury process was to make a selection and to distinguish between the large number of "good ideas" and the "next idea". In order to do so, the jury members were not just looking at the technical feasibility of the proposals, but also at a variety of other criteria. Especially important in this regard was the question of whether the proposed project is opening up a new field, and if it has the potential to spark fresh, not yet known ways of thinking and acting. Furthermore, the people behind the project were considered important, and within the jury sessions the question was asked: Could the individual or the group behind a proposal motivate others to work on this idea? Finally, the symbolic character of the project was very important, and the question debated was: Can this project become a symbol of change and an inspiring as well as empowering resource for others who are motivated to realize their own ideas? Judging the submitted concepts from that perspective allowed the jury members to understand the ideas in relation to their (future) context and to reflect on the possible social impact a next idea may have. Additionally, this perspective underlines the jury's understanding of innovation and positive change. It never happens alone, but always in relation to and with others, and the social context it is embedded in.

[the next idea] voestalpine Art and Technology Grant

SOYA C(O)U(L)TURE · XXLab—Irene Agrivina Widyaningrum, Asa Rahmana, Ratna Djuwita, Eka Jayani Ayuningtias, Atinna Rizqiana

The winning project *SOYA C(O)U(L)TURE* was developed by XXLab, an innovation lab managed by an interdisciplinary women's collective based in Indonesia. In their multi-faceted project they use the waste from soya production—which otherwise pollutes the water around the factories—to create eco-friendly products and accessories. Concentrating the expertise from science, technology, art and design, the XXLab team managed to create value at several levels; by using programmable bacteria and tissue culture, they turn soya liquid waste into edible cellulose, biofuel and bio leather and at the same time they help to reduce the water pollution. The bio-culture process is based on bacteria *(Acetobacter xylinium)* colonies. In a particular environment these colonies produce an enzyme that transforms the tofu waste into millions of fibers and forms edible cellulose. This project, based on a cheap, open and organic material, could develop into various valuable products in any home kitchen using DIY or DIWO (do-it-with-others) methods. The XXLab and their proposed strategies could also become an alternative sustainable economy, helping to increase or produce an income for women in the low-income areas. The jury finds that the interdisciplinary, collaborative, sustainable and creative aspects of this project meet all the criteria for a successful and a promising social innovation model and the XXLab women will certainly inspire many others.

Honorary Mentions

Beauty Technology · Katia Vega

The first Honorary Mention goes to *Beauty Technology* which truly expands the vision of make-up. With an interdisciplinary approach, it uses conductive make-up and invisible computing to convert body surfaces into interfaces. Blink your eye and the light goes on, or close your lips and the camera starts. Inspired by empowering human capabilities and magic, *Beauty Technology* is not merely a new tool of expression in fashion and art, but also a new way of communicating and interacting, for example in healthcare for people with disabilities. The project opens a new perspective on an existing field of wearables. It is an innovative and intimate interaction with technology, even respectful of the individual personality. The jury has seen a sequence of the designer's/scientist's range of works and awards an Honorary Mention for her visionary approach and the strategy behind it, which immediately inspires one to think of further potential.

TADCAD · Paula Te

The second Honorary Mention goes to *TADCAD*. This is a project that shows that forming (digital) 3D Objects with your bare hands in order to print them is not only playful, it is highly educational—not only—for kids. *TADCAD* is a learning environment that helps people to personally experience the growing intersection of our physical world with our virtual one. *TADCAD* is re-connecting the experience to our learning processes. By utilizing existing instruments or technologies such as camera tracking and gesture recognition, another door of perception is opened for the user. *TADCAD* does not stop at the perception of digital 3D objects and environments, as for example computer games do. Forming something with your hands is very intuitive, and forming a non-existent 3D-Object with your hands tells you a lot about the abstraction of 3D space. In this way *TADCAD* also addresses new perspectives on experience-based learning and education. Taking this into account, the jury selection is neither based on the project's technical innovations nor on its innovation in design. Rather it is based on the role model incorporated in the project: a smart way to combine existing tools and technologies, to raise the question of questions: "Why didn't I think of that ...?" *TADCAD* seems so obvious, once one has seen it.

SOYA C(O)U(L)TURE

XXLab–Irene Agrivina Widyaningrum, Asa Rahmana, Ratna Djuwita,
Eka Jayani Ayuningtias, Atinna Rizqiana

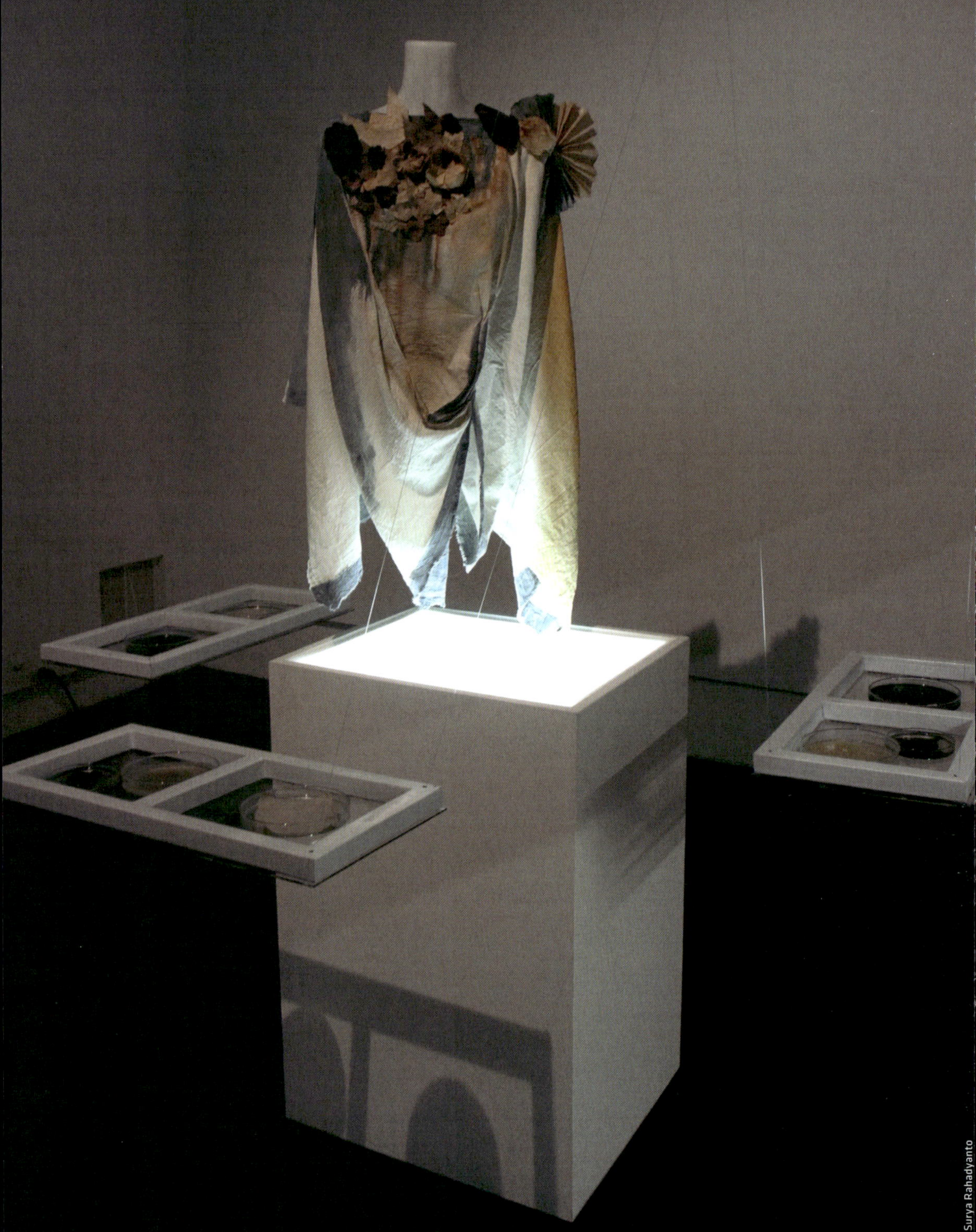

Tommy Surya Rahadyanto

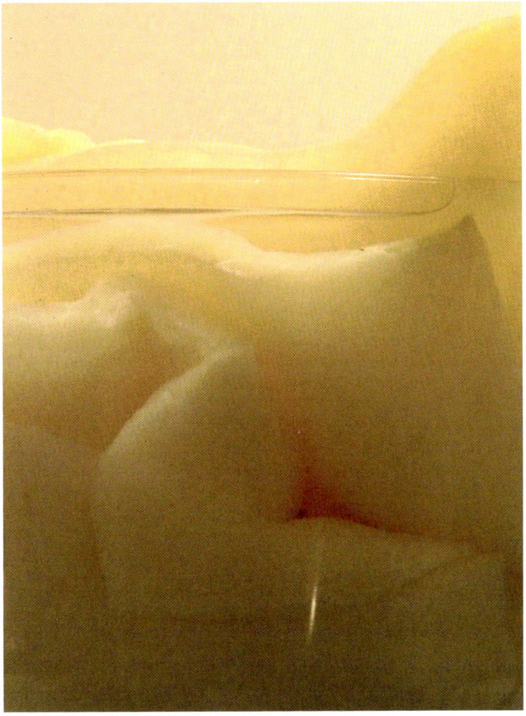

Irene Agrivina Widyaningrum

SOYA C(O)U(L)TURE is a research-based product development by XXLab. The research aim is to grow and program an alternative energy, food and bio material from liquid soya waste using bacteria and tissue culture. Tofu and tempeh made from soya beans are common healthy food for Indonesians, made by biological process. Indonesia has a lot of tofu and tempeh production, from small-scale (home industry) to large-scale (factory). But these produce liquid waste that pollutes the water and rivers around the factories. XXLab is a collective of women from various backgrounds, such as artists, designers and programmers, focusing on art, science and free technology facilitated and supported by the HONF Foundation, Yogyakarta, Indonesia. *SOYA C(O)U(L)TURE* is one of their recent projects that aims to reduce water pollution and poverty. XXLab creates and grows edible cellulose using *Acetobacter xylinum* as food, at the same time processing a microbial fuel cell and bio material that could in future be used as an eco-friendly alternative source of energy, food and organic fabric. This project uses cheap, organic material that could be developed into various products with an economic value. It could be produced and developed in any home using ordinary kitchen utensils, combining open-source software and hardware using DIY or DIWO (do-it-with-others) methods. This development could become an alternative solution for a sustainable economy to create or increase income for women in the low-income areas.

Supported and facilitated by:
HONF Foundation, *http://www.natural-fiber.com/*
HONFablab, *http://www.honfablab.org/*

Technical consultants:
Prof. Drs. Langkah Sembiring, Stephanus Yudianto Asmoro, Tommy Surya Rahadyanto

XXLAB (ID) is a group initiative by women from interdisciplinary backgrounds and practices supported and facilitated by the HONF Foundation. XXLAB focuses on the exploration of art, science and free technology using open-source software, hardware and material. Based in Yogyakarta, one of the most outstanding cities in Indonesia, and known as an art and education city, XXLAB runs numerous workshop with DIY and DIWO (do-it-with-others) methods. The XXLab has an open membership and was founded in 2013, as a continuation of a series workshop called Ms. Baltazar ID.

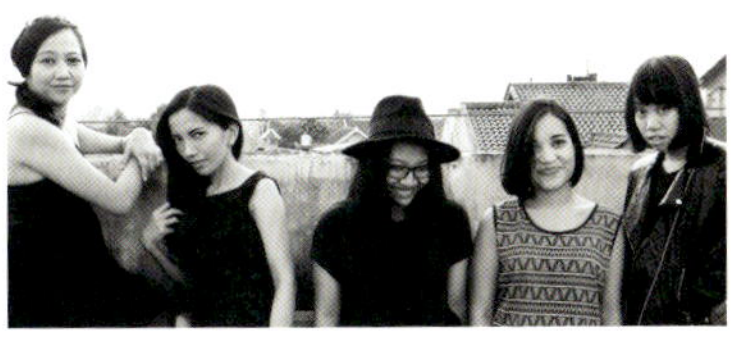

Purwa Anugerah

Beauty Technology

Katia Vega

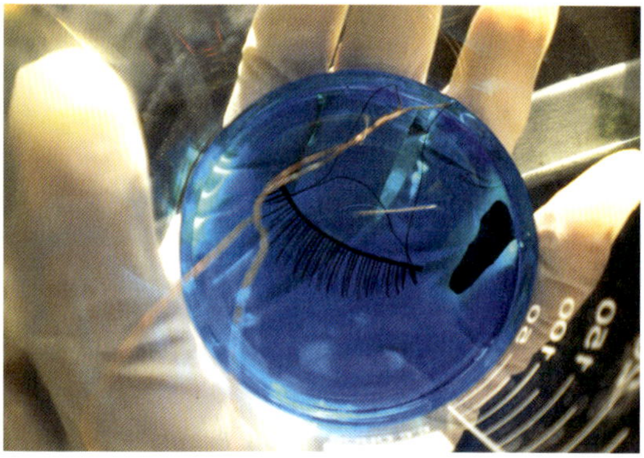

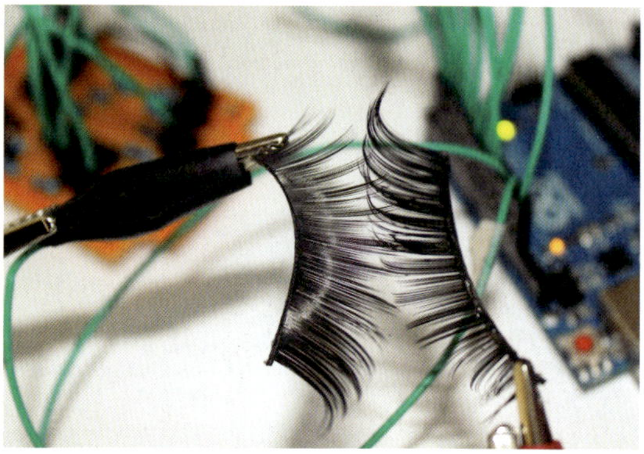

For centuries, moisturizer has been used for hydrating the skin, lipstick for coloring our lips, mascara for defining eyelashes. Several technologies have improved the manufacturing process of beauty products, but in the end their function has not changed over time. My proposal is to add a new function to beauty products, exploring them in relation to their use as wearable computers. *Beauty Technology* is a novel wearable-computing subfield that integrates electronics into beauty products applied directly to one's skin, fingernails, and hair. In this way, the body's surface becomes an interactive platform. Conductive Makeup, Tech Nails, Hairware and FX e-makeup are beauty technologies.

Felipe Esteves, a 33-year-old masters student who was a jujitsu world champion, inspired this project. He injured himself during a training session thirteen years ago. Since then he has a quadriplegic disability and depends on others to do common tasks such as changing TV channels. The idea is to take *Beauty Technology* to people with disabilities in hospitals. Instead of using wearables that have the electronics noticeable and are reminiscent of cyborgs, we will use *Beauty Technology*. Thus, users will have the confidence that beauty products give them but at the same time, they could be sufficiently independent to do simple tasks such as turning on devices. In this way beauty products will not just enhance their appearance, they also give them super-powers.

The Conductive Makeup and FX e-makeup are beauty technologies used in this project. We focus on the human agency to control facial muscles. In this way a voluntary movement will trigger appliances such as an air-conditioning, a television or a smartphone. Conductive makeup uses black conductive eyeliner to connect conductive false eyelashes to a circuit. These work like a switch, which is off when the eye is open, and, on when the eye is closed. The conductive eyelashes are given a metallic coating in order to mimic the natural black color of eyelashes. FX e-makeup uses special-effects makeup to hide sensors on the face that sense its muscles, looking like a second skin. The FX e-makeup sensors are switches that turn on when the skin furrows or creases. Kinisi shows the feasibility of this technology by answering the question, "Could your skin act as an interface?" A video shows the use of FX e-makeup for activating different light patterns with a smile, wink, raising the eyebrows and closing the lips.

Beauty Tech Designer: Katia Vega
Special thanks to my advisor Prof. Hugo Fuks for his support and guidance in this project, to Felipe Esteves for being our inspiration, Hugo Rojas for his support in the process of metalizing the eyelashes, and to the Kinisi video collaborators: director and editor: Juan Carlos Yanaura; electronics assistant: Abel Arrieta; make-up and character designer: Larca Meicap; model: Gabriella Chávez; producer: Pamela Ramos; cinematographer: Cesar Fajardo; camera assistant and gaffer: Renzo Rivas; lighting technicians: Iván Pflucker and Diego Valdivia; hairstyling: Carla Gonzales; music: Maribel Tafur

http://katiavega.com
http://youtu.be/7JrRo1U7c5o

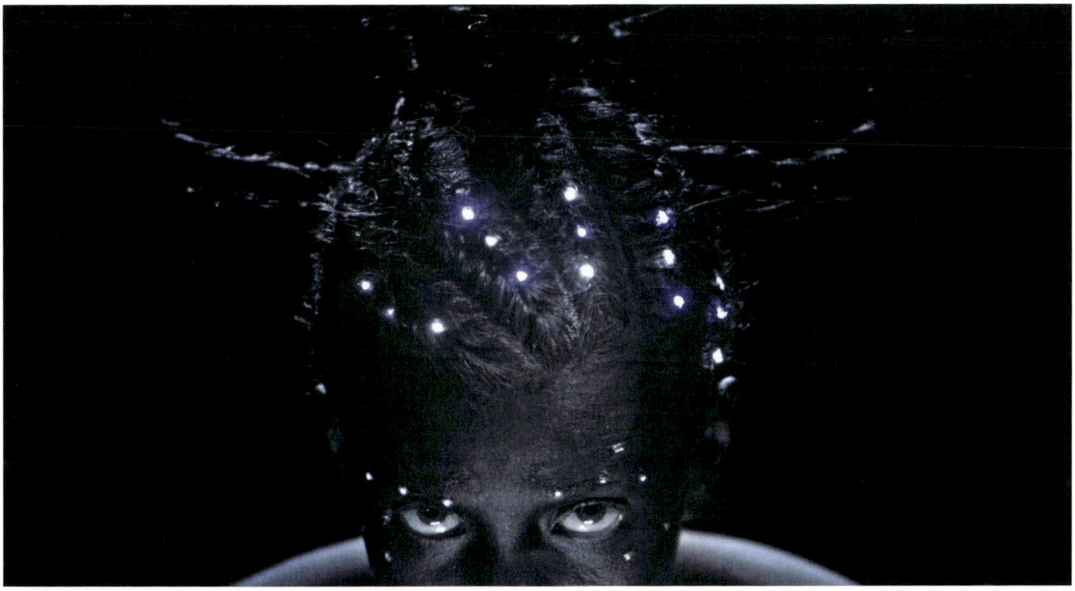

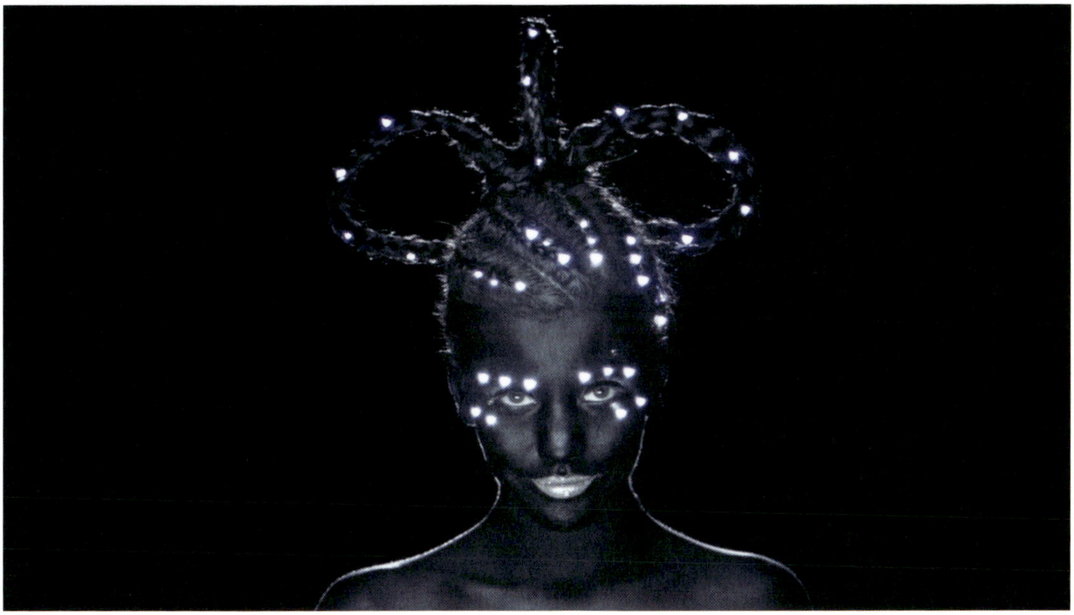

Yanaura

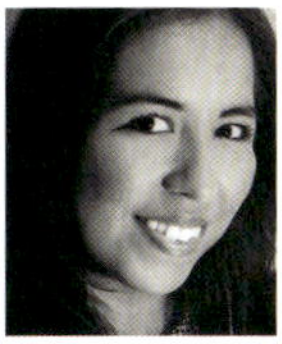

AnaPaulaDan

Katia Vega (PE) is a beauty-tech designer. Inspired by invisible computing, wearables and magic, she proposes novel ways to move from traditional to interactive cosmetics. Conductive Makeup, Tech Nails, Hairware and FX e-makeup are her beauty technologies that transform the body in an interactive platform. She is a postdoc in computer science at PUC-Rio (Brazil), where she also received her PhD and masters degrees. She received a BSc from UNMSM (Peru). She was a research assistant at HKBU (Hong Kong). Her work has been covered by the *New Scientist*, *Wired*, *Discovery*, CNN, PSFK and others.

TADCAD

Paula Te

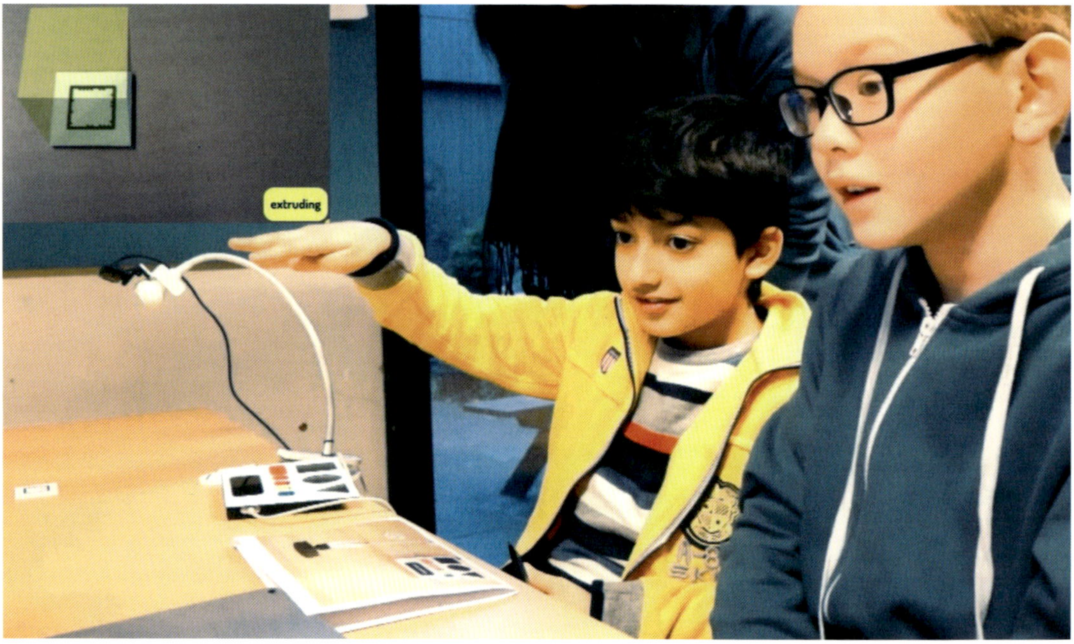

The rise of personal fabrication presents a future where there are 3D printers in every home and community, empowering people to design, build and iterate solutions that fit their own needs. While the production technologies are rapidly becoming more accessible, the tools for creation on these platforms are still mostly developed for domain experts.

Moreover, transferring an idea from imagination to real life can be limited by confidence and capacity to mentally model the creations in three-dimensional space. How might we improve this capacity and build confidence in these mental models?

TADCAD addresses this by providing a new interaction paradigm for 3D modeling. TADCAD is a gestural and tangible modeling platform for 3D printing. It recognizes 3D printed shapes on a build field that can be transformed using hand gestures. The transformations are seen in real time in an augmented reality view of the build field. The new creation can then be 3D printed.

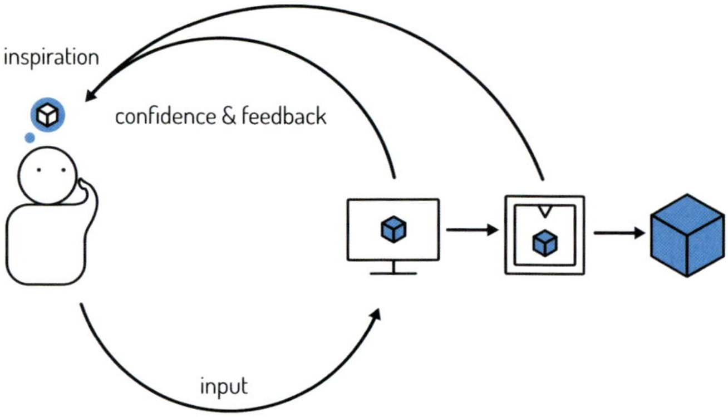

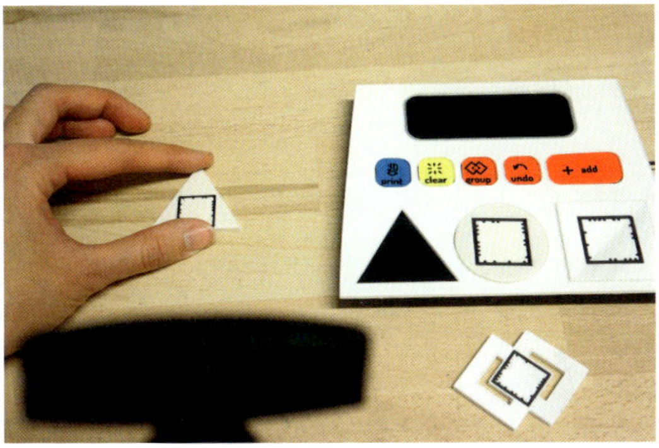

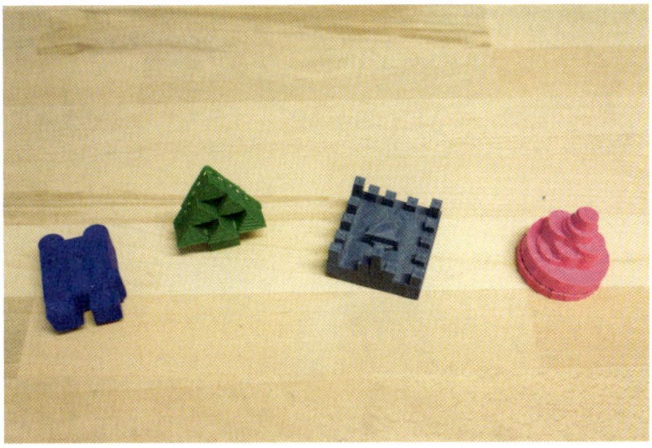

Ultimately, the platform's vision is to allow the creations to be built upon again and again; the system bridges tangible interaction with 3D printing in a way that facilitates the design process and iteration loop. TADCAD has been developed in the same spirit of maker education: to work in the platform, you build your own learning tools. The current prototype of TADCAD involves a webcam attached to an LED lamp, a game controller with a leap motion sensor, and 3D printed pieces with fiducial markers for identification. This prototype is helpful as a starting point to open up the discussion for applications of augmented reality, gestural interaction and tangible interfaces in new methods of working, learning, and creating in the domain of 3D modeling and elsewhere. The vision of TADCAD is much more than this current implementation, and I welcome you to join in the discussion of how to use technology to enable creation, fuel creativity and inspire learning in new ways while remaining sustainable and accessible.

Copenhagen Institute of Interaction Design
Bjørns Internationale Skole
http://codingpirates.dk
Copenhagen International School

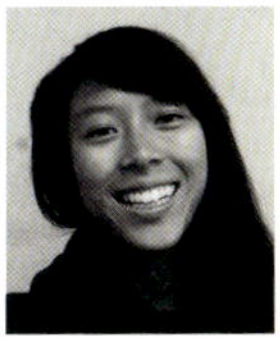

Paula Te (US) is an interaction designer and engineer whose focus is on crafting interfaces to empower people in creativity and learning. Her most recent area of exploration has been in tangible interfaces for digital fabrication and maker education. Previously she worked in design education at Karkhana in Kathmandu and at MIT in Boston. She studied at the Copenhagen Institute of Interaction Design and has a BSc in mechanical engineering from MIT.

Jury Prix Ars Electronica

2015

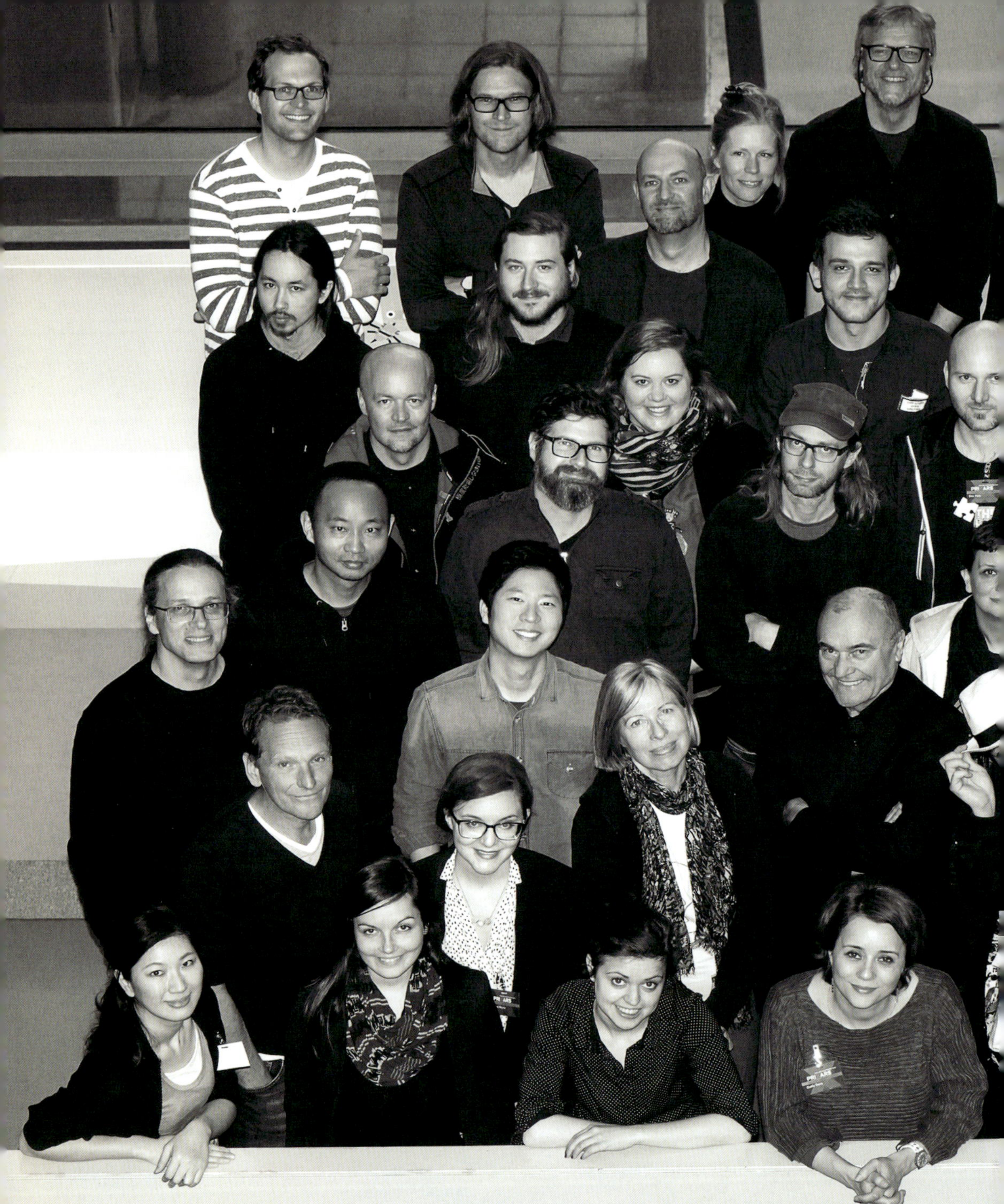

Prix Ars Electronica 2015–Jury

COMPUTER ANIMATION / FILM / VFX

Gaëlle Denis, Joe Gerhardt, Sabine Hirtes, Erick Oh, Rob O'Neill

HYBRID ART

Jens Hauser, Susanne Jaschko, Jurij V. Krpan, Victoria Vesna, Filip Visnjic

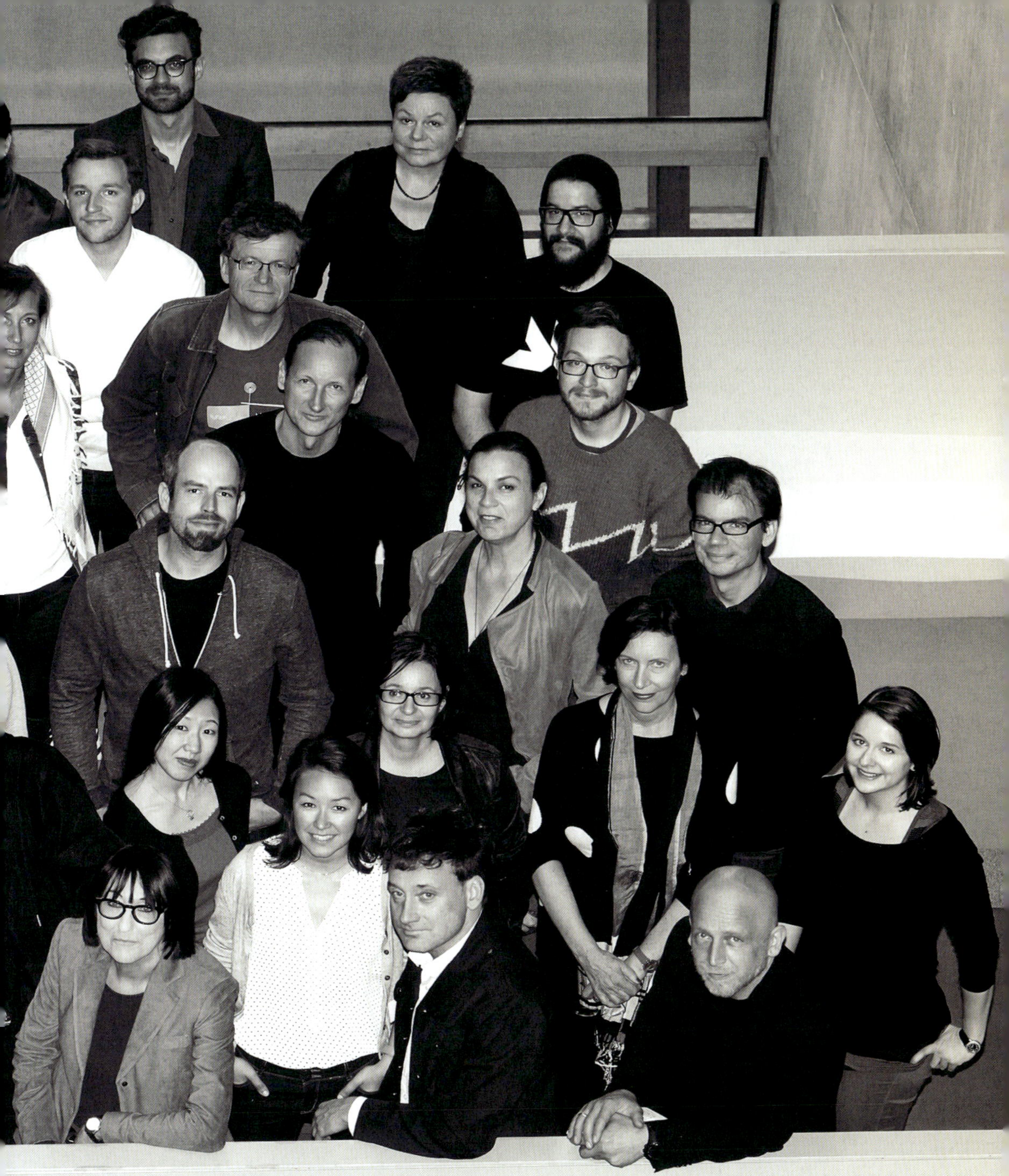

DIGITAL MUSICS & SOUND ART
Seppo Gründler, Sergey Kasich, Christina Kubisch, Valeria Rueda, Naohiro Ukawa

u19 – CREATE YOUR WORLD
Sirikit Amann, Conny Lee, Elisabeth Menasse-Wiesbauer, Peter Schernhuber, Erwin Wagenhofer

[the next idea] VOESTALPINE ART AND TECHNOLOGY GRANT
Yamina Aouina, Rikke Frisk, Horst Hörtner, Michael Sterrer-Ebenführer, Kazuhiko Washio

COMPUTER ANIMATION / FILM / VFX

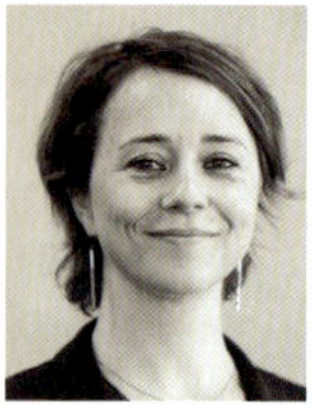

Gaëlle Denis (FR) came to London for an MA in animation at the Royal College of Art. She directed *Fish Never Sleep*, which won a BAFTA and a Cannes Cinéfondation selection. Later *City Paradise* collected more than 50 awards, including the prestigious Annecy Special Jury award and a BAFTA nomination. Her first live action short was *After the Rain* for Film 4 and the UK Film Council and her latest BFI-funded short, *Crocodile*, premiered at Cannes' Critics Week, where it won the Prix Canal+ for best short.

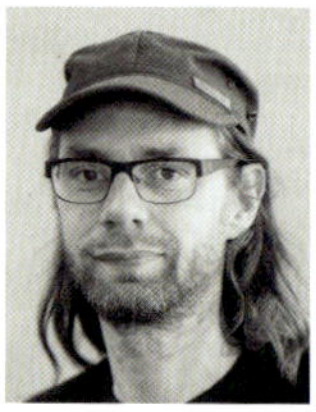

Joe Gerhardt (UK). Semiconductor is the UK artist duo Ruth Jarman and Joe Gerhardt. Through moving image works they explore the material nature of our world and how we experience it, questioning our place in the physical universe. Their unique approach has won them many awards and prestigious fellowships, most recently the 2012 Samsung Art + Prize for new media, the Golden Gate Award for New Visions at the 2012 San Francisco International Film Festival and the Art and Science Award at the Ann Arbor Film Festival USA.
http://www.semiconductorfilms.com

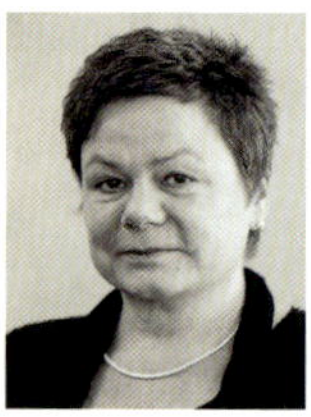

Sabine Hirtes (DE) has been teaching post-production and VFX at the University of Offenburg since 2010. Since graduating in visual communication at the FH Aachen, she has been involved in miscellaneous creative and educational activities in the field of digital print media and moving images, with a focus on computer animation and VFX in various companies, studios and schools in Germany and abroad, such as the Filmakademie Baden-Wuerttemberg, the Cairo Film Institute and the ZKM, Centre for Art and Media, Karlsruhe.

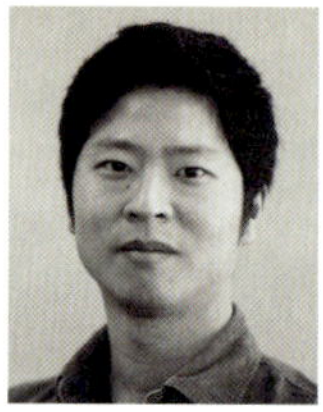

Erick Oh (KR) is a Korean filmmaker / painter based in California, USA. His work has been introduced and nominated at Annecy Animation Festival, Hiroshima Animation Festival, Student Academy Awards, Zagreb Film Festival, SIGGRAPH, Anima Mundi, Ars Electronica and numerous other international film festivals and galleries world wide. After receiving his BFA from the Fine Art Department at Seoul National University and his MFA from UCLA's film program, in 2010 Erick joined Pixar Animation Studios as an animator. Erick's most recent independent animated film, *The Dam Keeper*, was nominated for the Academy Awards this year.
http://www.erickoh.com

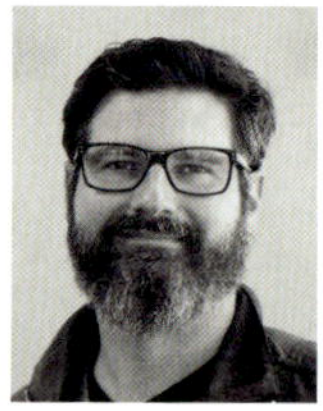

Rob O'Neill (US) is a Brooklyn-born, Los-Angeles-based writer / director / animator / programmer working in animated and live-action production. He is a character technical director supervisor at DreamWorks Animation. Rob has a BA in anthropology from Brooklyn College and an MFA in design and technology from Parsons School of Design. He was previously a researcher in cultural resources in anthropology at the American Museum of Natural History, studio technical director at Eyebeam, and director of the Digital Arts Research Laboratory at the Pratt Institute. Rob is the author of *Digital Character Development: Theory and Practice.*

DIGITAL MUSICS & SOUND ART

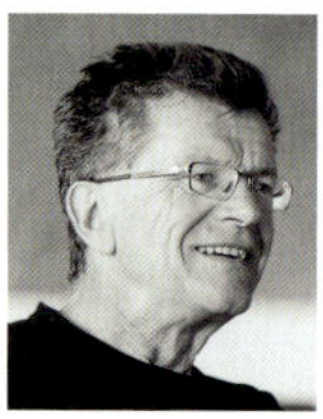

Seppo Gründler (AT), born in 1956, lives in Graz, Austria. He is the head of the master degree program in communication, media, sound and interaction design at University of Applied Sciences—FH Joanneum, visiting professor of sound design at Donau-University Krems, a member of the board of directors of the Institute for Media Archeology, and president of the Society for Dissemination and Distribution of New Music. His main instruments are guitar, electronics and software. He has been working in the field of new media since 1982. He has composed music for computer games, music for theater, film, media and sound installations. He is the creator of various CDs and two vinyls.
http://gruendler.mur.at

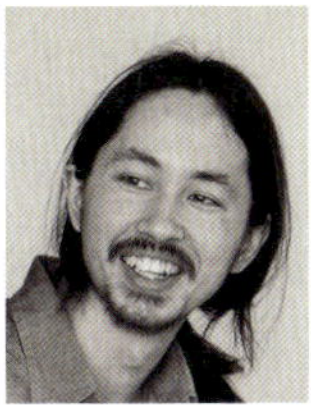

Sergey Kasich (RU) was born in Sevastopol (Crimea) in 1984. He graduated (with honors) in 2006 from Lomonosov's MSU (Moscow) as a psychologist. After attending the Moscow Theremin Center (2005-2010) he founded SoundArtist.ru, SA))—the community for experimental sound and technological arts. He curates and produces events and projects supported by residents of SA)), including an annual festival, monthly showcases and more. Sergey is the founder and curator of the Moscow Sound Art Gallery SA))_gallery and Moscow Sound Art Studio SA))_studio. Since 2011 he has been teaching a course on the technical basics of interactive arts at the Rodchenko Art School in Moscow.
http://soundartist.ru/kasich

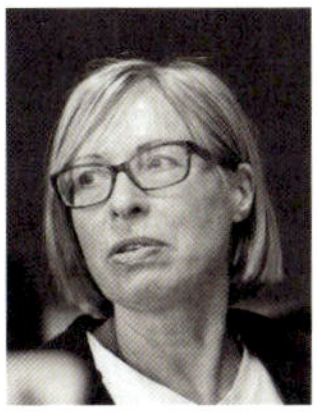

Christina Kubisch (DE) belongs to the first generation of sound artists. Trained as a composer, she has artistically developed such techniques as magnetic induction to realize her sound installations. Since 1986 she has added light as an artistic element to her work with sound. Christina Kubisch's work displays an artistic development which is often described as a "synthesis of arts"—the discovery of acoustic space and the dimension of time in the visual arts on one hand, and a redefinition of relationships between material and form in music on the other.

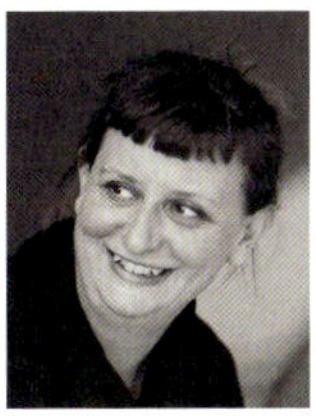

Valeria Rueda (ES) was born in Mexico and is now based in Berlin. She explores new territories with sound and emotion, a beautiful and inspirational place that has been sheltering her dreams for the past year. She has experimented in diverse areas of electronic music, from high end experimental sessions / pieces in some spectacular museums to a more club-oriented approach, participating in some important festivals in Europe and America. Signal Deluxe is her main project, Lila D. is her solo outfit, Blaqnet Records is a free platform for wide open and free experimentation, Blaq Records is her main label, Pantamuzik is her playground for house and underground club music.
http://signaldeluxe.wix.com/signaldeluxe

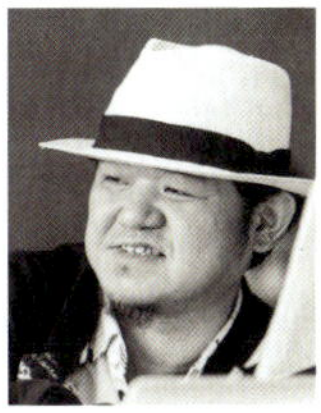

Naohiro Ukawa (JP), is an omnidirectional artist known for an extremely wide range of activities as a graphic designer, video artist, music video director, VJ, writer, college professor and Genzai artist among others. In March 2010, Ukawa founded a live streaming channel Dommune, which immediately attracted record-breaking number of viewers for its daily programs, very much discussed inside and outside Japan. Ukawa received Agency for Cultural Affairs' Japan Media Arts Festival encouragement award for Dommune as his very own form of art. Currently his occupation is Dommune. *www.dommune.com*

HYBRID ART

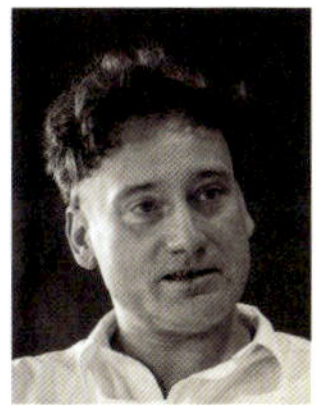

Jens Hauser (DE) is a Paris- and Copenhagen-based art curator and media studies scholar focusing on the interactions between art and technology. He has a dual research position at both the Department of Arts and Cultural Studies and at the Medical Museion at the University of Copenhagen, and is a distinguished affiliated faculty member of the Department of Art, Art History and Design at Michigan State University. His curated exhibitions include L'Art Biotech (Nantes, 2003), Still, Living (Perth, 2007), sk-interfaces (Liverpool, 2008/Luxembourg, 2009), the Article Biennale (Stavanger, 2008), Transbiotics (Riga 2010), Fingerprints (Berlin, 2011/Munich/2012) and Synth-ethic (Vienna, 2011).

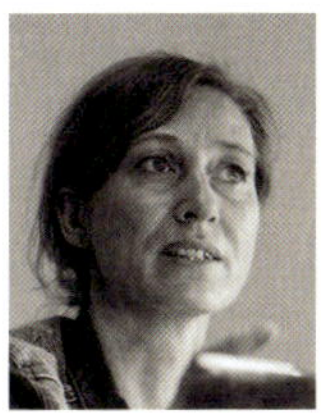

Susanne Jaschko (DE), born in 1967, is an independent curator and author with an international practice. Digital culture often serves as a starting point for her projects. With Prozessagenten, which she founded in 2012, she develops collaborative art and design projects. Previous positions include curator and deputy-director at Transmediale and Head of Exhibitions at the Netherlands Media Art Institute. She is based in Berlin.
http://sujaschko.de; http://prozessagenten.org

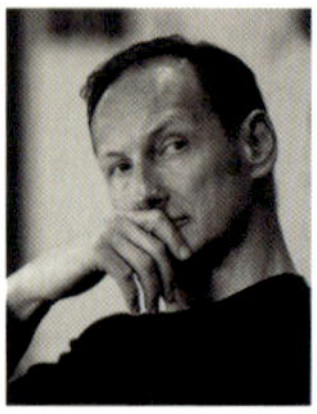

Jurij V. Krpan (SI), born in Postojna in 1961, lives and works in Ljubljana, Slovenia. At the initiative of the student organization of the University of Ljubljana he conceived the Kapelica Gallery—Gallery for Contemporary Investigative Arts, which he has been running since then. As curator and selector he has contributed to domestic and international festivals. In 2014 he co-curated the Designing Life section for the Product Design Biennale in Ljubljana and curated the Slovenian pavilion at the Venice Architecture Biennale. He started 2015 as curator of the Freies Museum Berlin. Jurij Krpan lectures on the artistic profile of the Kapelica Gallery in Slovenia as well as abroad.

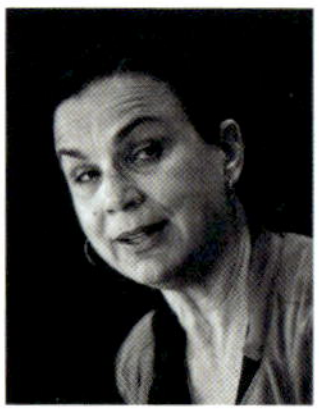

Victoria Vesna (US) Victoria Vesna, PhD, is an artist and professor at the UCLA Department of Design | Media Arts and Director of the Art|Sci center at the School of the Arts and California Nanosystems Institute (CNSI). With her installations she investigates how communication technologies affect collective behavior and perceptions of identity shift in relation to scientific innovation (PhD, University of Wales, 2000). Her work involves long-term collaborations with composers, nano-scientists, neuroscientists and evolutionary biologists, and she brings this experience to her students. She is the North American editor of *AI & Society* and in 2007 published an edited volume, *Database Aesthetics: Art in the Age of Information Overflow,* and another in 2011, *Context Providers: Conditions of Meaning in Media Arts.*

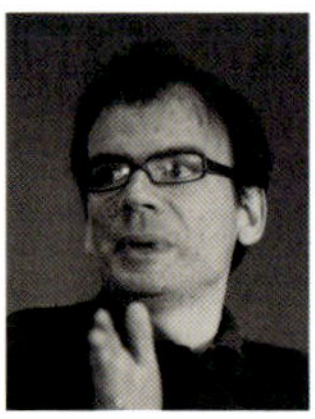

Filip Visnjic (UK) is a lecturer, curator and a media technologist born in Belgrade and now living in London. He is the founder and editor-in-chief of CreativeApplications.Net. The site tirelessly reports innovation across the field and catalogs projects, tools and platforms relevant to the intersection of art, media, and technology. In 2012, Filip co-founded Resonate, a new educational platform and a festival located in Belgrade, Serbia. In the same year, he co-launched *HOLO,* a magazine about art, science and technology, and is currently director of platform at FRM, working on a new canvas for digital art. He lectures at a number of universities in the UK. *http://fvda.co.uk*

[THE NEXT IDEA] VOESTALPINE ART AND TECHNOLOGY GRANT

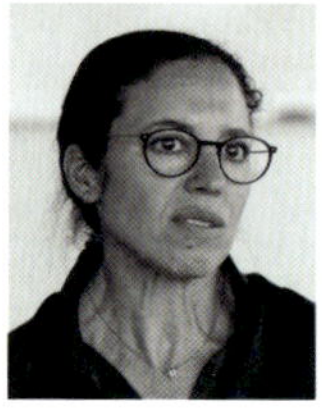

Yamina Aouina (DZ) For more than ten years Yamina Aouina has been involved with innovation and luxury, first as an advisor for big Swiss watch-making companies, then as Innovation Director at Cartier and now Head of Technology Intelligence at Richemont the Luxury Group. Through the different missions, her experience had one common focus: aligning tradition, history and outstanding craftsmanship with breakthrough technologies for the creation of fascinating products and experiences. As a member of Go-Beyond's business angle network, she was deeply immersed in the start-up world, helping young entrepreneurs with their business development and financing, and organized the first European Summit for sustainable investing, which was a very enriching experience.

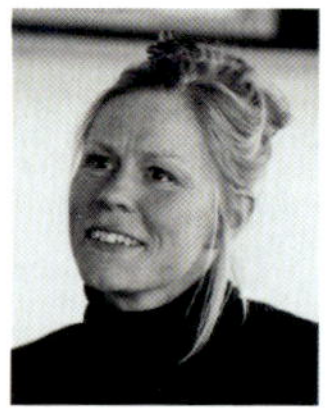

Rikke Frisk (DK), born in 1970, is the founder and co-director of the community focused culture planning company, Indgreb, based in Copenhagen. Indgreb specializes in participant-driven events, and has among other things created the international innovation and art competition and festival Afsnit I. She co-created and for several years managed Strøm—the leading festival for electronic music in Scandinavia—and later she was head of secretariat for the Copenhagen hosting of Womex—the world's biggest world music fair and festival. With a background in architecture and communication, she is an experienced and creative leader, with renowned relational abilities to develop people's skills and ideas. *http://www.indgreb.dk*

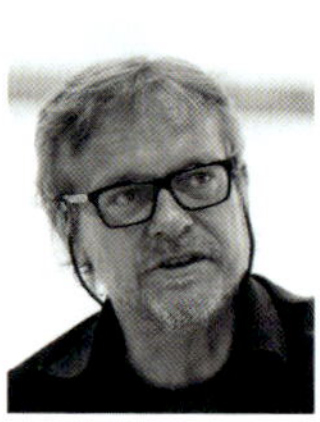

Horst Hörtner (AT) is a media artist and researcher. He is an expert in the design of human-computer interaction and holds several patents in this field. Hörtner was a founding member of the Ars Electronica Futurelab in 1996 and since then he has been the director of this atelier/laboratory. He started work in the field of media art in the 1980s and co-founded the media-art group "x-space" in Graz, Austria, in 1990. Horst Hörtner works at the nexus of art and science and gives lectures and talks at numerous international conferences and universities.

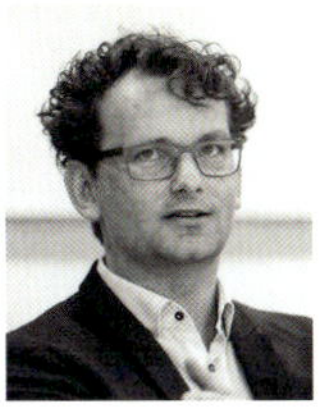

Michael Sterrer-Ebenführer (AT) Corporate Advertising and Sponsoring voestalpine AG

Kazuhiko Washio (JP) is a creative director/ producer at Hakuhodo Inc. a major advertising agency in Japan, and also is a chief research director at the Institute of Media Environment of Hakuhodo DY Media Partners Inc. Currently he is working for the creative platform in collaboration with Ars Electronica, "Future Catalysts", and aims to "invent new life experience from a future viewpoint" and support social innovation in the Japan and Asian region. He is the author of *Branding for Empathy* and also a photographic artist with a number of photography books and publications.
http://future-catalysts.com

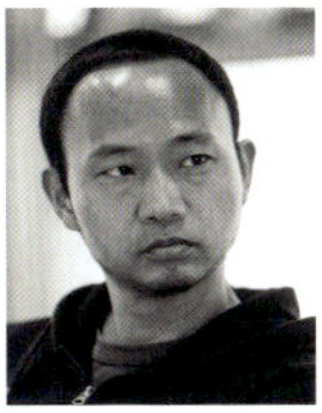

U19 – CREATE YOUR WORLD

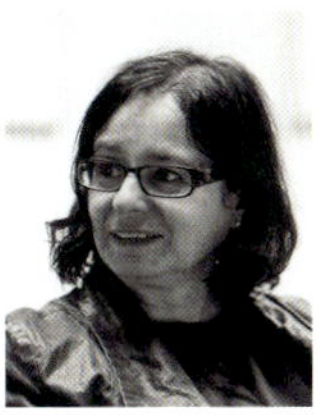

Sirikit Amann (AT) was born in 1961. She studied political science, theater and economics in Vienna. Since the 1980s, her activities in Austria and abroad have been focused on the interface of culture, education and new media: until 2007 she was a division manager for cultural education at KulturKontakt Austria. In 2008 she transferred to the newly-established staff position for artistic and cultural education at the Austrian Ministry of Education, Art and Culture. Since then she has worked as an advisor in the office of the Minister for Art and Culture. She curates Young Animation for the Prix Ars Electronica and has been an u19 juror since the category's inception.

Conny Lee (AT), born in 1985 in Vienna, studied the allegedly unpromising discipline of theatre, film and media studies. Since receiving her degree she has been working for Radio FM4 at the Austrian Broadcasting Corporation, where she produces and co-hosts the bilingual FM4 Morningshow and reviews games, literature and comics. In addition from that she also chairs events and public discussions.

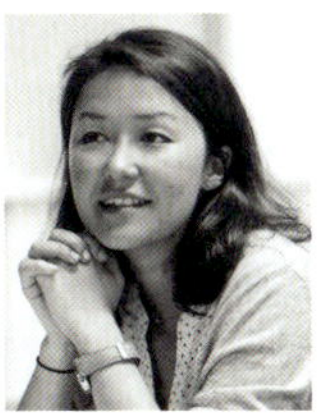

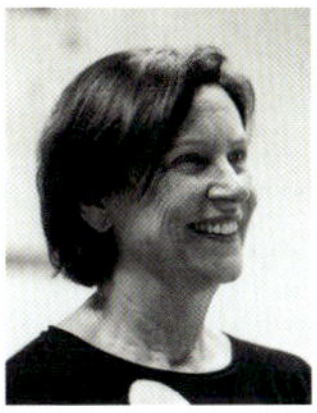

Elisabeth Menasse-Wiesbauer (AT), born in 1954, studied history, psychology and philosophy. After working as a teacher and researcher in the field of childhood history and the history of science, she organized the focus of xenophobia research at the Austrian Ministry of Science. Since 2003 Elisabeth Menasse-Wiesbauer has been the director of the ZOOM children's museum. Between 2003 and 2011 she was a board member of the European children's museum association "Hands on Europe".

Peter Schernhuber (AT), born in 1987 in Wels. Together with Sebastian Höglinger he was the head of the international youth media festival YOUKI until 2014. Since summer 2015, also together with Sebastian Höglinger, he has been head of the Diagonale festival of Austrian Film in Graz. So far Peter Schernhuber has also been involved in various (film) festivals (Crossing Europe, Diagonale, Music Unlimited, Vienna Design Week etc.), institutions (media-culture-house Wels, etc.) as well as in Ana Berlin Communications and various publications *(Edition netPOL, The Gap, FAQ, Swiss Cinema Yearbook,* etc.).

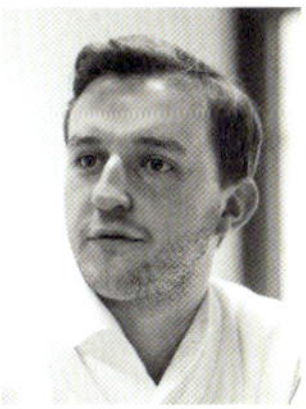

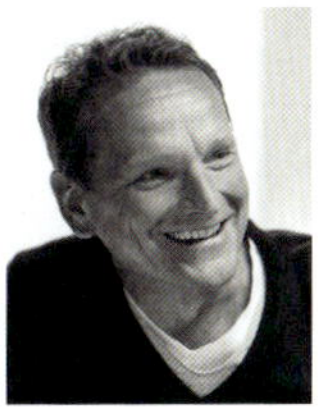

Erwin Wagenhofer (AT) studied telecommunications engineering and electronics in Vienna, and then spent three years working as a developer for Philips Austria. In 1983, Wagenhofer joined the ORF, the Austrian Broadcasting Corporation, as a freelance assistant director and cameraman. Since 1987 he has been a freelance author and filmmaker. He has also been a visiting lecturer at Danube University Krems and the University of Applied Arts Vienna. In 2005 Wagenhofer released his prize-winning documentary *We Feed the World,* which he followed up in 2008 with the internationally acclaimed documentary *Let's Make Money.* In 2010 Wagenhofer presented his first dramatic feature, *Black Brown White,* a fictional work in which he highlights egregious injustices in the social systems of industrialized countries. In his latest documentary, *Alphabet* he critically scrutinizes educational systems worldwide.

VISIONARY PIONEERS OF MEDIA ART 2015
International Experts

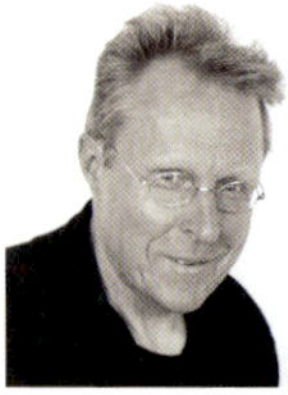

Erkki Huhtamo (FI/US) is known as a founding figure of media archeology. He has published extensively on media culture and media arts, lectured worldwide, given stage performances, curated exhibitions and directed TV programs. He is a professor at the University of California Los Angeles (UCLA), departments of design media arts, and film, television, and digital media. His most recent book is *Illusions in Motion: Media Archaeology of the Moving Panorama and Related Spectacles* (MIT Press, 2013).

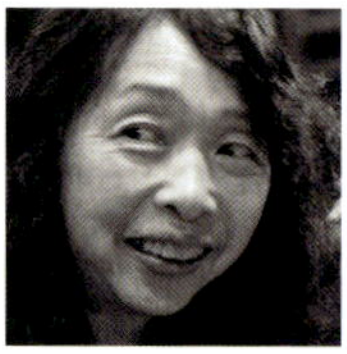

Masao Kohmura

Machiko Kusahara (JP) is a professor at the School of Culture, Media and Society of Waseda University. Her fields of theoretical research are media art and media archeology, with the focus on the interplay between media culture, technology and society in both early visual culture and contemporary media art. Since the mid 1980s she has curated, written, and given lectures internationally both on digital art and early visual media. She has served as a jury for major international competitions including Ars Electronica, SIGGRAPH, and ISEA.

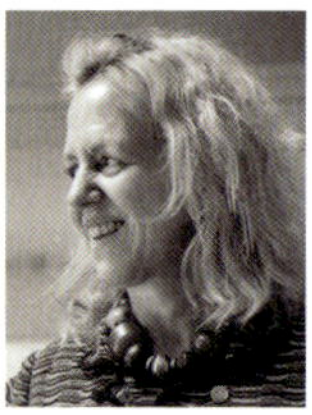

H Zernike

Barbara London (US) is a curator and writer who founded the video exhibition and collection programs at the Museum of Modern Art, where she worked between 1973 and 2013. The exhibitions she organized include solo shows featuring early mavericks Nam June Paik, Bill Viola, Steina Vasulka, Joan Jonas, Shigeko Kubota, Peter Campus, Gary Hill, Valie Export, Steve McQueen, and Laurie Anderson. She was the first curator in the United States to showcase the work of Asian artists Zhang Peili, Song Dong, Teiji Furuhashi, Feng Mengbo, and Yang Fudong. Her thematic projects have included Video from Tokyo to Fukui and Kyoto, New Video from China, Anime!, Stillness (Michael Snow and Sam Taylor-Wood), and Automatic Update, among others. Barbara London was the first to integrate the internet as part of curatorial practice. The projects where she put daily dispatches on-line include Stir-fry (1994), Internyet (1998), and dot.jp (1999.)
http://www.moma.org/dotjp

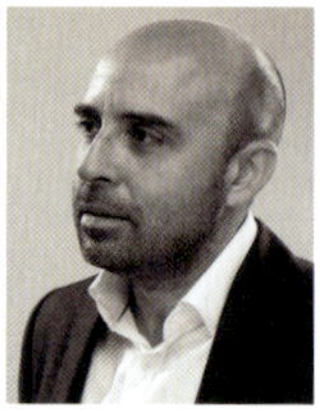

Wilber Dueñas

José-Carlos Mariátegui (PE), born in Lima in 1975, is a writer, curator and scholar on culture and new media. He studied biology and received his BSc in applied mathematics, and holds masters and doctoral degrees in information systems and innovation from the London School of Economics and Political Science (LSE). Dr. Mariátegui is the founder of Alta Tecnología Andina (ATA) and co-founder of Escuelab.org, spaces devoted to creativity, technology and innovation in Latin America. He is a member of the Advisory Board of the Ministry of Culture (2010/2012-2013) and an editorial board member for Leonardo Books at MIT Press. He lives in London and Lima.

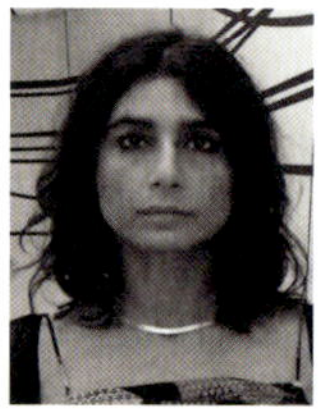

Monica Narula (IN) is a member of Raqs Media Collective, which enjoys playing a plurality of roles, often appearing as artists, occasionally as curators, and sometimes as philosophical agents provocateurs. They make contemporary art, have made films, curated exhibitions, edited books, staged events, collaborated with architects, computer programmers, writers and theater directors and have founded processes that have left deep impacts on contemporary culture in India. Raqs (pron. rux) follows its self-declared imperative of "kinetic contemplation" to produce a trajectory that is restless in terms of the forms and methods that it deploys even as it achieves a consistency of speculative procedures. Raqs was founded in 1992 by Jeebesh Bagchi, Monica Narula and Shuddhabrata Sengupta. It remains closely involved with the Sarai program at the Centre for the Study of Developing Societies, an initiative they co-founded in 2000. *http://www.sarai.net*
http://www.raqsmediacollective.net

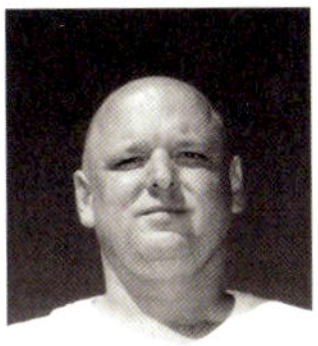

Marcus Neustetter (AT/ZA) is an artist and cultural activist in Johannesburg South Africa. Born in 1976 in Johannesburg, Marcus Neustetter gained his masters degree in fine arts in 2001 from the University of the Witwatersrand. As an artist and cultural activist, Neustetter has produced projects in the gallery, public and virtual domain. A consistent focus in his art practice has been on the intersections of art, science and technology, ranging from drawing, sculpture, installation, performance, video and multimedia to site-specific and socially engaged interventions. He has exhibited extensively in Europe, Africa and North America. He is the co-director of The Trinity Session.
http://www.thetrinitysession.com
http://www.marcusneustetter.com

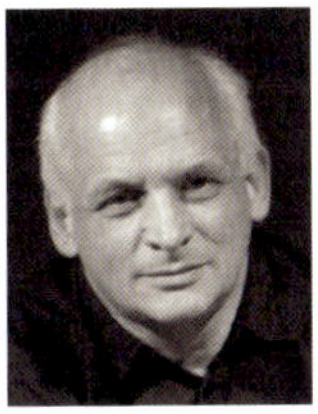

Andrey Smirnov (RU), born in 1956, is an interdisciplinary artist, performer, educator, independent curator, collector, writer and composer. He is the founding director of the Theremin Center in Moscow, a senior lecturer and a researcher at the Center for Electro-Acoustic Music at the Moscow State Conservatory and a lecturer at the Rodchenko School for Modern Photography and Multimedia, where he teaches courses on history and the aesthetics of electro-acoustic music, sound design and composition, new musical interfaces and physical computing. His ongoing research project is restoring the censored history of artistically utopian early 20th-century Russia. The project includes a series of exhibitions and the book *Sound in Z: Experiments in Sound and Electronic Music in Early 20th-Century Russia* (Walther Koenig, 2013).

Ars Electronica 2015

Festival for Art, Technology and Society

Organization
Ars Electronica Linz GmbH

Managing Directors
Gerfried Stocker, Diethard Schwarzmair
Ars-Electronica-Straße 1, 4040 Linz, Austria
Tel: +4373272720
Fax: +4373272722
info@aec.at

Co-organizers

ORF Oberösterreich
Director: Kurt Rammerstorfer

LIVA – Veranstaltungsgesellschaft m.b.H.
Directors: Hans-Joachim Frey, Wolfgang Lehner

OK Offenes Kulturhaus im OÖ Kulturquartier
Directors: Martin Sturm, Gabriele Daghofer

Partners
Kunstuniversität Linz – Universität für künstlerische und industrielle Gestaltung
Lentos Kunstmuseum Linz
Mariendom Linz
Österreichische Post AG

Akademie der bildenden Künste Wien
Backlab Collective
Bugnplay - Multimedianetzwerk
C3 - Multimedianetzwerk
Campus Genius Award
Central Linz
CPN Centre for the Promotion of Science
CERN
Connected Intelligence Atelier
Deutscher Multimediapreis – Multimedianetzwerk
DIG gallery
Empowerment Informatics
European Space Agency
European Southern Observatory
Etopia
FAB Verein zur Förderung von Arbeit und Beschäftigung
GV Art
ifva
Ingenieure ohne Grenzen Austria
Interface Cultures
Internationales Teletext Art Festival ITAF
International Students Creative Award
Internet Yami-Ichi and Body Paint
Japan Media Arts Festival
Kammer der Architekten und Ingenieurkonsulenten für Oberösterreich und Salzburg
Kapelica Gallery / Kersnikova
LABoral
Mons 2015
ORF Teletext
QUT Queensland University of Technology
Science Gallery
Stadtwerkstatt
Tourismusverband Linz
University of Tsukuba
V2 Institute for the Unstable Media
Zaragoza City of Knowledge Foundation

Directors Ars Electronica: Gerfried Stocker, Christine Schöpf
Head of Festival: Martin Honzik
Technical Head: Karl Julian Schmidinger
Finance & Organization: Veronika Liebl

Production Team: Katharina Bienert, Sigrid Blauensteiner, Florina Costamoling, Roman Dachsberger, Katharina Edlmair, Hannes Franks, Marion Friedl, Rosi Grillmair, Alexander Hinterlassnig, Georg Holzmann, Andrea Kohut, Sofie Kronberger, Theresa Lackner, Kristina Maurer, Hans Christian Merten, Manuela Naveau, Emiko Ogawa, Hideaki Ogawa, Elvis Pavic, Felix Pöchhacker, Christina Radner, Tina Reinthaler, Susanne Rosenlechner, Jutta Schmiederer, Mike Sarsteiner, Florian Sedmak, Tobias Tahler, Anna Titovets, Jochen Tuch, Joschi Viteka, Susi Windischbauer, Nina Wenhart, Michaela Wimplinger, Viktoria Wöß, Johanna Zauner, Jochen Zeirzer, Patrick Zorn

Co-curators
Ars Electronica Animation Festival: Christine Schöpf, Jürgen Hagler
Big Concert Night: Dennis Russell Davies, Heribert Schröder
Campus Exhibition: Jean-Luc Soret, Chu-Yin Chen
Connected Intelligence Atelier: Derrick de Kerckhove, Maria Pia Rossignaud
Spaceship Earth: Robert Meisner
Expanded Animation: Jürgen Hagler, Wilhelm Alexander
Interface Cultures Exhibition: Christa Sommerer, Laurent Mignonneau, Martin Kaltenbrunner, Michaela Ortner, Marlene Brandstätter, Reinhard Gupfinger
Knowledge Capital Curatorial Team
Music Monday: Werner Jauk
Naked Veriti: Javier Galán
Post City Nightline: Salon 2000

Prix Ars Electronica 2015

Co-organizers

ORF Oberösterreich
Director: Kurt Rammerstorfer

LIVA – Veranstaltungsgesellschaft m.b.H.
Directors: Hans-Joachim Frey, Wolfgang Lehner

OK Offenes Kulturhaus im OÖ Kulturquartier
Directors: Martin Sturm, Gabriele Daghofer

Idea: Hannes Leopoldseder
Conception: Christine Schöpf, Gerfried Stocker
Coordination: Martin Honzik, Emiko Ogawa
Technical Management: Karl Julian Schmidinger

Production Team: Katharina Bienert, Bernhard Böhm, Viktor Delev, Christoph Einfalt, Theresa Lackner, Veronika Liebl, Kristina Maurer, Hans Christian Merten, Elvis Pavic, Johannes Poell, Christina Radner, Tina Reinthaler, Jutta Schmiederer, Claudia Schnugg, Joschi Viteka, Florian Voggeneder

Press
Christopher Sonnleitner, Robert Bauernhansl, Martin Hieslmair, Magdalena Leitner

Marketing
Isabella Ematinger, Manuela Seethaler, Eva Tsackmaktsian

Ars Electronica Linz GmbH

Managing Directors
Gerfried Stocker, Diethard Schwarzmair

Ars Electronica Center
Andreas Bauer, Christoph Kremer, Renata Aigner, Katharina Aichinger, Viktoria Aistleitner, Reinhard Bengesser, Dietmar Bok, Sarah Breinbauer, Blanka Denkmaier, Johannes Egler, Erika Eiter, Julia Felberbauer, Melinda File, Andrea Fröhlich, Christoph Froschauer, Mitra Gazvini-Zateh, Christian Gerber, Elisabeth Gerhard-Mayrhofer, Tamara Geyerhofer, Nicole Grüneis, Ulrike Gschwandtner, Harald Haas, Gerid Maria Hager, Birgit Hartinger, Florian Heiml, Martin Hieslmair, Thomas Hillinger, Sri Rahayu Hofstadler, Gerold Hofstadler, Philip Huemer, Thomas Jannke, Erika Jungreithmayr, Elisabeth Kattner, Herwig Kerschner, Viktoria Klepp, Eva Klimesova, Martin Kneidinger, Michael Koller, Thomas Kollmann, Andreas Leeb, Daniel Lehner, Sabine Leidlmair, Juliane Leitner, Anna Katharina Link, Ulrike Mair, Reingard Medicus, Kathrin Meyer, Clemens Mock, Horst Morocutti, Claudia Moser, Marc Mühlberger, Daniel Murina, Heinrich Niederhuber, Michaela Obermayer, Benjamin Perndl, Svetlana Petrovic, Katharina Pilar, Armin Pils, Anna Polewiak, Ulrike Rieseneder, Andreas Roth, Michael Rottmann, Petra Saubolle-Hofmann, Alina Sauter, Birgitt Schäffer, Johann Schauer, Barbara Schmidt, Nina Schönberger, Thomas Schwarz, Markus Schwarzmair, Stefan Schwarzmair, Elio Seidl, Manfred Seifriedsberger, Margarethe Stöttner-Breuer, Johannes Strasser, Lioubov Studener, Johannes Stürzlinger, Istvan Szabo, Bhoomesh Tak, Kerstin Tak-Wakolbinger, Michaela Maria Tanzer, Michael Thaler, Linda Vankova, Thomas Viehböck, Florian Voggeneder, Karin Wabro, Damian Benno Wachlhofer, Manuel Walch, Florian Wanninger, Michael Wlaschitz

Ars Electronica Futurelab
Horst Hörtner, Christopher Lindinger, Roland Haring, Roland Aigner, Florian Berger, Bernhard Böhm, Chris Bruckmayr, Barbara Erlinger, Maria Eschböck, Peter Freudling, Matthew Gardiner, Martin Gösweiner, Peter Holzkorn, Andreas Jalsovec, Anna Lucia Kuthan, Magdalena Leitner, Martina Mara, Michael Mayr, Kristefan Minski, Stefan Mittlböck-Jungwirth-Fohringer, Martin Mörth, Otto Naderer, Nicolas Naveau, Kathrin Obernhumer, Hideaki Ogawa, Veronika Pauser, Marius Pfeffer, Michael Platz, Erwin Reitböck, Jonathan Rutherford, Clemens Francis Scharfen, Claudia Schnugg, Marianne Ternek

Ars Electronica Festival
Martin Honzik, Karl Julian Schmidinger, Katharina Bienert, Florina Costamoling, Stephanie Danner, Hannes F. Franks, Marion Friedl, Rosi Grillmair, Andrea Kohut, Theresa Lackner, Veronika Liebl, Kristina Maurer, Hans Christian Merten, Manuela Naveau, Emiko Ogawa, Elvis Pavic, Christina Radner, Tina Reinthaler, Susanne Rosenlechner, Viktoria Wöß, Johanna Zauner, Jochen Zeirzer, Patrick Zorn

Ars Electronica Management Services
Elisabeth Kapeller, Markus Jandl, Robert Bauernhansl, Bettina Danninger, Barbara Diesenreither, Isabella Ematinger, Michaela Frech, Bettina Gahleitner, Gerhard Grafinger, Gerold Hofstadler, Andrea Huemer, Heinrich Klambauer, Stephan Kobler, Dominic Lengauer, Zulfija Magomedova, Peter J. Nitzschmann, Julia Rabeder, Manuela Seethaler, Christopher Sonnleitner, David Starzengruber, Eva Tsackmaktsian, Michaela Wimplinger, Susi Windischbauer, Sebastian Zach

Ars Electronica Solutions
Michael Badics, Andreas Pramböck, Ina Badics, Lukas Bischof, Cecile Bucher, Stefan Dorn, Stefan Fuchs, My Trinh Gardiner, Yvonne Hauser, Barbara Hinterleitner, Christoph Hofbauer, Petros Kataras, Fadil Kujundzic, Thomas Lengauer, Pascal Maresch, Johanna Mathauer, Kathrin Agnes Meyer, Harald Moser, Patrick Müller, Ali Nikrang, Benjamin Olsen, Dietmar Peter, Poorya Piroozan, Stephan Pointner, Gerald Priewasser-Höller, Gabriele Purdue, Roland Reiter, Andrea Rovescalli, Stefan Rozporka, Gerald Sixt, Markus Wipplinger, Claus Zweythurm

OK Offenes Kulturhaus im OÖ Kulturquartier

OK CyberArts Team
Directors: Martin Sturm, Gabriele Daghofer
Public Relations: Maria Falkinger
Technical Manager: Rainer Jessl
Curator: Genoveva Rückert
Exhibition Manager: Martina Rauschmayer
Production Manager: Aron Rynda
Technical Head: Andreas Kurz

Production Team: Jarno Bachheimer, Stefan Brandmayr, Attila Ferenczi, Alfred Fürholzer, Martin Haselsteiner, Kraxberger David, Bernhard Kitzmüller, Daniel Mandel, Andreas Steindl, André Tschinder, Tom Vens, Hans-Jörg Weidinger, Gerhard Wörnhörer, Simon Wilhelm

Team: Verena Atteneder, Erika Baldinger, Katharina Baldinger-Hackl, Renate Berger, Julia Brunner, Michael Dalpiaz, Walter Eckerstorfer, Tamara Eder, Max Fabian, Werner Friesenecker, Michaela Fröhlich, Andrea Gintner, Josef Gruber, Manuela Gruber, Stephan Hadwiger, Dominik Harrer, Sabine Haunschmid, Evi Heininger, Robert Herbst, Susi Heuschober, Maximilian Höglinger, Fritz Holzinger, Christoph Kaltenböck, Sabrina Kamenar, Simon Lachner, Barbara Mair, Judith Maule, Franz Minichberger, Walter Mühlböck, Wolfgang Nagl, Josef Pfarrhofer, Franz Pfifferling, Wilhelm Pichler, Angelika Pöschl, Franz Quirchtmayr, Michaela Reisenberger, Gerda Sailer, Markus Schiller, Ulrike Schimpl, Helene Schoißengeyr, Marlies Stöger

LIVA – Veranstaltungsgesellschaft – Brucknerhaus
Directors: Hans-Joachim Frey, Wolfgang Lehner
Team: Wolfgang Scheibner, Wolfgang Schützeneder, Ursula Kislinger

Kunstuniversität Linz – Universität für künstlerische und industrielle Gestaltung
Rector: Reinhard Kannonier
Vice-Rectors: Rainer Zendron, Christine Windsteiger

ORGANIZER

ARS ELECTRONICA

Ars Electronica Linz GmbH is a company of the city of Linz.

BRUCKNER HAUS

OK imoökulturquartier

ORF OÖ

LINZ UNESCO City of Media Arts

COOPERATION PARTNERS

Akademie der bildenden Künste Wien
Anton Bruckner Privatuniversität
any:time Architekten mit Clemens Bauder, Felix Ganzer
Aquaponic-Austria
Art Council Tokyo
BRP ROTAX
bug`n`play
c3
Campus Genius Award
CDDV Centre for digital Documentation and Visualisation
Central Linz
Centre for the promotion of science
CERN
COMMOD-Haus
Crossing Europe
CTi – Culture and Technology International (Connected Intelligence Atelier)
CTIA – Chungnam Culture Technology Industry Agency
CUBUS
DIG gallery
Empowerment Informatics
Etopia
European Southern Observatory
European Space Agency
FAB Verein zur Förderung von Arbeit und Beschäftigung
FH Hagenberg - FH OÖ Studienbetriebs GmbH
Gelbes Krokodil
GV Art London
Hard-Chor Linz
holis market
ifva incubator for film & visual media in asia
Ingenieure ohne Grenzen Österreich
Integrationsbüro der Stadt Linz
Interface Cultures
Interio AG
International Students Creative Award
Internationales Teletext Art Festival ITAF
Japan Media Arts Festival
Kammer der Architekten und Ingenieurkonsulenten für Oberösterreich und Salzburg
Kapelica Gallery / Kersnikova
Kepler Salon - Verein zur Förderung von Wissensvermittlung
Kinderfreunde OÖ
KI-I - Kompetenznetzwerk Informationstechnologie zur Förderung der Integration von Menschen mit Behinderungen
KinderUni OÖ
Klimabündnis Oberösterreich
Kunst- und Kulturverein Backlab
Kunstuniversität Linz - Universität für künstlerische und industrielle Gestaltung
laboral - Centro de Arte y Creación Industrial
Lammerhuber KG
LENTOS Kunstmuseum Linz
maiz - Autonomes Zentrum von & für Migrantinnen
Mariendom Linz
mb21
Mons 2015
OPEN COMMONS LINZ
ORF Teletext
OTELO Linz und Vorchdorf
PANGEA | Werkstatt der Kulturen der Welt
QUT-Queensland University of Technology
Science Gallery
Sibelius AVID
Stadtwerkstatt
[tp3] architekten ZT Gmbh
The Alfred Fried Photography Award
The PELARS Project
Tourismusverband Linz
University of Tsukuba
V2 - Institute for the Unstable Media
WhatAVenture
Wirtschaftskammer OÖ
Zaragoza City of Knowledge Foundation

ARS ELECTRONICA RECEIVES SUPPORT FROM

Land Oberösterreich

Bundeskanzleramt

Bundesministerium für Wissenschaft, Forschung und Wirtschaft

Bundesministerium für Europe, Integration und Äusseres

KulturKontakt Austria

Creative Europe

EU Kultur

EU Council of Europe

Europäische Kommission

Erasmus+

DG Near

Japan Foundation

EU-Japan Fest Japan Commitee

Gobierno de Espana - Ministerio de education, cultura y deporte

Spain arts + culture

AC/E – Accion cultural Espanola

ARCADI

Ferderation Wallonie-Bruxelles

Institut Francais en Autriche

Ministry of Culture & Communication France

Creativ Industries Fund NL (CIFNL)

ARCUB

RKI Wien - Rumänisches Kulturinstitut Wien

Romanian Cultural Institute

SRE AMEXCID

SPONSORS

Linz AG

Hakuhodo

voestalpine

Hutchison 3

Mercedes-Benz

Liwest

ÖBB-Personenverkehr AG

Österreichische Post AG

LIVA

KNOWLEDGE CAPITAL

Greiner Holding AG

Industriellenvereinigung OÖ

netidee

SSI Schäfer Shop GmbH

Schäfer Shop GmbH

SilberHolz

NTS

Messe Linz

Rotary Club Linz-Altstadt

Ton + Bild

Sparkasse OÖ

FESTO

Quanta Arts Foundation

Casino Linz

Ableton

Smurfit Kappa

trotec

Rotes Kreuz

Cordial

Carl Zeiss GmbH

Hilti Austria Ges.m.b.H.

Kuka

Creative Region OÖ

PH Oberösterreich

Landestheater Linz

art:phalanx

JP IMMOBILIEN

Paris 8 University Vincennes-Saint-Denis

Université 8.0 Le pari numérique

Laboratoire d'Excellence Arts-H2H

Investissements d'Avenir

Initiative d'Excellence en formations innovantes, CreaTIC

École nationale supérieure des Arts Décoratifs

Yllisu

fuRo

MATULA Gartengestaltung GmbH

Otto Bock HealthCare Deutschland GmbH

Screenteam

ÖAMTC Oberösterreich

Vöslauer Mineralwasser AG

COMMOD-Haus GmbH

Siteco Österreich GmbH AN OSRAM BUSINESS

BIO AUSTRIA

AURO Naturfarben

Weinhaus Wakolbinger

Triple A

Donau Metall

Baumschule Ökoplant GmbH

STS Consulting & Trading GmbH

Johammer e-mobility GmbH

NTRY Ticketing OG

Marchfelder Bio-Edelpilze GmbH

Das Fraunhofer-Institut für Bildgestützte Medizin MEVIS

XI Machines GmbH

Red Bull GmbH

Future Catalysts

Rauch Recycling

TBF-PyroTec GmbH

Connecting Cities

art&science

MEDIA PARTNERS

OÖ Nachrichten

Ö1

FM4

Radio Fro

der Standard

Wired

CyberArts 2015
International Compendium – Prix Ars Electronica

International Compendium – Prix Ars Electronica
Computer Animation / Film / VFX – Hybrid Art – Digital Musics & Sound Art – Visionary Pioneers of Media Art
u19 - CREATE YOUR WORLD – [the next idea] voestalpine Art and Technology Grant

Editors: Hannes Leopoldseder, Christine Schöpf, Gerfried Stocker

Editing: Jutta Schmiederer
Translations (German–English): Mel Greenwald
Copyediting: Dave Westacott, Jutta Schmiederer, Ingrid Fischer-Schreiber

Graphic design and production: Gerhard Kirchschläger
Typeface: Klavika
Printed by: Gutenberg Werbering Gesellschaft m.b.H., Linz
Paper: Claro Bulk, 150 g/m², 300 g/m²
Photos: pp. 176–181: Florian Voggeneder

Published by
Hatje Cantz Verlag
Zeppelinstrasse 32
73760 Ostfildern
Germany
Tel. +49 711 4405-200
Fax +49 711 4405-220
www.hatjecantz.com
A Ganske Publishing Group company

Hatje Cantz books are available internationally at selected bookstores.
For more information about our distribution partners please visit our homepage at
www.hatjecantz.com.

ISBN 978-3-7757-4022-7

Printed in Austria

Cover illustration: Front: Alex Verhaest: *Temps Mort / Idle Times;* Agnes Meyer-Brandis: *Teacup Tools*
Back: Nobumichi Asai: *Omote / Real-Time Face Tracking & Projection Mapping;* Myriam Bleau: *Soft Revolvers*

PEFC
PEFC/06-39-27

This product is from
sustainably managed
forests and controlled sources.

printed climate-neutrally CP IKS-Nr.: 53401-1508-1002